Baillière's
CLINICAL
HAEMATOLOGY
INTERNATIONAL PRACTICE AND RESEARCH

Baillière's

CLINICAL HAEMATOLOGY

INTERNATIONAL PRACTICE AND RESEARCH

Volume 5/Number 1
January 1992

Epidemiology of Haematological Disease: Part I

A. F. FLEMING
Guest Editor

Baillière Tindall
London Philadelphia Sydney Tokyo Toronto

This book is printed on acid-free paper.

Baillière Tindall   24–28 Oval Road,
W.B. Saunders   London NW1 7DX

The Curtis Center, Independence Square West,
Philadelphia, PA 19106–3399, USA

55 Horner Avenue
Toronto, Ontario M8Z 4X6, Canada

Harcourt Brace Jovanovich Group (Australia) Pty Ltd,
30–52 Smidmore Street, Marrickville, NSW 2204, Australia

Harcourt Brace Jovanovich Japan, Inc.
Ichibancho Central Building, 22–1
Ichibancho, Chiyoda-ku, Tokyo 102, Japan

ISSN 0950-3536

ISBN 0-7020-1626-8 (single copy)

Baillière's Clinical Haematology is published four times each year by Baillière Tindall. Annual subscription prices are:

TERRITORY	ANNUAL SUBSCRIPTION	SINGLE ISSUE
UK and Europe	£65.00 post free	£27.50 post free
All other countries	Consult your local Harcourt Brace Jovanovich office for dollar price	

The editor of this publication is Stephen Handley, Baillière Tindall, 24–28 Oval Road, London NW1 7DX.

Baillière's Clinical Haematology was published from 1972 to 1986 as
Clinics in Haematology.

Typeset by Phoenix Photosetting, Chatham.
Printed and bound in Great Britain by Mackays of Chatham PLC, Chatham, Kent.

Contributors to this issue

R. A. CARTWRIGHT MA, MB, Bchir, PhD, MFCM, FFPHM, Director, Leukaemia Research Fund Centre for Clinical Epidemiology at the University of Leeds, 17 Springfield Mount, Leeds, West Yorkshire LS2 9NG, UK.

THERESA L. COETZER PhD, Senior Research Scientist, Department of Haematology, South African Institute for Medical Research, University of the Witwatersrand Medical School, York Road, Johannesburg 2193, South Africa.

STUART C. FINCH MD, UMDNJ-Robert Wood Johnson Medical School and the Cooper Hospital, One Cooper Plaza, Camden, New Jersey 08103, USA.

ALAN F. FLEMING, MA, MD, FRCPath, FMCPath, FWACP, Professor, Department of Haematology, South African Institute for Medical Research, University of Witwatersrand, Baragwanath Hospital, PO Bertsham, Soweto 2013, South Africa.

PILAR GALAN, Centre de Recherch sur les Anémies Nutritionnelles, Institut Scientifique et Technique de la Nutrition et de l'Alimentation, CNAM, 2 rue Conté, F-75003 Paris, France.

VICTOR R. GORDEUK MD, Assistant Professor of Medicine, Case Western Reserve University School of Medicine, Metro Health Medical Center, 3395 Scranton Road, Cleveland, OH 44109, USA.

SERGE HERCBERG MD, PhD, Groupe de Recherche sur les Minéraux et les Vitamines, Institut Scientifique et Technique de la Nutrition et de l'Alimentation, CNAM, 2 rue Conte, F-75003, Paris, France.

ADRIAN V. S. HILL DPhil, MRCP, Wellcome Senior Research Fellow in Clinical Science, Institute of Molecular Medicine, John Radcliffe Hospital, Oxford OX3 9DU, UK.

NAI KIONG HO MBBS, MMed, FRACP, Part-time Clinical Teacher, Department of Paediatrics, National University of Singapore; Senior Consultant and Head, Department of Neonatal Medicine 1, Kandang Kerbau Hospital, Hampshire Road, Singapore 0821.

RUTH F. JARRETT MBChB, Deputy Director, LRF Virus Centre, Veterinary School, Bearsden Road, Glasgow G61 1QH, UK.

HUXLEY H. M. KNOX-MACAULAY MA, MD, FRCP, FRCPE, FMCPath, DTM&H, Professor of Haematology, Departments of Internal Medicine and Pathology, College of Medicine and Medical Sciences, King Faisal University, Dammam 31451, Saudi Arabia; Present address: Department of Haematology, College of Medicine, Sultan Qaboos University, PO Box 32485 Al Khod, Muscat, Sultanate of Oman.

MARTHA S. LINET MD, Epidemiology and Biostatistics Program National Cancer Institute, Rockville, Maryland 20892, USA.

GEORGE TREVOR NURSE MB, ChB, PhD, DPH, FRAI, Medical Director, Highveld Blood Transfusion Service, PO Box 890522, Lyndhurst 2106; Honorary Professor in the Department of Haematology, The South African Institute for Medical Research and School of Pathology, University of the Witwatersrand, PO Box 1038, Johannesburg 2000, South Africa.

J. PALEK MD, Department of Biomedical Research, Division of Hematology/Oncology, St Elizabeth Hospital of Boston, Tufts University School of Medicine, Boston, MA 02135, USA.

BRACHA RAMOT MD, Professor of Medicine and Haematology, Incumbent of the Gregorio and Dora Shapiro Chair for Hematologic Malignancies at the Sackler School of Medicine, Tel-Aviv University, Tel-Aviv, Israel.

GIDEON RECHAVI MD, PhD, Senior Lecturer in Pediatrics & Hematology, Sackler School of Medicine, Tel-Aviv University, Tel-Aviv, Israel.

A. STAINES MB, BCh, BAO, BA, MSc, MRCPI, DCH, Research Fellow in Clinical Epidemiology, Leukaemia Research Fund Centre for Clinical Epidemiology at the University of Leeds, 17 Springfield Mount, Leeds, West Yorkshire, LS2 9NG, UK.

Table of contents

PREVIOUS ISSUES

FORTHCOMING ISSUES

Foreword

This is the first of two volumes devoted to the global epidemiology of haematological disorders. Emphasis has been on underlying factors determining the distribution of blood disorders, factors which include infective agents, chemical toxins, irradiation, nutrition and the selection for genetic variants. The ultimate purpose of the epidemiological approach is to discover aetiology and so develop policies for prevention, control and treatment.

Apart from the study of HIV, the last decade has seen remarkable research into infectious agents, both as aetiological agents of haematological disorders and as determining factors in their distribution. The advent of HIV and AIDS has led to a whole new epidemiology of marrow dysfunction, lymphomas, tuberculosis, sickle-cell disease and disorders of haemostasis. The original plan was to order the chapters logically in two issues, one with viruses and the other with malaria as their *leit motifs*. This scheme has been disrupted by the need to meet publication deadlines, the tardiness of some contributors, and even the withdrawal of others one year after commitment; if they read this, I send them my maledictions. Particular thanks have to be given to authors who have stood in at short notice, and to the authors from Dammam and Tel Aviv, Drs Knox-Macaulay, Rechavi and Ramot, who have contributed their scholarly chapters despite normal life being disrupted by the Gulf War.

One of the most intriguing epidemiological puzzles today is the distribution of common acute lymphoblastic leukaemia (cALL) in childhood; this must reflect interactions between the immune system and some unidentified aetiological factors being met for the first time in differing circumstances of age, pregnancy and herd immunity. Drs Cartwright and Staines present the state of the art in the rapidly moving field of the acute leukaemias. The interactions of genetic, infectious and environmental factors, including irradiation, in the aetiology of the chronic leukaemias are addressed by Drs Finch and Linet. Hodgkin's disease is emerging as a heterogeneous condition, with different aetiologies in different age groups. Dr Jarrett summarizes the evidence which suggests that the Epstein Barr virus plays a causative role in children and older adults, but that other agents, possibly viral, are involved in young adults. The non-Hodgkin's lymphomas and paraproteinaemias are a most diverse group of diseases, but there are common mechanisms in the multistep processes of aetiology. In the light of their experiences in a heterogeneous population undergoing rapid social change, Drs Ramot and Rechavi review constitutional factors, agents causing polyclonal proliferations (including well-characterized viruses), immune suppression (often caused by infectious agents such as malaria or HIV), and the final irreversible genetic change.

Some may find it surprising that a chapter is devoted to tuberculosis, but in many developing countries tuberculosis is the most common aetiological factor, with the exception of pregnancy, underlying anaemia in adults. The pandemic of HIV is having a catastrophic impact in Africa by allowing the recrudescence of latent tuberculosis and increasing transmission from adults to children, the latter being predominantly uninfected by HIV. The same parallel epidemics of HIV and tuberculosis may be anticipated in Asia during the coming decades. Dr Knox-Macaulay reviews the epidemiology and the protean haematological consequences of tuberculosis.

Neonatal jaundice and anaemia are major health problems in Asia and Africa, commonly causing severe morbidity and mortality. Dr Ho gives an account of a highly successful control programme in Singapore, and this should serve as a model for the rest of Asia and for Africa where there are precisely the same aetiological factors: sepsis, prematurity, glucose-6-phosphate dehydrogenase deficiency and ABO incompatibility. Two contrasting chapters cover haematinic deficiencies (Drs Hercberg and Galan) and iron overload (Dr Gordeuk). Dietary iron overload in southern Africa had been thought to be a thing of the past following the 'liberalization' of drinking laws, which allowed the majority of the population to drink bottled beer instead of beer brewed at home in iron pots. Dr Gordeuk points out that iron overload is still a problem in rural areas and that there is a putative genetic component in its aetiology.

The two final chapters concern inherited conditions occurring at polymorphic frequencies because of selection by malaria. Ovalocytosis and elliptocytosis had been thought to be relatively uncommon and perhaps unimportant, but Dr Nurse and co-authors review the classification of these inherited red cell skeleton disorders, and the role of malaria in the selection for ovalocytosis, which is found in up to 50% of some populations in south-east Asia and Oceania. Dr Hill summarizes the great diversity of mutations which give rise to the thalassaemias, their geographical distribution and evidence for selection by *P. falciparum*. Prenatal diagnosis programmes have been highly successful in reducing the frequency of thalassaemia major in Mediterranean populations and it is to be hoped that similar programmes can be established in Asia with immense benefit to families as well as huge savings for the national health budgets.

ALAN F. FLEMING

1

Acute leukaemias

R. A. CARTWRIGHT
A. STAINES

The acute leukaemias present major challenges for epidemiologists and others concerned with the public health. Their rarity means that investigations are time consuming and expensive, whilst the generally emotive nature of childhood lymphoblastic leukaemia and the high mortality associated with the adult myeloproliferative types add additional burdens to their investigation. Furthermore there is no other group of diseases accompanied by such a colourful folklore regarding occurrences and aetiologies, inevitably posing problems of bias in any survey.

Case ascertainment has been patchy in quality in the past (Alexander et al, 1989) and has been accompanied by major changes in concepts regarding classification and the elemental steps of pathogenesis. Despite these and other epidemiological problems a good deal of investment into epidemiological research has taken place recently and an increasing number of useful and viable studies have been produced in the last 5 years. Further noteworthy studies are currently anticipated and so this chapter must be regarded as a staging post in the evolution of our understanding of these conditions, rather than as a definitive essay.

INCIDENCE AND MORTALITY

The interpretation of incidence and mortality figures for leukaemia remains difficult. In earlier work mortality was invariably used as a proxy for incidence, and this was reasonably satisfactory at a time when most persons diagnosed as having acute leukaemia probably survived less than 6 months. With the increasing survival of people with leukaemia this is no longer adequate.

Coding systems for routine statistics often do not allow a distinction between acute leukaemias and chronic leukaemias. Thus in International Classification of Diseases-9 (ICD-9) the code 204 is for lymphoid leukaemia, 205 is myeloid leukaemia, and the acute/chronic distinction requires use of a fourth digit (WHO, 1977). Many published compilations of mortality and registration data use only three-digit codes, and many of the studies discussed here use either these codes, or even cruder classifications, such as 'leukaemia' or 'acute leukaemia' contrasted with 'chronic' leukaemia.

Baillière's Clinical Haematology—
Vol. 5, No. 1, January 1992
ISBN 0–7020–1626–8

1

The Leukaemia/Lymphoma Atlas of the United Kingdom, from the Leukaemia Research Fund (LRF) Data Collection Study (DCS) (Cartwright et al, 1990), is a major source for population-based incidence figures for the various subtypes of leukaemia and other haemopoietic malignancies. A discrepancy of about 20% between the figures from the LRF-DCS and the Office of Population Censuses and Surveys (OPCS) registration figures was found and is believed to be due to under registration by OPCS (Cartwright et al, 1990). The International Agency for Research on Cancer (IARC) publication *International Incidence of Childhood Cancer* (Parkin et al, 1988) provides a similar breakdown of leukaemia incidence for children only, but covering 51 countries, whilst further international data including adults are available elsewhere (Muir et al, 1987).

The most striking feature of the age-specific incidence figures for leukaemia is the peak at age 4 or so for childhood acute lymphoblastic leukaemia (ALL) (Table 1). In contrast acute myeloid leukaemia (AML), although relatively common in infancy, has its maximum incidence in late adult life. Court Brown and Doll (1962) have shown, from routine mortality statistics, how the 'modern' pattern of childhood ALL, with its distinctive early childhood peak, has evolved in Britain since the 1920s.

International comparisons show varying rates, with higher rates for childhood leukaemia in 'developed' countries (Table 2). Although good incidence data for Africa are lacking at present, the distribution of childhood neoplasms into different diagnostic groups is very different, and

Table 1. Incidence rates for the Leukaemia Research Fund (LRF) Data Collection Study (DCS) survey contrasted with the Office of Population Censuses and Surveys (OPCS) rates (rates/100 000/year).

Age (years)	OPCS 1980–1984		DCS 1984–1988	
	Male	Female	Male	Female
AML				
0– 4	0.38	0.47	1.18	0.94
5–14	0.33	0.41	0.49	0.53
15–24	0.64	0.43	0.82	0.83
25–34	0.81	0.76	0.84	0.91
35–44	1.06	1.04	1.25	1.39
45–54	1.84	1.69	2.53	2.36
55–64	3.83	3.23	5.77	3.65
65–74	8.02	6.78	10.82	7.16
ALL				
0– 4	4.39	4.04	5.10	5.54
5–14	2.26	1.67	2.05	1.60
15–24	1.10	0.51	1.25	0.57
25–34	0.48	0.27	0.50	0.32
35–44	0.25	0.21	0.36	0.21
45–54	0.30	0.31	0.52	0.37
55–64	0.66	0.65	0.75	0.48
65–74	0.86	1.20	0.91	0.43

From Cartwright et al (1990).

Table 2. Incidence of childhood (0–14 years) ALL: age standardised (rates/100 000/year).

	Male	Female
USA—New York (White)	3.6	3.1
Brazil—Recife	0.9	0.7
Costa Rica	4.8	4.2
China—Shanghai	2.0	1.6
India—Bombay	1.3	0.9
Kuwait—Kuwaiti	1.1	1.3
Israel—Jew	2.1	2.0
Japan—Osaka	2.3	1.9
Germany—FRG	3.9	3.4
Finland	3.0	2.2
France—Bas Rhin	2.5	2.8
England and Wales	3.4	2.6
Spain—Zaragoza	2.4	3.0
Italy—Turin	3.4	2.5
New Zealand—Maori	1.9	0.6

From Parkin et al (1988).

Table 3. Childhood (0–14 years) malignancies: lymphoma: leukaemia incidence.

	Male	Female
Africa		
Uganda—West Nile	23.3	15.5
Nigeria—Ibadan	5.8	7.3
America		
USA—New York—White	0.5	0.3
Brazil—Recife	0.8	0.6
Costa Rica	0.6	0.3
Asia		
China—Shanghai	0.4	0.2
India—Bombay	0.7	0.3
Kuwait—Kuwaiti	2.8	1.4
Israel—Jew	1.0	0.7
Japan—Osaka	0.3	0.2
Europe		
Germany—FRG	0.5	0.3
Finland	0.4	0.3
France—Bas Rhin	0.6	0.4
England and Wales	0.4	0.2
Spain—Zaragoza	0.7	0.3
Italy—Turin	0.4	0.3
Oceania		
Fiji—Fijian	0.6	0.7
New Zealand—Maori	0.7	0.7
Papua New Guinea	1.9	1.9

From Parkin et al (1988).

Table 4. Age standardized (world) incidence rates: all ages (rates/ 100 000/year).

	ALL		AML	
	Male	Female	Male	Female
Brazil—Recife	2.0	0.3	2.1	1.4
Costa Rica	2.9	2.4	1.7	1.7
USA—New York City	1.8	1.3	2.4	1.9
India—Bombay	0.8	0.5	0.9	0.6
Kuwait—Kuwaitis	1.2	0.5	1.6	1.3
Israel—Jews	1.3	1.1	1.9	1.5
Japan—Hiroshima	1.1	0.7	1.9	1.6
Germany—Hamburg	1.8	1.4	1.1	1.2
France—Bas Rhin	1.2	0.9	0.5	0.4
England and Wales	1.4	1.1	1.7	1.3
Spain—Zaragoza	0.7	0.8	1.1	1.0
New Zealand—Maori	1.9	1.2	4.6	2.6

From Muir et al (1987).

in particular lymphomas are far more common than leukaemias in most African studies, whereas the reverse is true in developed countries (Table 3). In most series the relative incidences of ALL and AML are such that ALL is more common in children, and AML is more common in adults (Muir et al, 1987; Parkin et al, 1988). There is some evidence that the usual childhood ALL peak is absent in Africa (Fleming, 1986), with relatively more childhood AML. Earlier studies from Japan had suggested that AML was the predominant type in childhood, but more recent work has suggested that this was due to histological misclassification, and that ALL is in fact more common (Bessho, 1989). Overall international rates for acute leukaemias are given in Table 4.

The overall incidence of leukaemia appears to have increased in England and Wales since the beginning of this century (Court Brown and Doll, 1962; Adelstein and White, 1976), and a slight rise in childhood leukaemia has continued in more recent years (Stiller and Draper, 1982; Birch et al, 1988). A similar rise, over a shorter time period, was observed in Sweden (Ericsson et al, 1978) and America (Roush et al, 1987), though not in Denmark (De Nully Brown et al, 1989). Over the last 20 years the case fatality rate for childhood leukaemia has fallen markedly (Birch et al, 1988; Stiller and Bunch, 1990). The reasons for the rise in incidence are presently unknown. It is plausible that improved diagnosis has played some role, but this is not likely to be the full story. The known association between social class and leukaemia allow speculation that some aspect of the modern life-style, possibly related to changes in the patterns of childhood antigenic stimulation and/or viral exposure, may be responsible.

CLUSTERING

Acute leukaemias are often described as 'clustered', most especially childhood ALL. This vague term is used to indicate several different phenomena and the reader should take great care in putting this descriptive term into its appropriate context. The phenomena can be classified into four broad types: (1) familial, (2) household, (3) having an obvious cause, and (4) having an obscure cause or no cause.

Familial clusters

Either there is an excess of acute leukaemias within blood relatives or an excess of leukaemia associated with a spectrum of possibly related malignancies. The former instances have been described as case reports (Anderson, 1951; Gunz, 1978); often there are striking excesses of adult myeloid leukaemia with preleukaemia. No epidemiological surveys are available to provide more information on this topic.

Syndromes featuring childhood acute leukaemias are rare but include the Li Fraumeni syndrome (Li and Fraumeni, 1982) and a familial microcephaly (Seemanova et al, 1985).

Household clusters

Observations on household cases are very old (Bie, 1910) and are either in unrelated householders (Ross et al, 1983) or in spouse pairs (Amos et al, 1967). No studies exist to indicate whether these rare reported incidents are due to anything other than chance.

Having an obvious cause

It is to be hoped that this group of cluster observations will increase as the years go by. At the present time acute adult leukaemia associated with the human T-cell lymphotropic virus type 1 (HTLV-1) infection in the Caribbean and Japan comprise the main group (Yoshida et al, 1982). In HTLV-1 endemic areas the lifetime risk of acquiring the associated leukaemia may be as high as 4% (Murphy and Blattner, 1988).

Having no obvious cause or chance

Although the majority of 'cluster' reports fall into this category, the first consideration should be whether the observation of the cluster is likely to be fortuitous or not.

This aspect has been an issue since the very early observations on clusters (Obrastzow, 1890; Aubertin and Grellety, 1923). A prolonged statistical debate started in the 1950s (Knox, 1964) and was eclipsed by a simulation study (Chen et al, 1984) which indicated that the available methods were not robust enough to detect clusters in many instances. This has led to a plethora of new statistical methods.

A parallel theme has been the acquisition of highly accurate incidence data sets to be used to apply the statistical methods. These objectives have been recently achieved (Cartwright et al, 1990). Analyses show ALL in childhood has heterogeneous distribution with higher rates in areas of isolation (Alexander et al, 1990a) and, in another data set, a firm indication of close neighbourhood clustering of ALL in similar areas (Draper, 1991).

There is less evidence to date that adult AML clusters in a similar fashion and most literature attention is devoted to childhood leukaemia clusters. Many such clusters can be described as 'neighbourhood' in type (Heath and Hasterlik, 1963; Day et al, 1989). No 'investigation' of a reported cluster has yet led to any conclusions or insights into the causes of the cluster itself or contributed to the study of the aetiology of the condition.

Some clusters are occupationally based (Frumkin, 1987) and again there has been little success in adding anything to the general knowledge of causation.

A promising line of investigation makes the assumption that close case aggregation of disease must be infectious in some way. If this is so, ALL cases must exhibit signs of clustering by either general community contact (Kinlen, 1988) or more direct case–case contact or case–contact–case contact. A variety of studies have addressed these issues by clinical observation (Kemmoona, 1974; Schimpff et al, 1975) and others have attempted population based approaches with negative results.

Recently the application of residential contact between cases by time-windows has proved very successful in accounting for the evolution of ALL clusters in several sites in the north of England (Alexander et al, un-published observations). It would seem likely, if this work is supported by other data sets, that such a phenomenon in young people with ALL is part of the natural history of the condition. This has two major consequences: it makes the search for local geographically based environmental factors associated with ALL fruitless (as it always has been); and it directs attention to the infectious disease structure within the 'isolated' and 'non-isolated' communities displaying such variation in ALL rates. The linkage of ALL with nuclear reprocessing plants, water supplies or overhead powerlines would thus be irrelevant. Even more importantly the successful search for infectious agents could result in public health measures and lead to a change in incidence of the condition.

IONIZING RADIATION

The adverse effects of radiation exposure have been known since the early years of this century. The long-term follow-up of the Hiroshima and Nagasaki survivors began in October 1950, but even before that date a marked excess of death from acute leukaemia and other haematological disorders had occurred (Ohkita, 1975; Ichimaru et al, 1976). The follow up study, now called the Life Span Study (LSS), has confirmed this excess, and along with the new (DS-86) dosimetry, has enabled a more precise quanti-fication of the risks from exposure to radiation (Preston and Pierce, 1987; BEIR V, 1990).

There is an increase in the risk of dying from leukaemia, which was maximal in the first years of follow-up (i.e. 1950 to 1952) and has declined steadily since. The excess mortality over the 35 years of follow-up is about

Table 5. BEIR V estimates of excess mortality from leukaemia due to radiation exposures: lifetime risks per 100 000 exposed persons.

Exposure	Male	Female
Single exposure to 100 mSv		
Excess deaths (90% CI)	110 (50–280)	80 (30–190)
Expected deaths	760	610
Excess as % of expected	15%	14%
Continuous lifetime exposure to 1 mSv/year		
Excess deaths (90% CI)	70 (20–260)	60 (20–200)
Expected deaths	790	660
Excess as % of expected	8.9%	8.6%
Continuous exposure to 10 mSv/years from age 18 to age 65		
Excess deaths (90% CI)	400 (130–1160)	310 (110–910)
Expected deaths	780	650
Excess as % of expected	52%	48%

From Table 4.2 in BEIR V (1990).

3.4 deaths per 10 000 person years at risk per gray of radiation dose to the marrow. The equivalent factor for whole body kerma is 2.75 excess deaths per 10 000 person years per gray. The risk is somewhat higher in men than in women, and higher in those who were older at the time of exposure.

A further analysis of the atomic bomb survivor figures is given in a report from the US Committee on the Biological Effects of Ionising Radiation— BEIR V (1990). The risk estimates in this report are approximately four times higher than those in the previous report from the same committee (BEIR III, 1980). BEIR V provides estimates of risk derived from various studies (Table 5).

Medical therapeutic irradiation

Risk estimates are available from a number of cohorts of people irradiated from various diseases, most notably a cohort of patients with ankylosing spondylitis irradiated in the United Kingdom (Smith and Doll, 1982; Darby et al, 1985, 1987). The ankylosing spondylitis data show a similar temporal pattern of risk to the LSS data, although the increase in risk with age at irradiation is steeper, and AML was more common.

Cohorts of women treated for cervical cancer provide another source of information on the leukaemogenic effects of radiation (Smith, 1977; Boice et al, 1987; Storm, 1988). A pattern of disease similar to that seen in the ankylosing spondylitis cohorts has been observed, but at higher doses the incidence curve flattens and this is attributed to a cell-killing effect of the higher (over 4 Gy) marrow doses. Further support for this interpretation comes from studies of women receiving pelvic irradiation for benign disease, who had lower doses of radiation and a higher excess risk of leukaemia (Smith, 1977).

It is harder to interpret the results from studies of second cancers after treatment for other malignancies, partly because chemotherapy of various kinds is used in most treatment regimens, and partly because the radiotherapy regimens are often complex. There is an increased incidence of most types of tumour in people who have been treated for malignancies and survived (Najean, 1987; Devereux et al, 1990; Hawkins, 1990). Most existing studies are of people treated for haemopoietic malignancies, or of children, because in these groups there is a substantial proportion of survivors. Boivin et al (1986) studied secondary leukaemias in a registry based case-control study and found that the risk of secondary cancer varied depending on the site of the primary tumour, with the greatest risk for uterine malignancies, and least for 'non-trunk' tumours. A similar, but larger, study is underway in England at present (Hawkins, 1990).

Medical diagnostic irradiation

Gibson et al (1972), in a case-control survey (the Tri-State study), showed an increase in the risk of acute and chronic myeloid leukaemia of about threefold for men exposed to over 40 films. Linos et al (1980), in a small case-control study, found no association between diagnostic X-ray exposure and leukaemia, however the method of control selection in this study has been criticized (BEIR V, 1990). Boice et al (1991), in a recent case-control study, suggested that this apparent relationship is an artefact induced by the early symptoms of leukaemia leading to X-rays being performed. However, other studies have found this relationship even when analyses excluded the few years before diagnosis (Preston-Martin et al, 1989).

Thorotrast, a colloid of thorium dioxide, was used as an X-ray contrast agent in continental Europe until the 1940s. The radiation emitted from Thorotrast is mainly α particles, and as a result the exposure is very different in character to most of the other categories of exposure (BEIR IV, 1988; Charles et al, 1990). Risk estimates from a large German study show a fourteenfold excess of deaths from 'bone marrow failure' and an eightfold excess of deaths from AML and related conditions (van Kaick et al, 1986).

In utero irradiation

Stewart et al (1956) observed a significant increase in the risk of leukaemia and other cancers in children who had been irradiated in utero. This unexpected finding was confirmed both by a more extensive analysis of their data by Stewart et al (1958) and by an independent study using a different methodology by MacMahon (1962) in the USA.

Although preliminary studies of those atomic bomb survivors exposed to in utero radiation, a small cohort, failed to confirm this observation, more recent studies of this group of children (Yoshimoto, 1990) have indicated the possibility of an increase in risk, which inevitably has considerable uncertainty in its estimates. Reasonable estimates of the in utero doses received as a result of diagnostic irradiation are between 5 and 50 mGy

(BEIR V, 1990) and, if the association is causal, this suggests a considerably enhanced susceptibility to the risks of ionizing radiation for the child in utero.

Occupational exposure

Radium dial workers

One of the few occupational groups exposed to large doses of α-irradiation were the women who applied luminous paint on watch and clock dials. Neither the British nor the USA studies of radium dial workers have shown clear evidence of an increased risk of dying from leukaemia (Spiers et al, 1983; Baverstock and Papworth, 1985), although early deaths from 'marrow failure' apparently occurred.

Radiologists

The largest American survey of radiologists' mortality has shown that the risk of dying from leukaemia was substantially higher amongst radiologists joining their professional association before 1940 compared with those joining from 1940 to 1949 (Matanoski et al, 1975). The equivalent British study showed a fourfold increase in risk for those joining before 1921, but the number of deaths was small and the result was not statistically significant (Court Brown and Doll, 1958). The largest study of this type to date comes from China (Wang et al, 1990), and reports qualitatively similar risks, with relative risks of 3.0 for those starting before 1969 and 1.3 for those who started work after 1969.

Occupation in the nuclear industry

One of the first epidemiological studies of occupational exposure to radiation was carried out by Archer et al (1973), of workers in a uranium mill. This showed a non-statistically significant rise in the Standard Mortality Ratio (SMR) for leukaemia, based on one case, and a larger, but equally statistically insignificant rise in the SMR for all cancers of haemopoietic tissues. A similar study of workers in a weapons grade uranium enrichment facility showed no evidence of a raised SMR for leukaemia, and no indication of a trend (Brown and Bloom, 1987).

A United Kingdom Atomic Energy Authority study found a raised, but not statistically significant, SMR for leukaemia compared with the general public among both radiation exposed and unexposed workers. The relationship between the risk of leukaemia and cumulative radiation exposure was complex, and the confidence limits on these estimates all include zero, so no firm interpretation is possible (Inskip et al, 1987), especially as 'non-exposed' men, i.e. workers without a radiation record, had higher rates of leukaemia mortality and incidence than those with a radiation record. Women with a radiation record had higher mortality rates from leukaemia than women without a record (Beral et al, 1985).

Workers at Sellafield, a nuclear fuel reprocessing plant, had mean accumulated doses of 124 mSv per radiation worker (Smith and Douglas, 1986). These workers had an SMR of 98 for all cause mortality. The equivalent SMRs for leukaemia mortality were 82 (10 deaths with 12.2 expected) in radiation workers, and 19 (1 death with 5.14 expected) in non-radiation workers. Amongst radiation workers there was a positive trend in leukaemia mortality with increasing dose which approached statistical significance (BEIR V, 1990).

Workers at the Atomic Weapons Establishment plants were studied by Beral et al (1988). There were no deaths from leukaemia in workers with a cumulative exposure of more than 10 mSv, and the SMR for leukaemia was 44 for radiation workers and 90 for non-radiation workers.

Checkoway et al (1985a) studied workers at the Oak Ridge National Laboratory in the USA. The SMR for leukaemia was 148, based on 16 deaths, but this was not statistically significant. Wing et al (1991) have extended the follow-up of this cohort for a further 7 years and found a statistically significant relationship between leukaemia and those workers who had both external dose (SMR 163) and internal dose monitoring (SMR 223).

Checkoway et al (1988) reported on workers at the Y-2 nuclear weapons manufacturing facility at Oak Ridge. There were only four deaths from leukaemia in the entire cohort (with eight expected), which precluded any investigation of dose–response curves.

Najarian and Colton (1978) carried out a proportionate mortality study of nuclear shipyard workers in Portsmouth, New Hampshire. They found a fivefold excess risk of dying from leukaemia in the 'radiation workers', a group with a trivial mean radiation exposure. There were further studies of this cohort by Rinsky et al (1981) as a cohort mortality study, by Stern et al (1986) as a case-control study of leukaemia cases only, and by Greenberg et al (1985) who reviewed sources of bias in determining the radiation exposure of the cases studied by Najarian and Colton. These more extensive studies failed to confirm the original findings.

Wilkinson et al (1987) studied workers at the Rocky Flats plutonium facility. Workers there were mainly exposed to internal α radiation from inhaled or ingested plutonium. There was a statistically significant increase (based on only four cases) in the incidence of all lymphopoietic malignancies in men with more than 2 nCi (75 Bq) of plutonium compared with those with less than this amount. Two cases of AML occurred in workers exposed to more than 10 mSv compared with none in those exposed to less than 10 mSv.

Of all the epidemiological studies of workers exposed to radiation, the one which has engendered the greatest difficulties in interpretation is the study of workers at the Hanford plant in Washington. This group of workers were first studied by Mancuso et al (1977) as a proportionate mortality study. Further studies followed from Kneale et al (1981, 1984a, 1984b), Gilbert and Marks (1979), Gilbert and Petersen (1985), Gilbert et al (1989) and Gilbert (1989). Of these papers only the last two address leukaemia mortality directly. Gilbert and colleagues conclude that the most likely estimate is of a negative association between radiation exposure and leukaemia mortality, but with wide confidence limits.

The occupational cohorts are one of the most important potential sources for information on low dose radiation effects. However there are a number of serious problems. No individual cohort has sufficient power reliably to identify small risks of the same order of magnitude as the BEIR estimates (Table 5). *A fortiori*, they lack power to detect a risk modestly in excess of the BEIR estimates (Darby, 1986). The exposures are very diverse, and the dosimetries used in different studies are not easy to compare. Also no study has yet been able to make any but the most rudimentary allowance for exposures to other chemicals. Thus Checkoway et al (1985a) used job categories as a proxy for this information and found evidence of excess leukaemia mortality among maintenance and engineering workers. Further, i.e. longer, follow-up of the US workers cohorts may clarify the picture (Wing et al, 1991).

Fall-out studies

There are two major groups of fall-out studies. The first studies the effects on civilian populations and the second studies the effect on those military so exposed. The main civilian study, apart from the Marshalese Islanders' study (Conrad, 1984) has been on the effect of living near the Nevada test site. As a result of local geography the bulk of the fall-out deposition on populated areas was in Utah (Voilleque and Gesell, 1990).

The first study of this population came from Lyon et al (1979), who found that leukaemia mortality among children in southern and eastern Utah (putatively high-exposure areas) was lower than that in north-western Utah before and after the periods affected by fall-out, and during the period affected by fall-out it had approximately doubled to the levels in the north-west. Beck and Krey (1983) presented dosimetry estimates by county for Utah, to indicate that Lyon's decision to divide Utah into 'high' and 'low' exposure counties was invalid. Land et al (1984) conducted another mortality study using slightly different time periods and showed that the original result was likely to be incorrect for a variety of reasons. Machado et al (1987) carried out a study of cancer mortality rates for the three south-western counties, compared with the rest of Utah. They found an increased rate of leukaemia after 1955, highest in children (odds ratio (OR) = 2.82), but raised in adults also (OR = 1.45 overall). The more recent study by Stevens et al (1990) was a case-control study of deceased cases, with controls matched for year of birth, year of death, and residence in Utah at death. Exposure was assessed using the results of the new dosimetry programme (Lloyd et al, 1990). This study showed a clear dose–response relationship, with an OR of 1.69 for exposure between 6 and 30 mGy to bone marrow.

An increase in the risk of leukaemia in that locality seems to be established, and fall-out from nuclear tests is a plausible but not the only possible explanation. The interpretation still awaits further considered clarification.

There are two major studies of military participants at nuclear test sites: Caldwell et al (1983), who studied American participants at one test in 1957, and Darby et al (1988), who studied a much larger group of participants in the UK test programme. Caldwell et al (1983) found a 2.5-fold increased risk of leukaemia, but with no evidence of a dose–response relationship, and they felt that this might be a chance finding. Darby et al (1988) found a 3.45-fold increased risk of leukaemia when contrasted with other servicemen, and a slight non-significant excess when compared to the UK public.

Living near nuclear facilities

Interest in this topic was first aroused in the UK when a television programme reported a 'cluster' of cases of leukaemia among young people living near the Sellafield reprocessing plant. The Government responded by setting up a Committee of Inquiry which concluded that there might be cause for concern, and recommended that a series of further studies should be carried out, both at Sellafield and elsewhere (Black, 1984). One finding of these studies was that there was evidence for an increased risk of leukaemia in children born in Seascale (the village near Sellafield), but no increased risk for children who moved into the area after birth (Gardner et al, 1987).

Similar studies were carried out around other nuclear facilities (Cook-Mozaffari et al, 1987; Roman et al, 1987; COMARE II, 1988), showing an increased number of leukaemias around these sites as well. However Cook-Mozaffari et al (1989) also studied sites which had been considered as candidate nuclear sites and found a similarly raised incidence of leukaemia. This evidence suggests that other factors besides radiation may be involved (see below). Studies on this topic in France (Hill and Laplanche, 1990) and America (Jablon et al, 1991) have been negative.

These results are not easy to interpret. Hills and Alexander (1989) discuss some of the problems of statistical inference involved. The problems of biological inference are perhaps even more difficult. In view of the dosimetry and other aspects of epidemiology it seems probable that the explanations for the raised leukaemia incidence around these plants have little to do with radiation, but rather may be indexes of aspects of life-style and isolation.

Natural sources of radiation

The possible role of natural radiation in leukaemogenesis has become the focus of an active research programme in several countries. So far the only data available are ecological correlations (Alexander et al, 1990b; Henshaw et al, 1990; Cohen, 1991), mostly using the National Radiological Protection Board (NRPB) radon survey data for the UK (Wrixon et al, 1988), or Cohen and Shah's (1991) data for the USA. In general these reports are difficult to interpret. The combined effect of the inevitable uncertainties in measurement (Lubin et al, 1990), and the difficulties of any ecological analysis, (Prentice and Sheppard, 1990) make secure inference almost impossible from this data.

A recent report from Bridges et al (1991) shows an association between home radon levels and the frequency of hypoxanthine guanine phosphoribosyl transferase gene mutations in peripheral blood T lymphocytes from 20 people. This is a preliminary report but, if confirmed, it will be of great interest. Studies are underway in which radon levels will be measured in the homes of people with leukaemia, and controls as part of a case-control study, and these may eventually settle the issue.

The largest studies of persons exposed to high levels of radon are of underground miners (BEIR IV, 1988), however almost all of the studies of these groups have mixed exposures and also considered lung cancer as the main end-point, and there is little information, mostly negative, on leukaemia deaths (Solli et al, 1985).

Conclusions

There is no doubt that higher doses of radiation (over 1 Gy) can cause acute leukaemia. Because the power of studies of low dose radiation to detect small excess risks of leukaemia is so limited, most estimates of risk at low doses come from extrapolation (Darby, 1986). Analyses of the high dose data have concluded that the evidence is consistent with a linear no-threshold relationship at these dose levels; that is to say that risk increases directly as dose, and that there is no dose below which no effect is possible (BEIR V, 1990). The high dose studies report people who have received large doses in a few seconds (for atomic bomb survivors), a few minutes (for ankylosing spondylitis patients), or over a few weeks (for those treated for malignant disease). Typical occupational or medical γ doses are of the same order of magnitude as background radiation (say 1 mSv per annum), and are received over long periods of time. The results of occupational studies are compatible with the view (but not confirmatory) that this extreme dose fractionation produces risks of the same order of magnitude as those derived from the high dose studies. The role of natural radon exposure, which is probably the most variable component of 'background' radiation (Wrixon et al, 1988; Cohen and Shah, 1991), remains to be determined.

ELECTRICAL AND MAGNETIC FIELD EXPOSURE

Individuals are exposed to both electrical and alternating magnetic fields in a variety of ways. Normally householders experience a widely varying flux depending on domestic appliances and the way the feeding cables configure in the neighbourhood. Rarely houses are sited within a few metres of an overhead high tension line, in which case the domestic background would be increased. Finally, some individuals are exposed as a result of their occupation or because of certain medical treatments. No studies have yet examined this last exposure, but the others have all been addressed in a variety of ways. There are no helpful biological experimental studies available which indicate that the leukaemias or any cancer are likely sequelae of exposure. Notwithstanding this, there are a myriad of reported biological experiments indicating that magnetic field exposures can alter aspects of cellular physiology. Electrical fields have little relevance as they only pass around the surface of the body and are not further discussed here. Despite the range of biological studies so far attempted, none has yet used animal systems relevant to leukaemogenesis. The lack of biological support has not deterred a considerable effort on the part of epidemiologists and others to further investigate potential harmful effects in a human population setting.

The initiating paper in this series (Wertheimer and Leeper, 1979), although showing a link between childhood leukaemias and estimated household magnetic field strengths from overhead lines, was heavily criticized and a reworking of the data considerably reduced the statistical significance of the original observation. All the other reported studies of childhood leukaemia and estimated household magnetic fields show no statistically significant excessive risks, although the risks of published studies themselves tend to be greater than unity (Fulton et al, 1980; Savitz et al, 1988; Myers et al, 1990). One similar study on adult leukaemia shows roughly analogous results (Youngson et al, 1991).

These studies may all be readily criticized on the grounds that their estimates of magnetic fields exposure are unrealistic in terms of real human exposure, as well as on many aspects of study design and execution (Cartwright, 1989). The main problem is that, because of recent personal dosimetric studies, it is apparent that households, irrespective of their proximity to overhead powerlines, vary considerably in the quantity of magnetic flux they contain. It would be essential to account for this to make sense of the earlier studies. This has yet to be achieved.

The other studies commonly associated with electrical and magnetic field exposures address the subject of 'electrically-related' occupations. These are a rag-bag of jobs loosely linked with electricity in some ways. They include linesmen, repair men and factory assembly workers (Coleman and Beral, 1988). All the studies, and there are many, assume they are exposed to 'excessive' magnetic fields, but none has provided evidence in support of this assertion. Nevertheless, there is some internal consistency within these studies, many of which have been reviewed by Coleman and Beral (1988), suggesting a link with AML with a risk of about 1.5. More recent studies have also supported this association (McKinney et al, 1989; Pearce et al, 1989; Juutilainen et al, 1990).

Because of the lack of an industrial hygiene input into these studies, the interpretation of the findings are speculative; although it is undoubtedly true that an association exists, it is not known whether it is due to magnetic field exposure or the many chemicals and their fumes used in the various workplaces.

It should be borne in mind that all these studies relate to exposures at the extremely low energy end of the electromagnetic spectrum, the fields in question being generated in the main by 50 or 60 Hz equipment. Studies on radio and radar exposure and other higher energy sources have yet to be undertaken in a satisfactory epidemiological fashion.

OCCUPATIONAL EXPOSURE TO CHEMICALS

The best established occupational leukaemogenic exposure is undoubtedly to benzene. Some controversy persists as to whether current exposure limits are 'safe' or acceptable (Infante, 1987). However, the work of Aksoy et al (1987), Infante et al (1977) and Yin et al (1987) leaves little room for doubt that exposure to high levels of benzene is a significant cause of AML (IARC, 1987). The latest and most detailed examinations of the dose–response relationship (Rinsky et al, 1987; Austin et al, 1988) suggest that an exposure equivalent to an annual exposure of 10 p.p.m. is associated with a markedly increased rate of death from acute leukaemia, mostly AML. Work relating to cigarette smoke exposure, probably the main source of individual benzene exposure (Wallace, 1989), is discussed elsewhere in this chapter.

Other groups of workers with diverse exposures, often including benzene, have been studied. Thus a series of studies of people employed in oil refineries and oil distribution services have shown evidence of a modestly increased risk of leukaemia and other haemopoietic malignancies (Rushton and Alderson, 1981; Wong and Raabe, 1989; Marsh et al, 1991). Similar studies in chemical industry employees have shown an excess of leukaemia in benzene exposed workers (Wong, 1987), and in workers with a more diverse pattern of exposures (Checkoway et al, 1985b; Rinsky et al, 1988). Many of the cohort studies have used mortality comparisons with the general population as their basis for comparison. As Wong (1987) has shown, this may lead to a systematic and substantial underestimation of the hazards of exposure. A further problem in interpreting the results of any such studies is the extreme diversity of possible exposures which can occur in modern chemical plants (Ott et al, 1989).

Other specific occupational exposures studied have included ethylene oxide and styrene. Ethylene oxide production and use have been associated with an increased incidence of leukaemia in small studies from Sweden (Hogstedt et al, 1986). A larger study from Connecticut (Greenberg et al, 1990) found that this association was confined to workers exposed to ethylene and propylene chlorhydrin in the manufacture of ethylene oxide. An increased number of sister chromatid exchanges, a marker of DNA damage, were found in workers using ethylene oxide to sterilize medical supplies (Yager et al, 1983). Styrene, widely used in the plastics manufacturing industry, has also been extensively studied, but with contradictory results suggesting little or no risk (Hodgson and Jones, 1985; Matanoski and Schwarz, 1987; Wong, 1990).

Farmers and other 'agricultural' workers have an increased risk of dying from leukaemia (Blair et al, 1985; Pearce et al, 1986; Pearce and Reif, 1990). Similar excesses have been observed in paper and sawmill workers, forestry workers, abattoir workers, and veterinarians (Blair and Hayes, 1982; Burkart, 1982; Pearce et al, 1988; Reif et al, 1989). Johnson et al (1986a, 1986b), in a very large study of meat workers, found an excess of AML confined to women working in meat packing and exposed to the thermal breakdown products of various plastics. Possible causes of the excess mortality in farmers include chemical and viral exposures (Blair et al, 1985; Pearce and Reif, 1990). The excess mortality in forestry workers remains unexplained but is probably not due to herbicide exposure (Reif et al, 1989).

Pesticides and herbicides have been implicated in the aetiology of leukaemia in case-control studies (McKinney et al, 1989; Brown et al, 1990).

A number of studies of phenoxy herbicide exposure have been undertaken (Axelson and Sundell, 1974; Hardell et al, 1981; Johnson et al, 1990; Coggon et al, 1991). Although there is an association with non-Hodgkin's lymphoma, there is presently no evidence for an association with acute leukaemia.

There are a very large number of studies of cancer mortality in other occupational groups. Leukaemia has been reported to be elevated in several studies of embalmers (Walrath and Fraumeni, 1984; Linos et al, 1990) and a study of anatomists (Stroup et al, 1986), possibly associated with formaldehyde exposure. Painters and printers, who have a complex range of exposures including solvents, dyes, and dusts, have been reported to have excess mortality from acute leukaemias in some studies but not in others (Greene et al, 1979; Zoloth et al, 1986; Lindquist et al, 1987; Bethwaite et al, 1990). Studies of 'chemists' and pharmaceutical industry staff have shown inconsistent results (Olin and Ahlbom, 1980; Hoar and Pell, 1981; Walrath et al, 1985; Harrington and Goldblatt, 1986). At present it is impossible to assess the proportion of acute leukaemia in the general population that can be attributed to occupational exposure. However, most occupations do not involve exposure to any of the putative leukaemogens discussed here, and many of the reports cited here have to be interpreted with caution. It seems unlikely that occupational exposure is quantitatively important in western countries.

PARENTAL OCCUPATION AND CHILDHOOD LEUKAEMIA

There have been numerous studies peripherally addressing the issue of links between diseases in children and specific exposures of parents. Overall the results have been somewhat variable, certainly for malignancies in the offspring (Savitz and Chen, 1990). In addition there has been considerable scepticism as to the biological basis for such links and a consequential debate, with very little experimental support regarding the possibilities of single gene changes, chromosomal rearrangements or epigenetic mechanisms. The outcome has been generally unsatisfactory so far, although new experimental systems are currently being investigated.

The available studies present a confusing array of parental occupations and putative exposures, and only a few studies present odds ratios which achieve statistical significance. These include motor vehicle mechanics and machinists, miners and lumbermen (Kwa and Fine, 1980; Lowengart et al, 1987; Buckley et al, 1989). Exposures to hydrocarbons (Vianna et al, 1984), spray paints (Lowengart et al, 1987) and other petroleum products (Buckley et al, 1989) also produce significantly high odds ratios. However, for each significant result there are more studies that report negative or non-significant results for that occupation or exposure.

The studies are readily criticized in that they usually aggregate together different types of leukaemia. An exception here is the study on childhood AML reported by Buckley et al (1989). In addition, they have very poor or non-existent assessments of true exposure and use job titles as exposure surrogates. Finally, they rarely examine their data with respect to length of exposure or the time of exposure with respect to the conception or birth of the case children. Some of these criticisms have been addressed in more recent studies where links have been described between female textile workers exposed at specific periods in their reproductive life for AML and ALL in their offspring (Magnani et al, 1990; Infante-Rivard et al, 1991) and similarly exposures to wood dust (McKinney et al, 1991).

Other possibly 'dusty' occupations associated with paternal exposures have also been described (Magnani et al, 1990; McKinney et al, 1991). More attention has been placed recently on the apparent association between male exposures to ionizing irradiation and subsequent childhood leukaemias (Gardner et al, 1990a, 1990b, Gardner, 1991; McKinney et al, 1991; Urquhart et al, 1991). In various and possibly overlapping ways these studies suggest there is a link before or around conception. These results have engendered considerable controversy, partly because they lack a 'mechanistic' or biological foundation. The interpretation of these statistical associations is not possible because further and more directed epidemiological surveys are underway.

CIGARETTE SMOKING

Although many case-control studies have failed to indicate a satisfactory link between cigarette smoking and adult acute leukaemia, there is now good and substantive evidence for an association. Kinlen and Rogot (1988) and McLaughlin et al (1989) examined a mortality cohort of 24000 US veterans and found an almost twofold risk leading to a substantial population attributable risk. A recent case-control study has confirmed this risk in AML (Severson et al, 1990), as have further independent cohort studies (Garfinkel and Boffetta, 1990). The latter also report results for women which show little overall risk and a generally lower or non-existent risk for lymphoid malignancies; however, these were not distinguished as 'acute' or 'chronic' leukaemia. Cigarette smoking represents the most common cause of AML, certainly in males, and might account for over 20% of the disease in certain situations.

INFECTIOUS AETIOLOGIES

The majority of work in this area has concentrated on the childhood leukaemias. There is little available in the literature to link adult acute leukaemia with the sequelae of infection or infectious agents of any types. However, the apparent tendency of childhood leukaemia to cluster has always made it a prime candidate as a virally related condition. This has been studied by case reports, for example, detailing influenza-like illnesses prior to diagnosis of ALL (Kemmoona, 1976). However, when epidemiological studies have been applied to the period prior to diagnosis (Leck and

Steward, 1972) or in pregnancy (Randolph and Heath, 1974), no clear links with influenza emerged.

The search for specific viruses associated with acute leukaemia has failed so far, despite the extensive research experience associated with animal leukaemia viruses, with the exception of identification of HTLV-1 causing an acute lymphoma/leukaemia-like condition (Blattner, 1989).

More recently the analysis of case aggregated data has tended to confirm clustering in ALL in childhood (Draper, 1991) and to stimulate further examination of the viral questions (Cartwright, 1991). In addition, two partially connected hypotheses have emerged attempting to explain childhood leukaemia. One (Greaves, 1988), biologically based, has some indirect epidemiological support and is arguably testable. Greaves suggests that the antigenic challenges experienced by young children are critical in creating a susceptible group, in that the lack of stimuli in the early months of life creates a potentially unstable situation in the developing lymphocytes, which are then critically challenged by common infections, leading to a rapidly developing leukaemia. The ideas are focused on common ALL of the childhood peak, and are partially supported by epidemiological evidence that ALL occurs more often in small families and in those children who lack infections early in life (van Steensel-Moll et al, 1986). In addition, the childhood peak of ALL is markedly different in isolated areas compared with urban centres (Alexander et al, 1990a). By this argument no specific infection is important.

Kinlen suggests that population mixing disrupts the spectrum of infections in a community by introducing 'new' viruses to a susceptible population. This hypothesis (Kinlen, 1988) is epidemiologically based with some survey based support, but is less clearly supported by biological models and is less readily testable. By these ideas, either a specific or a non-specific set of infections could be important.

Acknowledgements

We would like to thank Mrs A. Pickles for attending to the manuscript. Much of the work quoted is supported by the Leukaemia Research Fund of the UK.

REFERENCES

Adelstein A & White G (1976) Leukaemia 1911–1973: cohort analysis. *Population Trends* **3**: 9–13.
Aksoy M, Özeris S, Sabuncu H et al (1987) Exposure to benzene in Turkey between 1983 and 1985: a haematological study on 231 workers. *British Journal of Industrial Medicine* **44**: 785–787.
Alexander FE, Ricketts TJ, McKinney PA et al (1989) Cancer registration of leukaemias and lymphomas: results of a comparison with a specialist registry. *Community Medicine* **11**: 81–89.
Alexander FE, Ricketts TJ, McKinney PA et al (1990a) Community lifestyle characteristics and risk of acute lymphoblastic leukaemia in children. *Lancet* **336**: 1461–1465.
Alexander FEA, McKinney PA & Cartwright RA (1990b) Radon and leukaemia. *Lancet* **335**: 1336–1337.

Amos DA, Wellman WE, Bowie EJW et al (1967) Acute leukemia in a husband and wife. *Mayo Clinical Practices* **42**: 468–472.

Anderson RC (1951) Familial leukaemia. *American Journal of Diseases of Children* **81**: 313–322.

Archer VE, Wagoner JK & Lundin FE (1973) Cancer mortality among uranium mill workers. *Journal of Occupational Medicine* **15**: 11–14.

Aubertin CH & Grellety BP (1923) Contribution a l'étude de la leucémie aigue. *Archives du Mal de Coeur* **16**: 696–713.

Austin H, Delzell E & Cole P (1988) Benzene and leukaemia. A review of the literature and a risk assessment. *American Journal of Epidemiology* **127**: 419–439.

Axelson O & Sundell L (1974) Herbicide exposure, mortality and tumour incidence. An epidemiological investigation on Swedish railroad workers. *Work and Environmental Health* **11**: 21–28.

Baverstock KF & Papworth DG (1985) The UK radium luminiser survey: significance of a lack of excess leukaemia. *Strahlentherapie* **80**(supplement): 22–26.

Beck HL & Krey PW (1983) Radiation exposure in Utah from Nevada nuclear tests. *Science* **220**: 18–24.

BEIR III (1980) *The effects on populations of exposure to low levels of ionising radiation.* Washington, DC: National Academy Press.

BEIR IV (1988) *Health risks of radon and other internally deposited α-emitters.* Washington, DC: National Academy Press.

BEIR V (1990) *Health effects of exposure to low levels of ionising radiation.* Washington, DC: National Academy Press.

Beral V, Inskip H, Fraser P, Booth M, Coleman D & Rose G (1985) Mortality of employees of the United Kingdom Atomic Energy Authority 1946–1979. *British Medical Journal* **291**: 440–447.

Beral V, Fraser P, Carpenter L, Booth M, Brown A & Rose G (1988) Mortality of workers of the Atomic Weapons Establishment, 1951–1982. *British Medical Journal* **297**: 755–770.

Bessho F (1989) Acute non-lymphocytic leukaemia is not a major type of childhood leukaemia in Japan. *European Journal of Cancer and Clinical Oncology* **25**: 729–732.

Bethwaite PB, Pearce N & Fraser N (1990) Cancer risks in painters: study based on the New Zealand Cancer Registry. *British Journal of Industrial Medicine* **47**: 742–746.

Bie AV (1910) Two cases of leukaemia in the same household. *Ugeskrift for Laeger* **51**: 1607–1620.

Birch JM, Marsden HB, Morris Jones PH et al (1988) Improvements in survival from childhood cancer: results of a population based survey over thirty years. *British Medical Journal* **296**: 1372–1376.

Black D (chairman) (1984) *Investigation of the possible increased incidence of cancer in West Cumbria.* London: HMSO.

Blair A & Hayes HW (1982) Mortality patterns among US veterinarians, 1947–1977: an expanded study. *International Journal of Epidemiology* **11**: 391–397.

Blair A, Malker H, Cantor KP, Burmeister L & Wiklund K (1985) Cancer among farmers, a review. *Scandinavian Journal of Work and Environmental Health* **11**: 397–407.

Blattner WA (1989) Retroviruses. In Evans AS (ed.) *Viral Infections in Humans* 3rd edn, pp 545–592. New York: Plenum Medical.

Boice JD, Blettner M, Kleinerman RA et al (1987) Radiation dose and leukaemia risk in patients treated for cancer of the cervix. *Journal of the National Cancer Institute* **79**: 1295–1311.

Boice JD, Morin MM, Glass MM et al (1991) Diagnostic X-ray procedures and risk of leukemia, lymphoma and multiple myeloma. *Journal of the American Medical Association* **265**: 1290–1294.

Boivin JF, Hutchinson GB, Evans FB, Abou-Daoud KT & Junod B (1986) Leukemia after radiotherapy for first primary cancers of various anatomic sites. *American Journal of Epidemiology* **123**: 993–1003.

Bridges BA, Cole J, Arlett CF et al (1991) Possible association between mutant frequency in peripheral lymphocytes and domestic radon concentrations. *Lancet* **337**: 1187–1189.

Brown DP & Bloom T (1987) *Mortality among uranium enrichment workers*, PB87-188991. Ohio: National Institute for Occupational Safety and Health.

Brown LM, Blair A, Gibson R et al (1990) Pesticide exposures and other risk factors for leukaemia among men in Iowa and Minnesota. *Cancer Research* **50**: 6585–6591.

Buckley JD, Robinson LL, Swotinsky R et al (1989) Occupational exposures of parents of children with acute nonlymphocytic leukaemia: a report from the Children's Cancer Study Group. *Cancer Research* **49:** 4030–4037.

Burkart JA (1982) Leukaemia in hospital patients with occupational exposure to the sawmill industry. *Western Journal of Medicine* **137:** 440–441.

Caldwell GG, Kelley D, Zack M et al (1983) Mortality and cancer frequency among military nuclear test veterans (Smoky), 1957 thru 1979. *Journal of the American Medical Association* **250:** 620–624.

Cartwright RA (1989) Low frequency alternating electromagnetic fields and leukaemia: the saga so far. *British Journal of Cancer* **60:** 649–651.

Cartwright RA (1991) Lifestyle and leukaemia. *British Journal of Cancer* **64:** 417–418.

Cartwright RA, Alexander FE, McKinney PA et al (1990) *Leukaemia and Lymphoma: An Atlas of Distribution within Areas of England and Wales 1984–88.* London: Leukaemia Research Fund.

Charles M, Cox R, Goodhead D et al (1990) CEIR forum on the effects of high-LET radiation at low doses/low rates. *International Journal of Radiation Biology* **58:** 859–885.

Checkoway H, Mathew RM Shy CM et al (1985a) Radiation, work experience, and cause specific mortality among workers at an energy research laboratory. *British Journal of Industrial Medicine* **42:** 525–533.

Checkoway H, Wilcosky T, Wolf P & Tyroler H (1985b) An evaluation of the associations of leukaemia and rubber industry solvent exposures. *American Journal of Industrial Medicine* **5:** 239–249.

Checkoway H, Pearce N, Crawford-Brown DJ et al (1988) Radiation doses and cause-specific mortality among workers at a nuclear materials fabrication plant. *American Journal of Epidemiology* **127:** 255–266.

Chen R, Mantel N & Klingberg M (1984) A study of 3 techniques for time-space clustering in Hodgkin's disease. *Statistics in Medicine* **3:** 173–184.

Coggon D, Pannett B & Winter P (1991) Mortality and incidence of cancer at four factories making phenoxy herbicides. *British Journal of Industrial Medicine* **48:** 173–178.

Cohen B (1991) Radon exposure in homes and cancer. *Lancet* **337:** 790–791.

Cohen B & Shah RS (1991) Radon levels in United States homes by states and counties. *Health Physics* **60:** 243–259.

Coleman M & Beral V (1988) A review of epidemiological studies of the health effects of living near or working with electricity generation and transmission equipment. *International Journal of Epidemiology* **17:** 1–13.

COMARE II (1988) *Investigation of the possible increased incidence of leukaemia in young people near the Dounreay Nuclear Establishment, Caithness, Scotland.* London: HMSO.

Conrad RA (1984) Late radiation effects in Marshall Islanders exposed to fallout 28 years ago. In Boice JD & Fraumeni JF (eds) *Progress in Cancer Research and Therapy*, vol. 26 *Radiation Carcinogenesis*, pp 57–71. New York: Raven Press.

Cook-Mozaffari P, Ashwood FL, Vincent T et al (1987) *Cancer incidence and mortality in the vicinity of nuclear installations, England and Wales 1959–80.* Studies on medical and population subjects 51. London: HMSO.

Cook-Mozaffari P, Darby S & Doll R (1989) Cancer near potential sites of nuclear installations. *Lancet* **ii:** 1145–1147.

Court Brown WM & Doll R (1958) Expectation of life and mortality from cancer among British radiologists. *British Medical Journal* **ii:** 181–187.

Court Brown WM & Doll R (1962) Leukaemia in childhood and young adult life, trends in mortality in relation to aetiology. *British Medical Journal* **i:** 981–988.

Darby SC (1986) Epidemiological evaluation of radiation risk using populations exposed at high doses. *Health Physics* **51:** 269–281.

Darby SC, Nakashima E & Kato H (1985) A parallel analysis of cancer mortality among atomic bomb survivors and patients with ankylosing spondylitis given X-ray therapy. *Journal of the National Cancer Institute* **75:** 1–21.

Darby SC, Doll R, Gill SK & Smith PG (1987) Long term mortality after a single treatment course with X-rays in patients treated for ankylosing spondylitis. *British Journal of Cancer* **55:** 179–190.

Darby SC, Kendall GM, Fell TP et al (1988) A summary of mortality and incidence of cancer in men from the United Kingdom who participated in the United Kingdom's atmospheric nuclear weapons tests and experimental programmes. *British Medical Jo*

Day R, James H, Wartenberg D et al (1989) An investigation of a repo·
Randolph, Massachusetts. *Journal of Clinical Epidemiology* **42**: 1?

De Nully Brown P, Hertz H, Olsen JH et al (1989) Incidence of childhood
1943–1984. *International Journal of Epidemiology* **18**: 546–555.

Devereux S, Selassie TG, Hudson GV et al (1990) Leukaemia complicating ι
Hodgkin's disease: the experience of the British National Lymphoma Inve..
British Medical Journal **301**: 1077–1080.

Draper G (ed.) (1991) *The geographical epidemiology of childhood leukaemia and no.
Hodgkin's Lymphoma in Great Britain 1966–1983.* London: OPCS.

Ericsson JLE, Karnstrom L & Mattsson B (1978) Childhood cancer in Sweden 1958–1974. *Acta Paediatrica Scandinavica* **67**: 425–432.

Fleming AF (1986) Review. Epidemiology of the Leukaemias in Africa. *Leukaemia Research* **3**: 51–59.

Frumkin H (1987) Cancer clusters in the workplace: an approach to investigation. *Journal of Occupational Medicine* **289**: 1075.

Fulton JP, Cobb S, Preble L et al (1980) Electrical wiring configurations and childhood leukaemia in Rhode Island. *American Journal of Epidemiology* **111**: 292.

Gardner M (1991) Radiation workers and childhood leukaemia. *British Medical Journal* **302**: 907.

Gardner MJ, Hall AJ, Downes S et al (1987) Follow up study of children born elsewhere but attending schools in Seascale, West Cumbria (schools cohort). *British Medical Journal* **295**: 819–827.

Gardner MJ, Snee MP, Hall AJ et al (1990a) Results of case-control study of leukaemia and lymphoma among young people near Sellafield nuclear plant in West Cumbria. *British Medical Journal* **300**: 423–429.

Gardner MJ, Hall AJ, Snee MP et al (1990b) Methods and basic data of case-control study of leukaemia and lymphoma among young people near Sellafield nuclear plant in West Cumbria. *British Medical Journal* **300**: 429–434.

Garfinkel L & Boffetta P (1990) Association between smoking and leukaemia in two American cancer society prospective studies. *Cancer* **65**: 2356–2360.

Gibson R, Graham S, Lilienfield A, Schuman L, Dowd JE & Levin ML (1972) Irradiation in the epidemiology of leukemia among adults. *Journal of the National Cancer Institute* **48**: 301–311.

Gilbert ES (1989) Issues in analysing the effects of occupational exposure to low levels of radiation. *Statistics in Medicine* **8**: 173–187.

Gilbert ES & Marks S (1979) An analysis of the mortality of workers in a nuclear facility. *Radiation Research* **79**: 122–148.

Gilbert ES & Petersen GR (1985) A note on 'Job related mortality risks of Hanford Workers, and their relation to cancer effects of measured doses of external radiation'. *British Journal of Industrial Medicine* **42**: 137–139.

Gilbert ES, Petersen GR & Buchanan JA (1989) Mortality of workers at the Hanford site: 1945–1981. *Health Physics* **56**: 11–25.

Greaves MF (1988) Speculations on the cause of childhood acute lymphoblastic leukemia. *Leukemia* **2**: 120–125.

Greenberg ER, Rosner B, Hennekens C et al (1985) An investigation of bias in a study of nuclear shipyard workers. *American Journal of Epidemiology* **121**: 301–308.

Greenberg HL, Ott MG & Shore RE (1990) Men assigned to ethylene oxide production or other ethylene oxide related chemical manufacturing: a mortality study. *British Journal of Industrial Medicine* **47**: 221–230.

Greene MH, Hoover RN, Eck RL & Fraumeni JF (1979) Cancer mortality among printing plant workers. *Environmental Research* **20**: 66–73.

Gunz FW (1978) Thirteen cases of leukaemia in a family. *Journal of the National Cancer Institute* **60**: 1243–1250.

Hardell L, Eriksson M, Lenner P & Lundgren E (1981) Malignant lymphoma and exposure to chemicals, especially organic solvents, chlorophenols, and phenoxy acids: a case-control study. *British Journal of Cancer* **43**: 169–176.

Harrington JM & Goldblatt P (1986) Census based mortality study of pharmaceutical industry workers. *British Journal of Industrial Medicine* **43**: 206–211.

Hawkins MM (1990) Second primary tumours following radiotherapy for childhood cancer. *Journal of Radiation Oncology, Physics and Biology* **19**: 1297–1301.

Heath CW & Hasterlik RJ (1963) Leukemia among children in a suburban community. *American Journal of Medicine* **34**: 796–812.

Henshaw DL, Eatough JP & Richardson RB (1990) Radon as a causative factor in induction of myeloid leukaemia and other cancers. *Lancet* **335**: 1008–1012.

Hill C & Laplanche A (1990) Overall mortality and cancer mortality around French nuclear sites. *Nature* **347**: 755–757.

Hills M & Alexander FE (1989) Statistical methods used in assessing the risk of disease near a source of possible environmental pollution: a review. *Journal of the Royal Statistical Society (Series A)* **152**: 353–363.

Hoar SK & Pell S (1981) A retrospective cohort study of mortality and cancer incidence among chemists. *Journal of Occupational Medicine* **23**: 485–494.

Hodgson JT & Jones RD (1985) Mortality of styrene production, polymerization and processing workers at a site in Northwest England. *Scandinavian Journal of Work and Environmental Health* **11**: 347–352.

Hogstedt C, Aringer L & Gustavsson A (1986) Epidemiologic support for ethylene oxide as a cancer-causing agent. *Journal of the American Medical Association* **255**: 1575–1578.

IARC (1987) *IARC monographs on the evaluation of carcinogenic risks to humans. Overall evaluation of carcinogenicity: an updating of IARC monographs Volumes 1 to 42*, supplement 7. Lyon: IARC.

Ichimaru M, Ishimaru T, Belsky JL et al (1976) *Incidence of leukaemia in atomic bomb survivors, Hiroshima and Nagasaki 1950–1971*. RERF technical report 10–76. Hiroshima: Radiation Effects Research Foundation.

Infante PF (1987) Benzene toxicity: studying a subject to death. *American Journal of Industrial Medicine* **11**: 599–606.

Infante PF, Rinsky RA, Wagoner JK & Young RJ (1977) Leukaemia in benzene workers. *Lancet* **ii**: 76–78.

Infante-Rivard C, Mur P, Armstrong B et al (1991) Acute lymphoblastic leukaemia among Spanish children and mothers' occupation: a case-control study. *Journal of Epidemiology and Community Health* **45**: 11–15.

Inskip H, Beral V, Fraser P et al (1987) Further assessment of the effects of occupational radiation exposure in the United Kingdom atomic energy authority mortality study. *British Journal of Industrial Medicine* **44**: 149–160.

Jablon S, Hrubec Z & Boice JD (1991) Cancer in populations living near nuclear facilities. *Journal of the American Medical Association* **265**: 1403–1408.

Johnson CC, Feingold M & Tilley B (1990) A meta-analysis of exposure to phenoxy acid herbicides and chlorophenols in relation to risk of soft tissue sarcoma. *International Archives of Occupational Health* **62**: 513–520.

Johnson ES, Fischman HR, Matanoski GM & Diamond E (1986a) Occurrence of cancer in women in the meat industry. *British Journal of Industrial Medicine* **43**: 597–604.

Johnson ES, Fischman HR, Matanoski GM & Diamond E (1986b) Cancer mortality among white males in the meat industry. *Journal of Occupational Medicine* **28**: 23–32.

Juutilainen J, Laara E & Pukkala E (1990) Incidence of leukaemia and brain tumours in Finnish workers exposed to ELF magnetic fields. *International Archives of Occupational and Environmental Health* **62**: 289–293.

Kemmoona I (1974) Direct-contact clusters of acute lymphatic leukaemia. *Lancet* **i**: 994.

Kemmoona I (1976) Does influenza and contact with neoplasia predispose to leukaemia? *Irish Journal of Medical Science* **144**: 132–135.

Kinlen L (1988) Evidence for an infective cause of childhood leukaemia: comparison of a Scottish New Town with nuclear reprocessing sites in Britain. *Lancet* **ii**: 1323–1326.

Kinlen LJ & Rogot E (1988) Leukaemia and smoking habits among United States veterans. *British Medical Journal* **297**: 657–659.

Kneale GW, Mancuso TF & Stewart AM (1981) Hanford radiation study III: a cohort study of cancer risks from radiation to workers at Hanford (1944–1977 deaths) by the method of regression models in life-tables. *British Journal of Industrial Medicine* **38**: 156–166.

Kneale GW, Mancuso TF & Stewart AM (1984a) Identification of occupational mortality risks for Hanford workers. *British Journal of Industrial Medicine* **41**: 6–8.

Kneale GW, Mancuso TF & Stewart AM (1984b) Job related mortality risks of Hanford workers and their relation to cancer effects of measured doses of external radiation. *British Journal of Industrial Medicine* **41**: 9–14.

Knox G (1964) Epidemiology of childhood leukaemia in Northumberland and Durham. *British Journal of Medicine* **18**: 17–24.

Kwa SL & Fine LJ (1980) The association between parental occupation and childhood malignancy. *Journal of Occupational Medicine* **22**: 792–794.

Land CE, McKay FW & Machado SG (1984) Childhood leukaemia and fallout from the Nevada nuclear tests. *Science* **223**: 139–223.

Leck I & Steward JK (1972) Incidence of neoplasms in children born after an influenza epidemic. *British Medical Journal* **iv**: 631.

Li FP & Fraumeni JF Jr (1982) Prospective study of a cancer family syndrome. *Journal of the American Medical Association* **247**: 2692–2694.

Lindquist R, Nilsson B, Eklund G & Gahrton G (1987) Increased risk of developing acute leukaemia after employment as a painter. *Cancer* **60**: 1378–1384.

Linos A, Gray JE, Orvis AL, Kyle RA, O'Fallon M & Kurland LT (1980) Low dose radiation and leukemia. *New England Journal of Medicine* **302**: 1101–1105.

Linos A, Blair A, Cantor KP et al (1990) Leukaemia and non-Hodgkin's lymphoma among embalmers and funeral directors. *Journal of the National Cancer Institute* **82**: 66.

Lloyd RD, Grew DC, Simon SL et al (1990) Individual external exposures from Nevada test site fallout for Utah leukemia cases and controls. *Health Physics* **59**: 723–737.

Lowengart RA, Peters JM, Cicioni C et al (1987) Childhood leukaemia and parents' occupational and home exposures. *Journal of the National Cancer Institute* **79**: 39–46.

Lubin JH, Samet JM & Weinberg C (1990) Design issues in epidemiologic studies of indoor exposure to Rn and risk of lung cancer. *Health Physics* **59**: 807–817.

Lyon JL, Klauber MR, Gardner JW & Udall KS (1979) Childhood leukaemias associated with fallout from nuclear testing. *New England Journal of Medicine* **300**: 397–402.

Machado SG, Land CE & McKay FW (1987) Cancer mortality and radioactive fallout in southwestern Utah. *American Journal of Epidemiology* **125**: 44–61.

McKinney PA, Alexander FE, Roberts BE et al (1989) Yorkshire case-control study of leukaemias and lymphomas: parallel multivariate analyses of seven disease categories. *Leukaemia and Lymphoma* **2**: 67–80.

McKinney PA, Alexander FE, Cartwright RA et al (1991) Parental occupations of children with leukaemia in west Cumbria, north Humberside and Gateshead. *British Medical Journal* **302**: 681–687.

McLaughlin JK, Hrobes Z & Linet MS (1989) Cigarette smoking and leukaemia. *Journal of the National Cancer Institute* **81**: 1262–1263.

MacMahon B (1962) Prenatal X-ray exposure and childhood cancer. *Journal of the National Cancer Institute* **28**: 1173–1191.

Magnani C, Pastore G, Luzzatto L et al (1990) Parental occupation and other environmental factors in the etiology of leukemias and non-Hodgkin's lymphomas in childhood: a case-control study. *Tumori* **76**: 413–419.

Mancuso TF, Stewart AM & Kneale GW (1977) Radiation exposures of Hanford workers dying from cancer and other causes. *Health Physics* **33**: 369–384.

Marsh GM, Enterline PE & McCraw D (1991) Mortality patterns among petroleum refinery and chemical plant workers. *American Journal of Industrial Medicine* **19**: 29–42.

Matanoski GM & Schwarz L (1987) Mortality of workers in styrene–butadiene polymer production. *Journal of Occupational Medicine* **29**: 675–680.

Matanoski GM, Seltser R, Sartwell PE, Diamond EL & Elliot EA (1975) The current mortality rates of radiologists and other physician specialists: specific causes of death. *American Journal of Epidemiology* **101**: 199–210.

Muir C, Waterhouse J, Mack T et al (eds) (1987) *Cancer Incidence in Five Continents*, vol. V. Lyon: IARC.

Murphy EL & Blattner WA (1988) HTLV-I associated leukaemia: a model for chronic retroviral disease. *Annals of Neurology* **23**(supplement): S174–S180.

Myers A, Clayden AD, Cartwright RA et al (1990) Childhood cancer and overhead powerlines: a case-control study. *British Journal of Cancer* **62**: 1008–1014.

Najarian T & Colton T (1978) Mortality from leukaemia and cancer in shipyard nuclear workers. *Lancet* **i**: 1018–1020.

Najean Y (1987) The iatrogenic leukaemias induced by radio and/or chemotherapy. *Medical Oncology and Tumor Pharmacology* **4:** 245–257.

Obrastzow V (1890) Zwei Falle von actuer Leukamie. *Deutsche Medizinische Wochenschrift* **16:** 44.

Ohkita T (1975) Acute effects. *Journal of Radiation Research* **16**(supplement): 49–66.

Olin GR & Ahlbom A (1980) The cancer mortality among Swedish chemists graduated during three decades. *Environmental Research* **22:** 154–161.

Ott MG, Teta MJ & Greenberg HL (1989) Lymphatic and hematopoietic tissue cancer in a chemical manufacturing environment. *American Journal of Industrial Medicine* **16:** 631–643.

Parkin DM, Stiller CA, Draper GL et al (eds) (1988) *International Incidence of Childhood Cancer.* Lyon: IARC.

Pearce N & Reif J (1990) Epidemiologic studies of cancer in agricultural workers. *American Journal of Industrial Medicine* **18:** 133–148.

Pearce N, Sheppard RA, Howard JK et al (1986) Leukaemia among New Zealand agricultural workers. *American Journal of Epidemiology* **124:** 402–409.

Pearce N, Smith A & Reif J (1988) Increased risks of soft tissue sarcoma, malignant lymphoma and acute myeloid leukaemia in abattoir workers. *American Journal of Industrial Medicine* **14:** 63–72.

Pearce N, Reif J & Fraser J (1989) Case-control studies of cancer in New Zealand electrical workers. *International Journal of Epidemiology* **18:** 55–59.

Prentice RL & Sheppard L (1990) Dietary fat and cancer: consistency of the epidemiologic data, and disease prevention that may follow from a practical reduction in fat consumption. *Cancer Causes and Control* **1:** 81–97.

Preston DL & Pierce DA (1987) *The effects of changes in dosimetry on cancer mortality risk estimates in the atomic bomb survivors.* RERF technical report 9-87, Hiroshima: Radiation Effects Research Foundation.

Preston-Martin S, Thomas DC, Yu MC & Henderson BE (1989) Diagnostic radiography as a risk factor for chronic myeloid and monocytic leukaemia. *British Journal of Cancer* **59:** 639–644.

Randolph VL & Heath CW Jr (1974) Influenza during pregnancy in relation to subsequent childhood leukemia and lymphoma. *American Journal of Epidemiology* **100:** 399–409.

Reif J, Pearce N, Kawachi I & Fraser J (1989) Soft-tissue sarcoma, non-Hodgkin's lymphoma and other cancers in New Zealand forestry workers. *International Journal of Cancer* **43:** 49–54.

Rinsky RA, Zumwalde RD, Waxweiler RJ et al (1981) Cancer mortality at a naval nuclear shipyard. *Lancet* **i:** 231–235.

Rinsky RA, Smith AB, Hornung R et al (1987) Benzene and leukemia: an epidemiologic risk assessment. *New England Journal of Medicine* **316:** 1044–1050.

Rinsky RA, Ott G, Ward E et al (1988) Study of mortality among chemical workers in the Kanawha valley of West Virginia. *American Journal of Industrial Medicine* **13:** 429–438.

Roman E, Beral V, Carpenter L et al (1987) Childhood leukaemia in the West Berkshire and Basingstoke and north Hampshire health districts in relation to nuclear establishments in the vicinity. *British Medical Journal* **294:** 597–602.

Ross R, Dworsky R, Paganini-Hill A et al (1983) The occurrence of multiple lymphoreticular and hematological malignancies in the same households. *British Journal of Cancer* **47:** 853–856.

Roush GC, Holford TR, Schymura MJ et al (1987) *Cancer Risk and Incidence Trends: the Connecticut Perspective.* New Haven, CT: Hemisphere Publishing.

Rushton L & Alderson MR (1981) A case-control study to investigate the association between exposure to benzene and deaths from leukaemia in oil refinery workers. *British Journal of Cancer* **43:** 77–84.

Savitz D & Chen J (1990) Parental occupation and childhood cancer: review of epidemiological studies. *Environmental Health Perspectives* **88:** 325–337.

Savitz DA, Wachtel H, Barnes FA et al (1988) Case-control study of childhood cancer and exposure to 60-Hz magnetic fields. *American Journal of Epidemiology* **128:** 21.

Schimpff SC, Schimpff CR, Brager DM et al (1975) Leukaemia and lymphoma patients interlinked by prior social contact. *Lancet* **i:** 124–129.

Seemanova E, Passarge E, Beneskova D et al (1985) Familial microcephaly with normal intelligence, immunodeficiency, and risk for lymphoreticular malignancies: a new autosomal recessive disorder. *American Journal of Human Genetics* **20:** 639–648.

Severson RK, Scott D, Heuser L et al (1990) Cigarette smoking and acute nonlymphocytic leukaemia. *American Journal of Epidemiology* **132:** 418–422.

Smith PG (1977) Leukaemia and other cancers following radiation treatment of pelvic disease. *Cancer* **39:** 1901–1905.

Smith PG & Doll R (1982) Mortality among patients with ankylosing spondylitis after a single treatment course with X-rays. *British Medical Journal* **284:** 449–460.

Smith PG & Douglas A (1986) Mortality of workers at the Sellafield plant of British Nuclear Fuels. *British Medical Journal* **293:** 845–854.

Solli HM, Andersen A, Stranden E et al (1985) Cancer incidence among workers exposed to radon and thoron daughters at a niobium mine. *Scandinavian Journal of Work and Environmental Health* **11:** 7–13.

Spiers FW, Lucas HF, Rundo J et al (1983) Leukaemia incidence in the US dial workers. *Health Physics* **44**(supplement 1): 65–72.

Stern FB, Waxweiler RA, Beaumont JJ et al (1986) A case-control study of leukaemia at a naval nuclear shipyard. *American Journal of Epidemiology* **123:** 980–992.

Stevens W, Thomas DC, Lyon JL et al (1990) Leukaemia in Utah and radioactive fallout from the Nevada test site. *Journal of the American Medical Association* **264:** 585–591.

Stewart A, Webb J, Giles D et al (1956) Malignant disease in childhood and diagnostic irradiation in utero; preliminary communications. *Lancet* **ii:** 447.

Stewart A, Webb J & Hewitt D (1958) A survey of childhood malignancies. *British Medical Journal* **i:** 1495–1508.

Stiller CA & Draper GJ (1982) Trends in childhood leukaemia in Britain 1968–1978. *British Journal of Cancer* **45:** 543–551.

Stiller CA & Bunch KJ (1990) Trends in survival for childhood cancer in Britain diagnosed 1971–1985. *British Journal of Cancer* **62:** 806–815.

Storm HH (1988) Second primary cancer after treatment for cervical cancer. Late effects after radiotherapy. *Cancer* **61:** 679–688.

Stroup NE, Blair A & Erikson GE (1986) Brain cancer and other causes of death in anatomists. *Journal of the National Cancer Institute* **77:** 1217–1224.

Urquhart JD, Black RJ, Muirhead MJ et al (1991) Case-control study of leukaemia and non-Hodgkin's lymphoma in children in Caithness near the Dounreay nuclear installation. *British Medical Journal* **302:** 687–692.

van Kaick G, Muth H, Kaul A et al (1986) Report on the German Thorotrast study. *Strahlentherapie* **80**(supplement): 114–118.

van Steensel-Moll HA, Valkenburg HA & van Zanen GE (1986) Childhood leukaemia and infectious diseases in the first year of life: a register-based case-control study. *American Journal of Epidemiology* **124:** 590–594.

Vianna NJ, Kovasznay B, Polan A et al (1984) Infant leukaemia and paternal exposure to motor vehicle exhaust fumes. *Journal of Occupational Medicine* **26:** 679–682.

Voilleque PG & Gesell TF (eds) (1990) Evaluation of environmental radiation exposures from nuclear testing in Nevada: a symposium. *Health Physics* **59:** 501–746.

Wallace LA (1989) Major sources of benzene exposure. *Environmental Health Perspectives* **82:** 165–169.

Walrath J & Fraumeni F Jr (1984) Cancer and other causes of death among embalmers. *Cancer Research* **44:** 4638–4641.

Walrath J, Li FP, Hoar SK, Mead MW & Fraumeni JF (1985) Causes of death among female chemists. *American Journal of Public Health* **75:** 883–885.

Wang J, Boice JD, Inskip PD et al (1990) Leukemia among medical diagnostic X-ray workers in China. *Proceedings of the Chinese Academy of Medical Sciences and the Peking (Beijing) Union Medical College* **5:** 194–199.

Wertheimer N & Leeper E (1979) Electrical wiring configurations and childhood cancer. *American Journal of Epidemiology* **109:** 273–284.

WHO (1977) *Manual of the international statistical classification of diseases, injuries and causes of death*, vol. 1 (9th revision). Geneva: World Health Organization.

Wilkinson GS, Tietjen GL, Wiggs LD et al (1987) Mortality among plutonium and other radiation workers at a plutonium weapons facility. *American Journal of Epidemiology* **125:** 231–250.

Wing S, Shy CM, Wood JL et al (1991) Mortality among workers at Oak ridge national laboratory. *Journal of the American Medical Association* **265**: 1397–1402.

Wong O (1987) An industry wide study of chemical workers occupationally exposed to benzene. *British Journal of Industrial Medicine* **44**: 365–381.

Wong O (1990) A cohort mortality study and a case-control study of workers potentially exposed to styrene in the reinforced plastics and composites industry. *British Journal of Industrial Medicine* **47**: 753–762.

Wong O & Raabe GK (1989) Critical review of cancer epidemiology in petroleum industry employees, with a quantitative meta-analysis by site. *American Journal of Industrial Medicine* **15**: 283–310.

Wrixon AD, Green BMR, Lomas PR et al (1988) *Natural radiation exposure in UK dwellings*, NRPB-R190. Didcot: National Radiological Protection Board.

Yager JW, Hines CJ & Spear RC (1983) Exposure to ethylene oxide at work increases sister chromatid exchanges in human peripheral lymphocytes. *Science* **219**: 1221–1223.

Yin SN, Li GL, Tain FD et al (1987) Leukaemia in benzene workers: a retrospective cohort study. *British Journal of Industrial Medicine* **44**: 124–128.

Yoshida M, Miyoshi I & Hinuma Y (1982) Isolation and characterisation of retrovirus from cell lines of human adult T-cell leukemia and its implication in the disease. *Proceedings of the National Academy of Sciences of the USA* **79**: 2031.

Yoshimoto Y (1990) Cancer risk among children of atomic bomb survivors. *Journal of the American Medical Association* **264**: 596–600.

Youngson J, Clayden D, Myers A et al (1991) Adult lymphoma and leukaemia and overhead power lines. *British Journal of Cancer* **63**: 977–985.

Zoloth SR, Michaels DM, Villalbi JR & Lacher M (1986) Pattern of mortality among commercial pressmen. *Journal of the National Cancer Institute* **76**: 1047–1051.

2

Chronic leukaemias

STUART C. FINCH
MARTHA S. LINET

Human leukaemias first were recognized about 165 years ago, but a century passed before chronic lymphocytic leukaemia (CLL) and chronic myelogenous leukaemia (CML) were clinically differentiated (Minot et al, 1924). Only within the last few years has the clonal nature of each of these disorders been established. Differences between CLL and CML in basic biological mechanisms, clinical expression, demographic patterns, and epidemiological associations have become increasingly clarified, whereas the aetiology of most cases remains elusive.

The chronic leukaemias comprise a large proportion of all leukaemias among middle-aged persons and CLL is the most common type among the elderly in western populations. Therapy has improved the quality of life, but there has been little success in either curing (with the possible exception of bone marrow transplantation for CML) or substantially prolonging life for most persons with either type of chronic leukaemia. For these reasons it is important to identify aetiologic agents that can be eliminated or reduced in level to decrease incidence of these haematopoietic neoplasms.

Prior to the past decade, descriptive and analytic investigations often considered leukaemia as a single entity or as combined myeloid or lymphatic subtypes. Most of these studies did not utilize standardized criteria or expert haematopathology review to validate diagnoses. Registry and population-based investigations often lacked complete ascertainment of cases, particularly those diagnosed in outpatient settings. Despite these shortcomings, epidemiological work to date suggests risk factor differences among the chronic leukaemia subtypes. Epidemiological studies before the early 1980s and associated methodological issues have been reviewed previously (Cartwright and Bernard, 1985; Linet, 1985; Linet and Blattner, 1988; Linet and Devesa, 1990; Linet and Cartwright, in press). This review will emphasize more recent work and summarize newer approaches for distinguishing additional chronic leukaemia subtypes that should be considered in designing future epidemiological studies.

Baillière's Clinical Haematology—
Vol. 5, No. 1, January 1992
ISBN 0–7020–1626–8

Table 1. Nomenclature and basic epidemiology of lymphoid-related chronic leukaemias*.

Disease	Cell type	Other designations	Approximate % of all CLL	M:F ratio	Median age at diagnosis (years)	Median survival (months)	References
Chronic lymphocytic leukaemia	B	CLL, B-cell CLL, B-cell chronic lymphocytic leukaemia	90–95	1.5:1	64	96	Gale and Foon (1987); Pines et al (1987); Linet and Blattner (1988); Foon et al (1990)
	T	T-cell CLL, T-cell CLL CD4, T-cell CLL CD8, T-cell chronic lymphocytic leukaemia	1	M>F	60	—	
Prolymphocytic leukaemia	B	PLL, B-cell PLL, B-cell prolymphocytic leukaemia	0.7	1.5:1	70	24–36	Matutes et al (1986); Brito-Babapulle et al (1987); Stone (1990)
	T	T-cell PLL, T-cell lymphocytic leukaemia	0.2	M>F	—	6–7	
Hairy cell leukaemia	B	HCL, B-cell HCL, B-cell hairy cell leukaemia	5–10	4:1	50	>60	Gale and Foon (1987); Bernstein et al (1990)
	T	T-cell HCL, T-cell hairy cell leukaemia	rare	M>F	50	>60	
Leukaemic phase of poorly differentiated lymphoma	B	Leukaemic phase of B-cell lymphoma	<1	2:1	45	—	Mintzer and Hauptman (1983); Gale and Foon (1987)

Waldenstrom's macroglobulinaemia	B	Macroglobulinaemia	<1	1.2:1	60	56	Gale and Foon (1987)
T γ lymphocytosis	T	Chronic T-cell lymphocytosis, T suppressor cell chronic lymphocytic leukaemia, T-cell lymphocytosis with neutropenia, suppressor cell leukaemia, T-8-chronic lymphoproliferative disease, large granular leukaemia, TGLS, LGL CD8, CD8 CLL, LGLS	1	1:1	60	—	Chan et al (1986); Gale and Foon (1987); Berliner 1990
Cutaneous T-cell lymphoma	T	Sézary syndrome/mycosis fungoides, MF-Sézary	<1	2:1	50	24	Gale and Foon (1987)
Adult T-cell leukaemia/ lymphoma	T	ATL, ATLL, acute ATLL, chronic ATLL, acute ATL, chronic ATL, acute (or chronic) T-cell leukaemia/ lymphoma	**	**	58	Acute <12 Chronic 12–36	Ratner and Poiesz (1988); Blattner (1990); Wiktor and Blattner (1991)

* Most data relates to Caucasian populations as reported.
** Endemic disorder with M:F ratios from 1.5 to 0.8 and % of all CLL ranging from 75% to <1% in endemic and non-endemic areas, respectively.
Modified from Gale and Foon (1987).

PROBLEMS IN DIAGNOSIS AND CLASSIFICATION

Chronic lymphocytic leukaemia

Classification of leukaemia subtypes has become increasingly sophisticated because of advances over the past few years in histochemistry, immuno-phenotyping and cytogenetics (Bennett et al, 1990). Although diagnosis of most CLL is not difficult, underdiagnosis world-wide is probably consider-able. About 95% of persons with CLL have the mature B-cell type (Freedman, 1990), of which over 25% may be asymptomatic or indolent for many years and thus not routinely diagnosed in early stages. In developing countries, limited access to medical care and reduced life expectancy may also contribute to the lower reported incidence.

Diagnostic problems may occur in cases of classical B-cell CLL with atypical presentation, or among the 5% or more of persons who have either one of the four other major types of B-cell CLL or any of the six types of T-cell CLL (Gale and Foon, 1987) (Table 1). B-cell CLL cases which transform terminally into non-Hodgkin's lymphoma (Richter's syndrome) or acute leukaemia present another type of diagnostic problem (Zarrabi et al, 1977). Other diagnostic problems are the transformed lymphomas which present as leukaemias and the rare cases of multiple myeloma that transform into CLL (Mintzer and Hauptman, 1983; Saltman et al, 1989). Cases may also be incorrectly designated as having infectious, autoimmune, benign haematological or drug-induced disorders, or other haematopoietic malignancies.

Chronic myelocytic leukaemia

Although the diagnosis of CML generally is not difficult to establish, mis-classification has been estimated to occur in approximately 10–15% of patients with this disorder. Some patients are incorrectly diagnosed as having one of the closely related myeloproliferative diseases such as poly-cythaemia vera, myelofibrosis, or a chronic leukaemoid reaction, especially if they are among the 10% with Philadelphia (Ph[1]) chromosome-negative CML (Epner and Koeffler, 1990; Rowley, 1990). More important is the confusion of CML with various types of acute leukaemia, more likely to occur in patients initially presenting with accelerated late stage disease, or those undergoing either myeloblastic or lymphoblastic transformation, or loss of the Ph[1] chromosome during the terminal blastic stage. Cases initially observed during blast crisis who retain the Ph[1] chromosome can be confused with the 10–15% of adults with acute lymphoblastic leukaemia who are positive for the Ph[1] chromosome. Some persons with Ph[1]-negative CML have also been incorrectly designated as having chronic myelomonocytic leukaemia (Fenaux et al, 1987; Stark et al, 1987; del Canizo et al, 1989), chronic monocytic leukaemia (Bearman et al, 1981), or juvenile chronic myelomonocytic leukaemia (Castro-Malaspina et al, 1984; Altman, 1988), (Table 2).

Table 2. Nomenclature and basic epidemiology of myeloid-related chronic leukaemias.

Disease	Other designations	Approximate % of all CML	M:F ratio	Median age at diagnosis (years)	% Ph[1]	Median survival (months)	References
Chronic myelogenous leukaemia	CML, chronic granulocytic leukaemia, adult-type chronic myelogenous leukaemia	98–99	1.2–1.5:1	45	90–95	40–47	Sokal et al (1984); Altman (1988); Prischl et al (1989)
Chronic myelomonocytic leukaemia	CMML, erythromonocytic leukaemia, subacute myelomonocytic leukaemia	0.5–1	2:1	69	0	18–49	Fenaux et al (1987); Stark et al (1987); del Canizo et al (1989)
Chronic monocytic leukaemia	CMOL	Very rare	M>F	60 (33–80)	0	20	Bearman et al (1981)
Juvenile chronic myelocytic leukaemia	JCML, juvenile CML, juvenile chronic granulocytic leukaemia, juvenile chronic myelomonocytic leukaemia	2–3*	2:1	<2	0	9–16	Castro-Malaspina et al (1984); Altman (1988)

* This figure refers to % of all childhood leukaemias.

International classification of diseases

The leukaemia classification used to code death certificates and medical records internationally has undergone dramatic revisions during the past four to five decades. In the late 1940s, the Sixth Revision of the International Classification of Diseases considered leukaemia as a single entity, while the Ninth Revision, implemented in the late 1970s, designated lymphatic, myelocytic, monocytic and other and unspecified as the major categories, with acute, chronic and unspecified subtypes used to further characterize each of these major groupings. These changes have also been implemented at different times by individual countries, thus presenting major problems in comparison of incidence patterns, particularly over time. Despite implementation of the Eighth Revision in 1968 (which was similar to the Ninth Revision), some registries and key international registry references still do not routinely present incidence data for the acute and chronic subtypes of lymphoid and myeloid leukaemia. Death certificates often lack specification of leukaemia subtypes (Linet and Devesa, 1990).

Clinical classification approaches

Although the French–American–British (FAB) classification system, based on cellular morphological and histochemical criteria, has greatly increased clinical diagnostic precision for the acute leukaemias, the relative ease with which most chronic leukaemia cases are diagnosed delayed consideration of a similar approach for the latter. In recent years, however, there has been increasing recognition that a similar system for the chronic leukaemias might substantially improve accuracy of diagnosis. This has led to an international collaboration for the characterization of lymphocytic leukaemia subtypes by means of morphological, immunophenotypic and cytogenetic features (Brito-Babapulle et al, 1987; Gale and Foon, 1987; Bennett et al, 1990; Juliusson and Gahrton, 1990).

Diagnosis and classification of CML has become increasingly accurate as a result of increased use of banding techniques for chromosomal karyotyping and molecular probes to identify DNA abnormalities (Epner and Koeffler, 1990; Rowley, 1990). Increasing use of these more accurate approaches for diagnosing and designating subtypes of CLL and CML should appreciably reduce misdiagnosis.

CHRONIC LYMPHOCYTIC LEUKAEMIA

Demographic features

General considerations

Because of differing survival patterns and incomplete specification of leukaemia deaths by cell type on death certificates, the more accurate incidence data will be presented rather than mortality comparisons. However, chronic leukaemia incidence rates derived from registries employing standard reporting mechanisms are likely to be underestimates, since cases never diagnosed or treated in hospitals are more likely to be missed. Other problems described above (lack of physician access in developing countries, misdiagnosis, asymptomatic or indolent initial stages) may also affect rates.

CLL incidence patterns

CLL is rare in persons under 30 years old, but incidence increases dramatically with age for both sexes (Figure 1a). Elderly persons in western populations have higher rates of CLL than CML (Figures 1a and 1b). Rates are similar among Whites and Blacks in each age group, but exceptionally low among Asians because of the deficit of CLL among persons aged 55 and older (Kushwaha et al, 1985; Muir et al, 1987). Underdiagnosis and shortened life expectancy may contribute to the apparently low incidence of CLL in African populations, although cases have been described with onset in their twenties and thirties (Fleming, 1990).

CLL rates are consistently higher among males than females of the same age in the USA and most other populations, with male-to-female ratios generally ranging from 1.5–2.5 (Figure 1a) (Linet and Devesa, 1990). The male predominance is particularly notable in Australia with a M:F ratio of 4.7 whereas a low ratio of 1.0 is found in Colombia (Figure 2a). In Nigeria a female predominance has been reported among rural persons of low socio-economic status under age 45 (Williams and Bamgboye, 1983; Fleming, 1990). Fleming has hypothesized that young adult Nigerian women may be at higher risk because of relatively depressed immunity due to pregnancy. In a hospital series from Kenya, however, there was a male predominance and similar age distribution as in western populations (Oloo and Ogada, 1984).

Internationally, age-adjusted incidence rates differ more than tenfold among populations, CLL showing greater variation among populations than the other major leukaemia types (Figure 2a). This notable variation reflects real differences among populations (e.g. rarity of CLL among Asians over age 55) as well as differing levels of under-ascertainment of cases due to misdiagnosis and lack of access to medical care. For males, the highest rates are reported from Canada, Denmark and other Scandinavian countries (Figure 2a). Mid-level rates for men occur among US Whites and Blacks; eastern, western and northern European countries; among Israeli Jews; and Whites in Australia and New Zealand. In most of these populations, CLL comprises 30% of all leukaemias (Foon et al, 1990; Linet and Devesa, 1990). Caribbean and South American men have low rates, and CLL is rare among Asian men in Japan, Singapore, India, and other countries (the last not shown). In Asian populations CLL constitutes only 3–5% of total leukaemia (Foon et al, 1990). The rankings are generally the same for women, although females in Sao Paulo, Brazil and Zaragoza, Spain also have very low rates. CLL cases are not routinely further characterized by subtype, thus descriptive statistics are not separately available for B-cell CLL and for T-cell CLL (except to a limited extent for adult T-cell leukaemia, see below) or for the subtypes of these two groups.

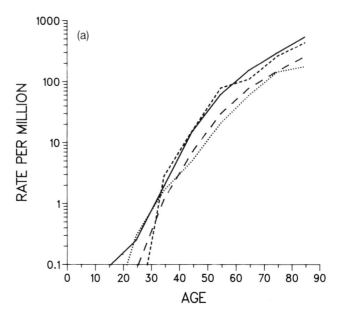

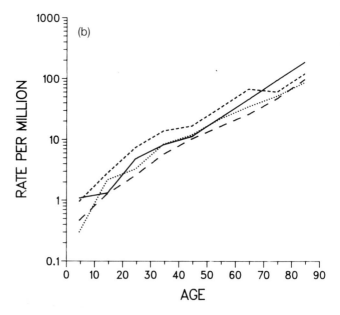

Figure 1. Age-specific rates by sex and race, US SEER programme, 1973–1987: (a) chronic lymphocytic leukaemia; (b) chronic myelogenous leukaemia. ——, White males; –––, White females; ---, Black males; ·····, Black females.

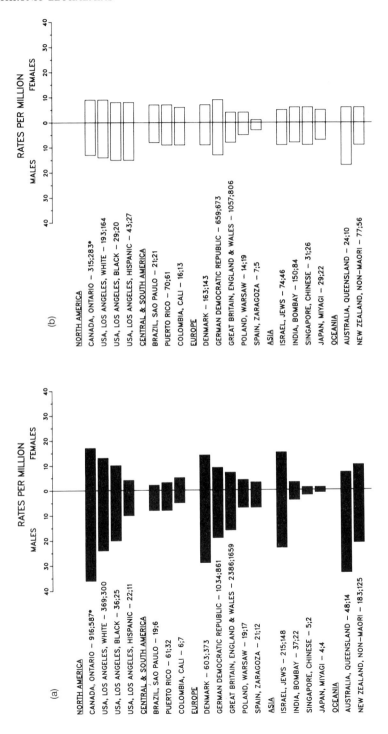

Figure 2. International incidence rates per million (age-adjusted—world standard) by sex, 1978–1982; (a) chronic lymphocytic leukaemia; (b) chronic myelogenous leukaemia. * Numbers of males and females (M:F) on which rates are based, provided by IARC. From Muir et al (1987).

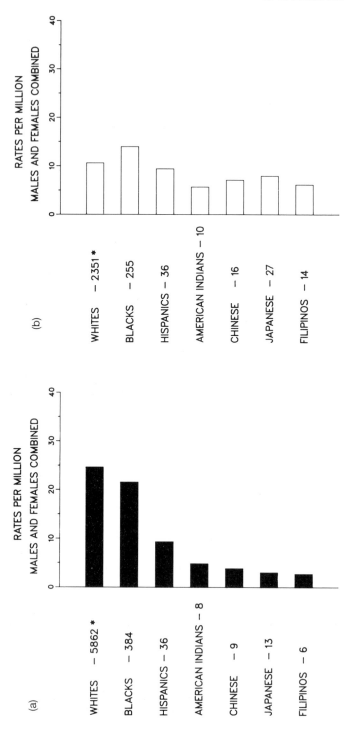

Figure 3. Ethnic and racial group variations in US incidence rates per million (age-adjusted—world standard), US SEER programme, 1976–1984: (a) chronic lymphocytic leukaemia; (b) chronic myelogenous leukaemia. * Total number of subjects, both sexes combined, on which the rates are based. Source of data: Whites and Blacks, nine SEER registries; Hispanics, New Mexico and Arizona; American Indians, New Mexico and Arizona; Chinese, Japanese and Filipinos, San Francisco and Hawaii.

Similarly, in the USA there is marked variability (eight to ninefold differences between lowest and highest) in age-adjusted rates among racial and ethnic groups, with rates highest among Whites, high though slightly lower among Blacks, mid-level among Hispanics, and very low among Asians (Chinese, Japanese and Filipinos) (Figure 3a). Although US data generally parallel international patterns, there is only a small difference in rates between US Whites and Blacks of the same sex, whereas CLL rates appear to be low in African Black populations compared with incidence among most Caucasian populations (Linet and Devesa, 1990; National Cancer Institute, 1990). An early US study described CLL rates among Jews to be 2.4-fold higher than those for non-Jewish Caucasians (MacMahon and Koller, 1957).

CLL time trends

The incidence of CLL has increased during the last 50 years among both sexes in Connecticut and Denmark, although this may partly reflect improvements in diagnosis and reduced mortality from competing causes (reviewed in Linet and Cartwright, in press). Male to female ratios for CLL in western countries decreased from a range of 2.5–3.0 some 50 to 75 years ago to current ratios of 1.5–2.5 (reviewed in Linet and Cartwright, in press). During the 1940s and 1950s, mortality rates increased for males age 45 and over and, to a lesser extent, for females age 60 and over in several countries (reviewed in Linet and Devesa, 1990). The reasons for these changes in mortality and sex ratios over time are unclear but again may reflect increased access to medical care and shifts in causes of death for both men and women due to competing risks.

CLL survival

Median survival for all patients with B-cell CLL is about 8 years. In the most favourable stages median survival ranges from 12 to 17 years whereas in the more unfavourable stages the range is from a few months to 5 or 6 years (Pines et al, 1987). Five-year survival ranged from 30 to 70% in a hospital based series, with survival strongly related to age, sex, subtype, stage of disease, cytogenetic characteristics and response to treatment (Catovsky et al, 1988). Five-year survival rates derived from US population based data have changed very little over the past 15 years, but neither stage nor other prognostic factors were considered (National Cancer Institute, 1990). Patients with the prolymphocytic variant of B-cell CLL or trisomy of chromosome #12 accompanied by another cytogenetic abnormality usually have aggressive disease with a survival measured in months rather than years (Rai and Sawitsky, 1987; Foon et al, 1990; Stone, 1990).

Adult T-cell leukaemia incidence patterns

Adult T-cell leukaemia (ATL) is an aggressive variant of CLL caused by the human T-cell lymphotrophic virus type one (HTLV-1) (Blattner, 1990). The world-wide distribution of ATL closely follows the world-wide distribution of HTLV-1 infection, as determined by seroepidemiological studies. The disease has an endemic distribution in certain tropical and subtropical regions, with reports of high incidence in southern Japan, Jamaica, Panama, and parts of Africa including Ghana, Nigeria, the Ivory Coast, Zaire and Rwanda (reviewed in Blattner, 1990). A study of patients with ATL in Brooklyn, New York, indicated that all were Black and either from the southern USA or the Caribbean (Dosik et al, 1988).

Hairy cell leukaemia incidence patterns

Hairy cell comprises about 2% of all leukaemias. The only population based incidence study of hairy cell leukaemia has shown that the disease is rare among persons under age 30 and increases with age in the fourth and fifth decades, reaching a plateau among men at age 50 and older and at younger ages among women (Bernstein et al, 1990). Risk was highest among white males, particularly Jewish men, with age-adjusted rates for males 4.8-fold higher than those for females. There were few cases among Black and Asian persons.

Environmental factors

Occupational exposures and CLL

Relationships between exposure to various chemicals, drugs and other environmental agents and the development of leukaemia are much less well established for CLL than for several forms of acute leukaemia. Occupational studies through the mid-1980s have been reviewed previously in detail (Linet and Blattner, 1988).

In addition to its clearly established role in the aetiology of AML, benzene has been associated with occurrence of CLL and hairy cell leukaemia (McMichael et al, 1976; Aksoy, 1988), although the evidence is weak (Austin et al, 1988). Most cohort studies include small numbers of CLL cases, with inadequate evaluation of exposure levels (including time-related changes), and confounding factors.

Mortality studies among some groups of rubber workers exposed to benzene and other solvents have shown an elevated risk for lymphocytic leukaemia (Delzell and Monson, 1984). Among the specific solvents implicated in this industry in addition to benzene are acetone, carbon disulphide, carbon tetrachloride, ethyl acetate and hexane (Checkoway et al, 1984). Duration and level of solvent exposure appear to influence risk (McMichael et al, 1976).

CLL has also been linked with exposure to acid-containing chemicals, 'other caustic substances', aliphatic hydrocarbons and chlorinated hydrocarbons in a case-control study (Malone et al, 1989). This investigation also demonstrated a weak association with benzene and aromatic hydrocarbons as a group.

Small to moderate increases of CLL have occurred in some cohorts of petroleum workers (Bertazzi et al, 1989; Wong and Raabe, 1989; Wongsri-chanalai et al, 1989), but not in many others (reviewed in Wong and Raabe, 1989). Elevated risks of lymphocytic leukaemias and lymphomas (primarily non-Hodgkin's lymphoma) have been reported among small cohorts of workers in plants producing, polymerizing and/or processing styrene monomers and butadiene, but not in other large cohort studies (Wong, 1990).

Slightly elevated risks (risk ratios 1.1–1.5) have been observed among farmers in some regions, with exposures to cattle, poultry, dairy farming and pesticides sometimes implicated. Farmers in other areas have not been found to have an excess occurrence (reviewed in Blair et al, 1985). Limited numbers of studies have demonstrated increased risks for CLL among underground coal miners (Gilman et al, 1985); flour mill workers with exposure to pesticides (Alavanja et al, 1990); agricultural extension agents (Alavanja et al, 1988); carpet manufacturing workers (O'Brien and Decoufle, 1988); and power line workers (Linet et al, 1988b). CLL has also been found to be elevated among those with exposure to wood products (Lynge, 1985; Flodin et al, 1988), diesel engine exhaust (Flodin et al, 1988), and asbestos (Schwartz et al, 1988). Lymphocytic leukaemia was increased among saw mill and lumber products workers (Burkhardt, 1982; International Agency for Research on Cancer, 1985) and among male barbers and hairdressers (Spinelli et al, 1984; Teta et al, 1984).

Other environmental exposures and CLL

Since 1986 a growing body of evidence has linked acute myeloid leukaemia with cigarette smoking (reviewed in Wald, 1988). More recently, excesses of lymphatic leukaemia have been reported in a few cohorts (Kinlen and Rogot, 1988; Garfinkel and Boffetta, 1990; Linet et al, in press), but additional studies are needed to confirm this association.

CLL has never been linked with acute or chronic exposures to ionizing radiation in any of the numerous populations evaluated for these exposures (Finch and Finch, 1988; National Research Council, 1990; Shimizu et al, 1990; Finch, 1991). To date, CLL has not been associated with residential exposure to non-ionizing electromagnetic radiation or solar radiation. In addition, there is no consistent evidence that the administration of any drug or combination of drugs has been responsible for the induction of CLL.

Genetic considerations

CLL clinical genetic observations

Familial aggregates of leukaemia with other cases of leukaemia and related lymphoproliferative disorders have been observed more frequently for CLL than for any other type of leukaemia (reviewed in Linet, 1985). The excess risk of leukaemia in persons with one or more first-degree relatives with CLL has been estimated as 2–7 times greater than the risk in individuals without affected first-degree relatives, with considerable concordance for this leukaemia type in afflicted families. Three of 25 twin pairs with one affected member have been reported to be concordant for CLL (Zeulzer and Cox, 1969).

There are other observations that strengthen genetic relationships. Familial CLL cases have been found to share common haplotypes, identical chromosomal defects, similar immunological alterations or be a consequence of consanguinity (reviewed in Linet, 1985). Increased autoimmune disorders have been observed in the close relatives of CLL probands (Conley et al, 1980). The continued low incidence of CLL in Japanese who have migrated to Hawaii also suggests that genetic influences are much stronger than environmental factors in disease expression (Nishiyama et al, 1969).

Although there are many observations which indicate a strong CLL genetic component, environmental influences also may play a role (Linet and Blattner, 1988). For example, the incidence of CLL in Israel is higher among European immigrants than among immigrants from Africa and Asia (Bartal et al, 1978), a difference which is ascribed to environmental rather than genetic factors.

HLA studies of CLL

HLA information in chronic lymphocytic leukaemia has been very inconsistent. In some studies A9 has been increased in association with CLL, whereas others have failed to demonstrate any significant association (reviewed in Linet, 1985; Dyer et al, 1986; Linet et al, 1988a).

CLL chromosome and oncogene abnormalities

Chromosomal aberrations of the peripheral blood lymphocytes are present in from 40 to 65% of patients with B-cell CLL (Juliusson and Gahrton, 1990). Chromosome banding studies have shown that about 50% of CLL patients have an abnormality involving chromosomes # 12 or #14 (Han et al, 1984). The most common aberration is trisomy #12, followed by deletion of the long arms of chromosomes #13 or #11 with translocation to the long arm of chromosome #14 (Foon et al, 1990; Juliusson and Gahrton, 1990). It is of interest that trisomy #12 also may be present in other B-cell lymphocytic malignancies such as lymphocytic lymphoma, hairy cell leukaemia and prolymphocytic leukaemia (Juliusson and Gahrton, 1990).

Neither trisomy #12 nor t(11:14) occur in lymphocytes with an apparently normal karyotype from patients with CLL (Einhorn et al, 1990). The additional observation that over half of the CLL patients have no abnormality of chromosome #12 suggests that a specific CLL gene is unlikely (Juliusson and Gahrton, 1990). Most of the abnormal karyotypes in CLL involve chromosomes containing either immunoglobulin coding genes such as #14 (heavy chain) or oncogenes such as those on chromosomes #12 (c-ras-Harvey) or #11 (c-ras-Kirsten) (Gale and Foon, 1985). Expression of most proto-oncogenes and oncogenes in CLL, however, is normal (Foon et al, 1990).

Viruses

HTLV-I

HTLV-I is a type C retrovirus which may be responsible for a broad spectrum of chronic neurodegenerative and lymphoid disorders in man other than acute T-cell leukaemia (ATL) (reviewed in Blattner, 1990). The most prominent other lymphoid diseases which have been suggested as possibly HTLV-I related are T-cell CLL, T-cell non-Hodgkin's lymphoma, the mycosis fungoides—Sézary syndrome, and persistent T-cell lymphocytosis (reviewed in Blattner, 1990).

ATL is usually an aggressive form of leukaemia characterized by generalized lymphadenopathy, skin involvement, lytic bone lesions, hepatomegaly, hypercalcaemia and a high white blood count (reviewed in Blattner, 1990). The fissured lymphocytes in the peripheral blood have often been identified as lymphosarcoma cells. The disease frequently behaves more like a lymphoma than a leukaemia, although in some cases it may have a chronic progression and a clinical picture resembling CLL. The diagnosis is confirmed by the presence of antibody to HTLV-I.

Transmission of HTLV-I can occur via breast-feeding from mother to child, sexually, or parenterally from blood transfusions or intravenous drug abuse (reviewed in Blattner, 1990). These modes of viral transmission are consistent with age-specific patterns of ATL, the latter rising steeply to age 60–70 and then decreasing in both sexes (reviewed in Blattner, 1990). Seroprevalence rates for HTLV-I range from 2 to 8% in endemic areas. The cumulative lifetime occurrence of ATL in seropositive persons has been estimated as 3–5% among those infected during childhood or less than 1% among persons infected during adulthood (reviewed in Blattner, 1990).

There is no proof that B-cell CLL is of viral origin, but the long preclinical viral incubation period prior to the development of clinical manifestations of ATL bears some resemblance to the long, often initially indolent, course of B-cell CLL. An indirect role for HTLV-I has been demonstrated in some cases of B-cell CLL (Mann et al, 1987). The leukaemic cells in these cases were not infected, but were found to synthesize antibody to the virus-related envelope protein. It was suggested that this type of CLL resulted from an immune response to the HTLV-I rather than being caused by the viral infection itself.

HTLV-II

HTLV-II is another human retrovirus whose role in human disease has not been clearly established. Two persons with a T-cell variant of hairy cell leukaemia and two with T-cell prolymphocytic leukaemia (T-Pl) have been found to be infected with HTLV-II (reviewed in Blattner, 1990). On the other hand, no evidence of an increased risk for hairy cell leukaemia, mycosis fungoides or CLL has been observed in a population of American Indian and Hispanic blood donors that is endemic for HTLV-II infection (Hjelle et al, 1991). A high rate of HTLV-II infection has also been found in several populations of US drug abusers without evident disease association (reviewed in Blattner, 1990; Wiktor and Blattner, 1991).

Other viruses linked with lymphocytic neoplasms

Other reports have linked human lymphocytic disorders with various other viral infections. Most notable have been the possible associations of acute and chronic lymphocytic leukaemias with feline leukaemia virus, acute lymphocytic leukaemia with Epstein–Barr virus, and lymphoid leukaemias with bovine leukaemia virus (reviewed in Linet, 1985). A recent study of the seroepidemiology of human herpes virus-6 did not substantiate any relationship to CLL (Clark et al, 1990), nor is there conclusive evidence that either the Epstein–Barr virus or cytomegalovirus is responsible for the development of CLL (Foon et al, 1990).

Other CLL associations

There are many reports in the medical literature of various acute and chronic illnesses, medical procedures and even medications which might be of importance in the aetiology of CLL. Most of these are small studies without statistical significance or are case reports that are difficult to interpret.

CLL has arisen subsequent to the onset of pernicious anaemia, thyroid disease, rheumatoid arthritis, myasthenia gravis and other autoimmune conditions (reviewed in Conley et al, 1980). A number of reports also have linked chronic infections, inflammatory disorders, allergic conditions, surgical excision of lymphoid tissue and various viral, plasmodial and parasitic infections with CLL, although none of these associations have been consistently observed (Linet and Blattner, 1988). Similarly, possible associations of CLL with rheumatoid arthritis, idiopathic thrombocytopenic purpura, diabetes, scleroderma, allergic disorders, tuberculosis, infectious mononucleosis, heart disease, skin cancer or migraine have not been consistently noted (reviewed in Linet and Cartwright, in press). It has been hypothesized that some of the apparent associations of autoimmune disorders with CLL may reflect underlying perturbations of immune mechanisms common to both disorders. The association with rheumatoid arthritis may be real, since CLL patients with this autoimmune disorder have been found to have the unusual subtype T-γ lymphocytic leukaemia (Berliner, 1990). The other reported CLL disease associations probably represent fortuitous occurrences.

CHRONIC MYELOGENOUS LEUKAEMIA

Demographic features

CML incidence patterns

CML is rare during childhood in western populations, but a small peak in incidence has been observed internationally in White males under age 5 (reviewed in Neglia and Robison, 1988). CML in this age group is frequently of the Ph[1]-negative juvenile type, whereas cases aged 5 and older are most likely to be of the Ph[1]-positive adult type of CML (Altman, 1988). Incidence of the adult type CML begins to rise in adolescence among both sexes and increases steadily with age (Figure 1b). African Blacks have been described as having a younger age of onset than among western populations, but in the absence of accurate population based incidence data this is difficult to evaluate (Essien, 1976; Lowenthal, 1976; Okany and Akinyanju, 1989). In each age group, rates are higher among males than among females, and generally higher among Blacks than among Whites, except for the elderly (Figure 1b). The M : F ratio for CML in most populations ranges from 1.0 to 2.0, with the highest ratio occurring in Queensland, Australia (2.8). None of the populations shown in Figure 2b has a ratio lower than 1.0.

Age-adjusted rates differ among populations by fivefold or less, CML showing the smallest variation in rates internationally of the major leukaemia types (Figure 2b). For males, highest rates occur among Australians in Queensland and Los Angeles Hispanics; mid-level rates are found in Central and South American populations; and lowest rates are seen in Zaragoza, Spain and Warsaw, Poland (Figure 2b). For females, the highest rates were reported for Los Angeles Whites and the German Democratic Republic, while mid- and low-level rankings were generally similar to those for males. In many western countries, age-adjusted rates for CLL are higher than those for CML in both sexes, but CML rates are higher than those for CLL among Los Angeles Hispanics, populations in Central and South America, and Asians (Indians, Chinese and Japanese). Reliable incidence data for CML from tropical Africa and South Africa are scanty, but most information suggests that rates in these populations are comparable with those of western countries (Williams and Bamgboye, 1983; Okany and Akinyanju, 1989).

Compared with CLL, there is much less variation (slightly over twofold) in age-adjusted rates among racial and ethnic groups in the USA (Figure 3b). As noted earlier, Whites have the highest CLL rates of all groups shown. For CML, Blacks have the highest rates (Figures 3a and 3b). Although CML rates in Israeli Jews of both sexes are lower than those in most US Caucasian populations, an early US study reported that rates in New York City Jews were almost twofold higher than rates in non-Jewish Caucasians (MacMahon and Koller, 1957). If this disparity is real, it may reflect differences in origin of American and Israeli Jews or environmental influences.

CML time trends

Incidence of CML decreased slightly for both males and females in the USA during the 15-year period 1973–1987, except for a slight increase among Black males aged 65 and older (National Cancer Institute, 1990). The overall decline and a similar one in parts of England and Wales (Cartwright et al, 1990) may reflect, at least in part, an increasing tendency to classify chronic myelomonocytic leukaemia with the myelodysplasias. The increase during 1973–1987 in elderly US Black males, and increases in elderly persons of both sexes in Connecticut during 1935–1980 (Heston et al, 1986), and between 1965–1970 and 1971–1976 in Lancashire, England (Geary et al, 1979), may be due to improved diagnosis.

CML survival

Survival in CML is extremely variable but on the average median survival is in the range of 40 to 47 months (Sokal et al, 1984; Herr et al, 1990). Various forms of chemotherapy have prolonged periods of remission and improved the quality of life, but have had little impact on overall survival, which has been basically unchanged over a period of the last 40 or 50 years. The only other exception is that cure or prolonged survival is now possible through the use of bone marrow transplantation (Delage et al, 1990). The best prognostic indicators appear to be spleen size, the percentage of circulating blast cells (Sokal et al, 1984) and the duration of first unmaintained remission following chemotherapy (Prischl et al, 1989). The presence of increased basophils and eosinophils, a high platelet count, an abnormal karyotype, or the absence of the Ph^1 chromosome portend an unfavourable prognosis (Sokal et al, 1984). On the other hand, Ph^1 mosaicism has been reported to influence survival favourably (Prischl et al, 1989). A recent study has concluded that cigarette smoking has an adverse effect on the development of both blast crisis and survival (Herr et al, 1990).

Environmental factors

Radiation

The single environmental agent consistently associated with CML is excessive exposure to ionizing radiation.

Atomic bomb survivors. The largest and most valuable source of information regarding radiation leukaemogenesis and induction of CML has been the follow-up of the atomic bomb survivors of Japan (Ichimaru et al, 1986; Finch and Finch, 1988; Shimizu et al, 1990). The Japanese information is derived from both incidence and mortality studies of a cohort of approximately 120 000 atomic bomb survivors and their controls followed since 1950. Radiation doses for this population ranged from usual background levels found in many geographical areas to near lethal levels from a single exposure of only a few seconds duration. Most of the radiation was relatively low energy γ, similar to the type of radiation received from background environmental or X-ray sources.

On the other hand, most background environmental radiation exposures are small (3.6 mSv/year) and are continuous over a period of many years (National Research Council, 1990). Despite these differences, the leukaemogenic effects of low dose radiation for man have been estimated only by means of extrapolation of results from high dose levels, such as those from the atomic bomb survivors, to low dose levels. Estimates of this type are not ideal but there are few alternatives as little reliable low dose information is available. It is likely that the leukaemogenic effect for man following various levels of low dose radiation exposure may never be obtained directly because of the large population that would be needed to generate reliable risk estimates.

The incidence of CML and other leukaemia types, except for CLL, increased with exposure dose for exposed persons in all age groups. The earliest cases of radiation-induced leukaemia occurred 3–4 years following exposure, with peak incidence 3 to 4 years later. For CML, the radiation effect largely disappeared 15 years following exposure for all age groups (Ichimaru et al, 1986; Finch and Finch, 1988; Shimizu et al, 1990). For other leukaemia types, the radiation-induced leukaemogenic effect for persons exposed under 15 years of age disappeared about 15 years following exposure, whereas the effect was more prolonged and slowly declined during the next 25–30 years in persons who were over age 30 at the time of exposure.

The highest risk in atomic bomb survivors for any type of radiation-induced leukaemia during peak incidence for exposures over 1 Gy was for CML in persons who were less than 15 years old at the time of exposure. The annual incidence rate for this group for CML for the period 1950–1955 was 66.3 per 100 000, in comparison to unexposed controls for whom the annual incidence rate at that time for all types of leukaemia was about 3 per 100 000. In this respect, CML has been considered the most characteristic atomic bomb radiation-induced human leukaemia (Ichimaru et al, 1986).

Males predominated in a ratio of about 2:1, similar to the sex ratio for non-radiation induced CML. Other laboratory and clinical characteristics were also similar between persons with radiation-induced CML and their unexposed controls.

Mortality data for leukaemia in atomic bomb survivors indicates that a linear-quadratic dose–response curve fits better than a linear model for all radiation-induced leukaemia (Shimizu et al, 1990). The risk coefficients for leukaemia were significant for air dose exposures under 0.5 Gy but not under 0.2 Gy. The lowest bone marrow radiation dose for which leukaemia mortality was significantly increased was 0.2–0.49 Gy (Shimizu et al, 1990). The number of excess deaths from leukaemia per 10^4 person-year-sievert was estimated to range from 2.40 to 2.95. No increased risk for CML or any other type of leukaemia has been observed in the population exposed in utero (Ichimaru et al, 1986; Yoshimoto et al, 1988).

Therapeutic irradiation. A second study which has been very valuable in the assessment of radiation-induced leukaemia has been the mortality follow-up to 48 years for over 14 000 patients in England who received an average bone marrow dose of 3.21 Gy of X-ray for therapy of ankylosing spondylitis during 1935–1954 (Smith and Doll, 1982; Darby et al, 1987).The peak relative risk of 4.61 for CML was observed during the period of 1–14.9 years after treatment. Thereafter, there was no evidence of an increased risk for this leukaemia type. The overall relative risk for CML during the total period of observation was 1.46. The excess relative risk of 0.98/Gy or excess absolute risk of 0.45 per 10^4 person-year-gray for all types of leukaemia are lower values than those observed in the study of atomic bomb survivors

(National Research Council, 1990). These differences are not unusual in view of the extreme differences in methods of radiation delivery and composition of the two populations.

A third study which has contributed appreciably to man's knowledge of radiation-induced leukaemia has been an international case-control study of about 30 000 women treated with X-irradiation therapy for carcinoma of the cervix (Boice et al, 1987, 1988). Excess leukaemia was 0.48 cases per 10^4 person-year-gray. The relative risk for all leukaemia was increased twofold. Risk was highest 1–4 years after treatment and decreased with increasing age at initiation of treatment (Boice et al, 1988). The relative risk of 4.2 for CML was not significantly different from a relative risk of 1.6 for acute leukaemia (Boice et al, 1987). The highest leukaemia rates were observed following the delivery of 2.5–5.0 Gy of X-ray exposure to the bone marrow. At higher radiation doses leukaemia rates were lower, presumably due to a cell killing effect.

Several other studies of fractionated radiation therapy for localized benign or malignant tumours have shown an increased risk for leukaemia in both adults and children. Most of the radiation-induced leukaemia has been acute non-lymphocytic in type following therapy for uterine corpus cancer, breast cancer, and menorrhagia. An increase in myeloid leukaemia has been reported following the intravenous administration of radium-224 for therapeutic purposes (reviewed in National Research Council, 1990; Linet and Cartwright, in press).

Diagnostic X-rays. Diagnostic X-ray exposure has been associated with the increased occurrence of CML, particularly following X-ray examination of the gastrointestinal tract, kidneys and back during the previous 3–20 years (Preston-Martin et al, 1989). Other studies of patients who received multiple chest fluoroscopy examinations for tuberculosis, or other types of diagnostic radiation, have shown little or no increase in any type of leukaemia (Linos et al, 1980; Boice et al, 1981; Evans et al, 1986). Increased leukaemia rates have not been reported in patients who have received radioactive iodine for diagnostic purposes. However, an increased incidence of CML has occurred in patients who received intravenous thorium dioxide for the purpose of diagnostic X-ray contrast studies (National Research Council, 1990). It has been estimated that about 1% of all leukaemia may be attributed to diagnostic radiation (Evans et al, 1986).

Environmental and occupational irradiation. An increased incidence of leukaemia, but not CML, has been reported in the proximity of nuclear installations in England and Wales (Cook-Mozaffari et al, 1989), but not in Canada (Clarke et al, 1991), France (Hill and Laplanche, 1990) or the USA (Jablon et al, 1991), with one possible exception in the USA (Clapp et al, 1987). A weak association between estimated bone marrow dose from radioactive fall-out in Utah and acute leukaemia, but not CML, has been reported (Stevens et al, 1990). Extensive observations have also been made in populations in a number of countries in locations with high background radiation. Most of these studies have shown no excess of leukaemia and the few reporting increased leukaemia rates did not find CML excesses (reviewed in National Research Council, 1990). Recent studies have also suggested that radon is a causative factor in the induction of myeloid leukaemia, but again not specifically CML (Henshaw et al, 1990).

Few studies in radiation-exposed industrial workers have demonstrated a increased risk specifically for CML. Early British and US mortality studies clearly showed an increased leukaemia risk for radiologists (Seltser and Sartwell, 1965; Smith and Doll, 1981). The types of leukaemia were not specified in the British report and most of the leukaemias observed in American radiologists were acute myeloid in type, although the risk for CML was somewhat increased. An increased incidence of all types of leukaemia with the exception of CLL has been demonstrated in a large cohort of Chinese medical diagnostic X-ray workers (Wang et al, 1990). The relative risk for CML in that study was 2.3. However, a 29-year follow-up study for a similar group of American army radiology technologists, did not show an increased risk for any type of leukaemia (Jablon and Miller, 1978).

Studies of radium dial workers, uranium miners, nuclear shipyard workers, and most studies of workers in the nuclear industry have also not shown an increased risk for leukaemia (reviewed in National Research Council, 1988, 1990). A few studies of nuclear workers with low levels of radiation exposure have demonstrated small, but non-significant increases in leukaemia risk (Checkoway et al, 1985; Cragle et al, 1988). A recent mortality study of workers at the Oak Ridge National Laboratory also describes a small increase in leukaemia risk (Wing et al, 1991), but it should be emphasized that the excess was limited to only one exposure group at the end of the follow-up interval. In none of these occupational cohorts was a specific radiation risk for CML identified.

In a 22-year follow-up study of 3072 American military participants in a 1957 above-ground nuclear detonation, 'Smoky', an excess leukaemia risk was observed with ten leukaemia cases identified, four of which were CML (Caldwell et al, 1983). However, medical follow-up of over 46 000 US military personnel involved in one or more of five other atmospheric nuclear test series between 1951 and 1958 did not show a significant excess of leukaemia in any or all of the series (Robinette et al, 1985). It is not known if Smoky had unique features compared with the other above-ground detonations. Cell type was not specified in a study of New Zealand military participants in British atomic weapons tests which showed increased leukaemia incidence and mortality (Pearce et al, 1990).

Other occupational and environmental exposures and CML

Although the link of AML with benzene exposure has been shown consistently in several populations (Rinsky et al, 1987), a few studies have also suggested an increase in CML, but the results have not been definitive (Aksoy and Erdem, 1978; Aksoy, 1988; Yin et al, 1989).

Most occupational studies concerned with benzene exposure have been conducted on workers in the rubber, shoe, petroleum, leather, printing and chemical industries (reviewed in Linet and Cartwright, in press). Welders have also been shown to have an increased risk of myeloid leukaemia, particularly CML (Stern, 1987; Preston-Martin and Peters, 1988). Butadiene and monomeric styrene are believed to have been responsible for an increased risk of leukaemia in workers in plants producing styrene monomers and butadiene (Spirtas et al, 1976; Ott et al, 1980). In three small cohort studies of workers with ethylene or ethylene oxide, increased leukaemia, including a few cases of CML, has been demonstrated (reviewed in Hogstedt et al, 1986). An increased incidence of CML has been associated with farming (Blair and White, 1981).

The cumulative lifetime risk of leukaemia secondary to treatment of children or adults with alkylating agents, either with or without radiation therapy, has been estimated as 5–10%. The usual latent period prior to the onset of secondary acute myelocytic or acute myelomonocytic leukaemia is from 2 to 10 years. CML has not been reported secondary to therapy with alkylating agents and there is little evidence that other medicinal agents are leukaemogenic for CML.

There have been several instances of transmission of Ph[1]-positive CML to the donor cells of a successful bone marrow transplantation for CML (Marmont et al, 1984). It was suggested that the agent responsible for the original leukaemia initiated leukaemogenesis in donor cells.

Most of the studies demonstrating a link between myeloid leukaemia and cigarette smoking either do not specify acute or chronic subtypes, or have demonstrated an association with AML (Wald, 1988). In one report, however, a small, elevated risk was found for CML (Williams and Horm, 1977).

The question of a possible role for electromagnetic radiation in the aetiology of CML has been raised in electrical workers and amateur radio operators (Milham, 1985) as well as in welders who may be exposed to magnetic fields (Preston-Martin and Peters, 1988). CML has not been associated to date with the use of electric blankets (Preston-Martin et al, 1988).

Genetic considerations

CML clinical genetic observations

Studies of familial leukaemia and twins with leukaemia provide strong evidence for genetic transmission of various forms of lymphocytic leukaemia, but not CML (Gunz, 1983). Multiple cases of CML in families are quite rare. Twin studies provide additional information concerning the genetics of inherited CML. Five pairs of identical twins have been described who were discordant for Ph[1] chromosome CML (Tokuhata et al, 1968). The presence of the Ph[1] chromosome only in the twins with leukaemia strongly suggests that the Ph[1] chromosome is acquired rather than inherited.

HLA studies of CML

There is no evidence to date for a significant association between HLA antigens and CML (Hester et al, 1977), although there have been few studies

(Linet, 1985). There is also little evidence of specificity for any type of leukaemia with red cell antigens, serum proteins or red cell enzyme polymorphisms (Gunz, 1983).

CML chromosome and oncogene abnormalities

The Ph[1] chromosome associated with CML was the first leukaemia chromosomal abnormality to be identified, and remains the most characteristic observed to date for any type of leukaemia (Rowley, 1990). The Ph[1] chromosome is a chromosome #22 that has lost most of its long arm due to a reciprocal translocation with chromosome #9. This translocation moves the Abelson proto-oncogene (*ABL*) from the long arm of chromosome #9 to a position adjacent to the breakpoint cluster region (*BCR*) gene on chromosome #22 (Rowley, 1990). Although the breakpoint on chromosome #9 varies widely, the breakpoint on #22 is restricted to 5–6 bp of DNA within the *BCR* gene. This combination produces an 8.5 kb *BCR–ABL* chimeric messenger RNA (mRNA), which translates into a larger protein than normal with in vitro tyrosine kinase activity (Epner and Koeffler, 1990; Rowley, 1990). Several growth factor receptors are tyrosine kinase and it is recognized that this abnormal protein can confer growth factor independence to several cell lines. This information suggests that intracellular signalling pathways for growth factors are activated by the variant ABL protein (Epner and Koeffler, 1990). The increased protein tyrosine kinase activity produced by the *BCR-ABL* gene indicates activation of the ABL proto-oncogene.

Approximately 10% of patients who are diagnosed as having CML do not have the Ph[1] chromosome (Epner and Koeffler, 1990). The malignant myeloid cells of these patients contain *ABL* and *BCR* which are molecularly juxtaposed in the absence of typical t(9:22) translocation. The exact mechanism of this molecular derangement is not known but it has been observed that the malignant cells express the same chimeric *BCR–ABL* mRNA and *BCR–ABL* fusion protein as occurs in the presence of the usual Ph[1] chromosome (Epner and Koeffler, 1990).

The polymerase chain reaction provides a very sensitive technique for the identification of the *BCR–ABL* mRNA in less than one leukaemic cell per 10 000 non-leukaemic cells (Dobrovic et al, 1988). This extremely sensitive and specific technique has the potential for identifying other CML variants, as well as determining the presence of a very small number of residual leukaemic cells (Epner and Koeffler, 1990).

It should be emphasized that the Ph[1] chromosome is not pathognomonic of CML since it is present in the blast cells of approximately 20% of adults and 5% of children with acute lymphocytic leukaemia (ALL) (Epner and Koeffler, 1990). These ALL patients usually have L1 blast cell morphology and, in comparison with Ph[1]-negative ALL, have higher white counts, more frequent involvement of the central nervous system and a poorer prognosis.

Chromosomal syndromes associated with CML

There are many hereditary or congenital disorders associated with acute lymphoid or myeloid leukaemias, but few have been linked with CML of the adult type. Some of the disorders linked with subsequent development of acute leukaemia are characterized by the presence of an extra chromosome (i.e. Down's syndrome, Klinefelter's and trisomy D) or chromosome breakage (i.e. Bloom's syndrome, Fanconi's anaemia, and ataxia-telangiectasia). Neurofibromatosis has been linked with CML of the juvenile type (Clark and Hutter, 1982). The leukaemia occurring in these cases is an unusual Ph[1]-negative form of CML, usually appearing before the age of 2, and often in association with cutaneous lesions and respiratory symptoms (Table 2). Other concomitants of these cases of neurofibromatosis include trisomy 8 and chronic Epstein–Barr virus infection (Palmer et al, 1983; Altman, 1988). An excess of leukaemia has not been demonstrated consistently in the relatives of patients with neurofibromatosis-associated juvenile CML (Sorensen et al, 1986).

SUMMARY

In recent years many subtypes of CLL and some CML variants have been recognized throughout the world by means of careful clinical, epidemiological, immunological, molecular biological and viral studies. Most striking has been the establishment of a close association between certain immunophenotypical subtypes of CLL and infection with HTLV-I and possibly HTLV-II. CLL has consistently been shown to have a strong genetic component and a low incidence among Asians, but a growing body of evidence also links this major leukaemia type with environmental factors including solvents, unidentified farming and other occupational exposures. In contrast, CML is characterized by few genetic associations, relatively homogenous world-wide distribution, greater frequency in Blacks than in Whites, little evidence of viral aetiology, and evidence that exposures to ionizing radiation, benzene and possibly other chemical agents are important aetiological factors. Most studies suggest that acquired rather than genetic factors are of greater importance in the aetiology of CML, but this conclusion is somewhat difficult to reconcile with the relatively small variation in incidence rates internationally. Common to both disorders in most populations are an increasing incidence with age, male predominance, and stability of incidence, survival and mortality over the years, exclusive of improved survival of CML following allogeneic bone marrow transplantation.

Acknowledgements

The authors are grateful for assistance provided by Dr Susan Devesa of the Epidemiology and Biostatistics Program, NCI, and for computer programming and graphics support provided by Mr Scott Gaetjen of Information Management Systems, Inc. in creating the figures used in this chapter. Dr Sharon Whelan and Dr Eric Masuyer of the Descriptive Epidemiology Unit, International Agency for Research on Cancer, deserve special thanks for providing the authors with the numbers of CLL and CML cases by sex for each of the countries shown in the international comparisons of age-adjusted rates shown in Figures 2a and 2b. The editorial and stenographic assistance of Ms Linda Rizzuto and Ms Susan Howell is also gratefully acknowledged.

REFERENCES

Aksoy M (1988) Benzene hematotoxicity. In Aksoy M (ed.) *Benzene Carcinogenicity*, pp 59–112. Boca Raton: CRC Press.

Aksoy M & Erdem S (1978) A follow-up study on the mortality and the development of leukemia in the pancytopenic patients associated with long-term exposure to benzene. *Blood* **52:** 285–292.

Alavanja MCR, Blair A, Merkle S et al (1988) Mortality among agricultural extension agents. *American Journal of Industrial Medicine* **14:** 167–176.

Alavanja MCR, Blair A & Masters M (1990) Cancer mortality in the US flour industry. *Journal of the National Cancer Institute* **82:** 840–848.

Altman AJ (1988) Chronic leukemias of childhood. *Pediatric Clinics of North America* **35:** 765–787.

Austin H, Delezell E & Cole P (1988) Benzene and leukemia: a review of the literature and a risk assessment. *American Journal of Epidemiology* **127:** 419–438.

Bartal A, Bentwich Z, Manny N et al (1978) Ethical and clinical aspects of chronic lymphocytic leukemia in Israel: a survey on 288 patients. *Acta Haematologica* **60:** 161–171.

Bearman RM, Kjeldsberg CR, Pangalis GA et al (1981) Chronic monocytic leukemia in adults. *Cancer* **48:** 2239–2255.

Bennett JM, Juliusson G & Mecucci C (1990) Morphologic, immunologic, and cytogenetic classification of the chronic (mature) B and T lymphoid leukemias: Fourth Meeting of the MIC Cooperative Study Group. *Cancer Research* **50:** 2212.

Berliner N (1990) T gamma lymphocytosis and T cell chronic leukemias. *Hematology/Oncology Clinics of North America* **4:** 473–487.

Bernstein L, Newton P & Ross RK (1990) Epidemiology of hairy cell leukemia in Los Angeles County. *Cancer Research* **50:** 3605–3609.

Bertazzi PA, Zocchetti C, Pesatori AC et al (1989) Ten-year mortality study of the population involved in the Seveso incident in 1976. *American Journal of Epidemiology* **129:** 1187–1200.

Blair A & White DW (1981) Death certificate study of leukemia among farmers from Wisconsin. *Journal of the National Cancer Institute* **66:** 1027–1030.

Blair A, Malker H, Cantor KP et al (1985) Cancer among farmers. A review. *Scandinavian Journal of Work, Environment and Health* **11:** 397–407.

Blattner WA (1990) *Human Retrovirology: HTLV*, pp 1–484. New York: Raven Press.

Boice JD Jr, Monson RR, Rosenstein M et al (1981) Cancer mortality in women after repeated fluoroscopic examinations of the chest. *Journal of the National Cancer Institute* **66:** 863–867.

Boice JD Jr, Blettner M, Kleinerman RA et al (1987) Radiation dose and leukemia risk in patients treated for cancer of the cervix. *Journal of the National Cancer Institute* **79:** 1295–1311.

Boice JD Jr, Engholm G, Kleinerman RA et al (1988) Radiation dose and second cancer risk in patients treated for cancer of the cervix. *Radiation Research* **116:** 3–55.

Brito-Babapulle V, Pittman S, Melo JV et al (1987) Cytogenetic studies on prolymphocytic leukemia. I. B-cell prolymphocytic leukemia. *Hematologic Pathology* **1:** 27–33.

Burkhardt JA (1982) Leukemia in hospital patients with occupational exposure to the sawmill industry. *Western Journal of Medicine* **137:** 440–441.

Caldwell GG, Kelley D, Zack M et al (1983) Mortality and cancer frequency among military nuclear test (Smoky) participants 1957 through 1979. *Journal of the American Medical Association* **250:** 620–624.

Cartwright RA & Bernard SM (1985) Epidemiology. In Whittaker JA & Delamore IW (eds) *Leukaemia*, pp 3–23. Oxford: Blackwell Scientific Publications.

Cartwright RA, Alexander FE, McKinney PA et al (1990) *Leukaemia and Lymphoma. An Atlas of Distribution within Areas of England and Wales 1984–88*. London: Leukaemia Research Fund.

Castro-Malaspina H, Schaison G, Passe S et al (1984) Subacute and chronic myelomonocytic leukemia in children (Juvenile CML): clinical and hematologic observations, and identification of prognostic factors. *Cancer* **54:** 675–686.

Catovsky D, Fooks J & Richards S (1988) The UK Medical Research Council CLL trials 1 and 2. *Nouvelle Revue Française D Hématologie* **30:** 423–427.

Chan WC, Link S, Mawle A et al (1986) Heterogeneity of large granular lymphocyte proliferations—delineation of two major subtypes with distinct origins, immunophenotypes, functional and clinical characteristics. *Blood* **68:** 1142–1153.

Checkoway H, Wilcosky T, Wolf P et al (1984) An evaluation of the associations of leukemia and rubber industry solvent exposures. *American Journal of Industrial Medicine* **5:** 239–249.

Checkoway H, Matthew RM, Shy CM et al (1985) Radiation, work experience, and cause specific mortality among workers at an energy research laboratory. *British Journal of Industrial Medicine* **42:** 525–533.

Clapp RW, Cobb S, Chan CK et al (1987) Leukaemia near Massachusetts nuclear power plant. *Lancet* **ii:** 1324–1325.

Clark DA, Alexander FE, McKinney PA et al (1990) The seroepidemiology of human herpesvirus-6 (HHV-6) from a can-control study of leukaemia and lymphoma. *International Journal of Cancer* **45:** 829–833.

Clark RD & Hutter JJ Jr (1982) Familial neurofibromatosis and juvenile chronic myelogenous leukemia. *Human Genetics* **60:** 230–232.

Clarke EA, McLaughlin J & Anderson TW (1991) *Childhood Leukaemia Around Canadian Nuclear Facilities: Phase II, Final Report*, pp 1–53. Ottawa, Ontario: Atomic Energy Control Board.

Conley CL, Misiti J, Laster AJ et al (1980) Genetic factors predisposing to CLL and to autoimmune disease. *Medicine* **59:** 323–331.

Cook-Mozaffari PJ, Darby SC, Doll R et al (1989) Geographical variation from leukaemia and in other cancers in England and Wales in relation to proximity to nuclear installations. *British Journal of Cancer* **59:** 476–485.

Cragle DL, McLain RW & Qualters JR (1988) Mortality among workers at nuclear fuels production facility. *American Journal of Industrial Medicine* **14:** 379–401.

Darby SC, Doll R, Gill SR et al (1987) Long-term mortality after a single treatment course with X-rays in patients treated for ankylosing spondylitis. *British Journal of Cancer* **55:** 179–190.

Delage R, Ritz J & Anderson KC (1990) The evolving role of bone marrow transplantation in the treatment of chronic myelogenous leukemia. *Hematology/Oncology Clinics of North America* **4:** 369–388.

del Canizo MC, Sanz G & San Miguel JF (1989) Chronic myelomonocytic leukemia-clinicobiological characteristics: a multivariate analysis in a series of 70 cases. *European Journal of Haematology* **42:** 466–473.

Delzell E & Monson RR (1984) Mortality among rubber workers. VII. Aerospace workers. *American Journal of Industrial Medicine* **6:** 265–271.

Dobrovic A, Trainor KJ & Morley AA (1988) Detection of the molecular abnormality in chronic myeloid leukemia by use of the polymerase chain reaction. *Blood* **72:** 2063–2065.

Dosik H, Denic S, Patel N et al (1988) Adult T-cell leukemia/lymphoma in Brooklyn. *Journal of the American Medical Association* **259:** 2255–2257.

Dyer PA, Ridway JC & Flanagan NG (1986) HLA-A, B and DR antigens in chronic lymphocytic leukaemia. *Disease Markers* **4:** 231–237.

Einhorn S, Meeker T, Juliusson G et al (1990) No evidence of trisomy 12 or t(11;14) by molecular genetic techniques in chronic lymphocytic leukemic cells with a normal karyotype. *Cancer Genetics and Cytogenetics* **48:** 183–192.

Epner DE & Koeffler HP (1990) Molecular genetic advances in chronic myelogenous leukemia. *Annals of Internal Medicine* **113:** 3–6.

Essien EM (1976) Leukaemia in Nigerians. II. The chronic leukaemias. *East African Medical Journal* **53:** 96–104.

Evans JS, Wennberg JE & McNeil BJ (1986) The influence of diagnostic radiography on the incidence of breast cancer and leukemia. *New England Journal of Medicine* **315:** 810–815.

Fenaux P, Jouet JP, Zandecki M et al (1987) Chronic and subacute myelomonocytic leukaemia in the adult: a report of 60 cases with special reference to prognostic factors. *British Journal of Haematology* **65:** 101–106.

Finch SC (1991) Radiation Injury. In Wilson JD, Braunwald E, Isselbacher KJ et al (eds) *Harrison's Principles of Internal Medicine*, pp 204–208. New York: McGraw-Hill.

Finch SC & Finch CA (1988) *Summary of the studies at ABCC-RERF concerning the late hematologic effects of atomic bomb exposure in Hiroshima and Nagasaki*. RERF technical report 23–88, pp 5–7. Hiroshima: Radiation Effects Research Foundation.

Fleming AF (1990) Chronic lymphocytic leukaemia in tropical Africa: a review. *Leukemia and Lymphoma* 1: 169–173.

Flodin U, Fredriksson M, Persson B et al (1988) Chronic lymphocytic leukaemia and engine exhausts, fresh wood and DDT: a case-referent study. *British Journal of Industrial Medicine* 45: 33–38.

Foon KA, Rai KR & Gale RP (1990) Chronic lymphocytic leukemia: new insights into biology and therapy. *Annals of Internal Medicine* 113: 525–539.

Freedman AS (1990) Immunobiology of chronic lymphocytic leukemia. *Hematology/Oncology Clinics of North America* 4: 405–429.

Gale RP & Foon KA (1985) Chronic lymphocytic leukemia: recent advances in biology and treatment. *Annals of Internal Medicine* 103: 101–120.

Gale RP & Foon KA (1987) Biology of chronic lymphocytic leukemia. *Seminars in Hematology* 24: 209–229.

Garfinkel L & Boffetta P (1990) Association between smoking and leukemia in two American Cancer Society prospective studies. *Cancer* 65: 2356–2360.

Geary CG, Benn RT & Leck I (1979) Incidence of myeloid leukaemia in Lancashire. *Lancet* ii: 549–551.

Gilman PA, Ames RG & McCawley MA (1985) Leukemia risk among US white male coal miners. *Journal of Occupational Medicine* 27: 669–671.

Gunz FW (1983) Genetic factors in human leukemia. In Gunz FW & Henderson ES (eds) *Leukemia* 4th edn, pp 313–328. New York: Grune & Stratton.

Han T, Ozer H, Sadamori H et al (1984) Prognostic importance of cytogenic abnormalities in chronic lymphocytic leukemia. *New England Journal of Medicine* 310: 288–292.

Henshaw DL, Eatough JP & Richardson RB (1990) Radon as a causative factor in induction of myeloid leukaemia and other cancers. *Epidemiology* 335: 1008–1012.

Herr R, Ferguson J, Meyers N et al (1990) Cigarette smoking, blast crises, and survival in chronic myeloid leukemia. *American Journal of Hematology* 34: 1–4.

Hester JP, Rossen R & Truijillo J (1977) Frequency of HLA antigens in chronic myelocytic leukemia. *Southern Medical Journal* 70: 691–693.

Heston JF, Kelly JB, Meigs JW et al (1986) Forty-five years of cancer incidence in Connecticut: 1935–79. *National Cancer Institute Monographs* 70, PHS (NIH). DHHS 86-2652, pp 555–561. Bethesda, MD: National Institutes of Health.

Hill C & Laplanche A (1990) Overall mortality and cancer mortality around French nuclear sites. *Nature* 374: 755–757.

Hjelle B, Mills R & Swenson S (1991) Incidence of hairy cell leukemia, mycosis fungoides, and chronic lymphocytic leukemia in first known HTLV-II-endemic population. *Journal of Infectious Diseases* 163: 435–440.

Hogstedt C, Aringer L & Gustavsson A (1986) Epidemiologic support for ethylene oxide as a cancer-causing agent. *Journal of the American Medical Association* 255: 1575–1578.

Ichimaru M, Ohkita T & Ishimaru T (1986) Leukemia, multiple myeloma, and malignant lymphoma. In Shigimatsu I & Kagan A (eds) *Cancer in Atomic Bomb Survivors, GANN Monograph on Cancer Research No. 32*, pp 113–127. Tokyo: Japan Scientific Societies Press.

International Agency for Research on Cancer (1985) *Monographs on the Evaluation of the Carcinogenic Risk of Chemicals to Man. Allyl Compounds, Aldehydes, Epoxides, and Peroxides*, vol. 36, pp 189–226. Lyon: IARC.

Jablon S & Miller RW (1978) Army technologists: 29-year follow up for cause of death. *Radiology* 126: 677–679.

Jablon S, Hrubec Z & Boice JD Jr (1991) Cancer in populations living near nuclear facilities: a survey of mortality nationwide and incidence in two states. *Journal of the American Medical Association* 265: 1403–1408.

Juliusson G & Gahrton G (1990) Chromosome aberrations in B-cell chronic lymphocytic leukemia. *Cancer Genetics and Cytogenetics* 45: 143–160.

Kinlen LJ & Rogot E (1988) Leukaemia and smoking habits among United States veterans. *British Medical Journal* 297: 657–659.

Kushwaha MRS, Chandra D, Misra NC et al (1985) Leukemias and lymphomas at Luchnow. *Leukemia Research* **9:** 799–802.

Linet MS (1985) *The Leukemias: Epidemiologic Aspects*, pp 14–27. New York: Oxford University Press.

Linet MS & Blattner WA (1988) The epidemiology of chronic lymphocytic leukemia. In Polliack S & Catovsky D (eds) *Chronic Lymphocytic Leukemia*, pp 11–32. Chur, Switzerland: Harwood Academic Press.

Linet MS & Cartwright RA (in press) The leukemias. In Schottenfeld D & Fraumeni JF Jr (eds) *Cancer Epidemiology and Prevention* 2nd edn. New York: Oxford University Press.

Linet MS & Devesa SS (1990) Descriptive epidemiology of the leukemias. In Henderson ES & Lister TA (eds) *Leukemia* 5th edn, pp 207–224. Philadelphia: WB Saunders.

Linet MS, Bias WB, Dorgan JF et al (1988a) HLA antigens in chronic lymphocytic leukemia. *Tissue Antigens* **31:** 71–78.

Linet MS, Malker HSR, McLaughlin JK et al (1988b) Leukemias and occupation in Sweden: a registry-based analysis. *American Journal of Industrial Medicine* **14:** 319–330.

Linet MS, Hsing AW, McLaughlin JK et al (in press) Cigarette smoking and leukemia: results from the Lutheran Brotherhood Cohort study. *Cancer Causes and Control.*

Linos A, Kyle RA, O'Fallon WM et al (1980) A case-control study of occupational exposures and leukemia. *International Journal of Epidemiology* **9:** 131–135.

Lowenthal MN (1976) Chronic myeloid leukemia in Zambians. *Tropical and Geographical Medicine* **27:** 132–137.

Lynge E (1985) A follow-up study of cancer incidence among workers in manufacture of phenoxy herbicides in Denmark. *British Journal of Cancer* **52:** 259–270.

MacMahon B & Koller EK (1957) Ethnic differences in the incidence of leukemia. *Blood* **12:** 1–10.

McMichael AJ, Spirtas R, Gamble JF et al (1976) Mortality among rubber workers: relationship to specific jobs. *Journal of Occupational Medicine* **18:** 178–185.

Malone KE, Koepsell TD, Daling JR et al (1989) Chronic lymphocytic leukemia in relation to chemical exposures. *American Journal of Epidemiology* **130:** 1152–1158.

Mann DL, DeSantis P, Mark G et al (1987) HTLV-I associated B-cell CLL: indirect role for retrovirus in leukemogenesis. *Science* **236:** 1103–1106.

Marmont TA, Frassoni F, Bacigalupo A et al (1984) Recurrence of Ph[1]-positive leukemia in donor cells after marrow transplantation for chronic granulocytic leukemia. *New England Journal of Medicine* **310:** 903–906.

Matutes E, Garcia Talavera J, O'Brian M et al (1986) The morphological spectrum of T-prolymphocytic leukaemia. *British Journal of Haematology* **64:** 111–124.

Milham S Jr (1985) Silent keys: leukaemia mortality in amateur radio operators. *Lancet* **i:** 812.

Minot GR, Buckman TE & Issacs R (1924) Chronic myelogenous leukemia. *Journal of the American Medical Association* **82:** 1489–1494.

Mintzer DM & Hauptman SP (1983) Lymphosarcoma cell leukemia and other non-Hodgkin's lymphomas in leukemic phase. *American Journal of Medicine* **75:** 110–120.

Muir C, Waterhouse J, Mack T et al (1987) *Cancer Incidence in Five Continents*, vol. 5. IARC Scientific Publications No. 88, pp 827–828. Lyon: IARC.

National Cancer Institute (1990) *Cancer Statistics Review 1973–1987*. US Department of Health and Human Services, NIH Publication No. 90-2789, pp 1.45–1.50. Bethesda, MD: National Institutes of Health.

National Research Council (Committee on the Biological Effects of Ionizing Radiation) (1988) *Health risks of radon and other internally-deposited alpha-emitters* (BEIR IV), p 483. Washington, DC: National Academy Press.

National Research Council (Committee on the Biologic Effects of Ionizing Radiation) (1990) *The effects on populations of exposure to low levels of ionizing radiation* (BEIR V), pp 242–351. Washington, DC: National Academy Press.

Neglia JP & Robison LL (1988) Epidemiology of childhood acute leukemias. *Pediatric Clinics of North America* **35:** 675–692.

Nishiyama H, Mokuno J & Inoue T (1969) Relative frequency and mortality rate of various types of leukemia in Japan. *Japanese Journal of Cancer Research* **60:** 71–81.

O'Brien TR & Decoufle P (1988) Cancer mortality among northern Georgia carpet and textile workers. *American Journal of Industrial Medicine* **14:** 15–24.

Okany CC & Akinyanju OO (1989) Chronic leukaemia: an African experience. *Medical Oncology and Tumor Pharmacotherapy* **6:** 189–194.

Oloo AJ & Ogada TA (1984) Chronic lymphocytic leukaemia (CLL): clinical studies at Kenyatta National Hospital (KNH). *East African Medical Journal* **61:** 797–801.

Ott MG, Kolesar RC, Scharnweber HC et al (1980) A mortality survey of employees engaged in the development or manufacture of styrene-based products. *Journal of Occupational Medicine* **22:** 445–460.

Palmer CG, Provisor AJ, Weaver DD et al (1983) Juvenile chronic granulocytic leukemia in a patient with trisomy 8, neurofibromatosis, and prolonged Epstein–Barr virus infection. *Journal of Pediatrics* **102:** 888–892.

Pearce N, Prior I, Methven D et al (1990) Follow up of New Zealand participants in British atmospheric nuclear weapons tests in the Pacific. *British Medical Journal* **300:** 1161–1166.

Pines A, Ben-Bassat B, Modan M et al (1987) Survival and prognostic factors in chronic lymphocytic leukemia. *European Journal of Haematology* **38:** 123–130.

Preston-Martin S & Peters JM (1988) Prior employment as a welder associated with the development of chronic myeloid leukaemia. *British Journal of Cancer* **58:** 105–108.

Preston-Martin S, Peters JM, Yu MC et al (1988) Myelogenous leukemia and electric blanket use. *Bioelectromagnetics* **9:** 207–213.

Preston-Martin S, Thomas DC, Yu MC et al (1989) Diagnostic radiography as a risk factor for chronic myeloid and monocytic leukaemia (CML). *British Journal of Cancer* **59:** 639–644.

Prischl FC, Haas OK, Lion T et al (1989) Duration of first remission as an indicator of long-term survival in chronic myelogenous leukaemia. *British Journal of Haematology* **71:** 337–342.

Rai KR & Sawitsky A (1987) A review of the prognostic role of cytogenic, phenotypic, morphologic, and immune function characteristics in chronic lymphocytic leukemia. *Blood Cells* **12:** 327–338.

Ratner L & Poiesz BJ (1988) Leukemias associated with human T-cell lymphotropic virus type I in a non-endemic region. *Medicine* **67:** 401–422.

Rinsky RA, Smith AB, Hornung R et al (1987) Benzene and leukemia: an epidemiologic risk assessment. *New England Journal of Medicine* **316:** 1044–1050.

Robinette CD, Jablon S & Preston TL (1985) *Mortality of nuclear weapons test participants.* Medical Followup Agency, National Research Council, Washington, DC: National Academy Press.

Rowley JD (1990) The Philadelphia chromosome translocation; a paradigm for understanding leukemia. *Cancer* **65:** 2178–2184.

Saltman DL, Ross JA, Banks RE et al (1989) Molecular evidence for a single clonal origin in biphenotypic concomitant chronic lymphocytic leukemia and multiple myeloma. *Blood* **74:** 2062–2065.

Schwartz DA, Vaughan TL, Heyer NJ et al (1988) B cell neoplasms and occupational asbestos exposure. *American Journal of Industrial Medicine* **14:** 661–671.

Seltser R & Sartwell PE (1965) The influence of occupational exposure on the mortality of American radiologists and other medical specialists. *American Journal of Epidemiology* **101:** 188–198.

Shimizu Y, Kato H & Schull W (1990) Studies of the mortality of A-bomb survivors. 9. Mortality, 1950–85; Part 2. Cancer mortality based on the recently revised doses (DS86). *Radiation Research* **121:** 120–141.

Smith PG & Doll R (1981) Mortality from cancer and all causes among British radiologists. *British Journal of Radiology* **54:** 187–194.

Smith PG & Doll R (1982) Mortality among patients with ankylosing spondylitis after a single treatment course with X-ray. *British Medical Journal* **284:** 449–460.

Sokal JE, Cox EB, Baccarani M et al (1984) Prognostic discrimination in 'good risk' chronic granulocytic leukemia. *Blood* **63:** 789–799.

Sorensen SA, Mulvihill JJ & Nielsen A (1986) Long-term follow-up of von Recklinghausen neurofibromatosis. Survival and malignant neoplasms. *New England Journal of Medicine* **314:** 1010–1015.

Spinelli JJ, Gallagher RP, Band PR et al (1984) Multiple myeloma, leukemia, and cancer of the ovary in cosmetologists and hair dressers. *American Journal of Industrial Medicine* **6:** 97–102.

Spirtas R, Van Ert M, Gamble J et al (1976) Toxicologic, industrial hygiene and epidemiologic considerations in the possible association between SBR manufacturing and neoplasms of lymphatic and hematopoietic tissues. *Proceedings of NIOSH Syrene-Butadiene Briefing, Covington, Kentucky, April 30, 1976.* DHEW publication no. (NIOSH), pp 77–129.

Stark AN, Thorogood J, Head C et al (1987) Prognostic factors and survival in chronic myelomonocytic leukaemia. *British Journal of Cancer* **56:** 59–63.

Stern RM (1987) Cancer incidence among welders: possible effects of exposure to extremely low frequency electromagnetic radiation (ELF) and to welding fumes. *Environmental Health Perspectives* **76:** 221–229.

Stevens W, Thomas DC, Lyon JL et al (1990) Leukemia in Utah and radioactive fallout from the Nevada test site: a case control study. *Journal of the American Medical Association* **264:** 585–591.

Stone RM (1990) Prolymphocytic leukemia. *Hematology/Oncology Clinics of North America* **4:** 457–467.

Teta MJ, Walrath J, Meigs JW et al (1984) Cancer incidence among cosmetologists. *Journal of the National Cancer Institute* **72:** 1051–1057.

Tokuhata GK, Neely CL & Williams DL (1968) Chronic myelocytic leukemia in identical twins and siblings. *Blood* **31:** 216–225.

Wald N (1988) Smoking and leukaemia. *British Medical Journal* **297:** 638.

Wang J-X, Inskip PD, Boice JD Jr et al (1990) Cancer incidence among medical diagnostic X-ray workers in China, 1950 to 1985. *International Journal of Cancer* **45:** 889–895.

Wiktor SZ & Blattner WA (1991) Epidemiology of human T-cell leukemia virus (HTLV-I). In Gallo RC & Jay G (eds) *The Human Retroviruses*, pp 175–192. San Diego: Academic Press.

Williams CKO & Bamgboye EA (1983) Estimation of incidence of human leukemia subtypes in an urban African population. *Oncology* **40:** 381–386.

Williams RR & Horm JW (1977) Association of cancer sites with tobacco and alcohol consumption and socioeconomic status of patients: interview study from the Third National Cancer Survey. *Journal of the National Cancer Institute* **58:** 525–547.

Wing S, Shy CM, Wood JL et al (1991) Mortality among workers at Oak Ridge National Laboratory. *Journal of the American Medical Association* **265:** 1397–1402.

Wong O (1990) A cohort mortality study and a case-control study of workers potentially exposed to styrene in reinforced plastics and composites industry. *British Journal of Internal Medicine* **47:** 753–762.

Wong O & Raabe GK (1989) Critical review of cancer epidemiology in petroleum industry employees, with a quantitative meta-analysis by cancer site. *American Journal of Industrial Medicine* **15:** 283–310.

Wongsrichanalai C, Delzell E & Code P (1989) Mortality from leukemia and other diseases among workers at a petroleum refinery. *Journal of Occupational Medicine* **31:** 106–111.

Yin S-N, Li G-L, Tain F-D et al (1989) A retrospective cohort study of leukemia and other cancers in benzene workers. *Environmental Health Perspectives* **82:** 207–213.

Yoshimoto Y, Kato H & Schull WJ (1988) Risk of cancer among children exposed in utero to A-bomb radiations, 1950–1984. *Lancet* **ii:** 665–669.

Zarrabi MH, Grunwald HW & Rosner F (1977) Chronic lymphocytic leukemia terminating in acute leukemia. *Archives of Internal Medicine* **137:** 1059–1064.

Zuelzer WW & Cox DE (1969) Genetic aspects of leukemia. *Seminars in Hematology* **6:** 4–25.

3

Hodgkin's disease

RUTH F. JARRETT

The aim of this chapter is to review recent data which provide evidence for the involvement of viruses in the pathogenesis of Hodgkin's disease (HD) and to relate these data to the epidemiological findings.

Since the first description of HD in 1832 it has been suggested that this disease may have an infectious aetiology (Hodgkin, 1832). This idea is based on both the clinicopathological and epidemiological features of the disease. Clinically HD usually presents with lymphadenopathy, which is often accompanied by constitutional symptoms such as fever, night sweats, tiredness and weight loss. The histological picture is characterized by the presence of the Reed–Sternberg (RS) cell, the putative malignant cell, admixed with an inflammatory infiltrate consisting of lymphocytes, plasma cells, eosinophils and histiocytes. The lineage of the RS cell is unknown but current opinion favours a lymphoid origin. RS cells are not unique to HD and therefore in order to make the diagnosis the RS cells must be present in an appropriate cellular background. The frequent presence of systemic symptoms, coupled with the polymorphous and predominantly reactive nature of the cellular infiltrate, distinguish HD from the non-Hodgkin's lymphomas (NHLs) and suggest the possibility that an infectious agent is involved.

There is a range of histological appearances and on this basis the disease is divided into four subtypes: nodular sclerosis (HDNS), mixed cellularity (HDMC), lymphocyte predominance (HDLP) and lymphocyte depleted (HDLD) (Lukes et al, 1966). Recent data suggest that HDLP is a distinct entity which should be classified separately from other forms of HD (Nicholas et al, 1990).

DESCRIPTIVE EPIDEMIOLOGY

HD is not common, although not rare. The overall incidence is 3.0 per 10^5 person years in the USA and 2.4 per 10^5 person years in the UK (Glaser, 1987; McKinney et al, 1989). However it is one of the most common forms of malignancy in young people and has an unusual age distribution which is quite distinct from that of the NHLs. The majority of studies have reported a bimodal age incidence curve, although the shape of this curve varies in different communities (MacMahon, 1966). These differences led Correa and O'Conor (1971) to suggest that there are at least three epidemiologica patterns of HD. In the type I pattern the first peak of the bimodal distribution occurs in childhood, there is a low incidence in the third decade and a second peak in older age groups. This pattern is found in developing countries. The type III pattern, which is seen in developed countries, is characterized by low rates in childhood and a pronounced first peak in young adults; a second peak is observed in older adults. An intermediate pattern, type II, is found in rural areas of developed countries, in central Europe and in the southern United States. This pattern is thought to represent a transition state between the type I and III patterns consequent upon improved living conditions. Although this interpretation is probably correct in many cases (Merk et al, 1990), a recent study from the UK suggests that the type II pattern may be a feature of rural as opposed to urban communities (Alexander et al, 1991a). Low rates of HD have been noted in China and other Asian populations, including Japan (Muir et al, 1987).

Many surveys have shown that the risk of HD in young adults is related to high socioeconomic status (Gutensohn and Cole, 1981; Glaser, 1987; Alexander et al, 1991b). In contrast, older patients are more likely to be of low socioeconomic status (Gutensohn, 1982; Alexander et al, 1991b). The possibility that racial differences contribute to the different epidemiological patterns has been reviewed by Glaser (1990a). The pattern of HD in Black Americans more closely resembles that of White Americans than that of Black Africans. HD variation therefore appears less dependent on race than on socioeconomic conditions.

The age incidence curves for HDNS and the other subtypes are quite distinct (McKinney et al, 1989; Glaser and Swartz, 1990; Alexander et al, 1991b). HDNS has a unimodal age incidence curve and accounts for the young adult peak in incidence. In contrast, the other subtypes grouped together show a gradually increasing incidence with increasing age, a pattern more similar to that seen for other lymphomas. The majority of the childhood cases in developing countries are HDMC and HDLP and the relative proportion of these subtypes, compared with HDNS, is increased in childhood cases in the UK (Correa and O'Conor, 1971; McKinney et al, 1989).

Overall there is a male predominance of HD cases with a male:female ratio of 1.5 (McKinney et al, 1989). The male excess is most pronounced in children but is also present in older adults. The incidence of female cases in the young adult group is increasing and a female excess has been reported in the 15–24 year age bracket (Spitz et al, 1986; McKinney et al, 1989; Glaser and Swartz, 1990).

Temporal studies suggest that young adult HDNS cases are increasing in incidence (Glaser and Swartz, 1990). This most probably reflects a change from the type I to III patterns described above. In a recent study from the UK the second peak in age incidence was not seen (McKinney et al, 1989). This study used high quality incidence data and had optimal case ascertainment and is therefore likely to accurately reflect HD incidence in the UK. Figure 1 shows the age incidence of HD obtained from an extension of this survey (Cartwright et al, 1990). The authors suggest that the failure to

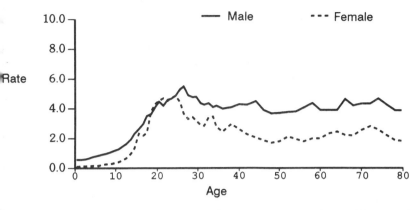

Figure 1. Incidence of HD in England and Wales (January 1984 to December 1988) by age and sex (——, male; –––, female). Reproduced, by kind permission of the Leukaemia Research Fund, from Cartwright et al (1990).

demonstrate a renewed rise in incidence in older patients is not due to a temporal change in disease incidence but rather to improved diagnostic accuracy in this age group. Updated HD incidence data from the USA show a decline in HD incidence in white persons over 40 years (Glaser and Swartz, 1990). Glaser and Swartz (1990) specifically addressed the issue of diagnostic accuracy. A comparison of initial and review diagnoses suggested that HD was over-diagnosed, particularly in older patients, however there appeared to be an improvement in accuracy in recent years. Therefore they concluded that the decrease in the reported incidence of HD in older adults did not represent a real secular trend.

On the basis of the above epidemiological findings, two hypotheses, which are not mutually exclusive, have been proposed regarding the aetiology of HD. These are considered below. The data obtaining to clustering or aggregation of cases are also discussed in more detail.

HYPOTHESES OF AETIOLOGY

Multiple aetiology hypothesis

In 1966 MacMahon put forward the hypothesis that HD is a grouping of at least three entities which probably have quite distinct aetiologies (MacMahon, 1966). He proposed that these groups could be distinguished on the basis of age at onset of clinical disease: 0–14 years; 15–34 years and 50 years and over. He suggested further that HD in young adults may be caused by an infectious agent. This hypothesis was based on the available data which suggested that the epidemiological features and histological subtype distribution were different in these three age groups. The idea that HD in young adults may have a different aetiology from HD in older patients has been supported by later epidemiological studies (Cole et al, 1968; Gutensohn, 1982; Alexander et al, 1991b). Most of these have concentrated on the adult age groups and therefore this model is often referred to as the 'two disease hypothesis'. Despite improved diagnostic accuracy in recent years the epidemiological risk factors for the development of HD correlate better with age at diagnosis than with histological subtype (Alexander et al, 1991b).

Delayed exposure hypothesis

infected later than normal

The delayed exposure hypothesis or late host response model suggests that the development of HD is related to late infection with a common childhood pathogen (Gutensohn and Cole, 1977). Paralytic polio has frequently been used as a model for this hypothesis. In the prevaccine era sanitary conditions determined the age at which infection with the polio virus was likely to occur and this in turn determined the likely outcome of infection. At all ages infection was usually silent. In children symptomatic infection usually involved the gastrointestinal tract and paralysis was rare; however when primary infection occurred in adults there was an increased likelihood of developing paralytic symptoms. In developing countries, with poorer standards of sanitation, exposure was ubiquitous in childhood and most people developed immunity before adolescence. Since all children were infected early in life paralytic manifestations were seen in this age group. In developed countries infection in childhood was rare and therefore older children and young adults were more likely to be susceptible to infection; in consequence paralytic polio was seen in these age groups. There are therefore similarities between the epidemiology of paralytic polio and HD. In both, disease risk is greatest in children with the least favourable living conditions and in young adults with the most favourable living conditions.

If this model applies to HD then factors which delay the age at which common pathogens are first encountered should be associated with an increased risk of HD. Several epidemiological studies have been designed to address this question. A detailed case-control study was carried out by Gutensohn and Cole in Massachusetts (1981). They found that young adults with a relatively high risk for the disease were those who were from small families, lived in single-family houses, had relatively few neighbourhood playmates and had relatively well-educated parents. The excess risk associated with any one of those variables was small, particularly following adjustment for confounding variables. However the risk factors are all in the same general direction, i.e. they all relate in the same way to childhood socioeconomic status. Other studies have shown that late birth order children are less likely to develop disease (Vianna and Polan, 1978), and in Israel, Abramson et al (1978) found that patients had better education and better sanitary facilities than controls.

Two additional findings support this model. First, Paffenbarger et al (1977) found that the risk of developing HD was lower in persons who had experienced more common contagious illnesses in childhood. Secondly, it has been shown that persons with a past history of infectious mononucleosis (IM) have an approximately threefold increased risk of developing HD. Gutensohn and Cole (1980) combined the data from six published studies: out of 41 600 individuals with a history of IM, a total of 37 HD cases were observed with 12 expected. The converse has also been found: HD cases are more likely to report a past history of IM than controls (Gutensohn and Cole, 1981; Evans and Gutensohn, 1984). IM is, of course, associated with late exposure to Epstein–Barr virus (EBV) and these data therefore provide support for the above model. However, there are additional data to specifically implicate EBV in the pathogenesis of HD (see below).

Clustering of Hodgkins disease

The possibility that HD cases occur in clusters has aroused great interest since the original report of case aggregation by Vianna et al (1971). It is difficult to assess the significance of the findings in this report as the cases were identified retrospectively on the basis of shared exposures, thus it was impossible to select a control population. However this study prompted other investigators to look for evidence of clustering of HD using a variety of statistical techniques. In general, studies of space–time interactions have given rise to inconclusive results (Kryscio et al, 1973; Greenberg et al, 1983); this is perhaps not surprising given the presumed long latent period of HD. Some studies of social linkage have found a slight increase in the relative risk of developing HD in schoolmates (Zack et al, 1977; Scherr et al, 1984); however others have reported negative findings (Smith et al, 1977).

A recent survey in the UK found no significant differences in the incidence rates for HD in 22 countries, i.e. the spatial pattern was uniform at this level (Alexander et al, 1989; Cartwright et al, 1990). However when the incidence figures were compared at the electoral ward level a non-random distribution was noted. This was investigated further using methods of analysis which are independent of census boundaries. Two methods of nearest neighbour analysis were employed. Significant evidence of spatial clustering was found, with 13% of young cases (0–34 years) identified as clustered. Similar results have been obtained in Scotland and in the USA (Urquhart et al, 1989; Glaser, 1990b).

Taken together, the recent data suggest that there is significant evidence for weak clustering of HD cases. This pattern of clustering would be consistent with an aetiology involving either delayed exposure to a common, but not ubiquitous, infectious agent or infection with a virus with a long latent period.

Seroepidemiological studies

Serological studies have investigated the potential role of many viruses in HD. Attention has focused primarily on the herpesvirus family as these viruses are widespread and common and some have been associated with lymphomas in man and animals.

Epstein–Barr virus antibodies

The most consistent findings have come from seroepidemiological studies of EBV. Infection by EBV is widespread and the majority of adults have been infected at some stage in their past (reviewed by Evans and Niederman, 1989). In developing countries most children have been infected by the age of 6 years but in developed countries infection is often delayed. Following primary infection the virus persists in a latent form in B-cells, replicates in the oropharynx and is shed in saliva. Different EBV antigens can be distinguished serologically; antibodies to the viral capsid antigen (VCA) are found in all individuals who have encountered EBV, whereas antibodies to early antigen (EA) are detected during primary infection and during viral reactivation.

Numerous case-control studies have shown that patients with HD, as a group, have elevated levels of antibody to EBV (Levine et al, 1971; Henderson et al, 1973; Henle and Henle, 1973; Langenhuysen et al, 1974; Hesse et al, 1977; Evans et al, 1978). The majority have found increased antibody titres to both VCA and EA. Antibody levels are higher in HD cases relative to their siblings, and cases reporting a past history of IM have higher titres than those with no such history (Evans et al, 1980; Evans and Gutensohn, 1984). Treatment has been shown to affect EBV antibody levels; however, studies utilizing samples collected at the time of diagnosis have also found elevated antibody levels (Hesse et al, 1977). Raised titres are found in both the young adult and older age groups. Studies which have analysed the data by histological subtype have produced inconsistent results (Levine et al, 1971; Hesse et al, 1977; Evans et al, 1978).

In order to investigate whether raised antibody levels antedate diagnosis, Mueller et al (1989) identified 43 HD patients from whom serum samples had been stored prior to the diagnosis of HD. Samples from these patients were matched with those from 96 controls and the association between elevated antibody titres to several EBV antigens and the subsequent development of HD analysed. The relative risk of developing HD was significantly increased in persons with elevated EBV antibody levels. The data further suggested that the pattern of antibody response differed in different age and sex groups. The results of this study demonstrate that the elevated EBV titres seen in HD do not simply reflect viral reactivation secondary to therapy or advanced disease. These data, coupled with the association between IM and HD mentioned above, raise the possibility that EBV is directly involved in the pathogenesis of the disease. It is also possible that the raised titres are the consequence of an underlying immune defect or are a marker for infection by another virus. It should be noted that not all HD patients have evidence of infection by EBV, therefore EBV cannot be implicated in all cases of HD.

Antibodies to the human herpesvirus-6

The second virus for which there is a consensus of opinion is human herpesvirus-6 (HHV-6). HHV-6 was first isolated in 1986 from patients with a variety of lymphoproliferative and immunosuppressive disorders (Sala-huddin et al, 1986). It has since been shown to be a ubiquitous virus with infection occurring early in life. Persistent infection can be detected in the majority of healthy adults (Jarrett et al, 1990). To date only three studies have examined HHV-6 antibody levels in HD (Ablashi et al, 1988; Biberfeld et al, 1988) and only one of these was a case-control study (Clark et al, 1990). However all three reported elevated antibody levels in HD. Clark et al (1990) found significantly elevated titres in all adult age groups but young adults were particularly likely to have high antibody levels. The difference between the geometric mean titres in young adults aged 15–34 years and the older age group was statistically significant. EBV serology performed on the same serum samples revealed that raised titres to these two herpesviruses are largely independent of each other (D. Clark, unpublished results).

Antibodies to other viruses

The results of serological analysis of the other human herpesviruses, *Herpes simplex* virus (HSV), *Varicella zoster* virus (VZV) and cytomegalovirus (CMV), are less consistent, with some studies reporting elevated titres (Catalano and Goldman, 1972; Henderson et al, 1973; Langenhuysen et al, 1974; Hesse et al, 1977) and others showing no significant differences between cases and controls (Levine et al, 1971; Evans et al, 1978; Evans and Gutensohn, 1984). No significant findings have emerged from studies of measles, rubella, adenovirus, parainfluenza viruses, papovavirus and human T-cell leukaemia virus (Hesse et al, 1977; Evans et al, 1978; Evans and Gutensohn, 1984; S. Crae, unpublished results).

In summary, seroepidemiological studies suggest that EBV and HHV-6 may be involved in HD. The results do not prove a causative association but suggest a direction for molecular and virological studies.

Epstein–Barr virus and Hodgkin's disease

Molecular studies of EBV

The most exciting development in HD research in the last few years is the demonstration of a molecular association between EBV and HD. Early studies using radiolabelled virus or cRNA as probe and liquid hybridization or early filter hybridization techniques failed to find EBV genomes in HD tumour biopsies (Pagano et al, 1973; Lindahl et al, 1974). In 1987 Weiss and colleagues reported the detection of EBV genomes in four out of 21 cases of HD. This study was facilitated by the use of the cloned EBV *Bam* HI-W fragment as the probe in the Southern blot analysis. This DNA sequence is repeated several times (usually 7–11) in the EBV genome and therefore provides a sensitive indicator for the presence of EBV (Arrand et al, 1981). A single EBV genome present in $<0.5\%$ of the cells in a sample containing DNA from approximately 1.5×10^6 cells can be detected using this probe (Jarrett et al, 1991b). Despite the scarcity of RS cells in some HD tumours this should allow the detection of EBV genomes, if they are present in RS cells, in the majority of HD cases.

Since the original report by Weiss et al (1987) a number of groups have reported similar findings (Table 1 and Figure 2) (Anagnostopoulos et al, 1989; Boiocchi et al, 1989; Staal et al, 1989; Weiss et al, 1989; Uccini et al, 1990; Gledhill et al, 1991). Studies from different geographical locales have

Table 1. Detection of EBV genomes in HD.

Study	Method of analysis	Total cases	EBV positive
Weiss et al (1987)	Southern blotting	21	4 (19)
Staal et al (1989)	Southern blotting	28	8 (29)
Weiss et al (1989)	Southern blotting	16	3 (19)
Boiocchi et al (1989)	Southern blotting	17	7 (41)
Anagnostopoulos et al (1989)	Southern blotting	42	7 (17)
Uccini et al (1990)*	Southern blotting	20	3 (15)
Jarrett et al (1991b)	Southern blotting	47	17 (36)
Uhara et al (1990)	In situ hybridization	31	8 (26)
Uhara et al (1990)	PCR	31	8 (26)
Bignon et al (1990)	PCR	16	8 (50)
Herbst et al (1990)	PCR	198	114 (58)
Pallesen et al (1991)	Immunohistochemistry	84	40 (48)

Values in parentheses are percentages.
* The figures presented here are from the HIV-negative patients included in this study.

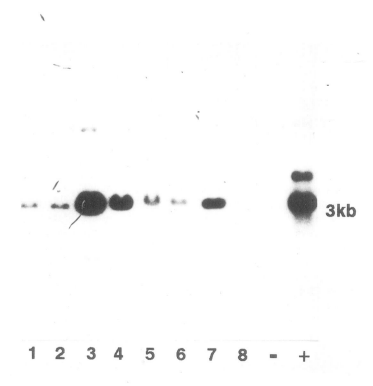

Figure 2. Detection of EBV genomes in HD samples by Southern blot analysis. DNA samples were digested with *Bam* HI and hybridized to the EBV *Bam* HI-W probe. A positive result is visualized as a band at 3 kb. Samples 1–7 were from HD cases positive for EBV; sample 8 is an EBV-negative HD case. The negative control is placental DNA and the positive control DNA from the B95-8 cell line. In sample 3 and the positive control additional bands represent fragments flanking the EBV *Bam* HI-W repeat sequence.

shown that EBV genomes are consistently found in HD tumour biopsies (Table 1). The proportion of positive cases varies from 15 to 41%. Using similar methodology, EBV genomes are only rarely found in reactive nodes and NHLs (Andiman et al, 1983; Staal et al, 1989; Jarrett et al, 1991b). Exceptions to this are Burkitt's lymphoma and lymphomas in immuno-suppressed persons (Andiman et al, 1983; reviewed by Miller, 1990).

Until recently the idea that EBV might be involved in the pathogenesis of HD was treated with scepticism. Following primary infection EBV is known to persist in a latent state in B cells and to replicate in the oropharynx (reviewed in Miller, 1990). Reactivation and increased viral replication may occur as a consequence of immune dysfunction; thus it seemed possible that the ability to detect EBV genomes in HD tumours was simply a reflection of increased viral load. To some it seemed unlikely that EBV was aetiologically involved in yet another malignancy. In order to show a meaningful association between the virus and the tumour it was therefore necessary to determine the clonality of the infected cells and the cellular localization of the EBV genomes.

It is possible to assess the clonality of EBV infected cells by examining the viral terminal repeat (TR) sequences (Raab-Traub and Flynn, 1986). This analysis indicates the number of infectious events that have taken place within a cell population and is explained in Figure 3. In the viral particle the EBV genome is linear (Figure 3A), but following infection of a cell the termini of the genome fuse to form a covalently closed circle (Figure 3B). At the fused termini is a DNA sequence, the TR, which is repeated a variable number of times. The number of TRs varies from one EBV genome to another; thus the size of restriction fragments including the TR sequence will vary from one genome to another. When a cell is infected at a low multiplicity of infection, all the EBV genomes within that cell will contain an identical number of TRs, and when that cell divides all the progeny will contain EBV genomes with an identical number of TRs (Figure 3C). Thus if this cell population is examined by Southern blot analysis, using restriction enzymes which cut the DNA flanking the TR and a probe from the terminal region, a single band will be visualized (Figure 3E). When the latent state is disrupted and productive viral replication ensues, the viral particles produced contain genomes with varying numbers of TRs (Figure 3D). The cells infected from this source will therefore contain genomes with varying numbers of TRs. Examination of this cell population by Southern blot analysis as above will reveal a ladder of bands (Figure 3F).

Several studies have assessed the clonality of the EBV genomes within HD tumours (Weiss et al, 1987, 1989; Anagnostopoulos et al, 1989; Boiocchi et al, 1989; Staal et al, 1989; Gledhill et al, 1991; Jarrett et al, 1991b). In the majority of cases the infected cells have been found to be clonal with respect to EBV; in one study clonality was demonstrable in 25/26 cases examined (Jarrett et al, 1991b). In three cases, from three different studies, Southern blot analysis revealed two or three different-sized fragments containing the TRs (Weiss et al, 1987; Boiocchi et al, 1989; Katz et al, 1989). This suggests either that, in these cases, the infected cells are oligoclonal with respect to EBV, or that the original infection took place at a high multiplicity of infection. Combining all the above studies, clonality has been demonstrated in 43/47 cases which have been successfully examined. This suggests that EBV has infected a single cell which has undergone clonal expansion. The ability to detect EBV DNA in HD is not therefore due to an

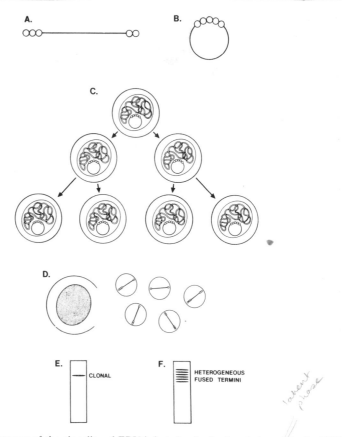

Figure 3. Assessment of the clonality of EBV-infected cells. In the viral particle the EBV genome is in a linear form (panel A) with a tandemly repeated sequence, the terminal repeat (TR), at each end. Each TR sequence is shown as an open circle (not to scale). Following infection of a cell the genome circularizes (panel B). The number of TRs varies from one EBV genome to another, therefore the size of restriction fragments containing the TR sequence will vary from one genome to another. When a cell is infected at a low multiplicity of infection all the EBV genomes within that cell will contain an identical number of TRs, and all the daughter cells will also contain identical viral genomes (panel C). If this cell population is examined by Southern blot analysis, using restriction enzymes which cut the DNA flanking the TR and a probe to the terminal region, a single band will be visualized (panel E). When the latent state is disrupted and productive viral replication ensues, the viruses produced contain genomes with varying numbers of TRs; this results from a process of concatemerization and cleavage of the genomes (panel D). Cells infected from this source will contain genomes with different numbers of TRs. Examination of this cell population by Southern blot analysis as above will reveal a ladder of bands (panel F). If a cell is infected at a high multiplicity of infection and several different viruses, with different numbers of TRs, infect the cell, a similar Southern blot result will be obtained.

increased viral load in polyclonal B cells, or to infection of RS cells following clonal expansion.

The cellular localization of EBV genomes has been shown using in situ hybridization. Weiss and colleagues (1989) showed that in five cases of HD the EBV genomes were present in cells with the morphology of RS cells, and shortly afterwards Anagnostopoulos et al (1989) reported similar findings in two cases. Since that time other groups have confirmed this observation (Uhara et al, 1990; Wu et al, 1990). Taken together, the results of the in situ hybridization and EBV clonality studies suggest that in a proportion of HD cases RS cells are a clonal expansion of a single EBV-infected cell.

Detection of EBV using the polymerase chain reaction

The use of the polymerase chain reaction (PCR) to detect EBV genomes should overcome problems of sensitivity associated with the examination of samples containing few RS cells. PCR is also faster and simpler to perform than either Southern blot analysis or in situ hybridization and can be carried out using archival material. However the use of such an exquisitely sensitive technique poses problems as the chance of detecting latent EBV infection in B cells is increased. Accurate quantification of the PCR may help to overcome this problem.

There are three published studies in which PCR has been used to detect EBV in HD tumours (Table 1) (Bignon et al, 1990; Herbst et al, 1990; Uhara et al, 1990). In each case the conditions used in the PCR were not designed for maximum sensitivity. Herbst et al (1990) scored the results of PCRs, which used extracted DNA as template, on ethidium bromide-stained gels, rather than scoring following hybridization, which would have resulted in an approximately 100-fold increase in sensitivity. In their study, 58% of HD samples and 10% of reactive nodes were found to be positive. Uhara et al (1990) used DNA extracted from paraffin-embedded material and performed only 25 cycles of amplification. This resulted in the detection of EBV DNA in 8/31 samples; identical results were obtained using in situ hybridization on the same samples. Bignon et al (1990) detected EBV in samples from 8/16 patients; however a positive result was obtained from a lymph node which appeared free of HD on histological examination. In an unpublished study in which 2 μg of DNA was used per reaction and 40 cycles of amplification were performed, EBV DNA could be detected in almost 90% of HD samples (R. Jarrett, unpublished results).

The use of PCR to detect EBV, and other herpesviruses, in pathological specimens is problematic and the optimal methodology has yet to be worked out. However, one important point emerges from these studies: EBV genomes are not detectable in all cases of HD.

EBV subtypes in Hodgkin's disease

There are two known subtypes of EBV: type 1 and type 2. EBV type 1 has a worldwide distribution and is thought to be the predominant strain in western countries. EBV type 2 is relatively more common in central Africa and Papua New Guinea and is found in approximately 40% of Burkitt's lymphomas from these areas (Zimber et al, 1986; Young et al, 1987). A recent study from the USA suggested that type 2 viruses may be more prevalent than previously recognized, particularly in individuals with immunosuppression (Sixbey et al, 1989). EBV subtyping has been performed on 30 DNA samples from cases of EBV-positive HD using a PCR strategy, and in all cases the EBV genomes were found to be subtype 1 (Gledhill et al, 1991; Jarrett et al, 1991b). This does not suggest that type 1 viruses are exclusively associated with HD but rather that type 2 viruses are not over-represented in this disease.

Expression of EBV genes in Hodgkin's disease

The EBV genome has the capacity to encode for over 80 proteins and there is evidence that many of these are transcribed during productive viral replication (Baer et al, 1984). In the latent state only a restricted group of genes are expressed (reviewed in Kieff and Liebowitz, 1990). B cells which have been immortalized by EBV in vitro are known to express nine proteins. These are six nuclear proteins, the EBNAs, and three membrane proteins, the latent membrane proteins (LMP-1, 2A and B); in addition, two small non-polyadenylated RNAs, EBER-1 and 2, which may play a role in viral RNA processing, are transcribed. The EBNA-1 protein is a DNA binding protein which enables the viral genome to persist in an episomal or plasmid state and may have additional functions. The EBNA-2 and LMP-1 proteins appear to play a critical role in cell immortalization. EBNA-2 is known to up-regulate the expression of LMP-1 and also the B-cell activation marker CD23. LMP-1 also up-regulates CD23 in addition to inducing the cellular adhesion molecules ICAM-1, LFA-1 and LFA-3 (Wang et al, 1990). The importance of EBNA-2 and LMP-1 in cellular transformation is exemplified by three sets of findings. First, viruses which lack the EBNA-2 gene do not immortalize B cells although they replicate efficiently; second, the constitutive expression of CD23 appears to be central to the process of immortalization of B cells; third, gene transfer studies have shown that the LMP-1 gene in isolation can transform rodent fibroblast cell lines. In addition, recent data suggest that the expression of LMP-1 can protect B cells from programmed cell death (Gregory et al, 1991).

There are three different patterns of latent gene expression in the tumours known to be associated with EBV. In lymphomas in immunosuppressed persons the pattern of expression seems to mirror that seen in B cells immortalized by EBV in vitro (Young et al, 1989). In Burkitt's lymphoma the EBNA-1 gene is expressed but EBNA-2 and LMP-1 are down-regulated (Rowe et al, 1986). It is therefore difficult to envisage the role, if any, that EBV plays in the maintenance of the malignant phenotype. The down-regulation of EBNA-2 and LMP-1, and consequent down-regulation of adhesion molecules, may allow the tumour cells to escape immune recognition (Gregory et al, 1988). In nasopharyngeal carcinoma, an epithelial malignancy associated with EBV, EBNA-1 is expressed and LMP-1 expression can be detected in many cases but EBNA-2 is silent (Young et al, 1988).

In order to investigate the role of EBV in HD it was important to establish which of the latent genes, if any, are expressed by RS cells. The first evidence that EBV latent genes are transcribed by RS cells was reported by Wu et al (1990). Using in situ hybridization and an antisense RNA probe to EBER-1 they examined eight cases of HD which had been shown previously to contain EBV genomes. In six of the cases expression of EBER-1 was detected in almost all of the tumour cells. Failure to detect transcripts in the remaining cases was thought to be due to technical reasons. The authors of this report also concluded that the EBER-1 probe was more sensitive than other EBV probes e.g. *Bam* HI-W, for the detection of EBV genomes in RS cells due to the abundance of the EBER-1 transcript. These observations have been confirmed by others (L. Young, personal communication).

The EBNA-1 gene appears to be expressed, by inference, since analysis of the viral TRs suggests that the EBV genomes in HD are maintained in the episomal state (Jarrett et al, 1991b). There is little direct evidence that EBNA-1 is expressed; this is largely for technical reasons as there are no good monoclonal reagents to EBNA-1 and thus immunohistochemical staining must be performed using polyclonal human sera. Poppema et al (1985) have reported EBNA-1 expression in RS cells in a case of chronic EBV infection with subsequent development of HD.

Most data exist for the expression of the LMP-1 protein. Three groups, using monoclonal or polyclonal antibody reagents directed against LMP-1, have found clear evidence of LMP-1 expression by RS cells and their variants (Herbst et al, 1991; Pallesen et al, 1991; A. A. Armstrong et al, unpublished data). Expression of LMP-1 can be demonstrated in sections from frozen and paraffin-embedded material and has a cytoplasmic and 'membrane' distribution. Pallesen et al (1991) detected expression of the protein in 40/84 cases (45%) stained using monoclonal antibodies to LMP-1. The results of LMP-1 expression studies show a good, although not absolute, correlation with the results of Southern blot analysis (A. A. Armstrong et al, unpublished data).

Using immunohistochemical staining there is, as yet, no evidence for EBNA-2 expression by RS cells. In their series of 84 cases, Pallesen and co-workers (1991) did not detect any EBNA-2 expression using the PE2 monoclonal antibody to EBNA2. Similarly, Herbst et al (1991) did not detect EBNA-2 expression in any of 47 cases examined.

There is therefore convincing evidence that EBV genes are expressed by RS cells. This suggests that EBV plays a role in the maintenance of the malignant state in HD. The pattern of EBV latent gene expression (EBNA-1 +ve, EBNA2 −ve, LMP-1 +ve) appears to differ from that found in the other lymphoid tumours associated with EBV but resembles that seen in nasopharyngeal carcinoma.

The function of LMP-1 in RS cells is not known. CD23 is detected only rarely in RS cells (Jarrett et al, 1991a) and does not appear to be induced by the expression of LMP-1 (A. A. Armstrong et al, unpublished data). Thus the role of LMP-1 in HD does not appear to involve the induction of the CD23 molecule. This again differentiates EBV-infected RS cells from B cells immortalized by EBV in vitro.

EBV and the origin of the Reed–Sternberg cell

The analysis of immunoglobulin (Ig) and T-cell receptor (TCR) genes has been used to study the lineage and clonality of RS cells and their mononuclear variants. Most studies have detected Ig heavy chain rearrangements at frequencies ranging from 6 to 26% of non-selected cases (O'Connor, 1987; Raghavachar et al, 1988; Herbst et al, 1989; Gledhill et al, 1991). In contrast, the results of TCR rearrangement studies have been conflicting, with some groups detecting rearrangements (Griesser et al, 1987; Herbst et al, 1989) while the majority have not (Weiss et al, 1986; O'Connor, 1987; Raghavachar et al, 1988; Gledhill et al, 1991). The reason for the latter discrepancy is obscure. The above findings provide some support for the lymphoid origin of RS cells, although it should be emphasized that there is only indirect evidence that the rearrangements are present in RS cells (Sundeen et al, 1987; Gledhill et al, 1991).

Since EBV is known to be tropic for B cells it was of interest to compare the results of the EBV analyses with the receptor gene rearrangement analyses. There does not appear to be a good correlation between Ig heavy chain gene rearrangement and EBV positivity (Weiss et al, 1987; Anagnostopoulos et al, 1989; Gledhill et al, 1991). Anagnostopoulos et al (1989) did find an over-representation of cases with TCR β-chain gene rearrangements in their EBV-positive cases but this has not been reported by others. The failure to detect Ig gene rearrangements in EBV-positive cases may in part reflect the relative sensitivities of the probes used in the two assays. Using 10 μg of DNA in the Southern blot analysis a single EBV genome present in <0.5% of the cell population can be detected, whereas an Ig gene rearrangement must be present in at least 2% of the cells in order to be detected (Gledhill et al, 1991; Jarrett et al, 1991b). This cannot explain the failure to detect Ig gene rearrangements in all cases. EBV-positive cases with large numbers of abnormal cells and germline Ig genes have been described; this suggests that in some cases of HD EBV is infecting a cell with germline Ig genes, such as an immature B cell or a cell of another lineage (Gledhill et al, 1991). In support of this idea, Gregory et al (1987) immortalized fetal B cells with EBV and succeeded in establishing B-cell lines at varying stages of differentiation. The cell lines lacked early lymphoid markers but expressed activation antigens, a phenotype reminiscent of that described for RS cells (Herbst et al, 1989).

Histological subtypes, age and EBV

The observation that only a proportion of HD cases are EBV positive does not necessarily detract from the association between the virus and the malignancy. There are several possible explanations for this result. The most likely is that since, as mentioned above, HD appears to be a heterogeneous condition, more than one agent will be involved in its causation. A second possibility is that defective, integrated EBV genomes are present in the so-called EBV-negative cases. If defective genomes lacked the *Bam* HI-W sequence they would not have been detected in most of the above studies. At the present time there is no evidence to support this idea but it has not yet been excluded.

If EBV is aetiologically involved in a subgroup of HD cases it would seem plausible that these cases can be differentiated on the basis of histological subtype or age at presentation. Most reports on EBV and HD have included the subtype distribution of their series of cases. However, most studies have been small, with relatively few cases of HDLP and HDLD, and have therefore lacked statistical power. In addition, histological subtyping is subjective and this may result in differences in the subtype distribution from different laboratories. Four studies have found an excess of positive cases in the HDMC subtype as compared with HDNS (Weiss et al, 1987; Staal et al, 1989; Uccini et al, 1990; Jarrett et al, 1991b). This excess is not statistically significant when these studies are analysed individually or collectively. Boiocchi et al (1989) analysed 17 cases of HD which were of a rather unusual age and subtype distribution. Statistical analysis of their results reveals a significant association between EBV positivity and HDLD as compared with HDNS. The significance is lost when one compares the HDNS cases with the HDLD and HDMC cases grouped together. In the reports by Weiss et al (1989) and Anagnastopoulos et al (1989) all of the EBV-positive cases were HDNS (Table 1).

In contrast to the above results obtained by Southern blot analysis, Pallesen et al (1991) found significant differences in EBV positivity by histological subtype. Using immunohistochemical staining and a cocktail of antibodies reactive with LMP-1 they found evidence of EBV infection in 1/10 cases of HDLP, 16/50 cases of HDNS and 23/24 cases of HDMC. Statistical analysis of these results reveals a highly significant association between EBV positivity and HDMC. The reasons for the difference between this study and the hybridization analyses is unclear and cannot be explained entirely by methodological differences (A. A. Armstrong et al, unpublished data). Overall there appears to be a trend towards fewer EBV-positive cases within the HDNS subtype.

As mentioned above, few studies have analysed their results with respect to age. Boiocchi et al (1989) studied 17 cases of HD, five of whom were aged over 50 years. There was an excess of positive cases among young adults, but following adjustment for histological subtype this result is not statistically significant. Libetta et al (1990) found a non-significant excess of EBV-positive cases among older patients compared with children and young adults. The results of the latter study are difficult to interpret as, in many of the cases scored as positive, the EBV *Bam* HI-W probe hybridized to a fragment of unexpected size. Uhara et al (1990) did not document the exact age distribution of the cases included in their in situ hybridization and PCR study. All of their eight EBV-positive cases were aged over 30 and four were aged over 50, leading them to suggest that EBV positivity might be age associated and should be investigated further. Herbst et al (1990), using PCR, did not find any association between EBV positivity and age.

Gledhill et al (1991) did find a significant association between increasing age and EBV. This prompted a larger study in which paediatric cases (<15 years) and older cases (>50 years) were specifically selected in order to augment numbers in these age groups (Jarrett et al, 1991b). This revealed a highly significant association between age and EBV positivity. In the older age group 27/38 (>70%) of cases were EBV positive. Similarly in the paediatric cases the majority, 7/13, were positive. In contrast to these results samples from only 4/28 cases in the young adult age bracket contained detectable EBV genomes (Figure 4a). It was also noted that within the young adult age group relatively fewer cases of HDNS were positive

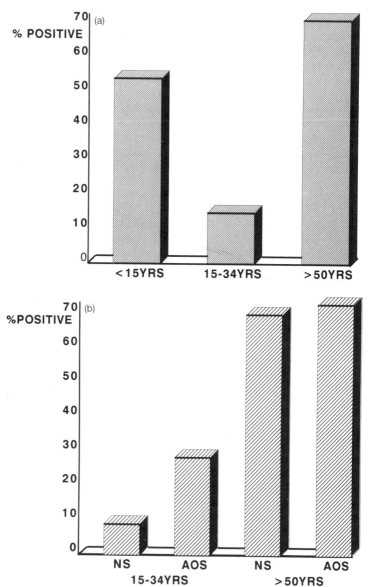

Figure 4. (a) EBV genome positivity in HD by age at diagnosis. **(b)** EBV genome positivity in HD by age and subtype. NS, nodular sclerosing HD; AOS, all other subtypes.

compared with the other subtypes grouped together, but this difference did not attain statistical significance (Figure 4b).

This study provides the first biological evidence to support the hypothesis, put forward by MacMahon, that HD in different age groups has different aetiologies (MacMahon, 1966). The results suggest that EBV has some role in the pathogenesis of HD in children and older patients but in young adults, particularly those with HDNS, other agents are involved. The failure to detect an association between EBV and age in other studies may well reflect the small numbers of paediatric and older cases likely to be present in non-selected series. In addition, these data emphasize the need to analyse age and subtype together as these variables will have confounding effects. More surveys from different laboratories, in different geographical locales and using different methodologies are needed to validate these observations.

The possibility that EBV genome positivity is associated with an unfavourable clinical outcome should be evaluated further as age over 50 years and HDMC, as compared with NDNS, are indicators of a poor prognosis (Gobbi et al, 1988; Walker et al, 1990).

Hodgkin's disease and HIV infection

The association between HD and human immunodeficiency virus (HIV) is not yet clear but HIV-infected persons appear to be at increased risk of developing HD (Ioachim et al, 1985; Beckhardt et al, 1988). There is a suggestion that HD may be more frequent in HIV-infected persons who are intravenous drug abusers as opposed to homosexuals (Roithmann et al, 1990; Serrano et al, 1990). It is generally accepted, however, that persons who develop HD in the context of HIV infection have aggressive disease and often present at late stages (Serrano et al, 1990). Uccini et al (1990) detected EBV genomes by Southern blot analysis and in situ hybridization in 5/7 HIV-positive patients, as compared with 3/20 HIV-negative patients, with HD. This suggests that HIV-positive persons may have an increased risk of developing EBV-positive HD and lends some support to the idea that an impairment of T-cell function may precede EBV-associated HD.

Other viruses

The studies presented above suggest that EBV is associated with only a proportion of HD cases. Young adult cases of HDNS appear to be least likely to be EBV positive. It is in this group that there is most evidence for involvement of a transmissible agent and so it would seem plausible that another virus is involved. One candidate virus is HHV-6 since, as mentioned above, antibody titres to this virus are elevated in HD, particularly in young adult cases (Clark et al, 1990). Despite this association, HHV-6 DNA sequences have not been detected in a total of 55 cases examined by Southern blot analysis (Josephs et al, 1988; Jarrett et al, 1988; Gledhill et al, 1991). It should be noted that the currently available probes used to detect HHV-6 are not as sensitive as the *Bam* HI-W probe for EBV. Despite this caveat the results suggest that HHV-6 is unlikely to play a direct role in the pathogenesis of HD. Elevated HHV-6 antibody titres may reflect recent infection or reactivation of the virus and may provide a marker for another virus which is aetiologically involved in HD. Molecular studies using probes for CMV have been similarly negative; CMV probes have been used as negative controls in some of the EBV studies (Weiss et al, 1987; Uhara et al, 1990). The possible role of another recently identified virus, human herpesvirus-7, is currently being investigated (Frenkel et al, 1990).

CONCLUSIONS AND FUTURE DIRECTIONS

Over the last 5 years data have accumulated which provide good evidence that EBV is involved in the pathogenesis of HD in a proportion of cases. EBV genomes are detected in approximately one-third of cases, the infected cells are clonal with respect to EBV, and the EBV genomes are present in RS cells. Furthermore, EBV latent gene products, including LMP-1, which is known to be important in the immortalization of B cells, are expressed by RS cells. Molecular studies examining the association between EBV and HD were prompted by seroepidemiological studies showing an association between EBV and HD and by the association between IM and HD. Future studies on the expression of EBV genes by RS cells, and on the interaction of EBV with cellular genes, should begin to shed light on the role which EBV plays in the pathogenesis of HD.

The available data suggest that EBV-positive HD cases are most likely to be children, older adults, or have HDMC rather than HDNS. Examination of a larger number of cases, from different geographical areas, with augmentation of case numbers within these groups, is required to establish this distribution. Statistical analyses should be performed with adjustment for the effects of age and histological subtype as these are likely to be confounding variables.

The age distribution of the EBV-positive cases provides support for the multiple aetiology hypothesis put forward by MacMahon (1966). The correlation between the above data and the delayed exposure hypothesis deserves further comment. If the paralytic polio model is correct, then one would expect the paediatric and the young adult cases to be caused by the same aetiological agent. The findings suggest that EBV is involved in children but is involved infrequently in the young adult peak incidence group. The observations are based on a small number of paediatric cases from a developed country and it is therefore important to establish whether EBV is involved in paediatric HD cases from countries with a type 1 disease pattern. The EBV data do not refute the hypothesis that delayed exposure to a common agent is aetiologically involved in HD in young adults but suggest that this agent is not EBV. This raises questions regarding the association between IM and HD. It would seem likely that EBV is involved in the pathogenesis of HD in those cases with a history of serologically-proven IM; however these cases may not be representative of the young adult group.

Spatial clustering of HD cases is, as yet, not explained. It is possible that

EBV may be associated with clustering of cases but it would seem more likely that this is attributable to infection by another agent. It is to be hoped that future studies will reveal the involvement of another virus which is responsible for this effect.

Finally, it is likely that HD has a multistep pathogenesis with involvement of cellular genes in addition to viruses. Oncogenes, tumour suppressor genes or genes which play a role in programmed cell death may be implicated and may be common to both EBV-positive and EBV-negative cases. The increasing sensitivity of molecular techniques and the ability to separate RS cells from the polymorphous cellular infiltrate in HD should help to unravel some of these issues.

SUMMARY

The epidemiological features of Hodgkin's disease (HD) suggest that it is a heterogeneous condition which may have different aetiologies in different age groups. The risk factors for the development of HD in young adults suggest that delayed exposure to a common infectious agent may be involved in this age group. Seroepidemiological studies have shown that HD patients have elevated antibody titres to Epstein–Barr virus (EBV) and the elevated titres have been shown to precede the diagnosis of HD. Recent molecular studies provide support for the idea that EBV is involved in the pathogenesis of HD. EBV genomes are consistently found in a proportion of tumour biopsies, the EBV-infected cells are clonal and the EBV genomes have been localized to Reed–Sternberg cells. Furthermore, EBV latent gene products are expressed by the Reed–Sternberg cells. The majority of HD samples from patients aged > 50 years and < 15 years are EBV positive, whereas the minority (< 15%) of samples from young adults contain detectable EBV DNA. The results suggest that EBV plays a role in HD in children and older adults but that other agents, possibly other viruses, are involved in young adults.

Acknowledgements

I would like to thank Maisie Riddell for preparing the manuscript and Freda Alexander and David Onions for helpful discussion. Our contribution to these studies was made possible by the Leukaemia Research Fund.

REFERENCES

Ablashi DV, Josephs SF, Buchbinder A et al (1988) Human B-lymphotropic virus (human herpesvirus-6). *Journal of Virological Methods* **21:** 29–48.

Abramson JH, Pridan H, Sacks MI, Avitzour M & Peritz E (1978) A case-control study of Hodgkin's disease in Israel. *Journal of the National Cancer Institute* **61:** 307–314.

Alexander FE, Williams J, McKinney PA, Ricketts TJ & Cartwright RA (1989) A specialist leukaemia/lymphoma registry in the UK. Part 2: Clustering of Hodgkin's disease. *British Journal of Cancer* **60:** 948–952.

Alexander FE, Ricketts TJ, McKinney PA & Cartwright RA (1991a) Community lifestyle characteristics and incidence of Hodgkin's disease in young people. *International Journal of Cancer* **48:** 10–14.

Alexander FE, McKinney PA, Williams J, Ricketts TJ & Cartwright RA (1991b) Epidemiological evidence for the 'Two-disease hypothesis' in Hodgkin's disease. *International Journal of Epidemiology* (in press).

Anagnostopoulos I, Herbst H, Niedobitek G & Stein H (1989) Demonstration of monoclonal EBV genomes in Hodgkin's disease and KI-1-positive anaplastic large cell lymphoma by combined Southern blot and in situ hybridization. *Blood* **74:** 810–816.

Andiman W, Gradoville L, Heston L et al (1983) Use of cloned probes to detect Epstein–Barr viral DNA in tissues of patients with neoplastic and lymphoproliferative diseases. *Journal of Infectious Diseases* **148:** 967–977.

Arrand JR, Rymo L, Walsh JE et al (1981) Molecular cloning of the complete Epstein–Barr virus genome as a set of overlapping restriction endonuclease fragments. *Nucleic Acids Research* **9:** 2999–3014.

Baer R, Bankier AT, Biggin MD et al (1984) DNA sequence and expression of the B95-8 Epstein–Barr virus genome. *Nature* **310:** 207–211.

Beckhardt RN, Farady N, May M, Torres RA & Strauchen JA (1988) Increased incidence of malignant lymphoma in AIDS: a comparison of risk groups and possible etiologic factors. *Mount Sinai Journal of Medicine* **55:** 383–389.

Biberfeld P, Petren A-L, Eklund A et al (1988) Human herpesvirus-6 (HHV-6, HBLV) in sarcoidosis and lymphoproliferative disorders. *Journal of Virological Methods* **21:** 49–59.

Bignon YJ, Bernard D, Cure H et al (1990) Detection of Epstein–Barr viral genomes in lymph nodes of Hodgkin's disease patients. *Molecular Carcinogenesis* **3:** 9–11.

Boiocchi M, Carbone A, De Re V & Dolcetti R (1989) Is the Epstein–Barr virus involved in Hodgkin's disease? *Tumori* **75:** 345–350.

Cartwright RA, Alexander FE, McKinney PA & Ricketts TJ (1990) *Leukaemia and Lymphoma. An Atlas of Distribution within Areas of England and Wales 1984–1988.* London: Leukaemia Research Fund.

Catalano LW Jr & Goldman JM (1972) Antibody to herpesvirus hominis types 1 and 2 in patients with Hodgkin's disease and carcinoma of the nasopharynx. *Cancer* **29:** 597–602.

Clark DA, Alexander FE, McKinney PA et al (1990) The seroepidemiology of human herpesvirus-6 (HHV-6) from a case-control study of leukaemia and lymphoma. *International Journal of Cancer* **45:** 829–833.

Cole P, MacMahon B & Aisenberg A (1968) Mortality from Hodgkin's disease in the United States: evidence for the multiple-aetiology hypothesis. *Lancet* **ii:** 1371–1376.

Correa P & O'Conor GT (1971) Epidemiologic patterns of Hodgkin's disease. *International Journal of Cancer* **8:** 192–201.

Evans AS & Gutensohn NM (1984) A population-based case-control study of EBV and other viral antibodies among persons with Hodgkin's disease and their siblings. *International Journal of Cancer* **34:** 149–157.

Evans AS & Neiderman JC (1989) Epstein–Barr virus. In Evans AS (ed.) *Viral Infections of Human Epidemiology and Control*, 3rd edn, pp 265–292. New York: Plenum.

Evans AS, Carvalho RPS, Frost P, Jamra M & Pozzi DHB (1978) Epstein–Barr virus infections in Brazil. II. Hodgkin's disease. *Journal of the National Cancer Institute* **61:** 19–26.

Evans AS, Kirchhoff LV, Pannuti CS, Carvalho RPS & McClelland KE (1980) A case-control study of Hodgkin's disease in Brazil. *American Journal of Epidemiology* **112:** 609–618.

Frenkel N, Schirmer EC, Wyatt LS et al (1990) Isolation of a new herpesvirus from human CD4⁺ T cells. *Proceedings of the National Academy of Science* **87:** 748–752.

Glaser SL (1987) Regional variation in Hodgkin's disease incidence by histologic subtype in the US. *Cancer* **60:** 2841–2847.

Glaser SL (1990a) Hodgkin's disease in black populations: a review of the epidemiologic literature. *Seminars in Oncology* **17:** 643–659.

Glaser SL (1990b) Spatial clustering of Hodgkin's disease in the San Francisco Bay area. *American Journal of Epidemiology* **132:** S167–S177.

Glaser SL & Swartz WG (1990) Time trends in Hodgkin's disease incidence: the role of diagnostic accuracy. *Cancer* **66:** 2196–2204.

Gledhill S, Gallagher A, Jones D et al (1991) Viral involvement in Hodgkin's disease: detection of clonal type A EBV genomes in tumour samples. *British Journal of Cancer* **64:** 227–232.

Gobbi PG, Cavalli C, Federico M et al (1988) Hodgkin's disease prognosis: a directly predictive equation. *Lancet* **i**: 675–678.

Greenberg RS, Grufferman S & Cole P (1983) An evaluation of space–time clustering in Hodgkin's disease. *Journal of Chronic Diseases* **36**: 257–262.

Gregory CD, Kirchgens C, Edwards CF et al (1987) Epstein–Barr virus-transformed human precursor B cell lines: altered growth phenotype of lines with germline or rearranged but nonexpressed heavy chain genes. *European Journal of Immunology* **17**: 1199–1207.

Gregory CD, Murray RJ, Edwards CF & Rickinson AB (1988) Down regulation of cell adhesion molecules LFA-3 and ICAM-1 in Epstein–Barr virus-positive Burkitt's lymphoma underlies tumor cell escape from virus-specific T cell surveillance. *Journal of Experimental Medicine* **167**: 1811–1824.

Gregory CD, Dive C, Henderson S et al (1991) Activation of Epstein–Barr virus latent genes protects human B cells from death by apoptosis. *Nature* **349**: 612–614.

Griesser H, Feller AC, Mak TW & Lennert K (1987) Clonal rearrangements of T-cell receptor and immunoglobulin genes and immunophenotypic antigen expression in different subclasses of Hodgkin's disease. *International Journal of Cancer* **40**: 157–160.

Gutensohn NM (1982) Social class and age at diagnosis of Hodgkin's disease: new epidemiologic evidence for the 'two-disease hypothesis'. *Cancer Treatment Reports* **66**: 689–695.

Gutensohn N & Cole P (1977) Epidemiology of Hodgkin's disease in the young. *International Journal of Cancer* **19**: 595–604.

Gutensohn N & Cole P (1980) Epidemiology of Hodgkin's disease. *Seminars in Oncology* **7**: 92–102.

Gutensohn N & Cole P (1981) Childhood social environment and Hodgkin's disease. *New England Journal of Medicine* **304**: 135–140.

Henderson BE, Dworsky R, Menck H et al (1973) Case-control study of Hodgkin's disease. II. Herpesvirus group antibody titers and HL-A type. *Journal of the National Cancer Institute* **51**: 1443–1447.

Henle W & Henle G (1973) Epstein Barr virus related serology in Hodgkin's disease. *National Cancer Institute Monographs* **36**: 79–84.

Herbst H, Tippelmann G, Anagnostopoulos I et al (1989) Immunoglobulin and T-cell receptor gene rearrangements in Hodgkin's disease and Ki-1-positive anaplastic large cell lymphoma: dissociation between phenotype and genotype. *Leukemia Research* **13**: 103–116.

Herbst H, Niedobitek G, Kneba M et al (1990) High incidence of Epstein–Barr virus genomes in Hodgkin's disease. *American Journal of Pathology* **137**: 13–18.

Herbst H, Dallenbach F, Hummel M et al (1991) Epstein–Barr virus latent membrane protein expression in Hodgkin and Reed–Sternberg cells. *Proceedings of the National Academy of Sciences (USA)* **88**: 4766–4770.

Hesse J, Levine PH, Ebbesen P, Connelly RR & Mordhorst CH (1977) A case control study on immunity to two Epstein–Barr virus-associated antigens, and to herpes simplex virus and adenovirus in a population-based group of patients with Hodgkin's disease in Denmark, 1971–73. *International Journal of Cancer* **19**: 49–58.

Hodgkin T (1832) On some morbid appearances of the absorbent glands and spleen. *Medical Chirurgical Transactions* **17**: 68–114.

Ioachim HL, Cooper MC & Hellman GC (1985) Lymphomas in men at high risk for acquired immune deficiency syndrome (AIDS). A study of 21 cases. *Cancer* **56**: 2831–2842.

Jarrett RF, Gledhill S, Qureshi F et al (1988) Identification of human herpesvirus 6—specific sequences in two patients with non-Hodgkin's lymphoma. *Leukemia* **2**: 496–502.

Jarrett RF, Clark DA, Josephs SF & Onions DE (1990) Detection of human herpesvirus-6 DNA in peripheral blood and saliva. *Journal of Medical Virology* **32**: 73–76.

Jarrett RF, Armstrong A, Wilkins BS & Jones DB (1991a) Immunohistochemical determination of CD23 expression in Hodgkin's disease using paraffin sections. *Journal of Pathology* **164**: 345–346.

Jarrett RF, Gallagher A, Jones DB et al (1991b) Detection of EBV genomes in Hodgkin's disease: association with age. *Journal of Clinical Pathology* **44**: 844–848.

Josephs SF, Buchbinder A, Streicher HZ et al (1988) Detection of human B-lymphotropic virus (human herpesvirus 6) sequences in B cell lymphoma tissues of three patients. *Leukemia* **2**: 132–135.

Katz BZ, Raab-Traub N & Miller G (1989) Latent and replicating forms of Epstein–Barr virus

DNA in lymphomas and lymphoproliferative diseases. *Journal of Infectious Diseases* **160:** 589–598.

Kieff E & Liebowitz D (1990) Epstein–Barr virus and its replication. In Fields BN, Knipe DM et al (eds) *Virology*, 2nd edn, pp 1889–1920. New York: Raven.

Kryscio RJ, Myers MH, Prusiner ST, Heise HW & Christine BW (1973) The space–time distribution of Hodgkin's disease in Connecticut, 1940–69. *Journal of the National Cancer Institute* **50:** 1107–1110.

Langenhuysen MMAC, Cazemier T, Houwen B et al (1974) Antibodies to Epstein–Barr virus, cytomegalovirus, and Australia antigen in Hodgkin's disease. *Cancer* **34:** 262–267.

Levine PH, Ablashi DV, Berard CW et al (1971) Elevated antibody titers to Epstein–Barr virus in Hodgkin's disease. *Cancer* **27:** 416–421.

Libetta CM, Pringle JH, Angel CA et al (1990) Demonstration of Epstein–Barr viral DNA in formalin-fixed, paraffin-embedded samples of Hodgkin's disease. *Journal of Pathology* **161:** 255–260.

Lindahl T, Klein G, Reedman BM, Johansson B & Singh S (1974) Relationship between Epstein–Barr virus (EBV) DNA and the EBV-determined nuclear antigen (EBNA) in Burkitt lymphoma biopsies and other lymphoproliferative malignancies. *International Journal of Cancer* **13:** 764–772.

Lukes RJ, Craver LF, Hall TC et al (1966) Report of the nomenclature committee. *Cancer Research* **26:** 1311.

McKinney PA, Alexander FE, Ricketts TJ, Williams J & Cartwright RA (1989) A specialist leukaemia/lymphoma registry in the UK. Part 1: Incidence and geographical distribution of Hodgkin's disease. *British Journal of Cancer* **60:** 942–947.

MacMahon B (1966) Epidemiology of Hodgkin's disease. *Cancer Research* **26:** 1189–1200.

Merk K, Bjorkholm M, Rengifo E et al (1990) Epidemiological study of Hodgkin's disease in Cuba and Sweden. *Oncology* **47:** 246–250.

Miller G (1990) Epstein–Barr virus: biology, pathogenesis and medical aspects. In Fields BN, Knipe DM et al (eds) *Virology*, 2nd edn, pp 1921–1928. New York: Raven.

Mueller N, Evans A, Harris NL et al (1989) Hodgkin's disease and Epstein–Barr virus. Altered antibody pattern before diagnosis. *New England Journal of Medicine* **320:** 689–695.

Muir CS, Waterhouse J, Mack T, Power J & Whelan S (1987) Cancer incidence in 5 continents, volume 5. *IARD Scientific Publications No. 88.* Lyon: International Agency for Research on Cancer.

Nicholas DS, Harris S & Wright DH (1990) Lymphocyte predominance Hodgkin's disease: an immunohistochemical study. *Histopathology* **16:** 157–165.

O'Connor NTJ (1987) Genotypic analysis of lymph node biopsies. *Journal of Pathology* **151:** 185–190.

Paffenbarger RS, Wing AL & Hyde RT (1977) Characteristics in youth indicative of adult-onset Hodgkin's disease. *Journal of the National Cancer Institute* **58:** 1489–1491.

Pagano JS, Huang CH & Levine P (1973) Absence of Epstein–Barr viral DNA in American Burkitt's lymphoma. *New England Journal of Medicine* **289:** 1395–1399.

Pallesen G, Hamilton-Dutoit SJ, Rowe M & Young LS (1991) Expression of Epstein–Barr virus latent gene products in tumour cells of Hodgkin's disease. *Lancet* **337:** 320–322.

Poppema S, van Imhoff G, Torensma R & Smit J (1985) Lymphadenopathy morphologically consistent with Hodgkin's disease associated with Epstein–Barr virus infection. *American Journal of Clinical Pathology* **84:** 385–390.

Raab-Traub N & Flynn K (1986) The structure of the termini of the Epstein–Barr virus as a marker of clonal cellular proliferation. *Cell* **47:** 883–889.

Raghavachar A, Binder T & Bartram CR (1988) Immunoglobulin and T-cell receptor gene rearrangements in Hodgkin's disease. *Cancer Research* **48:** 3591–3594.

Roithmann S, Tourani J-M & Andrieu J-M (1990) Hodgkin's disease in HIV-infected intravenous drug abusers. *New England Journal of Medicine* **323:** 275–276.

Rowe DT, Rowe M, Evan GI et al (1986) Restricted expression of EBV latent genes and T-lymphocyte detected membrane antigen in Burkitt's lymphoma cells. *European Molecular Biology Organization Journal* **5:** 2599–2607.

Salahuddin SZ, Ablashi DV, Markham PD et al (1986) Isolation of a new virus, HBLV, in patients with lymphoproliferative disorders. *Science* **234:** 596–601.

Scherr PA, Gutensohn N & Cole P (1984) School contact among persons with Hodgkin's disease. *American Journal of Epidemiology* **120:** 29–38.

Serrano M, Bellas C, Campo E et al (1990) Hodgkin's disease in patients with antibodies to human immunodeficiency virus. *Cancer* **65:** 2248–2254.

Sixbey JW, Shirley P, Chesney PJ, Buntin DM & Resnick L (1989) Detection of a second widespread strain of Epstein–Barr virus. *Lancet* **ii:** 761–765.

Smith PG, Pike MC, Kinlen LJ, Jones A & Harris R (1977) Contacts between young patients with Hodgkin's disease: a case-control study. *Lancet* **ii:** 59–62.

Spitz MR, Sider JG, Johnson CC et al (1986) Ethnic patterns of Hodgkin's disease incidence among children and adolescents in the United States, 1973–82. *Journal of the National Cancer Institute* **76:** 235–239.

Staal SP, Ambinder R, Beschorner WE, Hayward GS & Mann R (1989) A survey of Epstein–Barr virus DNA in lymphoid tissue. Frequent detection in Hodgkin's disease. *American Journal of Clinical Pathology* **91:** 1–5.

Sundeen J, Lipford E, Uppenkamp M et al (1987) Rearranged antigen receptor genes in Hodgkin's disease. *Blood* **70:** 96–103.

Uccini S, Monardo F, Stoppacciaro A et al (1990) High frequency of Epstein–Barr virus genome detection in Hodgkin's disease of HIV-positive patients. *International Journal of Cancer* **46:** 581–585.

Uhara H, Sato Y, Mukai K et al (1990) Detection of Epstein–Barr virus DNA in Reed–Sternberg cells of Hodgkin's disease using the polymerase chain reaction and in situ hybridization. *Japanese Journal of Cancer Research* **81:** 272–278.

Urquhart J, Black R & Blust E (1989) Exploring small area methods. In Rose G (ed.) *Methodology of Enquiries into Disease Clustering*, pp 41–49. London: London School of Hygiene.

Vianna NJ & Polan AK (1978) Immunity in Hodgkin's disease: importance of age at exposure. *Annals of Internal Medicine* **89:** 550–556.

Vianna NJ, Greenwald P & Davies JNP (1971) Extended epidemic of Hodgkin's disease in high-school students. *Lancet* **i:** 1209–1211.

Walker A, Schoenfeld ER, Lowman JT et al (1990) Survival of the older patient compared to the younger patient with Hodgkin's disease. *Cancer* **65:** 1635–1640.

Wang F, Gregory C, Sample C et al (1990) Epstein–Barr virus latent membrane protein (LMPI) and nuclear proteins 2 and 3C are effectors of phenotypic changes in B lymphocytes: EBNA-2 and LMPI co-operatively induces CD23. *Journal of Virology* **64:** 2309–2318.

Weiss LM, Strickler JG, Hu E, Warnke RA & Sklar J (1986) Immunoglobulin gene rearrangements in Hodgkin's disease. *Human Pathology* **17:** 1009–1014.

Weiss LM, Strickler JG, Warnke RA, Purtilo DT & Sklar J (1987) Epstein–Barr viral DNA in tissues of Hodgkin's disease. *American Journal of Pathology* **129:** 86–91.

Weiss LM, Movahed LA, Warnke RA & Sklar J (1989) Detection of Epstein–Barr viral genomes in Reed–Sternberg cells of Hodgkin's disease. *New England Journal of Medicine* **320:** 502–506.

Wu TC, Mann RB, Charache P et al (1990) Detection of EBV gene expression in Reed–Sternberg cells of Hodgkin's disease. *International Journal of Cancer* **46:** 801–804.

Young LS, Yao QY, Rooney CM et al (1987) New type B isolates of Epstein–Barr virus from Burkitt's lymphoma and from normal individuals in endemic areas. *Journal of General Virology* **68:** 2853–2862.

Young LS, Dawson CW, Clark D et al (1988) Epstein–Barr virus gene expression in nasopharyngeal carcinoma. *Journal of General Virology* **69:** 1051–1065.

Young L, Alfieri C, Hennessy K et al (1989) Expression of Epstein–Barr virus transformation-associated genes in tissues of patients with EBV lymphoproliferative disease. *New England Journal of Medicine* **321:** 1080–1085.

Zack MM Jr, Heath CW, Andrews M DeW, Grivas AS Jr & Christine BW (1977) High school contact among persons with leukemia and lymphoma. *Journal of the National Cancer Institute* **59:** 1343–1349.

Zimber U, Aldinger HK, Lenoir GM et al (1986) Geographical prevalence of two types of Epstein–Barr virus. *Virology* **154:** 56–66.

4

Non-Hodgkin's lymphomas and paraproteinaemias

BRACHA RAMOT
GIDEON RECHAVI

Epidemiological studies can provide important clues to the aetiological factors involved in the pathogenesis of malignant diseases, including lymphatic malignancies. However, such studies of the latter group have been complicated by variations in terminology and classification, which could cast doubt on the interpretation of regional differences. This is even further complicated by the marked variability in the quality of medical services, the level of cancer registration cohorts, and the variable age structure of the analysed populations. For the reasons mentioned, analysis of specific tumour syndromes that have characteristic clinical and diagnostic features may be more instructive for future epidemiological research. These assumptions will be stressed in this review.

BURKITT LYMPHOMA

Comprehensive epidemiological studies on Burkitt lymphoma (BL) illustrate the enormous contribution of epidemiology to the understanding of the biological features of this disease. It can probably serve as a model for the investigation of other lymphatic malignancies.

Having much in common, three types of BL have been characterized: the endemic type, the sporadic type and the type that is associated with acquired immunodeficiency states.

Endemic (African) type

The disease was characterized by Denis Burkitt, who noticed that the jaw and abdominal tumours in African children were features of the same clinical entity (Burkitt, 1958). These observations enabled the accurate diagnosis, and led Burkitt to an important epidemiological observation, namely the restricted geographical distribution and high incidence of the tumour in the wet tropical areas of Africa, with an incidence about 50 times higher than in the United States (Burkitt, 1970). Similar observations have also been made in Papua New Guinea in regions with humidity and

Baillière's Clinical Haematology—
Vol. 5, No. 1, January 1992
ISBN 0–7020–1626–8

temperature similar to tropical Africa (Wiley, 1973). In north Africa, south America and the Middle East an intermediate rate was found (Burkitt, 1970; Al-Attar et al, 1979; Stiller and Parkin, 1990).

The characteristic clinical features of African BL include not only the high frequency of jaw tumours but also extensive extranodal involvement, especially of kidneys, thyroid, ovaries and testes (Burkitt, 1970). The clinical features of the disease differ in various age groups; jaw tumours are very common at presentation in the young but their frequency declines progressively in older children. The cytology and histology of the tumour cells are typical and have been extensively described (Berard et al, 1969). Immunological studies confirmed the B-cell origin of BL cells (Guven et al, 1980; Magrath, 1984a, 1984b). The B cells carry low levels of surface immunoglobulins, predominantly IgM, and secrete very little immuno-globulin in culture (Benjamin et al, 1982; Magrath et al, 1983). Cell kinetic studies revealed that these cells have the shortest doubling time known for any human tumour cell, in vitro as well as in vivo (Iverson et al, 1972).

Very important virological and molecular findings emerged from the epidemiological studies; a previously unfamiliar herpes virus, the Epstein–Barr virus (EBV), was identified in cultured African BL cells (Epstein et al, 1964; Henle and Henle, 1966; Epstein and Achong, 1968). Practically all children with African BL were found to have high anti-EBV titres in serum, and the viral genome was found in the tumour cells, confirmed by molecular hybridization (Magrath, 1984a). In vitro and in vivo studies indicate that EBV is potentially an oncogenic virus that immortalizes B cells, resulting in B-cell proliferation (Purtilo, 1964). EBV is one of the most widespread of the known human viruses, therefore the aetiological relationship between EBV and the geographically restricted African BL syndrome cannot be easily settled. No significant differences have been demonstrated between EBVs isolated from African BL cells and viral isolates from other parts of the world. The pattern of EBV infection in equatorial Africa differs from that in the West by the very early age of infection in African children, the majority being infected before the age of one year (de Thé, 1977; Gerber et al, 1982). In addition, other cofactors seem to operate, including infestation by *Plasmodium falciparum*, via B-cell stimulation and suppression of regulatory T cells (Dalldorf, 1962; Morrow, 1985). An inverse relationship between the prevalence and intensity of malarial infection and the rate of BL was found. Additional factors, such as malnutrition and other infections may also play a role.

Characteristic chromosomal translocations involving chromosome 8 at the site of the c-*myc* proto-oncogene, have been demonstrated in virtually all BL studied (Manolov and Manolova, 1972; Zech et al, 1976; Croce et al, 1979; Erikson et al, 1981; Dalla-Favera et al, 1982; Taub et al, 1982; Croce and Nowell, 1986; Malcolm et al, 1989). In the majority of cases (85%), the translocation results in juxtaposition of c-*myc* sequences and immuno-globulin heavy chain gene sequences on chromosome 14. In the minority, the c-*myc* sequences are moved to the vicinity of immunoglobulin κ or λ light chain sequences on chromosomes 2 and 22 respectively. In most of the endemic BL, the breakpoints lie far 5' of the c-*myc* on chromosome 8, and involve the D_H or J_H on chromosome 14 (Haluska et al, 1986; Pelicci et al, 1986a). Analysis of several translocation breakpoints suggests that they are the result of 'false recombination' mediated by the immunoglobulin–T-cell receptor V-D-J 'recombinase'. In addition to the major chromosomal rearrangements, point mutations in the first exon of the c-myc gene were found in the majority of 8;14, 2;8 and 8;22 translocations (Pelicci et al, 1986a). It was suggested therefore that these mutations are involved in the dysregulation of c-myc expression in BL cells.

Based on the above data, a multistep model in the pathogenesis of African BL has been suggested by George Klein (Klein, 1979; Klein and Klein, 1985). The first step is the immortalization of B cells by EBV. The second involves the stimulation of the immortalized cells to proliferate, possibly by malarial infection or other immunosuppressive factors. The last step involves the chromosomal translocation, resulting in an irreversible c-myc activation and true malignant transformation. Experimental models support several aspects of this hypothesis (Lombardini et al, 1987).

Sporadic (American) type

The characterization of BL as a well-defined clinical and pathological entity led to the search for similar tumours in other regions of the world. Apart from endemic areas, BL cases have been reported sporadically from many countries.

Analysis of many sporadic BL cases has revealed clear differences between these two groups (Banks et al, 1975; Levine et al, 1982; Lombardini et al, 1987). The sporadic tumours only rarely involve the jaw but often involve the nasopharynx and the terminal ileum. Although the cytology and histology are indistinguishable from the endemic form, the biological characteristics differ. Less than 20% of the sporadic cases are associated with EBV infection, in contrast to almost all of the endemic BL (Klein and Klein, 1985). Sporadic tumours have a higher level of surface immuno-globulins, and secrete immunoglobulins in culture more frequently than the endemic tumours (Benjamin et al, 1982; McKeithan et al, 1986). No association with malaria or other known cofactors has been described. It seems, therefore, that the initial steps in the pathogenesis of African BL, namely the immortalization of B cells by EBV and the immune dysregu-lation by malarial infection, are not involved in the sporadic cases. Chromo-somal analyses suggested that the later step, c-myc dysregulation, is similar in the endemic and sporadic cases. Although the same chromosomal trans-locations (t(8;14), t(2;8) and t(8;22)) were described in both, detailed molecular studies, involving cloning of rearranged c-myc genes and mapping the chromosomal breakpoints, revealed that the rearranged genes found in the sporadic tumours differ from those found in the endemic BL (Manolov and Manolova, 1972; Zech et al, 1976; Croce et al, 1979; Erikson et al, 1981; Dalla-Favera et al, 1982; Taub et al, 1982; Croce and Nowell, 1986; Malcolm et al, 1989). The translocation breakpoint in the sporadic cases occurs usually immediately upstream or within the c-myc transcription unit, in contrast to the far 5' c-myc breakpoints in the endemic cases. The breakpoints found on chromosome 14 were clustered in the switch sequences, suggesting the involvement of a switch 'recombinase' system. Taking together the differences in the immunophenotype and the molecular findings, it seems that the endemic BL involves a less mature B lymphocyte which is actively rearranging the immunoglobulin genes, whereas the sporadic BL involves a more mature B cell at the stage of heavy chain switch.

BL in HIV-positive individuals

Malignant lymphomas have been known for many years as a fatal complication of primary immunodeficiency syndromes (Perry et al, 1980; Fasth, 1982; Merrell et al, 1986; Cunningham-Rundles et al, 1987). In recent years, acquired immunodeficiency, secondary to intensive immunosuppressive therapy or following infection with human immunodeficiency virus (HIV) (Hoover and Fraumenti, 1973; Kinlen et al, 1979; Ziegler et al, 1982; Penn and First, 1986), resulted in a significant increase in the susceptibility to lymphoproliferative disorders. Immunophenotyping and molecular studies demonstrated that the lymphoproliferative disorders complicating immunodeficiency syndromes represent a full spectrum of lymphocyte activation, ranging from polyclonal or oligoclonal reactive proliferation to monoclonal malignant lymphoma. We will limit ourselves in this review to lymphoproliferative disorders complicating HIV infection and the acquired immunodeficiency syndrome (AIDS), which have become major health problems during the last decade in both developing and developed countries. AIDS-associated lymphomas belong to the high (small non-cleaved, immunoblastic) or intermediate (large cell) grade categories, and are usually of B-cell origin (Ziegler et al, 1984; Levine and Gill, 1987; Samuels and Ultman, 1987). The most common among them are small non-cleaved lymphomas which for some unknown reason are very rare in other immunodeficiency states. Several clinical features characterize lymphomas in HIV-positive individuals. Central nervous system and bone marrow involvement are common and unusual extranodal sites such as skin, anus and rectum are also involved. The majority of patients present with systemic symptoms, such as unexplained fever, weight loss and night sweats. The primary step in the evolution of HIV-related small non-cleaved lymphomas (AIDS-BL) is similar to that of endemic BL, namely, dysregulation of the immune system which precedes the malignant transformation (Peterson et al, 1985). In analogy to the dysregulation induced by endemic malaria in the African BL model, HIV infection indirectly causes B-cell proliferation and hypergammaglobulinaemia. EBV sequences have been detected in approximately one-half of AIDS-BL, suggesting a role for other unidentified factors in the early events of B-cell proliferation and immortalization (Birx et al, 1986). Specific chromosomal translocations ((8;14), (2;8), (8;22)) involving the c-*myc* and immunoglobulin loci, similar to those defined in both endemic and sporadic BL, were described also in AIDS-BL (Chaganti et al, 1983; Groopman et al, 1986; Pelicci et al, 1986b). Although molecular studies in a few cases of AIDS-BL revealed rearrangement patterns of c-*myc* and immunoglobulin genes similar to those found in

African BL, the majority carry a sporadic BL pattern of gene rearrangement (Neri et al, 1988; Subar et al, 1988; Knowles et al, 1989). Taken together, the inconsistent presence of EBV sequences on the one hand and the prevalent type of chromosomal translocations on the other suggest a biological similarity of most AIDS-BL to the sporadic BL. It should be remembered, however, that most AIDS-BL studied so far were from HIV-positive individuals in developed countries. Studies of AIDS-BL from developing countries, especially from equatorial Africa are required in order to identify the molecular characteristics of such tumours.

In addition to environmental and immunological factors that were shown to operate in the pathogenesis of the various types of BL, a role for genetic factors has been suggested. Specific major histocompatibility complex haplotypes may be involved in the control of the immune response to the various infectious agents such as EBV, HIV and *P. falciparum*, as well as in the response to BL malignant cells. The occurrence of AIDS-BL in two haemophilic brothers sharing an identical HLA haplotype may stress the importance of genetic susceptibility (Rechavi et al, 1987).

ADULT T-CELL LEUKAEMIA/LYMPHOMA

The prevalence of endemic BL was found to be related to early age EBV seroconversion. Similarly, the epidemiology of malignant lymphomas in Japan and other parts of the world was found to be linked to the sero-epidemiology of the human T-cell lymphotropic virus type I (HTLV-I).

In 1977 Uchiyama et al described a distinct form of peripheral T-cell leukaemia/lymphoma (ATLL) that appeared to be prevalent in south-western Japan, particularly in the southern part, Kyushu island (Uchiyama et al, 1977). The characteristic clinical and histopathological features of ATLL enabled its accurate diagnosis and thus systematic epidemiological and virological studies. ATLL occurs in the adult population with an incidence peak in the sixth decade. The overall incidence of ATLL in Japan is 3.5 cases per 100 000 in persons less than 40 years of age and 5.7 cases per 100 000 in persons over 40 years of age (Hinuma et al, 1982; Levine et al, 1987). The Caribbean basin is also an endemic region of ATLL with 2.8 cases per 100 000 in Trinidad and Tobago and 1–2 cases per 100 000 in Jamaica (Matutes et al, 1986). South-eastern USA is another endemic area. Cases of ATLL have been reported from other non-endemic countries; however, most patients described are among immigrants from endemic areas. For example, five out of the first six ATLL cases described in England were among black patients born in the West Indies (Catovsky et al, 1982), and most patients diagnosed in Israel occurred among newcomers from the Jewish community in Mashaad, Iran (Meytes et al, 1990). The male to female ratio of ATLL is 1.4:1. The typical clinical features are lymph-adenopathy, hepatosplenomegaly, skin involvement and hypercalcaemia (Kikuchi et al, 1986). Many patients develop a secondary immunodeficiency and the incidence of opportunistic infections is high. ATLL is a very aggressive disease with an actuarial 50% survival rate of only 9 months. A smouldering variant of ATLL has been described (Yamaguchi et al, 1983), which can undergo blastic transformation to the more typical ATLL. The neoplastic cells exhibit extreme pleomorphism of the nuclei, variously described as cerebriform, gyriform and flower cells (Suchi et al, 1987). They are usually helper T cells (CD4+, CD8−) that functionally have suppressor activity.

The geographical distribution of ATLL suggested a role for an infectious agent in the pathogenesis of this disease entity (Uchiyama et al, 1977). The finding of C-type virus particles, designated ATLV, in cultured ATLL cells was reported by Hinuma et al (1981), and patients with ATLL were found to have antibodies to an antigen present in a cultured cell line. Independently, a retrovirus was isolated at the National Cancer Institute from cultured T cells of an ATLL patient, and designated HTLV-I (Poiesz et al, 1980, 1981). It was shown subsequently that ATLV and HTLV-I are identical. An association between the prevalence of antibodies to HTLV-I and the distribution of ATLL was found (Hinuma et al, 1982; Maeda et al, 1984; Tajima et al, 1987). The rate of seropositivity in different locations within the endemic areas of Japan varies significantly between 2 and 50% (Tajima et al, 1987) and the incidence increases continuously with age (Hinuma et al, 1982; Maeda et al, 1984). A similar age effect was also reported in the Caribbean where the rate of seropositivity was found to be 2% in persons below the age of 50 years and 6% in persons above this age (Hinuma et al, 1982; Sarin and Gallo, 1986; Levine et al, 1987). Some other areas were shown in recent years to be endemic for HTLV-I infection, such as eastern China and northern Kenya. The virus is also associated with a neurological disease known as tropical spastic paraparesis or HTLV-I-associated myelopathy (Weiss, 1987).

Similar to the relationship between African BL and EBV infection, only a minority of those infected with the HTLV-I will develop ATLL. The risk among Japanese is reported to be 2.2 per 1000 males and 0.8 per 1000 females, per annum (Wong-Staal and Gallo, 1985; Matutes et al, 1986; Yoshida and Seiki, 1986). The seropositivity to HTLV-I among Japanese ATLL patients is practically 100% and HTLV-I proviral DNA was demonstrated in all Japanese ATLL cases analysed. Nineteen out of 24 Jamaican ATLL patients were seropositive for the virus (Gibbs and Murphy, 1986). Analysis of ATLL cells revealed that the HTLV-I provirus sequences were integrated in a clonal or oligoclonal pattern, indicating that the viral infection occurred before the neoplastic transformation (Wong-Staal and Gallo, 1985). The site of HTLV-I integration, although unique for each tumour, varied from one patient to another. The variability of integration sites in different ATLL samples differs from the situation in other tumour models, where specific retroviral sequences were inserted regularly in the vicinity of a particular proto-oncogene (Hayward et al, 1981; Corcoran et al, 1984). The integration in this model resulted in the activation of that oncogene via a promoter-enhancer insertion mechanism. The diversity of integration sites of HTLV-I sequences in the different cases of ATLL suggests that the virus operates through a trans-activating mechanism (Sarin and Gallo, 1986). A striking feature of ATLL cell lines is the high level of expression of interleukin-2 receptor (IL-2R) and in some cases also interleukin-2 (IL-2). It can be speculated that overexpression of IL-2R with normal or elevated expression of IL-2 may be involved in an autocrine or paracrine mechanism as an early event in HTLV-I related lymphoproliferation. The HTLV-I trans-acting protein tax-1 was shown to increase the promoter activity of the IL-2R gene (Sarin and Gallo, 1986; Siekevitz et al, 1987), which may be important in the early steps of virus-related leukaemogenesis, but is by no means sufficient for induction of the malignant phenotype. As only a minority of HTLV-I infected individuals develop ATLL, other steps, including chromosomal translocations, appear to be necessary. The understanding of these later steps still awaits clarification. Several chromosomal translocations, similar to those described in non-HTLV-I-related high grade T-cell malignancies, were described in ATLL (Whang-Peng et al, 1985; Pandolfi, 1986). Some of these translocations can result in oncogene activation, again similar to the scenario of EBV-related BL where c-*myc* activation, superimposed on the viral-related lymphoproliferation, results in an irreversible malignant transformation. Further epidemiological studies are necessary to unravel other environmental factors as well as genetic factors involved in the pathogenesis of ATLL.

HODGKIN'S DISEASE

The incidence of Hodgkin's disease (HD) is characterized by a bimodal age peak, which has not been reported in other lymphomas (Grufferman and Delzell, 1984). Moreover, the age distribution of HD in developing countries differs from that observed in industrialized countries. Whereas the second peak occurs in late adulthood in both populations, the early peak varies. In developing countries, the early peak occurs before adolescence, and some cases are diagnosed in preschool children, while in industrialized countries, including the United States, it is extremely rare to diagnose HD before the age of 5, and the early peak occurs in the mid to late twenties (Schottenfeld, 1975; Gutensohn and Cole, 1977). In addition to the age shift, a difference in histological subtypes was reported between developing and industrialized countries. While the incidence of the mixed cellularity subtype is predominant among children in developing countries, it decreases in parallel with industrialization (Schottenfeld, 1975; Gutensohn and Cole, 1977). A slight overall age-dependent male predominance in the incidence of HD was reported. In children younger than 10 years there is a clear male predominance, whereas it is about equal in teenagers. Race was also shown to be an age-dependent factor; among teenagers older than 15 years and young adults the disease is more common in the white race (Spitz et al, 1986).

The racial differences, in addition to the numerous reports documenting HD in first-degree relatives, may suggest genetic factors to be culprits (Grufferman and Delzell, 1984; Fogel et al, 1985). Familial HD cases were described in the inbred Amish population and in another consanguineous family (Fraumeni, 1974; Buehler et al, 1975). Interestingly, HD affecting siblings occurs usually in those of the same gender. Similarly, HD in parents and children affects mainly parent–child concordant pairs. No association was described with specific HLA determinants. An underlying immunodeficiency may predispose affected individuals to HD (Gatti and Good, 1971). Familial primary immunodeficiency syndrome such as ataxia telangiectasia may explain some of the familial aggregations of HD. An increased incidence of HD was also described in families affected by other diseases of the lymphoreticular system. In addition to the primary immunodeficiency syndromes, secondary immunodeficiency states are associated with increased risk of lymphomas, including HD. In recent years AIDS has become the notable example of such secondary immunodeficiency (Ioachim et al, 1985).

The possibility that an environmental contagious factor plays a role in the pathogenesis of HD has been the focus of several epidemiological studies (Vianna et al, 1971; Smith and Pike, 1974). The correlation between the epidemiological patterns of the disease and socioeconomic status may reflect the effect of factors such as sibship size and hygiene. Such factors may influence the age when an individual encounters an aetiological agent in the environment. The relationship between a higher socioeconomic status and the pattern of HD distribution in young patients is similar to that described 50 years ago for paralytic poliomyelitis, thereby contributing to the hypothesis that an infectious agent plays a role in HD. The socioeconomic class is also related to the access to and quality of medical services. This may explain the findings in some surveys that tonsillectomy or appendicectomy are associated with a slightly elevated risk of HD (Gutensohn and Cole, 1977, 1981).

Case clusters of HD have been described among students in a particular high-school. Some studies reported that direct or indirect personal contacts several years prior to diagnosis of HD, among the affected subjects, again support an infectious agent involvement. However, other investigators suggested that these findings can be explained by mere chance, or result from exposure to an environmental non-infectious mitogen or carcinogen. Other studies did not confirm more than the expected linkages among HD patients (Vianna et al, 1971; Smith and Pike, 1974; Gutensohn and Cole, 1981).

Whereas the epidemiological studies searching for the role of an infectious agent have been inconclusive, cumulative evidence obtained from immunological and molecular studies suggest an association between HD and EBV. Increased titres of anti-EBV antibodies were detected in HD (Johnson et al, 1970; Levine et al, 1971; Mueller et al, 1989), and an increased risk of developing HD after infectious mononucleosis was reported (Rosdahl et al, 1974). EBV nuclear antigen-1 (EBNA-1) has been detected in the HD cells in a patient with chronic EBV infection (Poppema et al, 1985). EBV genomic sequences were detected in DNA extracted from HD biopsies, using Southern blot hybridization or the polymerase chain reaction (Weiss et al, 1987a; Staal et al, 1989; Masiah et al, 1990). The application of an in situ hybridization technique enabled the demonstration of EBV sequences in the tumour cells in 17–35% of HD samples (Amganastopoulos et al, 1989; Weiss et al, 1989). The use of EBV terminal repeats sequences as molecular probes showed that the EBV carrying cells were monoclonal (Weiss et al,

1987a; Amganastopoulos et al, 1989). In a recent study, 84 HD cases were studied by immunohistochemical labelling with monoclonal antibodies for the expression of EBV encoded latent membrane protein (LMP) and EBNA-2 (Pallesen et al, 1991). LMP, but not EBNA-2, was demonstrated in Reed–Sternberg (RS) cells of 48% of the cases. Interestingly, the LMP expression in RS cells varied according to the histological subtype. Ten per cent of lymphocyte predominant, 32% of nodular sclerosis and 96% of mixed cellularity type cases had LMP expression. The latent EBV infection phenotype (LMP+, EBNA-2−) of HD differs from other EBV-associated lymphoproliferative states: EBV-positive BL is LMP− EBNA-2− phenotype, whereas lymphomas related to immunodeficiency, nasal T-cell lymphomas, infectious mononucleosis and lymphoblastoid cell lines are LMP+EBNA+ (Klein, 1989; Young et al, 1989; Harabuchi et al, 1990; Pallesen et al, 1990). In analogy with the African BL model, where children are infected with EBV at a very young age and develop EBV-positive BL, mixed cellularity HD that is almost always EBV-positive is the prevalent type affecting young children in developing countries.

FOLLICULAR LYMPHOMA

Studies that characterized the epidemiology of the follicular lymphomas (FL) revealed that the distribution of this clinical entity varies in different parts of the world. Follicle centre cell lymphomas with a follicular growth pattern are the leading non-Hodgkin's lymphoma diagnosed in Europe and North America. In other areas, such as Japan, China, Africa and the Middle East, such lymphomas constitute only a small fraction of non-Hodgkin's lymphomas (Dorfman, 1963; Non-Hodgkin's Lymphoma Classification Project, 1982; Harrington et al, 1987). Several explanations were suggested for the variation in the representation of FL in distinct areas. Differences in the age structure of the studied populations may partially explain this discrepancy. As FL is rare in young persons, developing countries where the majority of the population is young are expected to have less FL. However, even allowing for this consideration, FLs are clearly underrepresented in these areas. Follicle centre cell lymphomas are known to have a natural progression from tumours composed predominantly of small cells with a follicular growth pattern to tumours composed mainly of large cells with a diffuse growth pattern. In an effort to explain the rarity of FL in developing countries it was argued that these lymphomas are diagnosed late in areas where the medical services are less organized and less accessible, and that because of the delay in diagnosis some of the FLs have already progressed to diffuse large cell lymphomas.

A characteristic translocation between chromosomes 14 and 18 has been described in about 75% of the FLs (Yunis et al, 1987). The breakpoint on chromosome 14 is in the immunoglobulin heavy chain locus and that on chromosome 18 involves the bcl-2 putative proto-oncogene (Tsujimoto et al, 1984; Bakhshi et al, 1985; Cleary and Sklar, 1985). Molecular analysis of several chromosomal breakpoints suggests that these translocations are the result of false recombination events, probably at the time of immuno globulin gene rearrangements during B-cell differentiation. The 14;1 translocations were detected both in the low-grade and the high-grade FL (Yunis et al, 1987; Tanagavelu et al, 1990). However, whereas in th low-grade variants the 14;18 translocation was usually the only detectabl chromosomal aberration, additional chromosomal abnormalities wer frequently demonstrated in the high-grade tumours. In addition to th frequent finding of the 14;18 translocation in FLs, this translocation wa detected in about 30% of diffuse large cell lymphomas. Some of thes diffuse lymphomas may represent a late stage in the progression of FLs. A analogous variant translocation t(2;18) in an FL involving the 5' end of *bcl-* and Ig κ light chain gene, was recently described (Hillion et al, 1991).

As the molecular details of the 14;18 chromosomal translocations ar known, it is possible to detect such translocation events using DNA probe neighbouring the frequently involved breakpoints (Weiss et al, 1987b) Moreover, it is possible to apply the polymerase chain reaction for th amplification of the sequences flanking the 14;18 breakpoints (Shibata et a 1990). The application of the molecular biology techniques for the detectio of *bcl-2*–immunoglobulin heavy chain sequences may facilitate epidemio logical studies to determine the frequency of the 14;18 translocations i lymphomas. It may even demonstrate that in some countries this trans location is present mainly in diffuse large cell lymphomas. Such studies ca lead to future research on the role of environmental factors in th pathogenesis of t(14;18) positive and negative FLs, and the factors tha govern the progression of FLs to high-grade diffuse lymphomas.

PRIMARY INTESTINAL LYMPHOMA AND α HEAVY CHAIN DISEASE

The relative incidence of malignant lymphomas is high in some countries i the Middle East, accounting for up to 10% of all neoplasms. A hig proportion of the lymphomas in this region are extranodal and, of these, th majority involve the gastrointestinal tract. The study of these gastro intestinal lymphomas led to the characterization of a distinct clinicopatho logical entity variously entitled 'Middle East lymphoma' or 'α heavy chai disease'. The association between intestinal malabsorption and small bowe lymphoma was first noted by Fairley and Mackie in 1937 (Fairley an Mackie, 1937). This syndrome, which is a very rare condition in the wester world, was described by Ramot et al in 1965 as quite a common clinical entit affecting young adult Arabs and non-European Jews, characterized by severe malabsorption syndrome terminating in a malignant lymphom (Ramot et al, 1965; Ramot, 1971). Further clinical information an characterization of intestinal biopsy findings were reported by Eidelman e al (1966). In 1968, Seligman's group described a new immunoglobuli aberration in a patient suffering from malabsorption associated with plasm cell infiltration of the gut, and termed it α heavy chain disease (Rambaud e al, 1968). It became apparent that these two clinical entities are part of th pectrum of small intestine lymphoproliferative syndromes observed in the Mediterranean region and in other developing countries (Ramot and Hulu, 975; WHO, 1976). Whereas sporadic cases were reported from different egions of the world, clusters were described mainly in Tunis, Morocco, Algiers, Lebanon, Israel, Iran and South Africa (WHO, 1976; Gary et al, 982; Khojasten, 1990). The premalignant phase of this entity, characterized by malabsorption as the dominant clinical feature, was designated uring a WHO workshop in 1976 by the term immunoproliferative small intestine disease (IPSID) (WHO, 1976). While intestinal lymphoma appears to be an important cause of malabsorption in developing countries, he available information concerning the incidence rates of this entity in ifferent countries is limited. A male to female ratio of 2.2 : 1 was observed. The only longitudinal epidemiological surveys were reported from Israel, where the mean annual incidence of primary intestinal lymphoma was 4.8 per million during the years 1960–1967, differing in various ethnic groups (Shani et al, 1969). This rate had dropped to 3.6 per million between 1966 and 1975 (Selzer et al, 1979). In parallel with the decrease in the rate of the disease, a significant change was noted in its age distribution. A remarkable decrease was noted in the rates among children and young adults, with a concomitant rise in the older age groups (Seligmann and Rambaud, 1969; Haghighi and Wolf, 1986). The lower rate of the disease observed in Israel in recent years, its occurrence in the older age population and the pattern of bowel involvement are now similar to those observed in western countries.

The evolution of α heavy chain disease suggests a two-step model (Rappaport et al, 1972; Nassar et al, 1978; Haghighi and Wolf, 1986). The first step is a lymphoplasmocytic proliferation, accompanied by synthesis of a defective α heavy chain protein. Patients at this premalignant stage (stage A according to the staging classification suggested by Salem et al) suffer from steatorrhoea and weight loss. Pathological staging at that stage usually reveals a diffuse benign-appearing mucosal cellular infiltrate without evidence of lymphoma. This premalignant stage can be reversible, following antibiotic therapy, with a disappearance of steatorrhoea and α heavy chain from the serum, and an improvement in the pathological intestinal findings (Ramot and Rechavi, 1990). A role for environmental factors in the pathogenesis of the early stage of the disease was suggested, based on the epidemiological studies linking this disease to low socioeconomic status, the decline in its incidence in parallel with industrialization, and finally the favourable response to antibiotic therapy. Because of the impressive response to antibiotics, an infectious enteric pathogen seems to be an attractive candidate as a causative factor. It may be, however, that antibacterial treatment affects a secondary bacterial overgrowth and not the primary causative factor. Other dietary non-infectious factors, such as dietary lectins, may have a proliferation-promoting activity on intestinal lymphocytes.

The high prevalence of defective α heavy chain proteins suggests a possible selective advantage favouring the proliferation of cells producing such protein. As all α heavy chain proteins described so far have been α_1 and not α_2 proteins, it was speculated that an external selective pressure

operates on IgA1 producing cells. Enteric growth of IgA1 protease
producing bacteria could suppress the proliferation of IgA1 producing cell:
so that only cells that synthesize an aberrant α_1 heavy chain protein would b
resistant to the proteolytic activity, because of deletions involving the hing
region or neighbouring sequences of the heavy chain (Ramot and Rechav
1990). Another possible explanation for a selective advantage is that th
membrane-bound abnormal heavy chain confers a growth advantage an
contributes to the uncontrolled proliferation that characterizes the earl
stages of the disease. Additional genetic changes are expected to operat
during the disease progression from a reversible process to a true maligna
disease. Some reports documenting chromosomal aberrations in intestin;
lymphoma cells support the role of secondary genetic events in the evolutio
of this tumour (Pellet et al, 1988).

ACUTE LEUKAEMIAS AND SOCIOECONOMIC STATUS

Significant changes in the patterns of α heavy chain disease and childhoo
lymphoblastic leukaemia subtypes presentation have recently bee
observed to occur concomitantly with an improvement in the socioeconom;
status of the afflicted population.

Childhood acute lymphoblastic leukaemia (ALL) is the most commo
childhood cancer in developed countries (Breslow and Langholz, 1983
ALL is phenotypically heterogeneous. The most common phenotype i
developed countries is common ALL (cALL) which is HLADR+, CD19+
CD10+; it accounts for 60–70% of ALL cases. Following in decreasin
order of frequency are pre-B (cytoplasmatic μ chain positive), T-ALL an
B-ALL (surface immunoglobulin positive) (Greaves, 1984). Epidemic
logical studies from developed countries revealed a peak incidence of AL
between the ages 2 and 5 (Court Brown and Doll, 1961). This age-relate
peak incidence is known to reflect the predilection of cALL for this ag
group (Court Brown and Doll, 1961; Ramot and Magrath, 1982). T-AL
accounts for 10–25% of the ALLs in the western world. It has a constar
incidence rate during childhood, a male preponderance and an older age ;
presentation than non-T-cell leukaemias.

Our group has reported a gradual increase in the number of childhoo
ALL from 1967 in the Arab population of the Gaza Strip, a regio
administered by Israel since that year (Ramot et al, 1982). Analysis of th
subtypes of ALL revealed a very high proportion of T-ALL, accounting fc
as much as 50% of these patients (Ramot et al, 1984). Recent data fron
Egypt and from India indicate a similar ratio of T-ALL:non-T-ALL a
observed in the Gaza Strip (Ramot, 1988). Even more interesting than th
findings of the high proportion of T-ALL are the results of the analysis of th
different leukaemia subtypes over the years (Ramot, 1988). While the tot;
number of ALL cases in the Gaza Strip did not change, the T-ALL:cAL
ratio steadily decreased since 1982. The changes of leukaemia subtyp
presentation were followed by marked socioeconomic changes that occu
red in the Gaza Strip at the same time, as evidenced by a continuous declin

n infant mortality and a rise in the per capita income (Ramot and Magrath, 1982). Changing patterns of acute leukaemia in American Blacks (Bowman et al, 1984) further support the notion that socioeconomic development is associated with changes in the types of leukaemia.

Two explanations were suggested for the differences in the T-ALL:cALL ratio between developing and developed countries. One hypothesis was that death in early childhood from infectious diseases obscured the true incidence rate of leukaemia in countries with less available and less sophisticated medical services (Stewart and Kneale, 1969). It is suggested that under-diagnosis of early childhood cases, most of them cALL, is expected to bias the analysis because T-ALL affects mainly older children who have a better chance to be diagnosed properly. An alternative explanation, proposed by our group, is that the higher proportion of T-ALL in developing countries is due to an absolute deficit of cALL, and that environmental factors, such as infancy infections, influence the incidence of the leukaemia subtypes (Magrath et al, 1984). The data from the Gaza Strip, where an increase in the incidence of cALL occurred concomitantly with the improvement in socio-economic state, support the latter hypothesis.

Recently it was suggested that cALL results from a spontaneous mutation in the proliferating pre-B-cell progenitor population (Greaves and Chan, 1986), and that this mutation occurs at a similar frequency throughout the world. We believe that the occurrence of mutations at a relatively constant rate could explain the higher incidence of T-ALL in developing countries, where the proliferating T-cell pool in children expands in response to various viral infections and increases the cell population at risk for mutations.

CONCLUSIONS

What are the lessons to be learned from epidemiology?

The epidemiological studies on lymphatic malignancies, and the infor-mation gathered from immunological, virological and molecular investi-gations that followed them, enhanced our knowledge of their pathogenesis. Although lymphomas and paraproteinaemias are a very heterogeneous group, there are some common mechanisms that seem to operate in their evolution. Analyses of the various tumour models described above and of animal lymphatic tumours indicate a multistep process. Future epidemio-logical studies may shed light on the genetic factors involved in the pathogenesis of lymphatic malignancies that could fill in many of the missing pieces in this puzzle.

Constitutional factors

Preliminary information concerning the clustering of haematological malignancies in some families, or a familial aggregation of the same disease, suggests that genetic factors may play a role. Defects in genes involved in the detoxification of environmental agents may predispose the haematopoietic stem cell or a more differentiated haematopoietic cell to malignant trans formation. In addition, immunodeficiency states resulting in impaired immune surveillance could fail to restrain uncontrolled cell proliferation, as in X-linked immunoproliferative (XLP) syndrome. Genetic defects of DNA repair predispose to chromosomal instability and may result in chromo somal aberrations. Ataxia telangiectasia is an example of such a genetic instability syndrome. Finally, genetic changes in cellular oncogenes that are involved in the regulation of cell growth and proliferation can convert them into transforming genes (Cooper, 1990). Lately, interest has been focused on recessive oncogenes, also known as antioncogenes or tumour suppressor genes (Cooper, 1990). In some tumours, in addition to somatic mutations germ-line mutations affecting such genes occur. The latter predispose some families to a significantly increased risk for malignant tumours. Epidemio logical and molecular studies are needed for the determination of the genetic changes in lymphatic malignancies.

Factors involved in early polyclonal cell proliferation

The first event in the evolution of a lymphatic malignancy is usually a polyclonal cell proliferation. For example, polyclonal B-cell proliferation precedes the development of BL and intestinal lymphoma, whereas poly clonal T-cell proliferation precedes the development of ATLL. One of the most important lessons that evolved from the studies mentioned above is the central role of infectious agents on the early events.

The best-studied infectious agent linked to lymphatic malignancies is the EBV. The EBV genome can be detected in the vast majority of African BL in 50% of HIV-related BL, in less than 20% of the sporadic cases, in organ transplant recipients and in all XLP. The presence of EBV sequences and the expression of viral proteins were documented in a significant number of RS cells in HD. An association with EBV was suggested in nasal T-cell lymphomas of the lethal midline granuloma type, in some hairy cell leukaemia cases and nasopharyngeal carcinoma. The ability of EBV to immortalize B-cells both in vivo and in vitro is well known (Miller, 1985) Inoculation of transforming EBV induced lymphomas in white-lipped marmosets (Johnson et al, 1983; Miller, 1985), illustrating its oncogenic potential in primates. Analysis of individual tumours in multifocal lymphomas of tamarins revealed that they arose from different clones suggesting that transformation by this virus is not a rare event. Some viral proteins were shown to be related to EBV transformation. It may be suggested that the main contribution of EBV is its role in the expansion of the B-cell pool, thereby increasing the risk for translocation events Alternatively, EBV-transformed cells may be more susceptible to chromo somal instability and false recombination events. In analogy with the role of EBV in the early, preneoplastic polyclonal B-cell proliferation, early T-cell proliferation is induced by HTLV-I. ATLL cells contain HTLV-I proviral DNA. The high levels of IL-2 receptor expression, and rarely the enhanced production of IL-2, suggest that an autocrine stimulation mechanism may play a role in the early T-cell proliferation in HTLV-I positive individuals (Siekevitz et al, 1987). It is, however, not known whether the role of HTLV-I is limited to the expansion of the T-cell pool or is also involved in converting the cells into a genetic instability that could contribute to the increased rate of mutations. Based on the impressive link between some infectious agents, such as EBV, HTLV-I and possibly other viruses such as HTLV-II and human herpes virus 6 and lymphatic malignancies, the search for other infectious agents should be continued. The possibility of non-infectious environmental factors in the induction of lymphatic cell proliferation must also be borne in mind. A speculative example for such factors may be lectins that are capable of inducing cell proliferation and transformation.

Since only a minority of those exposed to an infectious agent develop uncontrolled cell proliferation, other contributing factors must operate, i.e. primary or secondary immunodeficiency. Malaria and HIV infections are two such examples of environmental factors affecting the immune system. The inherent immunodeficiency in patients with the XLP syndrome, and possibly in some HD patients, may limit their ability to control EBV-induced proliferation.

Secondary, irreversible genetic changes

Once a large pool of expanded and/or immortalized cells is created, the risk for transforming genetic alterations is increased. Some B-cell tumour models illustrate the multistep process, starting by a polyclonal proliferation, followed by an irreversible genetic event. In the murine-induced plasmacytoma model, a preneoplastic stage was induced by intraperitoneal injection of mineral oil, followed by a malignant transformation due to a chromosomal translocation resulting in c-*myc* activation (Klein and Klein, 1985). In the analogous EBV-associated BL model, a similar chromosomal translocation activates the c-*myc*. It is yet unknown whether another infectious agent, not associated with EBV, is involved in the induction of the early proliferation in the BL cases. Several examples of lymphomas carrying both c-*myc* and *bcl*-2 rearrangements have been reported (Tanagavelu et al, 1990), suggesting that in some cases another genetic mutation, not related to an infectious agent, can result in early B-cell proliferation.

Studies performed during the last decade indicate clearly that activation of a single oncogene is insufficient for tumourogenesis (Cooper, 1990). Tests of the transforming activities of cellular oncogenes in primary rat embryo fibroblasts demonstrated that, while a single oncogene failed to induce transformation, it was induced by a combination of several oncogenes. A similar cooperation was demonstrated between oncogenes and DNA tumour virus genes. Transfection of EBV-immortalized B-cells with an activated c-*myc* oncogene resulted in the induction of B-cell tumours in nude mice, whereas the EBV-transformed lymphoblastic cells were not tumourogenic. These experiments illustrate the cooperation between viral and cellular genes in the induction of lymphatic malignancies.

REFERENCES

Al-Attar A, Al-Mondhiry H, Al-Baharani Z & Al-Saleem T (1979) *International Journal of Cancer* **23:** 14.
Amganastopoulos I, Herbst H, Niedobitek G et al (1989) *Blood* **74:** 810–816.
Bakhshi A, Jensen JP, Goldman P et al (1985) *Cell* **41:** 899.
Banks PM, Arseneau JC, Gralnick HR et al (1975) *American Journal of Medicine* **58:** 322.
Benjamin D, Magrath IT & Maguire R (1982) *Journal of Immunology* **129:** 1336.
Berard C, O'Conor GT, Thomas LB & Torloni H (1969) *Bulletin of the World Health Organization* **40:** 601.
Birx DL, Redfield RR & Tosat G (1986) *New England Journal of Medicine* **314:** 874.
Bowman WP, Presbury G, Melvin SL et al (1984) A comparative analysis of acute lymphoblastic leukemia in white and black children. In Magrath IT, O'Connor GT & Ramot B (eds) *Pathogenesis of Leukemias and Lymphomas: Environmental Influences*, pp 169–177. New York: Raven Press.
Breslow NE & Langholz B (1983) *International Journal of Cancer* **32:** 703.
Buehler SK, Fodor G et al (1975) *Cancer* **1:** 195.
Burkitt D (1958) *British Journal of Surgery* **46:** 218.
Burkitt DP (1970) In Burkitt DP & Wright DH (eds) *Burkitt's Lymphoma*, pp 186–197. Edinburgh: Livingstone.
Catovsky D, Greaves MS, Rose M et al (1982) *Lancet* **i:** 639.
Chaganti RSK, Jhanawar SC, Kozener B et al (1983) *Blood* **61:** 1265.
Cleary ML & Sklar J (1985) *Proceedings of the National Academy of Sciences of the USA* **82:** 7439.
Cooper GM (1990) *Oncogenes*. Boston: Jones & Bartlett.
Corcoran LM, Adams JM, Dunn AR & Cory S (1984) *Cell* **37:** 113–122.
Court Brown WM & Doll R (1961) *British Medical Journal* **26:** 981.
Croce CM & Nowell PC (1986) *Advances in Immunology* **38:** 245.
Croce CM, Shander M, Martinis J et al (1979) *Proceedings of the National Academy of Sciences of the USA* **76:** 3416.
Cunningham-Rundles C, Sigal EP & Cunningham-Rundles S (1987) *Clinical Immunology* **7:** 294.
Dalla-Favera R, Bregni M, Erikson J et al (1982) *Proceedings of the National Academy of Sciences of the USA* **79:** 7824.
Dalldorf G (1962) *Journal of the American Medical Association* **181:** 1026.
de Thé G (1977) *Lancet* **i:** 335.
Dorfman RF (1963) In Roulet FC (ed.) *Symposium on Lymphoreticular Tumours in Africa*, p 211. Basel: Karger.
Eidelman S, Parkins RA & Rubin CE (1966) *Medicine* **45:** 111–137.
Epstein MA & Achong BG (1968) *Journal of the National Cancer Institute* **40:** 609.
Epstein MA, Achong BG & Barr YM (1964) *Lancet* **i:** 702.
Erikson J, Martinis J & Croce CM (1981) *Nature* **294:** 173.
Fairley NH & Mackie EP (1937) *British Medical Journal* **1:** 375–380.
Fasth A (1982) *Journal of Clinical Immunology* **1:** 31.
Fogel TD, Peschel RE & Papac R (1985) *Cancer* **55:** 2495–2497.
Fraumeni JF Jr (1974) *Cancer Research* **34:** 1164.
Gary GM, Rosenber SA, Cooper AD et al (1982) *Gastroenterology* **82:** 143–152.
Gatti RA & Good RA (1971) *Cancer* **28:** 89–98.
Gerber P, Nkrumah FK, Pritchett F & Kieff E (1982) *International Journal of Cancer* **29:** 397.
Gibbs WN & Murphy EL (1986) *American Journal of Epidemiology* **124:** 501.
Greaves FM (1984) Subtypes of acute lymphoblastic leukemia: implications for the pathogenesis and epidemiology of leukemia. In Magrath I, O'Connor GT & Ramot B (eds) *Environmental Influences in the Pathogenesis of Leukemias and Lymphomas*, vol. 29, pp 129–139. New York: Raven Press.
Greaves MF & Chan Li C (1986) *British Journal of Haematology* **64:** 1.
Groopman JE, Sullivan JL & Mulder G (1986) *Blood* **67:** 612.
Grufferman SL & Delzell E (1984) *Epidemiologic Reviews* **6:** 76–106.
Gutensohn N & Cole P (1977) *International Journal of Cancer* **19:** 595.

Gutensohn N & Cole P (1981) *New England Journal of Medicine* **304:** 135–140.
Guven P, Klein G, Norin T & Singh S (1980) *International Journal of Cancer* **25:** 711.
Haghighi P & Wolf PL (1986) *Clinics in Laboratory Medicine* **6:** 477–489.
Haluska FG, Finver S, Tsujimoto Y & Croce CM (1986) *Nature* **324:** 158.
Harabuchi Y, Yamanaka N, Kataura A et al (1990) *Lancet* **335:** 128–130.
Harrington DS, Yuling YE, Weissenberger DD et al (1987) *Human Pathology* **18:** 924.
Hayward WS, Neel BG & Astrin SM (1981) *Nature* **290:** 475–480.
Henle G & Henle W (1966) *Journal of Bacteriology* **91:** 1248.
Hillion J, Maccuci C, Aventin A et al (1991) *Oncogene* **6:** 169–172.
Hinuma Y, Nagata K, Hanaoka M et al (1981) *Proceedings of the National Academy of Sciences of the USA* **78:** 6476.
Hinuma Y, Komoda H, Chosa T et al (1982) *International Journal of Cancer* **29:** 631.
Hoover R & Fraumenti JF Jr (1973) *Lancet* **3:** 55.
Ioachim HL, Cooper MC & Hellman GC (1985) *Cancer* **56:** 2831–2842.
Iverson U, Iverson OH, Ziegler JL et al (1972) *European Journal of Cancer* **8:** 305–310.
Johnson B, Klein G, Henle W et al (1970) *International Journal of Cancer* **6:** 450–462.
Johnson DR, Wolf LG, Levan G et al (1983) *International Journal of Cancer* **31:** 91.
Khojasten A (1990) *American Journal of Medicine* **89:** 483–490.
Kikuchi M, Mitsui T, Takeshita M et al (1986) *Hematological Oncology* **4:** 67.
Kinlen LJ, Sheil AGR & Peto J (1979) *British Medical Journal* **2:** 1461.
Klein G (1979) *Proceedings of the National Academy of Sciences of the USA* **76:** 2442.
Klein G (1989) *Cell* **58:** 5–8.
Klein G & Klein E (1985) *Nature* **315:** 190.
Knowles DM, Inghirami G, Ubriaco A et al (1989) *Blood* **73:** 792.
Levine AM & Gill PS (1987) *Oncology* **1:** 41.
Levine PH, Ablashi DV, Berard CW et al (1971) *Cancer* **27:** 416–421.
Levine PH, Kamaraju LS, Connelly RR et al (1982) *Cancer* **49:** 1016.
Levine PH, Blattner W, Biggar RJ et al (1987) *Viruses and Human Cancer*, pp 93–103. New York: Alan Liss.
Lombardini L, Newcomb EW & Dalla-Favera R (1987) *Cell* **49:** 161.
McKeithan TW, Shima EA & LeBeau MM (1986) *Proceedings of the National Academy of Sciences of the USA* **83:** 6636.
Maeda Y, Fukuhara M, Takehara Y et al (1984) *International Journal of Cancer* **33:** 717.
Magrath I, Benjamin D & Papadopoulos N (1983) *Blood* **61:** 726.
Magrath IT (1984a) In Mollander D (ed.) *Diseases of the Lymphatic System: Diagnosis and Therapy*, pp 103–139. Heidelberg: Springer Verlag.
Magrath IT (1984b) In Ford RJ, Fuller L & Hagermeister FB (eds) *New Perspectives in Human Lymphoma*, pp 201–212. New York: Raven Press.
Magrath IT, O'Conor GT & Ramot B (1984) *Pathogenesis of Leukemias and Lymphomas: Environmental Influences*. New York: Raven Press.
Malcolm S, Barton P, Murphy C et al (1989) *Proceedings of the National Academy of Sciences of the USA* **74:** 4957.
Manolov G & Manolova Y (1972) *Nature* **237:** 33.
Masiah A, Wickert R, Mitchell D et al (1990) *Laboratory Investigation* **62:** 64 (abstract).
Matutes E, Dalgleish AG, Weiss RA et al (1986) *International Journal of Cancer* **38:** 41.
Merrell D, Cromatie E & Swift M (1986) *Journal of the Cancer Institute* **77:** 89.
Meytes D, Schochat B, Lee H et al (1990) *Lancet* **336:** 1533.
Miller G (1985) In Fields BN, Knipe DM, Chanock RM, Melnick JL, Roizman B & Schope RE (eds) *Virology*, p 563. New York: Raven Press.
Morrow RH (1985) In Lenoir GM, O'Conor GT & Olweny CLM (eds) *Burkitt's Lymphoma: A Human Cancer Model*. Lyon: IARC Scientific Publications.
Mueller N, Evans A, Harris N et al (1989) *New England Journal of Medicine* **320:** 689–695.
Nassar VH, Salem PA, Shahid MJ et al (1978) *Cancer* **41:** 1340–1354.
Neri A, Barriga F, Knowles DM et al (1988) *Proceedings of the National Academy of Sciences of the USA* **85:** 2748.
Non-Hodgkin's Lymphoma Classification Project (1982) *Cancer* **49:** 2112.
Pallesen G, Hamilton-Dutoit SJ, Young L et al (1990) *Third Meeting of the European Association for Haematopathology*, Würzburg, September (abstract).
Pallesen G, Hamilton-Dutoit SJ, Rowe M et al (1991) *Lancet* **337:** 322.

Pandolfi F (1986) *Diagnostic Immunology* **4:** 61.
Pelicci P-G, Knowles DM II & Magrath I (1986a) *Proceedings of the National Academy of Sciences of the USA* **83:** 2984.
Pelicci PG, Knowles DM, Arlin Z et al (1986b) *Journal of Experimental Medicine* **164:** 2049.
Pellet P, Berger R, Bernheim A et al (1988) *Oncogene* **4:** 653–657.
Penn L & First MR (1986) *Transplantation Proceedings* **18:** 210.
Perry GS III, Spector BD, Schuman LM et al (1980) *Journal of Pediatrics* **97:** 72.
Peterson JM, Tubbs RR, Savage RA et al (1985) *American Journal of Medicine* **78:** 141.
Poiesz BJ, Ruscetti FW, Gazdar AF et al (1980) *Proceedings of the National Academy of Sciences of the USA* **77:** 7415.
Poiesz BJ, Ruscetti FW, Reitz MS et al (1981) *Nature* **294:** 268.
Poppema S, van Imhoff G, Torensma R et al (1985) *American Journal of Clinical Pathology* **84:** 385–390.
Purtilo D (1964) *Lancet* **i:** 702.
Rambaud JC, Bognel C, Prost A et al (1968) *Digestion* **1:** 321–326.
Ramot B (1971) *Annual Review of Medicine* **22:** 19–24.
Ramot B (1988) Environment and malignancies of the lymphatic system. In Miller R et al (eds) *Unusual Occurrences As Clues to Cancer Etiology*, pp 87–94. London: Taylor & Francis.
Ramot B & Hulu N (1975) *British Journal of Cancer* **31:** 343–349.
Ramot B & Magrath I (1982) *British Journal of Haematology* **50:** 183.
Ramot B & Rechavi G (1990) Primary intestinal lymphoma and alpha heavy chain disease. In Magrath IT (ed.) *The Non-Hodgkin's Lymphomas*, p 352. London: Edward Arnold.
Ramot B, Shahin N & Bubis JJ (1965) *Israel Journal of Medical Sciences* **1:** 221–226.
Ramot B, Ben-Bassat I, Many A et al (1982) *Leukemia Research* **6:** 679.
Ramot B, Ben-Bassat I, Brecher A et al (1984) *Leukemia Research* **8:** 691.
Rappaport H, Ramot B, Hulu N et al (1972) *Cancer* **29:** 1502–1511.
Rechavi G, Ben-Bassat I, Berkowicz M et al (1987) *Blood* **70:** 1713–1717.
Rosdahl L, Larsen SO & Clemmesen J (1974) *British Medical Journal* **2:** 253–256.
Samuels BL & Ultman JE (1987) *Annals of Oncology* **3:** 10.
Sarin PS & Gallo RC (1986) *Scientific American* **225:** 88.
Schottenfeld D (1975) Epidemiology of Hodgkin's disease. In Lacher MG (ed.) *Hodgkin's Disease*, p 5. New York: Wiley.
Seligmann M & Rambaud JC (1969) *Israel Journal of Medical Sciences* **5:** 151–157.
Seligmann M, Mihaesco E, Preud'homme JL et al (1979) *Immunological Reviews* **48:** 145–167.
Selzer G, Sacks M, Sherman G et al (1979) *Israel Journal of Medical Sciences* **15:** 390–396.
Shani M, Modan B, Goldman B et al (1969) *Israel Journal of Medical Sciences* **5:** 1173–1177.
Shibata D, Hee, Weiss LM et al (1990) *Human Pathology* **21:** 199.
Siekevitz M, Feinberg MB, Holbrook N et al (1987) *Proceedings of the National Academy of Sciences of the USA* **84:** 5389.
Smith PG & Pike MC (1974) *Cancer Research* **34:** 1156–1160.
Spitz MR, Sider JF, Johnson CC et al (1986) *Journal of the National Cancer Institute* **76:** 235–239.
Staal SP, Ambinder R, Beschorner WE et al (1989) *American Journal of Clinical Pathology* **91:** 1–5.
Stewart A & Kneale GW (1969) *Nature* **233:** 741.
Stiller CA & Parkin DM (1990) *Paediatric and Perinatal Epidemiology* **4:** 303–324.
Subar M, Neri A, Inghirami G et al (1988) *Blood* **72:** 667.
Suchi T, Lennert K, Tu L-Y et al (1987) *Journal of Clinical Pathology* **40:** 995.
Tajima K, Kamura S, Ito S et al (1987) *International Journal of Cancer* **40:** 741.
Tanagavelu M, Olopade O & Beckman E (1990) *Genes, Chromosomes and Cancer* **2:** 147–158.
Taub R, Kirsch I, Morton C et al (1982) *Proceedings of the National Academy of Sciences of the USA* **79:** 7837.
Tsujimoto Y, Finger LR, Yunis J et al (1984) *Science* **226:** 1097.
Uchiyama T, Yodoi J, Sagawa K, Tatasuki K & Uchino H (1977) *Blood* **50:** 481.
Vianna NJ, Greenwald P & Davies JNP (1971) *Lancet* **i:** 1209–1211.
Weiss LM, Stricker JG, Warnke RA et al (1987a) *American Journal of Pathology* **129:** 86–91.
Weiss LM, Warnke RA, Sklar J et al (1987b) *New England Journal of Medicine* **317:** 1185.
Weiss LM, Movahed LA, Warnke RA et al (1989) *New England Journal of Medicine* **320:** 502–506.

Weiss RA (1987) *Journal of Clinical Pathology* **40:** 1064.
Whang-Peng J, Bunn PA, Knutsen T et al (1985) *Journal of the National Cancer Institute* **74:** 357.
WHO (1976) *Bulletin of the World Health Organization* **54:** 615–624.
Wiley IS (1973) *Journal of the National Cancer Institute* **50:** 1703.
Wong-Staal F & Gallo RC (1985) *Nature* **317:** 395.
Yamaguchi K, Nishimura H, Kawano F et al (1983) *Japanese Journal of Clinical Oncology* **13:** 189.
Yoshida M & Seiki M (1986) *Hematological Oncology* **4:** 13.
Young L, Alfieri C, Hennessy K et al (1989) *New England Journal of Medicine* **321:** 1080–1085.
Yunis JJ, Frizzera G, Oken MM et al (1987) *New England Journal of Medicine* **316:** 79.
Zech L, Haglund U, Nilsson K & Klein G (1976) *International Journal of Cancer* **17:** 47.
Ziegler JL, Drew WL, Miner RC et al (1982) *Lancet* **ii:** 631.
Ziegler JL, Beckstead JA, Volberding PA et al (1984) *New England Journal of Medicine* **311:** 565.

5

Tuberculosis and the haemopoietic system

HUXLEY H. M. KNOX-MACAULAY

Tuberculosis (TB) has been known to man probably since the dawn of history. It was not until the early part of the sixteenth century that Fracastorius suspected its infectious nature, but it was left to Villemin in 1865 to show that the disease was transmissible to animals by the inoculation of tuberculous material. Almost 20 years later, on 24 March 1882, Dr Robert Koch, a German physician and one of the leading pioneers of modern medical bacteriology, reported his findings on the aetiology of TB in a paper read to the Physiological Society in Berlin. He demonstrated organisms, which he designated tubercle bacilli, in tuberculous material, and was able to establish a causal relationship between the disease and the bacilli. Despite the availability of effective antituberculosis (anti-TB) chemotherapy for almost 50 years, TB still ranks with malnutrition, malaria and the diarrhoeal diseases as one of the major causes of morbidity and mortality in the developing Third World. The strong connection between the current pandemic of the human immunodeficiency virus (HIV) infection and the increased prevalence of clinically active TB, particularly in the developing world, has brought this old disease back to the headlines to occupy the attention of clinicians, laboratory scientists, epidemiologists, health planners, economists and many Third World governments.

Though primarily an infectious disease, the interactions of TB with the haemopoietic system have not only fascinated but puzzled haematologists for several decades. The descriptions of numerous predictable and unpredictable haematological abnormalities in patients with *Mycobacterium tuberculosis* infection, coupled with the frequent occurrence of clinically active disease in patients suffering from a variety of serious blood dyscrasias, have led investigators to reflect on the possibility of a special relationship between TB and the haemopoietic system (Cameron, 1974). This association is particularly striking in patients with cryptic disseminated disease, in whom the clinical and laboratory evidence of tuberculous infection is not obvious. Many such patients present with prominent abnormalities of their blood simulating a primary haematological disorder (Proudfoot, 1971).

GLOBAL EPIDEMIOLOGY OF TUBERCULOSIS AND INTERACTION WITH HIV INFECTION

Though its prevalence in industrialized countries is at present low, TB can

Baillière's Clinical Haematology—
Vol. 5, No. 1, January 1992
ISBN 0–7020–1626–8

still be regarded as a truly global disease with unacceptably high prevalence in the developing countries of Africa, Asia and Latin America. Currently about 1.7 billion people are infected with *M. tuberculosis*, and more than 20 million individuals suffer from clinically active disease (Kochi, 1990). There are also about eight million new illnesses and three million deaths annually (Styblo, 1989; Kochi, 1990). In comparison *M. leprae*, a related bacillus accounts for about one million new cases annually and very few deaths. Approximately four million of the eight million new tuberculous infections are smear-positive pulmonary cases; the remainder are extrapulmonary and smear-negative pulmonary infections (Styblo, 1989).

Epidemiology in Europe and USA

Since the earliest part of the twentieth century, there has been a progressive decline in prevalence and annual incidence in western Europe and north America. In western Europe, the proportion of young people with new infections is low and has been decreasing rapidly, so that at the beginning of the 1990s the risk of fresh infection in this group is virtually negligible

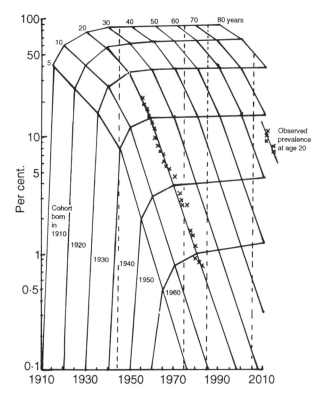

Figure 1. Estimated prevalence of tuberculous infection in cohorts born from 1910 to 1960 in 1945, 1975, 1985 and 2005, the Netherlands. From Styblo (1989) with permission.

(Styblo, 1988). Accompanying this significant fall in the risk of new infections, a reduction in mortality of about 3% annually was achieved between 1900 and 1920 and by about 5.5% over the succeeding two decades. Improved hygiene, nutrition, socioeconomic conditions and effective chemotherapy of infected individuals contributed to this fall in mortality, and facilitated the rapid decrease in the annual risk of infection to about 14% (Styblo, 1989). Between 1954 and 1984 the prevalence of *M. tuberculosis* infection in 20-year-old unvaccinated Dutch recruits fell from about 20 to 0.7%. A further fall to around 0.5% occurred between 1984 and 1987 (Styblo, 1988, 1989). In the mid-1950s the annual incidence of infection in the same age group of Dutch recruits was approximately 220 per 100 000 of the population, while a dramatic decrease to an extremely low figure of < 10 infections per 100 000 per year was recorded during the 1980s. However, during the mid- to late 1980s, there has been a progressive increase in the estimated prevalence with increasing age: about 2% in subjects aged 30 years, about 7% in subjects aged 40 years and about 20% in 50-year-old individuals (Figure 1) (Styblo, 1989). In low prevalence western European countries there is a small but significant pool of infected older persons whose disease is mainly the result of endogenous reactivation of infection acquired in earlier life. Though this pool is declining, it has been estimated that, assuming conditions remain stable, it may take at least 35–40 years before TB is eradicated from low prevalence countries (Styblo, 1989). Pockets of high prevalence are also to be found among the immigrant populations of many western European countries. In the United Kingdom, for example, notification rates for TB are lowest for native Whites, three to four times as great for Caribbean immigrants, and highest (> 50 times) for immigrants from the Indian subcontinent: Indians, Pakistanis and Bangladeshis (Sutherland et al, 1984).

The overall epidemiological situation in the USA was essentially similar to that of western Europe, in that there had been a progressive decline in prevalence and annual incidence until recently (Figure 2). In the early 1980s the fall in incidence was much less among non-Whites than among Whites, so that the risk ratio between these two groups has been increasing progressively, from 2.9 in 1953 to 5.3 in 1987 (Figure 3; Rieder et al, 1989) to almost 9.0 in 1988 (Centers for Disease Control, 1990). The fall in the number of reported cases ceased with the onset of the HIV epidemic, so that between 1985 and 1987 an estimated number of 9226 excess patients accumulated (Rieder et al, 1989), while between 1985 and 1988 there were 14 768 excess cases (see Figure 2). The largest increase in annual incidence (4.7% from the previous year) since national reporting was instituted in 1953 occurred in 1989. Between 1985 and 1989 the number of observed cases exceeded that of expected cases by over 22 000 (D. E. Snider, personal communication). This unprecedented excess is believed to be due to the effect of HIV infection. Case incidence by State showed a very wide range, with 0.0 in Wyoming to 17.8 per 100.000 in New York. These figures represented a decrease in 21 States, no change in two, but an increase in 27 States of the USA (D. E. Snider, personal communication).

There is considerable variation in annual risk, with Black males having the

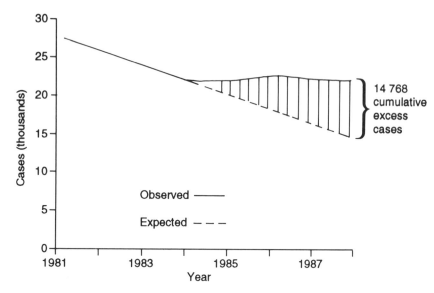

Figure 2. Observed and expected tuberculosis cases, United States of America, 1981–1988. From Centers for Disease Control (1990), with permission.

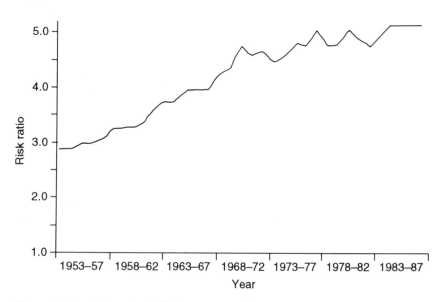

Figure 3. Ratio of tuberculosis risk between non-whites and whites from 1953 to 1987. From Rieder et al (1989), with permission.

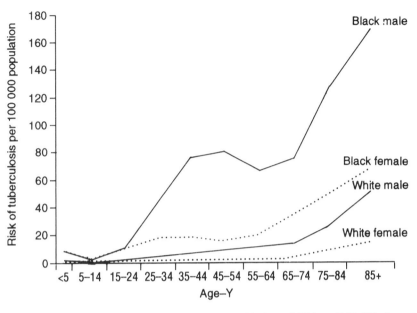

Figure 4. Risk of tuberculosis by age and sex among Blacks and Whites, 1987. (Blacks and Whites here include Hispanics.) From Rieder et al (1989), with permission.

greatest risk of infection (Figure 4). The disease is more prevalent in the younger age groups among Blacks and Hispanics, but among non-Hispanic Whites its epidemiology is similar to that of western Europe, where TB is encountered mainly in older age groups and represents activation of latent foci. It has been shown recently that elderly Americans living in groups, such as in nursing homes, are at a markedly increased risk of acquiring new infections which are likely to develop into clinically active disease (Stead et al, 1985).

Epidemiology in developing countries

The situation in developing countries is gloomy since TB affects and kills all age groups, including children. It has a devastating effect on a poor community's socioeconomic fabric, for not only is it one of the biggest killers, but the heaviest burden falls on the most productive members of society: those between the ages of 15 and 59 years (Murray, 1990). Eighty per cent of all cases of TB are found in this age group, and of all avoidable deaths from whatever cause in this same group, TB accounts for more than a quarter; in women there are more TB deaths than maternal deaths (Kochi, 1990; Murray and Feachem, 1990). The world's TB burden is being borne by the low income countries of Africa, Asia and Latin America, while middle income developing countries have shown an encouraging decrease caused by socioeconomic improvement combined with effective application of various control methods. In many developing countries of Africa, such as Tanzania, there was an annual fall in TB incidence of around 3–5% in the pre-HIV epidemic years 1979–1984, but since 1985 the number of cases has steadily increased (Styblo, 1988). Estimated risks of tuberculous infections in developing countries and the estimated incidence of smear-positive pulmonary TB are shown in Table 1. Because of the difficulty in obtaining

Table 1. Estimated risks of tuberculous infection (1985–1990) and estimated incidence rates of smear-positive TB in developing countries (1990).

Area	Estimated risk of tuberculous infection (%)	Estimated incidence of smear positive TB per 100 000 population
Sub-Saharan Africa	1.5–2.5	103
North Africa and Western Asia	0.5–1.5	54
Asia	1.0–2.0	79
South America	0.5–1.5	54
Central America and Caribbean	0.5–1.5	54

From Murray et al (1990), with permission.

reliable direct figures from inadequate health information systems in the Third World, certain epidemiological parameters have been used. Based on these indirect estimates it has been shown that more than three million new cases of smear-positive TB and more than seven million new cases of all forms of TB occur every year in developing countries (Murray et al, 1990). Poverty, overcrowding, ignorance and severely limited financial and organizational resources with which to execute effective therapeutic and prevention programmes are the main causes of these grim statistics. The recent explosive epidemic of HIV infection in sub-Saharan Africa has further aggravated an already serious situation.

Interaction with HIV infection and HIV disease

The relationship between TB and HIV infection was first recognized in immigrant Haitians living in Florida (Pitchenik and Fischl, 1983), and later in intravenous drug abusers (Sunderam et al, 1986). Since then, numerous reports and epidemiological studies have confirmed this association, both in the USA and Africa. In the USA, however, because of the relatively low background prevalence of TB, pulmonary TB does not feature as prominently in acquired immune deficiency syndrome (AIDS) cases as does *Pneumocystis carinii* pneumonia. The evidence linking HIV infection and disease to the change in prevalence and annual incidence of TB, particularly among Blacks and Hispanics in the USA, is convincing and has been summarized by Pitchenik and co-workers (1988). Moreover, in HIV infected persons, tuberculosis is frequently extrapulmonary and disseminated (Modilevsky et al, 1989). In over 60% of patients in a US study, TB preceded the diagnosis of AIDS (Modilevsky et al, 1989), suggesting activation of latent *M. tuberculosis* infection by HIV. The frequency of mycobacteraemia and disseminated TB appears much greater in HIV seropositive than seronegative individuals (Shafer et al, 1989). Parenteral drug abuse is a more frequent risk factor for HIV infection in US patients with TB.

It is generally agreed that the major mode of transmission of HIV infection on the African continent is through heterosexual activity, though blood transfusion, transplacental vertical transmission and use of inadequately sterilized needles are important but less frequent causes. Of sexually active adults in some urban populations of sub-Saharan Africa between the ages of 20 and 40 years, 20–30% are already HIV infected, primarily through heterosexual activity (Mann et al, 1986a). In Latin America and the Caribbean the prevalent sexual modes of transmission are through both homosexual and heterosexual activities, i.e. epidemiological patterns 1 and 2 (Mann and Chin, 1988). In the Caribbean, as in many other countries, heterosexual transmission is now predominant. In Asia and other pattern 3 regions (Mann and Chin, 1988), the incidence is low though rising rapidly, primarily through intravenous drug use and high risk heterosexual behaviour with persons from high prevalence areas. Thus, globally, heterosexual transmission now accounts for the greatest number of cases of HIV infection and disease.

Thus the explosive spread of this viral infection, with its devastating effects on cell-mediated immunity, has been accompanied by a disastrously rapid rate of increase of tuberculous infection and active disease. This has been particularly evident in the young men, women and children of the poor developing countries of Africa which had a background of high TB prevalence before the HIV epidemic. Therefore HIV seroprevalence rates (17–55%) in both urban and rural populations are much higher in TB patients (Table 2) than the 5–20% rates reported for the rest of the populations (Mann et al, 1988). Also, HIV infection rates are lower in rural than urban TB patients (Meeran, 1989) and higher (up to 67%) in patients presenting with extrapulmonary TB (Fleming, 1990).

All the foregoing data refer to HIV-1 infection, but recently a strong relationship has been demonstrated between HIV-2 infection and TB in West Africa (Corrah et al, 1988). HIV seropositive tuberculous subjects are

Table 2. HIV infection in TB patients in some sub-Saharan African countries (1985–1988).

Country	No. of TB patients	HIV seropositive (%)	References
Zaire	159	33	Mann et al (1986b)
Zaire	231	40	Colebunders et al (1988)
Zaire	235	36	Slutkin et al (1988a)
Zaire	509	17	Williame et al (1988)
Burundi	328	54	Slutkin et al (1988a)
Uganda	150	45	Slutkin et al (1988a)
Uganda	31	30	Slutkin et al (1988a)
Central African Republic	55	55	Mbolidi et al (1988)
Central African Republic	165	30	Cathebras et al (1988)
Zambia	54	50	Meeran (1989)
Malawi	125	26	Kool et al (1990)

Table 3. Crude global estimates of HIV infection and TB.

Global distribution (HIV)	No. of cases ($\times 10^6$)
North America	1.0
Latin America including Caribbean	1.0
Western Europe	0.5
Asia and Pacific	0.5
Sub-Saharan Africa	≥ 5.0
Total (HIV)	≥ 8.0
Total (with HIV and TB)	~ 3.0

The above estimates, as of early 1991, were kindly provided by Dr James Chin, Chief, Surveillance, Forecasting and Impact Assessment Unit, Office of Research, WHO Global Programme on AIDS.

more infectious for *M. tuberculosis* than HIV seronegative individuals (Standaert et al, 1989) and cause an increase not only in the overall frequency of TB in the general population but also in HIV seronegative children under the age of 10 years. World Health Organization (WHO) crude global estimates as of early 1991 are shown in Table 3. The independent effects of HIV infection on the haemopoietic system have been described fully (Holland and Spivak, 1990). A bewildering array of haematological abnormalities may therefore develop when both HIV and *M. tuberculosis* infections affect the same patient. In such cases it may be difficult to separate the haemopoietic disorders associated with each specific infection.

MYCOBACTERIOLOGY AND IMMUNOPATHOLOGY

The tubercle bacillus (*M. tuberculosis*)

Many of the biological properties of this organism, including its immunogenicity, are determined primarily by the subcellular structure of its cell wall, which is rich in lipids and contains a protein skeleton. This skeleton comprises a peptidoglycan to which molecules of arabinogalactan mycolate are covalently linked. On the outer face of the cell wall are complex glycolipids and peptidoglycolipids (including wax D) termed mycosides. When virulent strains of bacilli are grown in a synthetic medium they form long filaments, strands or 'cords' due to the presence of a so-called cord factor, a 6,6'-dimycolate of α,α-D-trehalose. Cord factor is an immunostimulant which induces granuloma formation, probably secondary to macrophage chemotaxis and stimulation; it also activates the alternative complement pathway, thereby provoking an inflammatory response. Other constituents of the mycobacterial cell wall with antigenic properties are proteins, polysaccharide–protein complexes, peptides, phospholipids and arabinomannan.

When acid-fast bacilli (AFB) cannot be demonstrated directly on smears by Ziehl–Neelsen staining, accurate diagnosis of *M. tuberculosis* infection has rested on the traditional but rather slow method of growing the organisms in appropriate culture media followed by identification based on accepted taxonomic characteristics. Newer and more rapid techniques for detecting the presence of tubercle bacilli include DNA amplification (polymerase chain reaction) methods, competitive ELISA with monoclonal antibodies against a 38 kDa mycobacterial antigen, use of species-specific oligonucleotide probes, detection of tuberculostearic acid and latex particle agglutination tests. In disseminated disease, histology and culture of appropriate biopsy specimens can enhance substantially the chances of an accurate diagnosis. The liver and bone marrow are the preferred sites in patients with cryptic disseminated miliary TB. Diagnostic yield from the liver (60–100%) is higher than from the bone marrow (15–50%). Biopsies from both sites will further improve the diagnostic accuracy. An advantage of bone marrow over liver biopsy is that the former procedure can be performed quite safely even in the presence of haemostatic failure. Blood cultures in appropriate BACTEC media are proving increasingly useful for demonstrating mycobacteraemia in disseminated TB, especially in the group of patients with concomitant HIV infection (Shafer et al, 1989).

Immunopathological mechanisms

Resistance against *M. tuberculosis* infection by most immunocompetent individuals represents mainly an expression of active immunity which is cell-mediated and dependent on T lymphocytes and monocytes/macrophages. Bacilli are initially taken up by resident scavenger macrophages at the site of the lesion; the mycobacteria multiply rapidly until a primary tubercle granuloma is formed. Large numbers of monocytes from the peripheral blood migrate to the lesion and become responsible for bactericidal activity. The monocytes/macrophages are activated by lymphokines (especially γ-interferon) released by specifically sensitized T cells following their exposure to specific processed mycobacterial antigens in the granuloma. Activated macrophages also play an important immune regulatory role by releasing a number of cytokines—interleukin 1 (IL-1), α- and β-interferons and tumour necrosis factor (TNF-α or TNF)—which in turn regulate the activity of various components of the immune system (Edwards and Kirkpatrick, 1986; Collins, 1989). TNF, otherwise known as cachectin, is a mature 17 kDa protein comprising 157 amino acids produced from a pro-hormone of 233 amino acids by cleavage of a 76-residue signal peptide. It shares a 28% amino acid sequence homology with another cytokine named lymphotoxin or TNF-β, which possesses some similar biological activities. Though these two molecules may compete for the same receptor, they are encoded for by separate genes on the short arm of chromosome 6. The biological actions of TNF overlap those of IL-1, which is also a 17 kDa protein. IL-1 is structurally different from TNF and does not compete for the same receptor. TNF is synthesized by various activated phagocytic and non-phagocytic cells. It plays a central role in a wide variety of infections and inflammatory processes, including tuberculosis; it is also implicated in the pathogenesis of the anaemia of chronic inflammatory disorders. It is of interest that TNF has an autocrine effect, which means that it stimulates appropriate cells to synthesize more of itself.

Live mycobacteria are also a powerful trigger for TNF release from monocytes/macrophages activated by γ-interferon or calcitriol ($1,25$-$(OH)_2$-cholecalciferol). Calcitriol at physiological concentrations is the most potent activator of the antimycobacterial mechanisms of human monocytes (Rook et al, 1989). Lipoarabinomannan and cell wall peptidoglycan fragments (Moreno et al, 1989; Rook et al, 1989), 46 kDa and 20 kDa mycobacterial protein fractions (Wallis et al, 1990) and cord factor (Silva and Faccioli, 1988) also stimulate the release of TNF by macrophages and monocytes. Though the actions of membrane-associated and systemic TNF are intimately linked with the adverse pathological processes of *M. tuberculosis* infection including granuloma formation (Kindler et al, 1989), in certain situations TNF may also play a limited but essential role in protective immunity (Rook et al, 1989). However, necrosis in tuberculous granuloma does not appear related to TNF release since TNF production is also a prominent feature of non-necrotic granulomata such as leprosy and sarcoidosis. An increase in the circulatory level of agalactosyl immunoglobulin G (IgG), a glycosylation variant of IgG, has been found in tuberculosis though not in leprosy or sarcoidosis; it appears to act as a marker for necrotizing granulomata but its functional role is at present obscure (Rook et al, 1989). Immune suppression from various causes (including steroid and cytotoxic therapy, haemopoietic malignancies and HIV infection) is frequently associated with tuberculous lesions in which there is impaired cellular reactivity (areactive or non-reactive disease), marked necrosis, numerous tubercle bacilli and a tendency to dissemination.

NUTRITION AND TUBERCULOSIS

Vegetarianism and malnutrition

There is now considerable evidence which indicates that deficiencies of certain single nutrients, cobalamin, iron and folic acid as well as protein energy malnutrition (PEM) impair cell-mediated immunity. The incidence of TB in the predominantly vegetarian Indian Hindu immigrant population in England and Wales is about 40 times as high as in native Whites. In a large questionnaire study involving 1187 adult Indians, Chanarin and Stephenson (1988) showed that there was a highly significant difference in the prevalence of tuberculosis in vegetarians (133 per 1000) as compared with those on mixed diets (48 per 1000) containing fish, chicken or meat eaten not less than twice weekly. Though the cobalamin status of the subjects questioned was not determined at the time of the study, an analysis of previously recorded serum cobalamin values of samples from Indians living in the same area had shown that 54.6% of 1000 consecutive sera had lower than normal cobalamin concentration. Impairment of bactericidal killing activity of macrophages because of cobalamin deficiency could explain the high incidence of TB in vegetarians (Chanarin and Stephenson, 1988). Iron deficiency due to poor availability of iron in a vegetarian diet also contributes to the impairment of cell-mediated immunity in vegetarians (Strauss, 1978). The results of animal experimental work, together with abnormal in vitro responses of folate-deficient lymphocytes to mitogenic stimuli, provide strong evidence of disordered cellular immune function in folate-deficiency states. Thus, insufficiency of this vitamin, which is a common feature of malnourished individuals, may increase the risk of acquiring tuberculous infection and active disease.

Cell-mediated immunity is defective in children and adults who suffer from PEM and the degree of immune suppression is related to the severity of the malnutrition. Glycolytic and oxidative metabolic activities necessary for ingestion and killing of microorganisms by leukocytes are reduced in PEM but revert to normal after correction of the malnourished state. Bhaskaram and Sundaramma (1990) studied three groups of Indians: TB patients, non-tuberculous close contacts with positive Mantoux and non-tuberculous controls with negative Mantoux readings. All subjects were shown to have a lower than normal body mass index (BMI), which reflected poor nutritional status. The authors demonstrated that the BMI of the TB patients was lower than that of the close contacts, which in turn was also lower than that of the controls. These findings clearly show that TB worsens malnutrition. Results of studies of the generation of H_2O_2, O_2 and IL-1 activity in the monocytes of these three groups also indicate a lack or impairment of monocyte activation by *M. tuberculosis* in the presence of coexisting malnutrition. Such derangement of cell-mediated immunity could explain not only the enhanced susceptibility to tuberculous infection and active disease but also the frequent occurrence of disseminated non-reactive miliary TB in malnourished patients.

Folate metabolism

Frank megaloblastic anaemia due to folate deficiency is not frequently observed in untreated localized or disseminated tuberculosis, but derangements in folate metabolism are common. Low serum folate levels representing incipient folate depletion were found in 45% of a group of 33 untreated British TB patients (Line et al, 1971), while extremely low values of < 4.5 nmol/l (2.0 μg/l) were detected in 16 out of 148 Nigerian patients (Knox-Macaulay, 1989). Reduced red cell folate values reflecting depletion of tissue stores were found in 15% of the British group. Eleven per cent (16/148) of Nigerians had extremely low red cell folate concentrations of < 227 nmol/l (100 μg/l), but a larger number were mildly deficient (Knox-Macaulay, 1989). Other studies concerning folate metabolism in tuberculosis are mentioned by Cameron and Horne (1971). The aetiology of incipient folate depletion and overt folate deficiency in TB patients includes poor dietary intake associated with alcoholism (Klipstein et al, 1967) and an intrinsically low dietary folate which is further reduced by excessive cooking of green vegetables, a common practice in many tropical countries. Anorexia in debilitated patients and folate malabsorption, even in the absence of small bowel involvement, are possible contributory factors. Investigations based on tuberculous folate-deficient western Europeans suggested that excessive utilization of folate by the active inflammatory process contributes to the deficiency state (Cameron and Horne, 1971). On the other hand it was observed that in a large group of Nigerian patients suffering from pulmonary TB, the extent of the inflammatory process *per se* did not influence folate status to any significant degree, nor was there any relationship between red cell or serum folate and severity of anaemia (Knox-Macaulay, 1989).

Cobalamin metabolism

Unlike folate metabolism, aberrations in cobalamin metabolism do not feature prominently in localized or disseminated TB except in vegans and possibly other vegetarians. Relatively high serum cobalamin concentrations with increased unsaturated B_{12} binding capacity and raised transcobalamin values are found in the healthy non-vegetarian populations of high TB-prevalence countries (Hift, 1966; Fleming et al, 1978). Thus, large cobalamin stores coupled with a relatively low average daily requirement of about 2.5 μg ensure that significant deficiency does not occur even in very ill, anorectic, malnourished TB patients (Knox-Macaulay, 1990). Also, no significant difference was detected between mean serum cobalamin concentration (300.7 pmol/l, 407.5 pg/ml) of 126 Nigerians with localized active organ involvement and that of 21 Nigerians (311.1 pmol/l, 421.5 pg/ml) with disseminated disease. Furthermore, it does not appear that cobalamin status influences the severity of anaemia in pulmonary and disseminated TB patients (Knox-Macaulay, 1990). Extensive caseating granulomatous involvement of the terminal ileum may result in cobalamin deficiency with or without megaloblastic anaemia.

Iron metabolism

Disturbances of iron metabolism in TB are in general similar to those of other chronic inflammatory and malignant disorders. The essential features are reduced or absent marrow sideroblasts, a redistribution of tissue iron with most of the circulating iron being directed into the mononuclear phagocytic cells, low serum iron, low to normal serum total iron binding capacity (TIBC), reduced transferrin saturation ($< 16\%$), increased serum ferritin and increased red cell protoporphyrin. There is experimental evidence that some of these changes, which are exaggerated in anaemic subjects, represent an acute-phase response to the presence of infection and result from the secretion of IL-1 by monocytes (Lee, 1983). Recent studies by Baynes and colleagues (1986a), in a group of 59 South African patients (45 anaemic, 14 non-anaemic) with active pulmonary TB, reveal certain differences from findings obtained previously in a heterogeneous population of patients suffering from a variety of chronic disorders. The South African subjects exhibited hypoferraemia, hyperferritinaemia but a normal transferrin saturation ($\bar{x} \sim 30\%$). There was also evidence of (1) a direct correlation between serum ferritin and C-reactive protein (a marker of inflammation); (2) a direct correlation between marrow non-haem iron and C-reactive protein; (3) an inverse correlation between serum ferritin and serum TIBC; and (4) an inverse correlation between marrow iron stores and serum TIBC. Following anti-TB therapy, serum ferritin and C-reactive protein concentrations fell, indicating that the raised serum ferritin was at least in part an acute phase response to the tuberculous inflammatory process. Evidence was also adduced which indicated that body iron stores are probably a more important factor influencing the level of serum ferritin in TB. Marrow iron may be absent in some patients with concomitant chronic gastrointestinal blood loss, as in hookworm infestation (Henderson, 1984), or in vegetarians, as well as in anorectic debilitated patients whose dietary iron intake is low. Iron deficiency from iron malabsorption secondary to disease involvement of the upper small bowel is unusual.

HAEMATOLOGICAL ABNORMALITIES

Pulmonary tuberculosis

In the early stages of localized reactive fibrocaseous pulmonary TB, peripheral blood counts are usually normal. Persistent infection and local extension of disease give rise to a normochromic normocytic or hypochromic microcytic anaemia of mild to moderate severity (haemoglobin (Hb) 80–100 g/l). Mean values for red cell volume distribution width (RDW) are increased in untreated anaemic TB patients and in anaemic patients during treatment. RDW is similarly increased in non-anaemic TB patients, but it is not a useful index for distinguishing the hypochromic microcytic anaemia of chronic disease from that of iron deficiency for it is also raised in the latter condition (Baynes et al, 1986b). Aetiological factors in the anaemia of localized and disseminated disease are summarized in Table 4.

Table 4. Aetiological factors contributing to the anaemia of TB.

Causes	Comments
Anaemia of chronic disease	Main aetiological factor
Folate deficiency	Common in malnourished patients
Cobalamin (B$_{12}$) deficiency	Occurs primarily in vegetarians
Iron deficiency	Associated with vegetarianism, malnutrition and concomitant chronic blood loss
Leucoerythroblastic anaemia	'Metastatic' reactive caseating granulomata in bone marrow
Aplastic anaemia	Usually antedates overt TB
Haemopoietic malignancies	TB is opportunistic
HIV infection	Contributes significantly to anaemia of HIV-infected TB patients
Anti-TB drugs	Refer to Figure 5
Dyserythropoiesis, red cell aplasia and *autoimmune haemolytic anaemia	Unusual causes

* Murray, 1978.

Changes in white cell counts and morphology, which are more often encountered in disseminated non-reactive TB (see Table 5), may occasionally be observed in localized pulmonary and extrapulmonary disease. These include absolute neutrophilia (even in the absence of secondary pyogenic infection), eosinophilia, monocytosis, lymphocytosis and lymphopenia (Corr et al, 1964). Moderate to marked reactive thrombocytosis, with platelet counts sometimes exceeding $1000 \times 10^9/l$, is a feature of many patients (Baynes et al, 1987). There is a significant inverse correlation between the platelet count and mean platelet volume, while platelet survival is considerably shortened with a preponderance of circulating small young platelets which aggregate excessively in vitro (Baynes et al, 1987). The degree of thrombocytosis also correlates significantly with the severity of inflammation as determined by the erythrocyte sedimentation rate and C-reactive protein (Baynes et al, 1987). The exact nature of the chemical mediators involved in the thrombocytosis of TB patients is unclear but thrombopoietic stimulating activity is increased in their sera.

Erythropoiesis is usually normoblastic or micronormoblastic due to chronic infection with or without concomitant iron deficiency but, less often, it may be megaloblastic (Cameron and Horne, 1971; Line et al, 1971; Cameron, 1974; Oluboyede and Onadeko, 1978; Chanarin and Stephenson, 1988). In patients without complicating iron deficiency, marrow non-haem iron in the macrophages (reticulum cells) is either adequate or increased. Bone marrow plasmacytosis and eosinophilia are observed not infrequently and represent reactive changes; megakaryocytic and granulocytic hyperplasia are found in the marrow of patients who present with neutrophilia and thrombocytosis.

Extrapulmonary tuberculosis

Sites affected commonly are lymph nodes, abdomen (peritoneal and/or intestinal), genitourinary and skeletal systems, and meninges. Peripheral blood and bone marrow changes in early and advanced disease are essentially similar to those found in pulmonary TB. However, the effects on the haemopoietic system may vary depending on the particular site and extent of disease. Retrospective studies carried out in different areas of the world have shown that 50–75% of all patients suffering from extrapulmonary TB are anaemic, with Hb $< 1.86 \, \text{mmol/l}$ (120 g/l); relevant references are to be found in Al-Freihi et al (1987). In abdominal tuberculosis, a common problem in the Third World, Hb values were $1.55–2.02 \, \text{mmol/l}$ (100–130 g/l) in 47 Indian patients (Singh et al, 1969), $0.81–1.86 \, \text{mmol/l}$ (52–120 g/l) with a mean of $1.12 \, \text{mmol/l}$ (72 g/l) in 65 Nigerian females, and $0.33–2.11 \, \text{mmol/l}$ (21–136 g/l) in 35 Nigerian males (Francis, 1972). In a larger review of 178 Nigerian patients with abdominal tuberculosis treated at University College Hospital, Ibadan, the haematocrits (Hct) of all the patients were between 0.18 and 0.5, with 40% of them having an Hct < 0.3; the total white cell count was $2.5–21 \times 10^9/l$, with 64% having a normal count and 26% a neutrophilia (Lewis and Abioye, 1975).

Table 5. Haematological manifestations of disseminated non-reactive miliary TB.

Red cells
Normochromic normocytic/hypochromic microcytic anaemia
Leucoerythroblastic anaemia

White cells
Abnormal morphology:
  Acquired Pelger–Huët anomaly
  Transformed lymphocytes
  Toxic granulation of neutrophils
Leucocytosis (neutrophilia, eosinophilia, monocytosis, lymphocytosis)
Leucopenia (neutropenia, lymphopenia)
Leukaemoid reactions (granulocytic, monocytic, lymphocytic, basophilic)

Platelets
Thrombocytosis
Thrombocytopenia

Disseminated tuberculosis (Table 5)

There are essentially two histological types of disseminated TB: reactive and non-reactive. The disseminated reactive variety is less common and comprises scattered ('metastatic') fibrocaseous granulomata which may give rise to a leucoerythroblastic anaemia, pancytopenia or selective cytopenias when the marrow is extensively involved. Affected patients are usually more severely anaemic than those with localized fibrocaseous disease.

Disseminated non-reactive tuberculosis, a frequent complication of immune-compromised individuals, is characterized by the widespread development of non-reactive tubercles consisting primarily of necrotic foci teeming with large numbers of bacilli, and with minimal or no surrounding cellular inflammatory reaction. Major haematological abnormalities may dominate the clinical picture which often presents as a cryptic disorder, so that the true diagnosis is made frequently only at post mortem. The spectrum of abnormalities of the haemopoietic system and the interacting blood dyscrasias in disseminated miliary non-reactive tuberculosis are summarized in Tables 5–7. Some of the white cell changes have already been mentioned under localized disease. Standard textbooks of haematology emphasize the diagnostic importance of monocytosis or lymphocytosis in localized or disseminated TB. In some series, however, neutrophilia was almost as common as monocytosis, while lymphocytosis was relatively rare (Corr et al, 1964). It is also interesting to note that, in a retrospective review, Glasser and colleagues (1970) reported an absolute monocytosis in only three out of 40 patients suffering from miliary TB. Basophilia or a basophilic leukaemoid reaction is extremely uncommon, but eosinophilia, which is more likely related to endemic parasitism than to mycobacterial infection, is frequently observed in African TB patients (H. H. M. Knox-Macaulay, unpublished data). Pancytopenia and selective cytopenias have also been described (Cameron, 1974). It is important to remember that absolute lymphopenia, which is rarely seen in TB, is a fairly consistent feature of HIV infection. Therefore an absolute lymphopenia in a case of suspected or confirmed TB should be regarded as sufficient justification for an HIV antibody assay.

Interaction with blood dyscrasias (Table 6)

Observations of an intimate relationship between miliary TB and blood dyscrasias were made as early as the latter half of the nineteenth century. Many of the reports of TB presenting as 'acute or chronic leukaemia' were of unusual leukaemoid responses to disseminated infection (see Table 5). Such leukaemoid responses with significant leftward shift, including blasts in the peripheral blood, may occur with a leucocytosis, normal total white cell count or a leucopenia. A review of collected cases suggests that the neutrophilic granulocytic leukaemoid reaction is probably the most common form (Twomey and Leavell, 1965). Eosinophilic and basophilic leukaemoid variants have also been observed, though rarely.

Reports of ante-mortem acute leukaemic blood pictures (including Auer rods in blasts) in some patients in whom at post mortem no evidence of leukaemic infiltration but only miliary TB was found, are puzzling. It is likely that in many of these cases, miliary TB developed either as a new opportunistic infection or as a result of reactivation of old lesions due to loss

Table 6. Blood dyscrasias associated with disseminated non-reactive TB.

Acute leukaemias
Chronic (granulocytic and lymphocytic) leukaemias
Hairy cell leukaemia
Myeloproliferative diseases (polycythaemia vera, idiopathic myelofibrosis)
Myelodysplastic syndrome
Haemophagocytic syndrome
Agranulocytosis
Pancytopenia
Hypoplastic ('aplastic') anaemia
Lymphoproliferative diseases
Myeloma

Table 7. Morphology of bone marrow in disseminated TB (reactive and non-reactive).

Morphology	Comments
Caseating granuloma $\pm$ AFB	Virtually diagnostic of TB
Non-caseating granuloma	Not diagnostic except AFB demonstrated
Bone marrow necrosis	Not diagnostic except AFB demonstrated
Hypoplasia of bone marrow	TB is usually a complication and not a cause
Red cell aplasia	Rare occurrence
Megaloblastosis	Present in patients with folate or B_{12} deficiency
Haemophagocytosis	Rare occurrence; other causes include VIAH and HMR
Myelodysplasia	Rare association
Lymphocytic infiltration of marrow	May simulate chronic lymphocytic leukaemia

AFB, acid fast bacilli; VIAH, viral infection associated haemophagocytosis; HMR, histiocytic medullary reticulosis.

of, or diminution of, cell-mediated immunity caused by a primary disorder of the haemopoietic system (Coburn et al, 1973). Increased frequency of tuberculous infections has been noted in the chronic leukaemias (Morrow and Anderson, 1965; Coburn et al, 1973), though not in the acute leukaemias. However, TB occurs twice as frequently with myeloid than it does with lymphocytic leukaemias (Lowther, 1959). An incidence of tuberculous infection of 5.4% has also been reported in hairy cell leukaemia (Marie et al, 1977). Other blood dyscrasias occasionally associated with disseminated miliary TB (Table 6) are polycythaemia vera, agnogenic myeloid metaplasia (Cameron, 1974), myelodysplastic syndrome (Hunt et al, 1987) and haemophagocytic syndrome (Chandra et al, 1975; Weintraub et al, 1984; Browett et al, 1988). In TB presenting as the haemophagocytic syndrome there is a benign histiocytic proliferation in the marrow with haemo-phagocytosis, a picture resembling histiocytic medullary reticulosis (HMR); reported cases responded clinically and haematologically to anti-TB drug therapy, with normalization of the bone marrow. It is therefore reasonable to carry out intensive investigations to exclude TB in patients with apparent HMR and, where appropriate, to consider seriously a trial of anti-TB therapy before embarking on a regimen of cytotoxic drugs.

The results of in vitro culture experiments suggest that severe neutropenia which may occur in isolation or as part of a pancytopenia in untreated disseminated areactive TB may be the result of inhibition of granulopoiesis by T cells (Bagby and Gilbert, 1981). The factors responsible for inducing T-cell inhibition are at present unknown. Rarely, neutropenia and pancyto-penia may be due to hypersplenism caused by tuberculous splenomegaly. More often, pancytopenia is the result of an inapparent underlying 'malignant' blood disorder in which disseminated TB develops as an opportunistic infection (Katzen and Spagnolo, 1980; Hunt et al, 1987). Reports that are not entirely convincing indicate that aplastic anaemia may be caused by miliary TB (Cameron, 1974). However, based on the recovery of the bone marrow and the peripheral blood counts following anti-TB therapy, a fairly convincing case has been made implicating disseminated TB in the aetiology of marrow hypoplasia (Mangion and Schiller, 1971). Nevertheless, it should be emphasized that recovery of peripheral counts after anti-TB therapy does not necessarily exclude the presence of a primary disorder of the haemopoietic system. Long-term follow-up in these circum-stances may ultimately reveal an underlying malignant disorder such as a leukaemic or myelodysplastic process (Katzen and Spagnolo, 1980; Hunt et al, 1987).

Pathogenesis of the anaemia of tuberculosis

A number of factors may be operative in the anaemia of an individual TB patient (see Table 4). However, the anaemia of TB is basically that associated with chronic inflammation or infection, and is designated the anaemia of chronic disease (ACD). The features of ACD have been well described previously (Lee, 1983). Although some of the underlying mechanisms involved in the pathogenesis of ACD are still obscure, a large body of information which has shed considerable light on the subject is being accumulated.

Red cell life span is slightly shortened in patients with TB and other chronic inflammatory processes. Anaemia therefore develops in those cases in which compensatory red cell production is inadequate. Possible reasons for impaired erythropoiesis are (1) an intrinsic marrow cellular defect, (2) a disorder of iron metabolism, (3) inadequate levels of serum erythropoietin (EPO), and (4) inhibition of erythropoiesis. The absence of significant dyserythropoiesis in most TB patients makes an intrinsic marrow defect unlikely and, to date, no major chromosomal or other nuclear and/or cytoplasmic abnormalities have been observed in the erythroid marrow of affected subjects. It is also equally unlikely that reduced red cell production represents an adaptation to low O_2 tissue demand, because an increase in whole blood $P_{50}O_2$ and in red cell 2,3-diphosphoglycerate (2,3-DPG) in anaemic patients with chronic disease reflects a response to increased tissue O_2 demand. Inappropriately low levels of serum EPO are found in patients with ACD (Ward et al, 1971; Zucker et al, 1974). Some studies have demonstrated the lack of an inverse correlation between Hb or venous Hct and serum EPO levels in ACD, unlike that observed in other types of anaemia such as iron deficiency anaemia (Ward et al, 1971; Zucker et al, 1974). Though in some other investigations a significant inverse correlation between serum EPO and Hb values was observed, the regression coefficient was significantly lower for the ACD patients than for iron deficiency anaemia (Hochberg et al, 1988). Marrow responsiveness to EPO stimulation in vitro appears normal and, so far, EPO inhibitors have not been detected in ACD (Zucker et al, 1974). Inadequate increases of serum EPO in ACD do not necessarily represent decreased production as increased catabolism of EPO would also result in relatively low serum EPO concentrations. It is surprising that there are no data available on EPO catabolism in anaemic or non-anaemic TB patients, or in any other chronic disorder. Disturbances in iron metabolism in ACD result in a reduced recycling of storage iron by macrophages, thus rendering iron stores unavailable to the red cell. Such defects in iron metabolism may also contribute to the anaemia of TB patients.

The role of certain cytokines in the pathogenesis of the anaemia of TB and other chronic disorders is being increasingly recognized. TNF and IL-1 have been shown in experimental studies to induce certain features of ACD (Tracey et al, 1988; Moldawer et al, 1989). TNF administered in sublethal doses to rats by intraperitoneal injections causes a reduced red cell survival and a decrease in red cell mass and red cell count by about 25%, without plasma volume expansion and without an increase in the absolute number of circulating reticulocytes. TNF administration also results in certain metabolic changes, including a reduction in food intake, weight loss and depletion of whole body protein. The haematological changes are independent of these metabolic changes. IL-1 probably does not play a significant role in ACD for it does not cause a decrease in red cell mass, though it reduces red cell life span slightly. TNF and IL-1 also cause abnormalities of iron metabolism in the experimental animal similar to ACD in man except that IL-1, unlike TNF, does not reduce the daily amount of iron incorporated into erythrocytes. TNF has a stimulating effect on haemopoiesis by inducing the secretion of other cytokines such as GM-CSF, which in turn induce differentiation of haemopoietic stem cells. Nevertheless, the net effect of TNF on erythropoiesis following chronic in vivo administration is inhibitory. Likewise, in vitro, TNF inhibits directly the expression of BFU-E. It is therefore likely that in chronic disorders such as TB, endogenous TNF produced by activated monocytes/macrophages under the influence of inflammatory stimuli, especially live mycobacteria (Rook et al, 1989), causes a significant inhibition of erythropoiesis with resultant anaemia. This hypothesis, which is based on experimental data, has received substantial support from human studies. TNF activity was measured in the sera of 39 Brazilian patients suffering from pulmonary TB and 72 non-tuberculous (purified protein derivative (PPD) positive and negative) controls. Markedly elevated TNF levels were demonstrated in the TB patients in contrast to the non-tuberculous controls, whose sera showed little or no TNF activity (Silva et al, 1988).

Miscellaneous observations

Erythrocyte sedimentation rate (ESR)

The ESR is usually elevated in TB but is not a useful diagnostic marker of active disease as many seriously ill patients often have a normal value. Moreover, it should be remembered that there is considerable overlap between ESRs of the sick and apparently healthy populations of many developing countries (Ahme et al, 1977). Plasma viscosity is a more sensitive indicator of the presence and severity of localized and disseminated tuberculous infection (Harkness, 1971) but its routine measurement is not a practical proposition, especially in hospitals in Third World countries. A polyclonal increase in immunoglobulins and a rise in the level of various acute phase proteins, including fibrinogen, contribute to the elevation of plasma viscosity in TB.

Blood groups and haemoglobin phenotypes

Studies attempting to demonstrate a relationship between blood group phenotypes and the incidence of TB have produced conflicting results. A large study in India involving 1600 TB patients and 3799 healthy subjects found some relationship between blood group AB individuals and increased susceptibility to TB (Jain, 1970). In a similar study carried out in Zaria, northern Nigeria, no relationship between the frequency of the various ABO blood groups and the different forms of TB was detected (H. H. M. Knox-Macaulay, unpublished data). Likewise, there are conflicting data concerning the relative frequency of sickle-cell trait in African and black American TB patients (Sears, 1978). A recent unpublished study (H. H. M. Knox-Macaulay) in Nigeria confirms earlier work in the USA which showed that the frequency of sickle-cell trait is no greater among pulmonary TB patients than among non-tuberculous persons (Sears, 1978). Though sickle cell anaemia patients are prone to respiratory infections, there is no evidence indicating a predilection for pulmonary TB.

Haemostasis

Bleeding complications are usually caused by thrombocytopenia secondary either to selective or total marrow failure. Immune thrombocytopenia may rarely complicate anti-TB therapy. Anaphylactoid non-thrombocytopenic purpura simulating the Henoch–Schönlein syndrome is another uncommon feature which has been reported in some pulmonary TB patients. Extensive liver involvement in disseminated miliary tuberculosis may lead to abnormal haemostasis with bleeding. Disseminated intravascular coagulation, with or without haemorrhagic manifestations, may in rare instances complicate widespread areactive miliary TB, particularly in patients with mycobacter-aemia (Manzella et al, 1985).

Antituberculosis drugs and the haemopoietic system

Despite extensive and intensive use of the antituberculosis (anti-TB) drugs, the incidence ($<5\%$) of major adverse reactions is in general low (Slutkin et al, 1988b). A substantially higher incidence (18%) is observed in patients with advanced HIV infection (Small et al, 1991). Most of the drug-induced abnormalities of the haemopoietic system are relatively minor and disappear on withdrawal of the offending drug. Occasionally, serious life-threatening and even fatal blood dyscrasias may develop. Some of the blood disorders such as eosinophilia and immune haemolysis represent manifestations of drug hypersensitivity, while others, for example aplastic anaemia, are probably idiosyncratic responses. The haematological abnormalities caused by 12 tuberculocidal and tuberculostatic drugs are described briefly and summarized (Figure 5). Readers are referred to the review by Holdiness (1987) for further details. It may be difficult on many occasions to ascribe with any degree of certainty a particular adverse haematological effect to a specific drug since anti-TB drug therapy is usually administered as a combination of two or more drugs. Evidence incriminating a specific drug is frequently based on reproducing symptoms following exposure to a challenging dose, but in several cases rechallenge may be considered dangerous so that the evidence then becomes circumstantial and at times inconclusive.

Streptomycin

Immune haemolysis, accompanied by allergic manifestations including diffuse erythema and peripheral eosinophilia, has been reported (Nachman et al, 1962; Letona et al, 1977). The haemolysis was predominantly intravascular, resulting in haemoglobinaemia and haemoglobinuria with renal shut-down. Serological studies demonstrated streptomycin-specific IgG antibodies which fixed complement on to red cells and bound streptomycin

	Streptomycin	PAS	INAH	Rifampicin	Pyrazinamide	Ethambutol	Thiacetazone	Cycloserine	Ethionamide	Capreomycin	Kanamycin	Viomycin
Sideroblastic anaemia			+		+			+				
Immune haemolysis	+	+	+	+			+					
Aplastic anaemia	+	+	+	+			+					
Pure red cell aplasia			+				+					
Megaloblastic anaemia		+	+									
Folate deficiency			?					+				
B12 deficiency		+										
Eosinophilia	+	+	+	+						+		
Neutropenia		+	+	+			+			+		
Agranulocytosis		+	+	+				+				
Leukaemoid reaction			+	+								
Thrombocytopenia	+	+	+	+	+	+	+					
Methaemoglobinaemia		+										
Acute porphyria			?	+	?							
G6PD haemolysis	+	?		?								

Figure 5. Haematological complications of 12 antituberculosis drugs. +, complication definitely occurs irrespective of frequency; ?, evidence for complication is questionable; blank spaces represent absence of reports of the particular complications; G6PD haemolysis, haemolysis of glucose 6-phosphate dehydrogenase deficient red cells.

to the red cell membrane through chemical groups definitely related to the M antigen, and possibly also to the D antigen (Letona et al, 1977). Extremely rare attacks of haemolysis in individuals whose red cells are genetically deficient in the enzyme glucose 6-phosphate dehydrogenase (G6PD) have also been documented during streptomycin therapy. Immune thrombocytopenia with fever, skin rash, wheezing and demonstrable drug-dependent antiplatelet antibodies may also develop; withdrawal of the drug is usually followed by recovery of the platelet count. Soon after the introduction of streptomycin in 1945, a number of reports appeared in the literature describing the development of invariably fatal aplastic anaemia following its administration (as the sole therapeutic agent) to TB patients.

Though the evidence was mainly circumstantial, it would seem that marrow hypoplasia may occur, probably as an idiosyncrasy during streptomycin therapy. More recently this tuberculocidal drug was one of a combination of anti-TB drugs which caused fatal marrow aplasia in three Nigerian patients (Williams et al, 1982). However, its aetiological role in these cases seems unclear. Selective depression of platelet production (hypomegakaryocytic thrombocytopenia) may occasionally complicate streptomycin therapy.

Para-aminosalicylic acid (PAS)

Most of the more important side-effects of PAS therapy are related to the gastrointestinal tract. Blood disorders include eosinophilia, which may be accompanied by pulmonary infiltration (Loeffler's syndrome), leukaemoid reactions, agranulocytosis, thrombocytopenia and haemolytic anaemia. The haemolytic anaemia may be caused by PAS degradation products (toxic) or by drug-dependent complement-fixing antibodies (immune). Immune haemolysis may be of such intensity as to precipitate severe renal dysfunction (MacGibbon et al, 1960). Intravenous PAS may also cause haemolysis, during which PAS-specific agglutinating antibodies with a negative direct antiglobulin test are detected. This pattern of immune haemolysis has not been observed with oral preparations. Fatal haemolysis with methaemoglobinaemia and Heinz body formation may follow the administration of oral PAS solutions which have been standing for prolonged periods in hot moist weather, and is caused by toxic decarboxylation products. This complication is not observed with the use of stable oral resin preparations. Though this drug is an oxidant, its potential for inducing haemolysis in red cell G6PD deficiency states is doubtful. It interferes selectively with ileal absorption of cobalamin, resulting in low serum cobalamin levels; this decrease is proportional to the duration of therapy (Heinivaara and Palva, 1965; Toskes and Deren, 1972). PAS-induced megaloblastic anaemia is, however, an extremely uncommon event. Reversible agranulocytosis, isolated neutropenia and immune thrombocytopenia are other uncommon side-effects. It is interesting to note that an IgG circulating antibody to a glycine-conjugated metabolic product of PAS, but not to the drug itself, was reported to cause immune thrombocytopenia in a TB patient.

Isonicotinic acid hydrazide (INAH)

This drug occasionally causes a drug-dependent Coombs' positive haemolytic anaemia (Robinson and Foadi, 1969). Immune haemolysis with marrow erythroblastopenia (pure red cell aplasia) has been described, but pure red cell aplasia may also complicate INAH treatment in the absence of haemolysis. About 20% of patients treated with INAH for prolonged periods develop antinuclear antibody (ANA) with evidence of various immune cytopenias and LE cells in the peripheral blood. These patients do not show any of the clinical features of systemic lupus erythematosus. Cytopenias are reversed and ANA disappears on drug withdrawal. When administered with streptomycin and thiacetazone, INAH may contribute to the development of marrow hypoplasia (Williams et al, 1982). Sideroblastic anaemia is probably the most important disorder of haemopoiesis in patients receiving INAH. It tends to occur 4–40 weeks after the start of therapy, especially in patients with a pre-existing haematological abnormality. The mean corpuscular haemoglobin (MCH) and mean corpuscular volume (MCV) are in general low, and the morphology of the peripheral smear shows a dimorphic pattern comprising predominantly hypochromic microcytic red cells and a smaller population of normochromic normocytic or macrocytic red cells (Bottomley, 1982). Basophilic stippling and Pappenheimer bodies may also be seen in the blood film. Neutropenia and/or thrombocytopenia may complicate the sideroblastic process in some patients. The bone marrow is moderately cellular or hypercellular with erythroid hyperplasia which affects primarily the early basophilic erythroblasts. Erythroid maturation is essentially normoblastic with many ringed sideroblasts but a variable number of frank or transitional megaloblasts may be observed. Withdrawal of INAH, with or without pyridoxine administration, reverses the pathological process (McCurdy and Donohoe, 1966), though in some individuals the morphological abnormality of the red cells persists. Addition of folic acid may improve the blood counts in a proportion of those with megaloblastic erythropoiesis. When INAH is combined with cycloserine, folate deficiency may develop (Klipstein et al, 1967).

Rifampicin

Antibody-mediated haemolytic anaemia and thrombocytopenia may complicate rifampicin therapy occasionally. These reactions are more likely to occur with relatively high dose, irregular or intermittent therapy (Blajchman et al, 1970; Poole et al, 1971; Lakshminarayan et al, 1973). Intravascular haemolysis may be mild, and accompanied by a pyrexial flu-like syndrome, or it may be massive, with acute renal failure. Complement-fixing rifampicin-dependent red cell and antiplatelet antibodies are responsible for the immune haemolysis and immune thrombocytopenia (Blajchman et al, 1970; Lakshminarayan et al, 1973). The drug-dependent red cell antibodies may also be demonstrable in the absence of haemolysis. Other infrequent complications (Holdiness, 1987) are shown in Figure 5.

Pyrazinoic acid amide (pyrazinamide)

This drug may cause a sideroblastic anaemia similar in all respects to that induced by INAH. Many of the cases reported have occurred when pyrazinamide was administered in combination with other anti-TB drugs but its withdrawal resulted in correction of the sideroblastic anaemia. Other rare effects are included in Figure 5.

Thiacetazone

Several studies have revealed, with varying frequency, the occurrence of haemolytic anaemia, agranulocytosis, thrombocytopenia, pure red cell aplasia and fatal aplastic anaemia (Holdiness, 1987). Overall incidence of these reactions is probably quite low, particularly if it is borne in mind that this cheap, effective drug is one of the more widely used anti-TB chemotherapeutic agents in developing countries.

Cycloserine

This drug acts synergistically with INAH and pyrazinamide producing a pyridoxine-responsive sideroblastic anaemia. Folate-deficient megaloblastic anaemia may develop occasionally especially when cycloserine is administered in combination with INAH (Klipstein et al, 1967).

Other anti-TB drugs

Asymptomatic eosinophilia is a common finding, while neutropenia occurs infrequently during capreomycin therapy. Thrombocytopenia and neutropenia have been reported rarely in patients receiving ethambutol. Ethionamide is virtually free of haematological effects; no data are available so far on viomycin and kanamycin which are used infrequently for resistant cases.

MANAGEMENT, PREVENTION AND CONTROL

Effective management of disturbances of the haemopoietic system caused by or associated with TB comprises the following steps: (1) specific anti-TB chemotherapy, (2) specific treatment of any underlying blood dyscrasia, (3) specific treatment of other concomitant disorders such as HIV disease, malnutrition and haematinic deficiencies, and (4) supportive therapy which includes blood transfusion. The majority of patients in low-risk countries are usually not severely anaemic at presentation, unlike the situation in high-risk countries where a significant proportion of patients present with advanced disease and severe anaemia (Hb < 0.93 mmol/l, 60 g/l). For such patients, packed red cell transfusion is urgently indicated to prevent anaemic heart failure. In these countries TB is one of the most common causes of anaemia in adult males and non-pregnant females. It is probably also the most common underlying disease which requires blood transfusion for the management of associated anaemia in parts of southern Africa (A. F. Fleming, personal communication). Unfortunately, in regions with limited or no HIV antibody testing facilities, red cell transfusion could act as a vehicle for transmission of HIV infection. The post-transfused, HIV-seropositive TB patient then becomes considerably more dangerous as an agent for passing on his tubercle bacilli (Standaert et al, 1989).

   The proper prevention and control of TB and HIV infection, which are beyond the scope of this review, will avert the anaemia and other blood disorders caused by these interacting conditions. TB chemotherapy and BCG immunization are some of the most cost effective public health measures available to poor countries (Murray, 1990). The current frightening increase in the annual risk of infection in high prevalence areas, coupled with cost-effectiveness of available interventional strategies, should make the control and possible eradication of tuberculosis a health priority at national and international levels.

Acknowledgements

I wish to express my thanks to Professor B. Onadeko and Dr K. Twum-Danso for their helpful suggestions.

REFERENCES

Ahme E, Fleming AF, Oduloju D & Pasa Y (1977) The erythrocyte sedimentation rate (ESR) in male patients and symptom-free blood donors at Zaria and Kaduna. *Nigerian Medical Journal* **7**: 426–428.

Al-Freihi HM, Al-Mohaya SA, Ibrahim EM, Al-Idrissi HY & Baris I (1987) Extrapulmonary tuberculosis: diverse manifestations and diagnosis challenge. *East African Medical Journal* **64**: 295–301.

Bagby GC & Gilbert DN (1981) Suppression of granulopoiesis by T-lymphocytes in two patients with disseminated mycobacterial infection. *Annals of Internal Medicine* **94**: 478–481.

Baynes RD, Flax H, Bothwell TH et al (1986a) Haematological and iron-related measurements in active pulmonary tuberculosis. *Scandinavian Journal of Haematology* **36**: 280–287.

Baynes RD, Flax H, Bothwell TH et al (1986b) Red blood cell distribution width in the anemia secondary to tuberculosis. *American Journal of Clinical Pathology* **85**: 226–229.

Baynes RD, Bothwell TH, Flax H et al (1987) Reactive thrombocytosis in pulmonary tuberculosis. *Journal of Clinical Pathology* **40**: 676–679.

Bhaskaram P & Sundaramma MN (1990) Peripheral blood monocyte function in malnourished subjects with pulmonary tuberculosis. *European Journal of Clinical Nutrition* **44**: 245–248.

Blajchman MA, Lowry RC, Pettit JE & Stradling P (1970) Rifampicin-induced immune thrombocytopenia. *British Medical Journal* **3**: 24–26.

Bottomley SS (1982) Sideroblastic anaemia. *Clinics in Haematology* **11**: 389–409.

Browett PJ, Varcoe AR, Fraser AG & Ellis-Pegler RB (1988) Disseminated tuberculosis complicated by the hemophagocytic syndrome. *Australian and New Zealand Journal of Medicine* **18**: 79–80.

Cameron SJ (1974) Tuberculosis and the blood—a special relationship? *Tubercle* **55**: 55–72.

Cameron SJ & Horne NW (1971) The effect of tuberculosis and its treatment on erythropoiesis and folate activity. *Tubercle* **52**: 37–48.

Cathebras P, Vohito JA, Yete ML et al (1988) HIV infection among patients with tuberculosis in Bangui (Central African Republic): a prospective study. XIIth International Congress for Tropical Medicine and Malaria. *International Congress Series* **810**: 66.

Centers for Disease Control (1990) Tuberculosis elimination: update. *Weekly Epidemiological Record* no. 46 (16 November 1990), 358–360; based on *Morbidity and Mortality Weekly Report* (**1990**) 39, no. 10.

Chanarin I & Stephenson E (1988) Vegetarian diet and cobalamin deficiency: their association with tuberculosis. *Journal of Clinical Pathology* **41**: 759–762.

Chandra P, Chaudhery SA, Rosner F & Kagen M (1975) Transient histiocytosis with striking phagocytosis of platelets, leukocytes and erythrocytes. *Archives of Internal Medicine* **135**: 989–991.

Coburn RJ, England JM, Samson DM et al (1973) Tuberculosis and blood disorders. *British Journal of Haematology* **25**: 793–799.

Colebunders RL, Karahunga C, Ryder R et al (1988) Seroprevalence of HIV-1 antibody among tuberculosis patients in Zaire, 1985–1987. XIIth International Congress for Tropical Medicine and Malaria. *International Congress Series* **810**: 222.

Collins FM (1989) Mycobacterial disease, immunosuppression and acquired immunodeficienc syndrome. *Clinical Microbiology Reviews* **2:** 360–377.

Corr WP, Kyle RA & Bowie EJW (1964) Hematologic changes in tuberculosis. *America Journal of the Medical Sciences* **248:** 709–714.

Corrah T, Hughes A, Tang C et al (1988) HIV infections in West Africa: a clinico-epidemiologi study. *Abstracts of the Fourth International Conference on AIDS* (Stockholm) **1:** 316.

Edwards D & Kirkpatrick CH (1986) The immunology of mycobacterial diseases. *America Review of Respiratory Disease* **134:** 1062–1071.

Fleming AF (1990) Opportunistic infections in AIDS in developed and developing countries *Transactions of the Royal Society of Tropical Medicine and Hygiene* **84** (supplement 1) 1–6.

Fleming AF, Ogunfunmilade YA & Carmel R (1978) Serum vitamin B_{12} levels and vitami B_{12}-binding proteins of serum and saliva of healthy Nigerians and Europeans. *America Journal of Clinical Nutrition* **31:** 1732–1738.

Francis TI (1972) Abdominal tuberculosis in Nigerians: a clinico-pathological study. *Tropica and Geographical Medicine* **24:** 232–239.

Glasser RM, Walker RI & Herion JC (1970) The significance of hematologic abnormalities i patients with tuberculosis. *Archives of Internal Medicine* **125:** 691–695.

Harkness J (1971) The viscosity of human blood plasma; its measurement in health and disease *Biorheology* **8:** 171–193.

Heinivaara O & Palva IP (1965) Malabsorption and deficiency of vitamin B_{12} caused b treatment with para-aminosalicylic acid. *Acta Medica Scandinavica* **177:** 337–341.

Henderson A (1984) Ferritin levels in patients with microcytic anaemia complicating pulmonar tuberculosis. *Tubercle* **65:** 185–189.

Hift W (1966) The vitamin-B_{12} binding capacity in health and disease. *South African Medica Journal* **40:** 437–441.

Hochberg MC, Arnold CM, Hogans BB & Spivak JL (1988) Serum immunoreactive erythro poietin in rheumatoid arthritis: impaired response to anemia. *Arthritis and Rheumatisi* **31:** 1318–1321.

Holdiness MR (1987) A review of blood dyscrasias induced by the antituberculosis drugs *Tubercle* **68:** 301–309.

Holland HK & Spivak JL (1990) The haematological manifestations of acquired immun deficiency syndrome. *Clinical Haematology* **3:** 103–114.

Hunt BJ, Andrews V & Pettingale KW (1987) The significance of pancytopenia in miliar tuberculosis. *Postgraduate Medical Journal* **63:** 801–804.

Jain RC (1970) ABO blood groups and pulmonary tuberculosis. *Tubercle* **51:** 322–323.

Katzen H & Spagnolo SV (1980) Bone marrow necrosis from miliary tuberculosis. *Journal o the American Medical Association* **244:** 2438–2439.

Kindler V, Sappino AP, Grau GE, Piguet PF & Vassalli P (1989) The inducing role of tumo necrosis factor in the development of bactericidal granulomas during BCG infection. *Cel* **56:** 731–740.

Klipstein FA, Berlinger FG & Reed LJ (1967) Folate deficiency associated with drug therap for tuberculosis. *Blood* **29:** 697–712.

Knox-Macaulay HHM (1989) Folate status in tuberculosis: a study in the guinea savanna o Nigeria. *European Journal of Clinical Nutrition* **43:** 411–420.

Knox-Macaulay HHM (1990) Serum cobalamin concentration in tuberculosis. *Tropical an Geographical Medicine* **42:** 146–150.

Koch R (1882) The aetiology of tuberculosis: translation (of paper read before the Physio logical Society in Berlin, March 24, 1882 and from the *Berliner Klinische Wochenschrif* (1882) **19:** 221) by Pinner B & Pinner M (1982) *Bulletin of the International Union agains Tuberculosis* **56:** 87–100.

Kochi A (1990) WHO's role for tuberculosis control in the world. *Bulletin of the Internationa Union against Tuberculosis and Lung Disease* **65:** 94.

Kool HEJ, Bloemkolk D, Reeve PA & Danner SA (1990) HIV seropositivity and tuberculosi in a large general hospital in Malawi. *Tropical and Geographical Medicine* **42:** 128–132.

Lakshminarayan S, Sahn SA & Hudson LD (1973) Massive haemolysis caused by rifampicin *British Medical Journal* **2:** 282–283.

Lee GR (1983) The anemia of chronic disease. *Seminars in Hematology* **20:** 61–80.

Letona JM-L, Barbolla L, Frieyro E et al (1977) Immune haemolytic anaemia and renal failure induced by streptomycin. *British Journal of Haematology* **35:** 561–571.

Lewis EA & Abioye AA (1975) Tuberculosis of the abdomen in Ibadan: a clinicopathological review. *Tubercle* **56:** 149–155.

Line DH, Seitanidis B, Morgan JO & Hoffbrand AV (1971) The effects of chemotherapy on iron, folate and vitamin B_{12} metabolism in tuberculosis. *Quarterly Journal of Medicine* **40:** 331–340.

Lowther CP (1959) Leukemia and tuberculosis. *Annals of Internal Medicine* **51:** 52–56.

McCurdy PR & Donohoe RF (1966) Pyridoxine-responsive anaemia conditioned by isonicotinic acid hydrazide. *Blood* **27:** 352–362.

MacGibbon BH, Loughridge LW, Hourihane DO'B & Boyd DW (1960) Autoimmune haemolytic anaemia with acute renal failure due to phenacetin and *p*-amino-salicylic acid. *Lancet* **i:** 7–10.

Mangion PD & Schiller KF (1971) Disseminated tuberculosis complicated by pancytopenia. *Proceedings of the Royal Society of Medicine* **64:** 1000.

Mann JM & Chin J (1988) AIDS: A global perspective. *New England Journal of Medicine* **319:** 302–303.

Mann JM, Francis H, Quinn TC et al (1986a) HIV seroprevalence among hospital workers in Kinshasa, Zaire. *Journal of the American Medical Association* **256:** 3099–3102.

Mann J, Snider DE, Francis H et al (1986b) Association between HTLV-III/LAV infection and tuberculosis in Zaire. *Journal of the American Medical Association* **256:** 346.

Mann JM, Chin J, Piot P & Quinn T (1988) The international epidemiology of AIDS. *Scientific American* **8:** 82–89.

Manzella JP, Kellogg J & Sanstead JK (1985) Mycobacterium tuberculosis bacteremia and disseminated coagulation. *Journal of the American Medical Association* **254:** 2741.

Marie JP, Degos L & Flandrin G (1977) Hairy-cell leukemia and tuberculosis. *New England Journal of Medicine* **297:** 1354.

Mbolidi CD, Cathebras P & Vohito MD (1988) Parallel increase in the prevalence of pulmonary tuberculosis and infection with HIV in Bangui. *Presse Médicale* **17:** 872–873.

Meeran K (1989) Prevalence of HIV infection among patients with leprosy and tuberculosis in rural Zambia. *British Medical Journal* **298:** 364–365.

Modilevsky T, Sattler FR & Barnes PF (1989) Mycobacterial disease in patients with human immunodeficiency virus infection. *Archives of Internal Medicine* **149:** 2201–2205.

Moldawer LL, Marano MA, Wei H, Fong Y & Silen ML (1989) Cachectin/tumor necrosis factor-α alters red blood cell kinetics and induces anemia in vivo. *FASEB Journal* **3:** 1637–1643.

Moreno C, Taverne J, Mehlert A et al (1989) Lipoarabinomannan from *Mycobacterium tuberculosis* induces the production of tumour necrosis factor from human and murine macrophages. *Clinical and Experimental Immunology* **76:** 240–245.

Morrow LB & Anderson RE (1965) Active tuberculosis in leukemia, malignant lymphoma and myelofibrosis. *Archives of Pathology* **79:** 484–493.

Murray CJL (1990) World tuberculosis burden. *Lancet* **335:** 1043–1044.

Murray CJL & Feachem RG (1990) Adult mortality in the developing world. *Transactions of the Royal Society of Tropical Medicine and Hygiene* **84:** 21–22.

Murray CJL, Styblo K & Rouillon A (1990) Tuberculosis in developing countries: burden, intervention and cost. *Bulletin of the International Union against Tuberculosis and Lung Disease* **65:** 6–24.

Murray HW (1978) Transient autoimmune hemolytic anemia and pulmonary tuberculosis. *New England Journal of Medicine* **299:** 488.

Nachman R, Javid J & Krauss S (1962) Streptomycin-induced hemolytic anemia. *Archives of Internal Medicine* **110:** 187–190.

Oluboyede OA & Onadeko BO (1978) Observation on haematological patterns in pulmonary tuberculosis in Nigerians. *Journal of Tropical Medicine and Hygiene* **81:** 91–95.

Pitchenik AE & Fischl MA (1983) Disseminated tuberculosis and the acquired immunodeficiency syndrome. *Annals of Internal Medicine* **98:** 112.

Pitchenik AE, Fertel D & Bloch AB (1988) Mycobacterial disease: epidemiology, diagnosis, treatment and prevention. *Clinics in Chest Medicine* **9:** 425–441.

Poole G, Stradling P & Worlledge S (1971) Potentially serious side effects of high-dose twice-weekly rifampicin. *British Medical Journal* **3:** 343–347.

Proudfoot AT (1971) Cryptic disseminated tuberculosis. *British Journal of Hospital Medicine* 5: 773–780.

Rieder HL, Cauthen GM, Kelly GD, Bloch AB & Snider DE (1989) Tuberculosis in the United States. *Journal of the American Medical Association* 262: 385–389.

Robinson MG & Foadi M (1969) Hemolytic anemia with positive Coombs' test: association with isoniazid therapy. *Journal of the American Medical Association* 208: 656–658.

Rook GAW, Al Attiyah R & Foley N (1989) The role of cytokines in the immunopathology o tuberculosis and the regulation of agalactosyl IgG. *Lymphokine Research* 8: 323–328.

Sears DA (1978) The morbidity of sickle cell trait. *American Journal of Medicine* 64: 1021–1036.

Shafer RW, Goldberg R, Sierra M & Glatt AE (1989) Frequency of *Mycobacterium tuberculosis* bacteremia in patients with tuberculosis in an area endemic for AIDS. *American Review o Respiratory Disease* 140: 1611–1613.

Silva CL & Faccioli LH (1988) Tumor necrosis factor (cachectin) mediates induction o cachexia by cord factor from mycobacteria. *Infection and Immunity* 56: 3067–3071.

Silva CL, Faccioli LH & Rocha GM (1988) The role of cachectin/TNF in the pathogenesis o tuberculosis. *Brazilian Journal of Medical and Biological Research* 21: 489–492.

Singh MM, Bhargava AN & Jain KP (1969) Tuberculous peritonitis. *New England Journal o Medicine* 281: 1091–1094.

Slutkin G, Leowski J & Mann J (1988a) Tuberculosis and AIDS. The effects of the AIDS epidemic on the tuberculosis problem and tuberculosis programmes. *Bulletin of the International Union against Tuberculosis and Lung Disease* 63: 21–24.

Slutkin G, Schecter GF & Hopewell PC (1988b) The results of 9-month isoniazid–rifampir therapy for pulmonary tuberculosis under program conditions in San Francisco. *American Review of Respiratory Disease* 138: 1622–1624.

Small PM, Schecter GF, Goodman PC et al (1991) Treatment of tuberculosis in patients with advanced human immunodeficiency virus infection. *New England Journal of Medicine* 324: 289–294.

Standaert B, Niragira F, Kadende P & Piot P (1989) The association of tuberculosis and HIV infection in Burundi. *AIDS Research and Human Retroviruses* 5: 247–251.

Stead WW, Lofgren JP, Warren E & Thomas C (1985) Tuberculosis as an epidemic and nosocomial infection among the elderly in nursing homes. *New England Journal o Medicine* 312: 1483–1487.

Strauss RG (1978) Iron deficiency, infections and immune function: a reassessment. *American Journal of Clinical Nutrition* 31: 660–666.

Styblo K (1988) The potential impact of AIDS on the tuberculosis situation in developed and developing countries. *Bulletin of the International Union against Tuberculosis and Lung Diseases* 63: 25–28.

Styblo K (1989) Overview and epidemiologic assessment of the current global tuberculosis situation with an emphasis on control in developing countries. *Reviews of Infectious Diseases* 11 (supplement 2): S339–S346.

Sunderam G, McDonald RJ, Maniatis T et al (1986) Tuberculosis as a manifestation of the acquired immunodeficiency syndrome (AIDS). *Journal of the American Medical Association* 256: 362–366.

Sutherland I, Springett VH & Nunn AJ (1984) Changes in tuberculosis notification rates in ethnic groups in England between 1971 and 1978/9. *Tubercle* 65: 83–91.

Toskes PP & Deren JJ (1972) Selective inhibition of vitamin B_{12} absorption by para-aminosalicylic acid. *Gastroenterology* 62: 1232–1237.

Tracey KJ, Wei H, Manogue KR, Hesse DG & Nguyen HT (1988) Cachectin/tumor necrosis factor induces cachexia, anemia and inflammation. *Journal of Experimental Medicine* 167: 1211–1227.

Twomey JJ & Leavell BS (1965) Leukemoid reactions to tuberculosis. *Archives of Internal Medicine* 116: 21–28.

Wallis RS, Amir-Tahmasseb M & Ellner JJ (1990) Induction of interleukin 1 and tumor necrosis factor by mycobacterial proteins: the monocyte western blot. *Proceedings of the National Academy of Sciences of the USA* 87: 3348–3352.

Ward HP, Kurnick JE & Pisarczyk MJ (1971) Serum level of erythropoietin in anemias associated with chronic infection, malignancy and primary hematopoietic disease. *Journal of Clinical Investigation* 53: 1132–1138.

Weintraub M, Siegman-Ingra Y, Josiphov J, Rahmani R & Liron M (1984) Histiocytic hemophagocytosis in miliary tuberculosis. *Archives of Internal Medicine* **144:** 2055–2056.

Williame JC, Nkoko B, Pauwels P et al (1988) Tuberculose et sero-positive anti VIHA, Kinshasa, Zaire. *Annales de la Société Belge de Médecine Tropicale* **68:** 165–167.

Williams CKO, Aderoju EA, Adenle AD, Sekoni G & Esan GJF (1982) Aplastic anaemia associated with antituberculosis chemotherapy. *Acta Haematologica* **68:** 329–339.

Zucker S, Friedman S & Lysik RM (1974) Bone marrow erythropoiesis in the anemia of infection, inflammation and malignancy. *Journal of Clinical Investigation* **53:** 1132–1138.

6

Neonatal jaundice in Asia

NAI KIONG HO

DEFINITION

Neonatal jaundice is a clinically recognizable condition of the newborn, with yellow discoloration of the skin, sclera and other organs as a result of an accumulation of bilirubin. Jaundice becomes apparent at serum bilirubin levels of approximately 85–120 μmol/l (5–7 mg/dl) (Maisels, 1987). If the reference plasma bilirubin range in the human adult is taken as normal (5–17 μmol/l or 0.3–1.0 mg/dl), almost all babies in the neonatal period have levels exceeding such values and could therefore be considered abnormal.

There is no consensus on the definition of neonatal hyperbilirubinaemia. Turkel (1990) from the USA mentioned that hyperbilirubinaemia can usually be recognized clinically as 'jaundice', even without biochemical determination of elevated bilirubin levels. Also in the USA, Maisels (1987) indicated a bilirubin level of more than 222 μmol/l (13 mg/dl) as hyperbilirubinaemia. In Australia, Palmar and Drew (1983) defined it as a total serum bilirubin of 154 μmol/l (9 mg/dl) or more. In India, Menon and Mohapatra (1987) diagnosed hyperbilirubinaemia when a newborn had a bilirubin level exceeding 140 μmol/l (8 mg/dl). Lee et al (1970) in Hong Kong defined neonatal jaundice as a total bilirubin of 255 μmol/l (15 mg/dl) or more. Later in Hong Kong, hyperbilirubinaemia was arbitrarily divided into: (1) minimal: serum bilirubin level of 120 μmol/l (7 mg/dl) or less; (2) mild: 120–204 μmol/l (7–12 mg/dl); and (3) moderate/severe: 204 μmol/l (12 mg/dl) or more (Fok et al, 1986). Similarly, in Beijing, China, it was minimal (204–255 μmol/l or 12–15 mg/dl), moderate (306–340 μmol/l or 18–20 mg/dl) and severe (513–855 μmol/l or 30–50 mg/dl) (Huang and Wang, 1989).

In Singapore, we considered a serum bilirubin of 255 μmol/l (15 mg/dl) or more as hyperbilirubinaemia (Tan, 1981; Ho et al, 1988). In the past, before there were sufficient phototherapy units, we initiated close observation and treatment of jaundiced neonates when they reached this level.

It is felt that knowledge of the incidence of neonatal jaundice (both physiological and pathological) has less significance in clinical practice than that of the incidence of hyperbilirubinaemia. We should first agree on an acceptable definition. Hyperbilirubinaemia should be the clinical stage when neonatal jaundice is considered pathological rather than physiological, and is the bilirubin level beyond which babies might develop kernicterus without intervention. Since criteria for intervention vary in different clinical situations, one expects to see different definitions of hyperbilirubinaemia in different groups of babies, for example low birthweight infants or infants with early onset of neonatal jaundice. Ideally, one should compare the trends of hyperbilirubinaemia in babies with ABO incompatibility, glucose-6-phosphate dehydrogenase (G6PD) deficiency, infections, prematurity and other causes.

INCIDENCE

With such varied definitions of neonatal jaundice and hyperbilirubinaemia, it is difficult to compare the magnitude of the problem in neonatal units from different regions or areas.

In the United States, the National Collaborative Perinatal Project (Hardy et al, 1979) revealed that 6.2% of infants weighing more than 2500 g had serum bilirubin concentrations exceeding 220 μmol/l (12.9 mg/dl), and Maisels (1987) found 6% of 2297 babies (2500 g or more) had serum bilirubin concentration higher than 220 μmol/l (12.9 mg/dl). Data based on 12 587 babies (2500 g or more), born in Singapore from 1986 to 1989 (Ho, 1991), showed a frequency of this degree of neonatal jaundice of only 4.6%; Asian full-term babies are smaller in size but, if normal birth weight is defined as more than 2270 g, still only 5.2% had bilirubin concentrations in this range. We postulate that since we have been able to treat our babies early following acquisition of more phototherapy units and the adoption of a more liberal policy to institute treatment for milder jaundiced infants, we have reduced the incidence of severe jaundice.

In Hong Kong, from 1966 to 1969, 2687 (12.1%) of 22 122 newborn babies had serum bilirubin levels of 255 μmol/l (15 mg/dl) or more (Lee et al, 1970) when exchange transfusion was the only available method of treatment. During the period 1982–1985, 3.23% of all Singapore newborn infants also had serum bilirubin levels of 225 μmol/l (15 mg/dl) or more, but from 1986 to 1989 the prevalence was only 2.11%, a reduction attributed to early intervention and phototherapy (Ho, 1991).

When babies who have phototherapy are considered as the number of cases of neonatal jaundice, the reported frequency of neonatal jaundice rises if phototherapy is used more liberally for babies with minimal jaundice. For example, 7.9% of all babies born in the Toa Payoh Hospital, Singapore between 1982 and 1985 had neonatal jaundice, and the incidence rose to 10% for 1986–1989 although there were fewer hyperbilirubinaemic babies (serum bilirubin of 255 μmol/l (15 mg/dl) or more).

Ethnic group difference

Neonatal jaundice is prevalent in Asia (Gartner and Lee, 1983), especially in south-east Asia. Almost a quarter of a century ago, Brown and Wong (1965) documented that Chinese newborns are more prone than others to neonatal jaundice. This is also true for Taiwan Chinese (Lu et al, 1963) and

Hong Kong Chinese babies (Lee et al, 1970). Other Asian ethnic groups, including Malays, Indians and Japanese, are also prone to neonatal jaundice (Horiguchi and Bauer, 1975).

Asian newborn infants have higher peak serum bilirubin levels. They could have a different genetic expression in bilirubin metabolism. Fok et al (1986) showed that there was an association between hyperbilirubinaemia in newborn babies and a similar history in their elder siblings, and strongly suggested the presence of a genetically determined tendency towards development of neonatal jaundice. How much influence environmental factors exert is not completely understood.

AETIOLOGIES

Among the known causes of neonatal jaundice in Asian newborn infants are ABO incompatibility, G6PD deficiency, low birth weight and sepsis. The Rhesus (Rh) negative genotype occurs in less than 1% of the population so that Rh incompatibility is uncommon, although it is slightly more common in babies of Indian origin. We have encountered 32 cases of Rh incompatibility from 1982 to 1989, half of them were Indians and only 22% were hyper-bilirubinaemic (serum bilirubin > 255 μmol/l or 15 mg/dl).

ABO incompatibility

Infants with group A or B red blood cells may develop haemolysis and jaundice with a positive Coombs' test because of the transfer of maternal immune IgG anti-A or anti-B antibodies into the fetal circulation. In Asia, between 10 and 20% of jaundiced babies have ABO incompatibility (Table 1). The Australian experience was 7.1% (Palmar and Drew, 1983). When compared with Rh incompatibility, the jaundice is usually mild and characteristically late in onset, and associated anaemia rarely occurs.

Table 1. Neonatal jaundice due to ABO incompatibility.

Country	Percentage among cases of jaundice	References
China, Beijing	20	Huang and Wang (1989)
Hong Kong	15.6	Lee et al (1970)
	12.5	Fok et al (1986)
Singapore	16.6	Ho et al (1988)
	15.9	Ho (1991)
India, New Delhi	12.2	Madan and Sood (1987)
India, Bombay	38.2	Madan and Sood (1987)

Asian ABO incompatible infants are different from Australian infants. In Australia, 77.1% infants have blood group A and about 22.9% blood group B, whereas in Singapore it was 56.2% and 43.8% respectively (Han et al, 1988). In our study of all babies jaundiced due to ABO incompatibility, we encountered 37.5% A–O and 62.5% B–O combinations in 1986–1989.

Group A (especially A_1) infants are reported to be more antigenic (Oski and Naimen, 1982), but we have not been able to see significantly more hyper-bilirubinaemic infants belonging to the A–O combination; in our 1982–1985 (Ho et al, 1988) and 1986–1989 series (Ho, 1991), we saw more with the B–O combination, 58.4% and 62.5% respectively.

ABO incompatibility is not synonymous with ABO haemolytic disease (ABO-HD), nor does the presence of immune anti-A or anti-B antibodies in the mother's serum mean that haemolysis will take place. The Coombs', or direct antiglobulin test (DAT), and the elution test are not specific for ABO-HD because positive results occur frequently in infants who are not affected with the disease. However, Toy et al (1988) considered the DAT to be the best laboratory predictor of severity of ABO-HD. Menon and Mohapatra (1987) found the quantitative estimate of spherocytes a good predictor of ABO incompatibility, whereas the direct Coombs' test was a better predictor of severe haemolytic disease. However, Quinn et al (1988) mentioned that, in the individual case, Coombs' positivity and/or a strong positive elution test may be a helpful predictor of jaundice, but not of its severity. Brouwers et al (1988) suggested that the combination of the antibody-dependent cell-mediated cytotoxicity (ADCC) assay with the density of A or B antigens on cells provides a good screening test for ABO incompatibility. Unfortunately these tests are not widely available.

From the clinical point of view, it would be useful to be able to predict the occurrence of haemolytic disease in ABO incompatible infants as well as the severity of neonatal jaundice, since babies are often discharged early because of shortage of hospital beds. In practice, babies who are known to be ABO incompatible with the mother should be under close surveillance, so that those with moderately severe jaundice can be readmitted to the paediatric unit. Singapore has a very well-organized primary health care service and all newborn babies discharged from hospital are seen by trained and experienced primary health care nurses who can detect jaundice. Those babies who become more jaundiced are referred to hospital immediately. However, logistically it is difficult for larger countries in the Asian region to keep track of all newborn babies once they are discharged from hospital. They may live in rural areas inaccessible by ordinary road transport or live on one of the many thousands of islands. Furthermore, many babies are still delivered at home.

Glucose-6-phosphate dehydrogenase deficiency

G6PD deficiency is prevalent in south-east Asia, in particular in Indo-China, and makes a significant contribution to neonatal jaundice in this region (Table 2).

About 25 years ago many babies in Singapore developed kernicterus; nearly 50% of them had G6PD deficiency and many died (Wong, 1980). A kernicterus surveillance project was initiated in 1964 and, since then, death from this cause declined sharply. The project, strongly supported by the Government, included:

Table 2. Neonatal jaundice due to G6PD deficiency in Asia.

Country	Percentage among cases of jaundice	References
China		
Southern China (Canton or Guangdong)	4.4	Yu (1986)
Northern China (Shanghai)	0.2	Wu (1980)
(Nanjing)	0.97	Qi and Deng (1990)
South-west China (Sichuan)	4.6	Chinese Medical Science College Hospital (1980)
Hong Kong (Chinese)	3.74	Yue and Strickland (1965)
	4.4	Fok et al (1985)
India	1.0	Gupta et al (1970)
	3.5	Ahmed and Ahmad (1983)
Indonesia	3.61	Marnoto et al (1979)
Iran	8.5	Walker and Bowman (1959)
Iraq	9–15	WHO (1966)
Japan	0	Motulsky and Campbell-Kraut (1961)
Malaysia*		
West Malaysia—Chinese 3.2%	3.48	Balakrishnan and Lim (1985)
—Malay 2.3%	3.11	Singh (1986)
—Indian 1.3%		
East Malaysia	6.8	Luan Eng et al (1964)
Pakistan	2.54	Imran M (1986)
Philippines	6.6	Motulsky et al (1963)
Singapore*—Chinese 2.6%	1.5–2	Ho et al (1988); Ho (1991)
—Malay 1.35%		
—Indians 1.17%		
Taiwan (Chinese)	3.0	Motulsky et al (1965)
Thailand	6.77	Hathirat et al (1980)
	11.5	Flatz et al (1963)
	12.8	Phornphutkul et al (1969)

* Denotes more than 10 000 tests.

1. G6PD estimation on cord blood of all babies born in Singapore hospitals.
2. Keeping G6PD-deficient babies in the hospital for a minimum of 2 weeks for observation and early treatment of jaundice; hospitalization of these babies has the additional advantage of preventing contact with drugs or chemicals which can trigger severe haemolysis.
3. Education by health professionals and dissemination of information through the mass media to warn the lay public of the serious consequences of neonatal jaundice.
4. Giving all families where G6PD deficiency has been detected a letter addressed to the obstetrician who delivers the next baby so that he or she can be alerted to the possibility of severe jaundice in future babies and take preventative steps.
5. Good history taking from mothers for jaundice in previous babies, as jaundice seems to reoccur in the same family.

6. The issue of cards to parents of G6PD-deficient babies; these cards are produced at each visit to a doctor so that the prescription of potentially haemolysing drugs, listed on the cards, can be avoided.

It is gratifying to note that in Singapore we have not encountered a single case of kernicterus for more than 10 years. In Malaysia, parents of G6PD-deficient babies are given instructions to avoid herbs and drugs which trigger haemolysis (Singh, 1986), and the incidence of kernicterus has also been reduced there.

Low birth weight

Low birth weight (LBW) is usually defined as a weight of less than 2500 g but, as Asian babies tend to be smaller than others, a birth weight of 2270 g (5 lb.) has been used as the cut-off point. LBW infants are grouped into the following categories:

1. Extremely low birth weight (ELBW) infants weighing 1000 g or less at birth.
2. Very low birth weight (VLBW) infants weighing 1001–1500 g.
3. Premature infants, weighing 1501–2270 g.
4. Intrauterine growth retardation (IUGR) or small for gestational age (SGA) infants, weighing less than 2270 g at birth but considered clinically to be term or more mature than the gestational age.

Of babies in Singapore who had a peak serum bilirubin of 225 µmol/l (15 mg/dl) or more, 17% had a birth weight of less than 2500 g. The figures for Hong Kong (Lee et al, 1970) and Indonesia (Marnoto et al, 1979) were 8.9% and 21.3% respectively. The number of LBW babies who died before reaching the peak serum bilirubin level in the days before neonatal intensive care was widely available is not known.

These LBW infants are more prone to kernicterus than the full-term babies, especially when coexisting conditions such as acidosis, hypoxia, raised carbon dioxide tension, exposure to drugs or chemicals, sepsis, low albumin level and hyperosmolarity increase the likelihood of brain damage by bilirubin at lower levels (Gartner et al, 1970). Pathological staining of basal ganglia of the brain was noted in 20–25% of LBW infants who died (Ahdab-Barmada and Moosy, 1984), but it is not clear whether this was due to bilirubin entry into the brain during life, with consequent damage, or to post-mortem bilirubin staining. Surviving premature infants followed up to 2 years showed a dose–response relationship between maximal neonatal bilirubin level and risk for impaired neurodevelopmental outcome and for cerebral palsy (Van de Bor et al, 1989). In some studies bilirubin was shown to be an effective liquid-soluble antioxidant in vitro, which may have some physiologically beneficial effects. The role of bilirubin in these LBW infants is unknown and more studies are needed (McDonagh, 1990).

LBW infants require treatment of jaundice at lower serum bilirubin concentrations than do mature infants, but there is no definition of hyper-bilirubinaemia for the various groups of LBW infants. It is therefore difficult to compare the outcome in the control of neonatal jaundice in the LBW infants. In the 1982–1985 period, 268 (35%) of our LBW infants had either phototherapy or exchange transfusion; of these, 11 (4.1%) had exchange transfusion (Ho et al, 1988). This figure increased to 61% for the 1986–1989 period (Ho, 1991). Survival of more LBW babies contributes more problems in management than in the past as these babies used either to die before they developed severe jaundice or were considered too ill to receive treatment.

Infection

It is difficult to assess the contribution of infection as a single causative factor to neonatal jaundice as it may coexist with other adverse factors. This is particularly true in premature infants who are prone to infection. Many explanations are given for the development of neonatal jaundice in the infected baby, including haemolysis, cholestasis, endotoxin, fever and haem-oxygenase inducing agents (Rodgers and Stevenson, 1990).

In Beijing, China, neonatal infections (omphalitis, pneumonia, sepsis) were noted to be the cause of hyperbilirubinaemia in 53 and 59% of the newborn infants for the 1978–1980 and 1981–1983 periods respectively. With provision of neonatal care, it has declined to 33.5% (Huang and Wang, 1989). In Hong Kong 7.7% of neonatal jaundice was attributed to sepsis.

Jaundice of apparently unknown cause

There remains a group of babies whose cause of jaundice is unknown. Liver immaturity was propounded by many authors as the aetiological factor (Brown and Wong, 1965; Tan et al, 1984; Fok et al, 1986). Asian babies, in particular the Chinese, have this problem. More than half of the Hong Kong Chinese babies had no attributable cause for neonatal jaundice (Lee et al, 1970). Wong (1980) recounted that 25% of the cases of kernicteric babies were due to liver immaturity, and postulated the delay in liver conjugation of indirect bilirubin glucuronidase was most likely to be due to cultural habits such as taking of herbs and other drugs during pregnancy; his studies in 1964 revealed that about one-half of all Chinese mothers admitted to taking Chinese herbs during pregnancy. However, Fok et al (1986) did not show any significant association between herb consumption by mothers and the occurrence of hyperbilirubinaemia in their offspring, although 50% of the Hong Kong Chinese mothers also took herbs during pregnancy. Self-medication during pregnancy is also common in western countries, where 65–80% of pregnant women have been found to have such a habit, while 92–100% of expectant mothers take at least one drug prescribed by their physicians.

There are individual or ethnic variations of bilirubin elimination by neonates, the mechanisms of which are unknown. Valaes (1976) suggested that exposure to high bilirubin levels in utero could accelerate the maturation of the bilirubin conjugating mechanisms, as there was evidence that bilirubin itself is a natural endogenous inducing agent. This might explain the limited clearance of bilirubin of the newborn as a consequence of the absence in utero of an endogenous stimulus responsible for the maturation of the bilirubir elimination mechanism, and not as the inevitable result of 'liver immaturity (Valaes and Harvey-Wilkes, 1990). We do not know whether herbs or drug can interfere with such a maturation mechanism through the removal ir utero of endogenous bilirubin or other endogenous inducing agents. It is stil not known whether the presence of environmental factors or geneti predisposition, or both, contribute to the high prevalence of neonata jaundice in Chinese babies.

Chinese materia medica

Is the severity of neonatal jaundice aggravated by consumption of Chinese herbs by the pregnant mother and the newborn baby? Has Chinese materia medica any beneficial effect in the treatment and prevention of neonata jaundice? Unfortunately the study of Chinese materia medica is difficult as doctors trained in traditional medicine often prescribe a variety of herbs foι both prevention and treatment of neonatal jaundice. Furthermore, herbs contain many pharmacological substances and taking many herbs means ingesting multiple pharmacological agents. To make the study more difficult, 'western' drugs, such as phenobarbitone, and even hydrocortisone, have been used in conjunction with traditional medicines (Guan, 1986; Guan et al, 1989). As a result, it is not possible to tell whether the herbs or drugs were responsible for the 'success' of the management. Do herbs and drugs act synergistically or otherwise?

Two common herbs are popularly used in the treatment of jaundice by the Chinese: *yin chen hao* and *huang lian*. *Yin chen hao* is derived from a plant *Artemisia capillaris*, the main constituent of which is 6,7-dimethoxycoumarin. This chemical is said to cause an increase in bile flow (Jiangsu Medical College, 1977). Chen (1987) has also reported a beneficial effect of *Artemisia compositae* in preventing and treating neonatal haemolysis and hyper-bilirubinaemia. However, these plant products have been reported to cause cardiac arrhythmia and even Stokes–Adams syndrome (Bi, 1986). For many generations *huang lian*, derived from the plant *Coptis chinensis*, has been used by the Chinese for the treatment of neonatal jaundice. It contains 7–9% berberine, together with other alkaloids (Nadkarni, 1954). Berberine is said to increase bile flow, bilirubin excretion and intestinal peristalsis (Velluda et al, 1959; Jiangsu Medical College, 1977). Possibly by reducing the transit time, peristalsis decreases the amount of unconjugated bilirubin remaining in the small bowel and hence the amount which is reabsorbed. Berberine has also been found to have an antimicrobial effect and an anti-inflammatory action. Babies are usually fed one teaspoonful of *huang lian* (about 5 ml) mixed with honey 2–3 days after birth. This enhances the passage of meconium, which is excreted together with the large amount of bilirubin in it. Unfortunately the alkaloids of *huang lian* can trigger severe haemolysis in babies who are G6PD deficient, and as a result the sale of the herb is prohibited in Singapore.

Anaemia associated with jaundice

It is not our experience to see babies who have neonatal jaundice also develop severe anaemia. Haemolysis does occur, especially in G6PD-deficient infants (Tan, 1981), but anaemia is usually mild. Previous studies have shown that the mean haematocrit and mean haemoglobin levels of a group of G6PD-deficient and ABO-incompatible babies were lower, and the mean reticulocyte count was higher, compared with a control group of babies (Wong, 1983; Fok et al, 1986).

MANAGEMENT

Indications for exchange blood transfusion

Before the advent of phototherapy, exchange transfusion was administered frequently to babies with severe jaundice due to G6PD deficiency and ABO incompatibility. As a result of cord blood screening and effective phototherapy, as well as early treatment of jaundice due to G6PD deficiency, we observed a change in the pattern and incidence of the various causes of neonatal hyperbilirubinaemia which requires exchange transfusion. Severe jaundice due to G6PD deficiency was the most common indication in the 1960s; 26.3% (Hong Kong) to 34% (Singapore) of all babies who required exchange transfusion had G6PD deficiency. It is now a much less common indication: during the period 1986–1989 we performed 46 exchange transfusions but only two (4.3%) were for severe jaundice due to G6PD deficiency. There has been no significant fall in the number of babies who required exchange transfusion because, as a result of advances in neonatal intensive care, there are more premature babies who survive long enough to develop jaundice. Neonatologists are more aware of the risk of bilirubin encephalopathy and are more willing to perform exchange transfusion at lower serum bilirubin levels. Of the 46 exchange transfusions in the period 1986–1989, 18 (39%) were done for LBW infants, whereas it was only 9% during the period 1982–1985. The criteria for management of neonatal jaundice during this period are shown in Table 3. They have since been considerably revised.

Table 3. Indications for phototherapy and exchange blood transfusion in the management of neonatal jaundice, as applied in Singapore, 1986–1989.

	Start phototherapy at		Exchange transfusion at	
Weight	Normal babies	Abnormal babies	Normal babies	Abnormal babies
< 1500 g	170	136	255	221
1500–2250 g	205	170	306	290
> 2250 g	255	204	340	306

The values are for serum bilirubin in μmol/l.
Abnormal babies are those with haemolytic jaundice (ABO and Rh incompatibility, G6PD deficiency, DCT-positive), jaundice within 48 hours, severe acidosis, hypoglycaemia and uncontrolled sepsis. These guidelines have since been revised.

SUMMARY

Neonatal jaundice is a major clinical problem globally, especially in the Asian and south-east Asian regions. There is no universal definition of hyperbilirubinaemia, and comparisons of management and control of hyperbilirubinaemia in infants at different centres are difficult. G6PL deficiency, ABO incompatibility, low birth weight and sepsis are the common causes of neonatal jaundice, but there is a group of babies whose cause of neonatal jaundice has yet to be found. Genetic factors may be responsible for ethnic differences in the ability to eliminate bilirubin, while unidentified environmental factors may also play a role in the prevalence of neonatal jaundice. As a result of a surveillance programme for neonatal jaundice in Singapore, involving health education of doctors, nurses and the lay public, screening of the newborn and the early treatment of jaundice, we have not seen a single case of kernicterus in Singapore for more than 1(years.

REFERENCES

Ahdab-Barmada M & Moosy J (1984) The neuropathology of kernicterus in the premature neonate: diagnostic problems. *Journal of Neuropathology and Experimental Neurology* **43:** 45–56.

Ahmed P & Ahmad KN (1983) Screening of the newborn for glucose-6-phosphate dehydro genase deficiency. *Indian Pediatrics* **20:** 351–355.

Balakrishnan S & Lim MK (1985) G6PD screening for newborn in Hospital Sultanah Aminah Johore Bahru. *Abstracts of the 5th Asian Congress of Paediatrics*, Kuala Lumpur, 204.

Bi CS (1986) Qinghao. In Cheng HM & But PPH (eds) *Pharmacology and Applications of Chinese Materia Medica*, vol. 1, pp 685–693. Philadelphia: World Scientific Publishing.

Brouwers HAA, Overbeeke MAM, van Ertbruggen I et al (1988) What is the best predictor of the severity of ABO haemolytic disease of the newborn? *Lancet* **ii:** 641–644.

Brown WR & Wong HB (1965) Ethnic group differences in plasma bilirubin levels of full-term healthy Singapore newborns. *Pediatrics* **36:** 745–651.

Chen HY (1987) Artemisia composita for the prevention and treatment of neonatal hemolysis and hyperbilirubinemia. *Journal of Traditional Chinese Medicine* **7(2):** 105–108.

Chinese Medical Science College Hospital—Hematology Unit (1980) A study of glucose-6-phosphate dehydrogenase deficiency and abnormal haemoglobin in Jian-yang region. Sichuan Province. *Chinese Journal of Hematology* **1:** 95 (in the Chinese language).

Flatz G, Sringam S & Kokris V (1963) Neonatal jaundice in glucose-6-phosphate dehydrogenase deficiency. *Lancet* **i:** 1382–1383.

Fok TF, Lau SP & Fung KP (1985) Cord blood G6PD activity by quantitative enzyme assay and fluorescent spot test in Chinese neonates. *Australian Paediatric Journal* **21:** 23–25.

Fok TF, Lau SP & Hui CW (1986) Neonatal jaundice: its prevalence in Chinese babies and associating factors. *Australian Paediatric Journal* **22:** 215–219.

Gartner LM & Lee KS (1983) Jaundice and liver disease. In Fanaroff AA & Martin RJ (eds) *Behrman's Neonatal-Perinatal Medicine, Diseases of the Fetus and Infant*, p 758. St Louis: CV Mosby.

Gartner LM, Snyder RN, Chabon RS et al (1970) Kernicterus: high incidence in premature infants with low serum bilirubin concentrations. *Pediatrics* **45:** 906–917.

Guan XJ (1986) Prenatal prevention of hyperbilirubinemia in erythrocyte glucose-6-phosphate dehydrogenase deficiency in neonates. *Abstracts of Scientific Presentation XVIII International Congress of Pediatrics*, Honolulu, Hawaii, No. 500.

Guan XJ, Yu SJ & Chen XT (1989) Study of prevention and treatment of glucose-6-phosphate dehydrogenase deficiency of the neonates erythrocytes in perinatal period. *Chinese Journal of Pediatrics* **1:** 58 (abstract).

Gupta S, Ghai OP & Chandra RK (1970) Glucose-6-phosphate dehydrogenase deficiency in the newborn and its relation to serum bilirubin. *Indian Journal of Pediatrics* 37: 169–175.

Han P, Kiruba R, Ong R et al (1988) Haemolytic disease due to ABO incompatibility: Incidence and value of screening in an Asian population. *Australian Paediatric Journal* 24: 35–38.

Hardy JB, Drage JS & Jackson EC (1979) The first year of life. In Hardy JB (ed.) *The Collaborative Perinatal Project of the National Institutes of Neurological and Communicative Disorders and Stroke*, p 104. Baltimore: Johns Hopkins University Press.

Hathirat P, Sasanakul W, Bintadish P et al (1980) The erythrocyte G-6PD level in the first year of life. *Journal of the Medical Association of Thailand* 63: 651–654.

Ho NK (1991) Neonatal jaundice—a second 4-year experience in Toa Payoh Hospital (1986–1989). *Journal of the Singapore Paediatric Society* 34: 79–85.

Ho NK, Gomez JM & Lim SB (1988) Neonatal Jaundice. A 4-year experience in Toa Payoh Hospital. *Journal of the Singapore Paediatric Society* 30: 72–76.

Horiguchi T & Bauer C (1975) Ethnic differences in neonatal jaundice: comparison of Japanese and Caucasian newborn infants. *American Journal of Obstetrics and Gynecology* 121: 71–74.

Huang DM & Wang DW (1989) Causes and management of neonatal unconjugated hyperbilirubinemia. *Chinese Journal of Pediatrics* 27: 58 (abstract).

Imran M (1986) Neonatal jaundice due to G6PD deficiency in Peshawar, Pakistan. *Abstracts of Scientific Presentations, XVIII International Congress of Pediatrics*, Honolulu, Hawaii, No. 116.

Jiangsu Medical College (1977) *Zhong Yao Da Zi Dian* (A dictionary of Chinese medicine), vol. 2, pp 1588–1591. Shanghai: Shanghai Scientific Technology Publishers (in the Chinese language).

Lee KH, Yeung KK & Yeung CY (1970) Neonatal jaundice in Chinese newborns. *Journal of Obstetrics and Gynaecology of the British Commonwealth* 77: 561–564.

Lu TC, Lee TC & Chen CL (1963) Studies of serum bilirubin levels and its fractions in the Chinese newborn infants. *Acta Paediatrica Sinica* 4: 1.

Luan Eng Li, Chin J & Ti Ts (1964) Glucose 6 phosphate dehydrogenase deficiency in Brunei, Sabah and Sarawak. *Annals of Human Genetics* 28: 173–176.

McDonagh AF (1990) Is bilirubin good for you? *Clinics in Perinatology* 17: 359–369.

Madan N & Sood SK (1987) Role of G6PD, ABO Incompatibility, low birth weight and Infection in neonatal hyperbilirubinemia. *Tropical and Geographical Medicine* 39: 163–168.

Maisels MJ (1987) Neonatal jaundice. In Avery GB 3rd (ed.) *Neonatology—Pathophysiology and Management of the Newborn*, pp 534–629. Philadelphia: Lippincott.

Marnoto BW, Monintja HE, Kadri N et al (1979) The incidence and etiological factors of neonatal jaundice in the Dr Ciptomangunkusumo Hospital, Jakarta. In Karim SMM & Tan KL (eds) *Problems in Perinatology*, pp 555–559. Lancaster, England: MTP Press.

Menon PSN & Mohapatra SS (1987) Predictability of severity of ABO hemolytic disease. *Indian Pediatrics* 24: 313–315.

Motulsky AG & Campbell-Kraut JM (1961) In Blumberg BS (ed.) *Proceedings of the Conference on Genetic Polymorphisms and Geographic Variations in Disease*, pp 159–191. New York: Grune & Stratton.

Motulsky AG, Stransky E & Fraser GR (1963) Glucose-6-phosphate dehydrogenase (G6PD) deficiency, thalassemia and abnormal haemoglobins in the Philippines. *Journal of Medical Genetics* 1: 102–106.

Motulsky AG, Lee TC & Fraser GR (1965) Glucose-6-phosphate dehydrogenase (G6PD) deficiency, thalassemia and abnormal haemoglobins in Taiwan. *Journal of Medical Genetics* 2: 18–26.

Nadkarni AK (1954) Coptis chinensis. *Indian Materia Medica* 1: 376.

Oski FA & Naimen JL (eds) (1982) Erythroblastosis. In *Hematologic Problems in the Newborn*, chap. 10. Philadelphia: Saunders.

Palmar DC & Drew JH (1983) Jaundice: a 10 year review of 41 000 live born infants. *Australian Paediatric Journal* 19: 86–89.

Phornphutkul C, Whitaker JA, Worathumrong N (1969) Severe hyperbilirubinemia in Thai newborns in association with erythrocyte G6PD deficiency. *Clinical Pediatrics* 8: 275–278.

Qi C & Deng CD (1990) An investigation on gene frequency of RBC-G6PD deficiency in children of Nanjing Area. *Chinese Journal of Pediatrics* **28:** 63 (abstract).

Quinn MW, Weindling AM & Davidson DC (1988) Does ABO incompatibility matter *Archives of Disease in Childhood* **63:** 1258–1260.

Rodgers PA & Stevenson DK (1990) Developmental biology of heme oxygenase. *Clinics in Perinatology* **17:** 275–291.

Singh H (1986) Glucose-6-phosphate dehydrogenase deficiency: a preventable case of mental retardation. *British Medical Journal* **292:** 397–398.

Tan KL (1981) Glucose-6-phosphate dehydrogenase status and neonatal jaundice. *Archives of Disease in Childhood* **56:** 874–877.

Tan KL, Loganath A, Roy AC et al (1984) Cord plasma alpha-fetoprotein values and neonatal jaundice. *Pediatrics* **74:** 1065–1068.

Toy PT, Reid ME, Papenfus L et al (1988) Prevalence of ABO maternal–infant incompatibility in Asians, Blacks, Hispanics and Caucasians. *Vox Sanguinis* **54:** 181–183.

Turkel SB (1990) Autopsy findings associated with neonatal hyperbilirubinemia. *Clinics in Perinatology* **17:** 381–396.

Valaes T (1976) Bilirubin metabolism: review and discussion of inborn errors. *Clinics in Perinatology* **3:** 177–209.

Valaes TN & Harvey-Wilkes K (1990) Pharmacologic approaches to the prevention and treatment of neonatal hyperbilirubinemia. *Clinics in Perinatology* **17:** 245–273.

Van de Bor M, Van Zeben-van der Aa TM, Verloove-Vanhorick SP et al (1989) Hyperbilirubinemia in preterm infants and neurodevelopment outcome at 2 years of age. Results of a national collaborative survey. *Pediatrics* **83:** 915–920.

Velluda CC et al (1959) The pharmacological effect of berberine. *Chemical Abstracts* **53:** 15345a.

Walker DG & Bowman JE (1959) Glutathione stability of erythrocytes in Iranians. *Nature* **184** (supplement 17): 1325.

Wong HB (1980) Singapore kernicterus. *Singapore Medical Journal* **21:** 556–567.

Wong HB (1983) Erythrocytic glucose 6 phosphate dehydrogenase deficiency. *Journal of the Singapore Paediatric Society* **25:** 6–13.

World Health Organization (1966) *Haemoglobinopathies and Allied Disorders*. Technical Report Series 338. Geneva: WHO.

Wu Y (1980) Study of RBC-G6PD deficiency in 1000 newborn babies in the Shanghai region. *Shanghai Medicine* **3:** 278 (in the Chinese language).

Yu SJ (1986) A study of glucose 6 phosphate dehydrogenase deficiency in the newborn. *Journal of Neonatology* **1:** 32 (in the Chinese language).

Yue PCK & Strickland M (1965) Glucose-6-phosphate dehydrogenase deficiency and neonatal jaundice in Chinese male infants in Hong Kong. *Lancet* **i:** 350–351.

7

Nutritional anaemias

SERGE HERCBERG
PILAR GALAN

Anaemias due to specific deficiencies are usually collectively referred to as nutritional anaemias. The term 'nutritional' is used without regard to aetiology, and may apply to dietary deficiency, excessive losses or increased metabolic requirements. In most cases, this type of anaemia is the result of a single or a combined deficiency in iron, folic acid and vitamin B_{12}. Other, more unusual types of deficiency status include pyridoxin (vitamin B_6), copper and riboflavin deficiency and protein malnutrition, which may also produce mild anaemia.

Nutritional anaemia is recognized as a major public health problem throughout the world. In 1980, a review of epidemiological data estimated that some 1300 million people were affected by anaemia, especially in developing countries (DeMaeyer and Adiels-Tegman, 1985). Infants, young children, menstruating and especially pregnant women are most affected (Table 1). The highest overall prevalence of anaemias is found in southern Asia and Africa.

Although many nutrients and cofactors are involved in the maintenance of normal haemoglobin synthesis, there is sufficient evidence to suggest that iron deficiency is the most common cause of nutritional anaemia in the world. Even by conservative estimates, 600 to 700 million individuals suffer from anaemia due to iron deficiency (FAO/WHO, 1988). Numerous surveys using reliable, sensitive indicators of iron status have shown that iron depletion is even more prevalent than iron deficiency anaemia (Cook et al, 1976; INACG, 1981; Hercberg et al, 1986a). Folate deficiency is considered as the second most common cause of nutritional anaemia (Baker and DeMaeyer, 1979). To understand why nutritional anaemia is so widely prevalent in the world, it is necessary to understand the nutritional inadequacy of iron and folate requirements versus iron and folate intake, particularly in different age/sex categories. It is thus essential to determine the amounts of iron and folate involved in daily exchange and how these can be modified by the nature of the diet and by physiological and pathological variations in losses and requirements.

Baillière's Clinical Haematology—
Vol. 5, No. 1, January 1992
ISBN 0–7020–1626–8

Table 1. Estimated prevalence of anaemia by region and age/sex category (around 1980).

	Children						Men			Women 15–49 years					
	0–4 years			5–12 years			15–59 years			Pregnant			All		
	Total	Anaemic		Total	Anaemic		Total	Anaemic		Total	Anaemic		Total	Anaemic	
		%	No.		%	No.		%	No.		%	No.		%	No.
Africa	85.7	56	48.0	96.6	49	47.3	116.8	20	23.4	17.9	63	11.3	106.4	44	46.8
North America	19.6	8	1.6	27.5	13	3.6	76.3	4	3.1	3.4	NA	NA	64.2	8	5.1
Latin America	52.9	26	13.7	69.8	26	18.1	98.1	13	12.8	9.9	30	3.0	86.5	17	14.7
East Asia	16.1	20	3.2	25.4	22	5.6	55.8	11	6.1	2.7	20	0.5	46.9	18	8.4
South Asia	212.0	56	118.7	278.4	50	139.2	386.3	32	123.6	41.7	65	27.1	329.4	58	191.0
Europe	33.4	14	4.7	55.0	5	2.7	147.2	2	3.0	5.7	14	0.8	117.5	12	14.1
Oceania	2.3	18	0.4	3.6	15	0.5	6.9	7	0.5	0.4	25	0.1	5.5	19	1.0
USSR	23.1	NA	NA	3.1	NA	NA	80.3	NA	NA	4.0	NA	NA	68.7	NA	NA
World	445.1	43	193.5	587.6	37	217.4	967.7	18	174.2	85.8	51	43.9	825.0	35	288.4
Developed	86.1	12	10.3	130.7	7	9.1	346.5	3	12.0	14.8	14	2.0	285.5	11	32.7
Developing	359.0	51	183.2	456.8	46	208.3	621.2	26	162.2	71.0	59	41.9	539.5	47	255.7

NA, not available.
The figures do not include data from China. Populations are given in millions.
All calculations were made before rounding, figures may thus not add to totals.
Anaemia is defined as a haemoglobin concentration below WHO reference values for age, sex and pregnancy status.
Regions are drawn following United Nations designations; more developed regions include North America, Japan, Europe, Australia, New Zealand and the USSR.
From DeMaeyer and Adiels-Tegman (1985).

IRON DEFICIENCY

Iron balance

Although present in very small amounts in the human body (4 g in adult men, 2.5 g in adult women), iron plays a major role in important metabolic functions (Table 2). The major portion intervenes in the synthesis of haemoglobin and myoglobin, and is linked to many enzymes (Hercberg and Galan, 1989). The bulk of the remainder is present in the form of storage iron, as tissue ferritin and haemosiderin. The amount of iron stores varies between 0 and 1000 mg, depending on the previous iron nutrition status of the subject (Bothwell et al, 1979).

In healthy, well-nourished subjects, nutritional balance generally exists in which the quantity of daily iron absorbed from the diet is sufficient (1) to compensate for daily iron losses, (2) to permit metabolic iron utilization, and (3) to maintain adequate body iron stores. This status can be unbalanced by a variety of factors such as low dietary iron intake, poor iron absorption, increased iron losses and/or increased requirements.

Disturbances in the iron balance by one or more of these factors will initially lead to mobilizing the iron stores. When iron stores are exhausted (and perhaps even before total exhaustion), functions in which iron intervenes may be disturbed. Classically, three stages of deficiency are described, although clear-cut distinctions do not always exist between them (Cook, 1982). The first stage corresponds to the depletion of iron stores, the second to the inadequacy of iron transport to the bone marrow, and the third to anaemia. Anaemia is usually considered to be present when the haemoglobin level has decreased below a cut-off point defined according to sex, age and other physiological considerations. The most frequently used limits of 'normal haemoglobin concentrations' are values given by WHO (1968). Though these are often challenged, many surveys have used them, and they can be considered as rough guidelines. For people living at sea level, cut-off points of WHO are: children from 6 months to 6 years, 110 g/l; children from 6 to 14 years, 120 g/l; adult males, 130 g/l; adult females, 120 g/l; pregnant women, 110 g/l.

Cut-off limits are higher for individuals living at high altitudes. It has been suggested that an approximate correction for altitude may be obtained by increasing the haemoglobin values by 4% per 1000 m elevation. But this correction is based on work done in the early 1940s (Hurtado et al, 1945) and is also being challenged (Tufts et al, 1985; Estrella et al, 1987).

Physiological iron excretion

Iron losses from the human body are related mainly to desquamation of cells from external and internal surfaces. About two-thirds are from the gastrointestinal tract. Most of the remainder occur from the skin, and only a tiny fraction from the urine. Iron losses in sweat are now considered negligible, even in a tropical context: skin losses are not significantly increased by excess sweating in hot, humid climates (Brune et al, 1986).

Table 2. The iron-containing proteins: localization and functions. From Galan et al (1984).

		Subcellular localization	Principal organs studied	Functions
Haem iron				
Haemoglobin			Red blood cells	Oxygen carrier
Myoglobin			Heart, skeletal muscle	Oxygen carrier
Cytochromes	a, a$_3$	Mitochondria	Skeletal muscle, heart, liver, brain	Terminal oxidase in the transport chain of electron
	b	Mitochondria	Heart	Electron transport
	c$_1$	Mitochondria	Heart, brain	Electron transport
	c	Mitochondria	Liver, skeletal muscle, heart, brain	Electron transport
	b$_5$	Endoplasmic reticulum	Brain, liver	Electron transport in the microsomal chain
	P$_{450}$	Endoplasmic reticulum	Liver, intestinal mucous, adrenals	Hydroxylation of steroids, oxidation of foreign compounds
Catalase		Peroxisomes	Brain, liver, red blood cells	Peroxide breakdown
Lactic peroxidase			Milk, external secretions, neutrophils	Peroxide breakdown
Tryptophan pyrrolase		Cytosol	Liver	L-tryptophan→ formylkynurenine
Non-haem iron				
NADH cytochrome c reductase		Mitochondria	Liver, heart	Mitochondrial respiratory system
Succinic cytochrome c reductase		Mitochondria	Liver, heart	Mitochondrial respiratory system
Succinic dehydrogenase		Mitochondria	Heart	Mitochondrial respiratory system
NADH ferrocyanide oxidoreductase		Microsomal mitochondria	Heart, liver	Mitochondrial respiratory system
Aldehyde oxidase		Mitochondria	Brain, liver	Serotonin metabolism
Phenylalanine hydroxylase		Cytosol	Liver, kidney	Phenylalanine, β-tyrosine
Aconitase		Mitochondria	Heart, kidney	Citric acid cycle
Adrenodoxin		Mitochondria	Adrenal cortex	Steroid hydroxylation
Fe-S protein complex III		Mitochondria	Heart	Electron transport
Fe-S protein succinate dehydrogenase		Mitochondria	Heart	Electron transport
Plasmaprotein succinic dehydrogenase		Mitochondria	Heart	Electron transport
NADH dehydrogenase		Mitochondria	Liver, kidney, cardiac muscle	Electron transport
Xanthine oxidase		Mitochondria	Milk, liver, intestinal mucosa	Hypoxanthine, uric acid
Transferrin			Plasma	Iron transport
Lactoferrin			Milk, external secretions	Iron transport
Ferrum			All tissues	Iron storage
Hemosiderin			Liver, spleen, bone marrow	Iron storage
Monoamine oxidase*		Mitochondria	Brain, liver, blood platelets	Metabolism of catecholamines
Ribonucleotide reductase*		Ribosome Nucleus	Lymphocytes, haematopoietic tissue	DNA synthesis

*It is not known at what level iron acts.

Iron excretion in men

Using radioisotopic techniques, calculations based on the decrease in specific activity of ^{55}Fe in red cells over several years in different groups of healthy men (Green et al, 1968) showed a mean iron loss of $14\,\mu g\,kg^{-1}\,day^{-1}$, corresponding, in an adult man, to about 0.9–1 mg/day. These losses are reduced in the elderly (Finch, 1959).

Iron excretion in women

Extrapolated to women on the basis of body weight, basal iron losses may be estimated at 0.8 mg/day. But for women from puberty to menopause, menstrual iron losses must be added to basal losses. Menstrual iron losses have been studied in women in developed countries (Sweden: Hallberg et al, 1966; United Kingdom: Cole et al, 1971; Canada: Beaton et al, 1970) and in developing countries (Egypt: Hefnawi et al, 1980; India: Apte and Venkatachalam, 1963; Burma: Aug-Than-Batu et al, 1971). In all surveys, median monthly blood losses were around 30 ml; 90% of healthy women had losses of less than 80 ml. For 50% of the women these data corresponded to monthly supplemental iron losses of 15 mg or, expressed as a loss averaged over the whole month, to 0.5 mg daily. It is probable that 90% of women had supplemental daily iron losses of less than 1.4 mg.

Thus, average total iron losses (basal losses + menstrual iron losses) in menstruating women may be estimated at approximately 1.4 mg/day (0.8 + 0.6 mg/day) and 90% of healthy women may be considered as having iron losses of less then 2.2 mg/day (0.8 + 1.4 mg/day). Iron losses are reduced by about 50% in women using oral contraceptives; intrauterine devices can increase them by about 100% (INACG, 1981). It is probable that other factors such as body length and parity play a role in determining menstrual blood losses and, therefore, in iron requirements.

Finally, taking into account the greater physiological iron losses, menstruating women may be considered to be at higher risk of iron deficiency than men.

Special iron requirements

Pregnancy

Iron requirements are considerably increased during pregnancy because of the increase in the maternal red cell mass (about 500 mg of iron), active iron transport to the fetus (about 290 mg), the constitution of the placenta (about 25 mg) and the compensation of basal losses (about 220 mg for the duration of pregnancy despite the interruption of menstrual blood losses) (INACG, 1981). Total requirements are greater than 1000 mg for the duration of pregnancy, but they are more concentrated during the second and third trimesters of gestation. The size of iron stores at the beginning of pregnancy plays an important role. Iron requirements are higher in mothers who begin pregnancy with depleted or low iron stores, a situation very common in developing countries, but also not unusual in developed countries.

Lactation

During lactation, iron is secreted in breast milk. The iron concentration o breast milk is low, varying from 0.3 to 0.5 mg/l (Macy et al, 1953), but thi supplemental loss represents an added strain upon women at a time whei their iron stores are at their lowest level because of the previous burden o pregnancy. Moreover, at delivery and in the puerperium, it is not uncom mon to observe supplemental iron losses related to haemorrhage. Thes losses may be greater in cases of traumatic delivery. The return of iron afte the decline in red cell mass following delivery, and the 'iron economy', du to the absence of menstruation for several weeks, suggest that iron require ments in lactating women are just slightly higher during the first 6 months o lactation than in menstruating women. In many developing countries breast-feeding is often greatly prolonged, up to 10 or 12 months. Thi assumes higher iron requirements after 6 months of lactation.

Infants, children and adolescents

In addition to basal iron losses, infants, children and adolescents need iror for the expansion of their red cell mass and growing body tissues (Dallman e al, 1980). During the first 4–6 months of life, iron is redistributed betweei the decreasing haemoglobin mass and expanding tissue iron. It is assumec that, in breast-fed infants, the iron content of breast milk is adequate to mee basal losses (except for premature children and children of low birtl weight). After 4–6 months, total body iron increases, as does basal loss, witl the continued growth of the individual. When expressed as kilogram/body weight, iron requirements during childhood are very high. This is particu larly true during periods of rapid growth.

Acceleration of growth, particularly during the years of sexual matu ration, imposes increased requirements for iron, primarily in the productior of haemoglobin. In adolescent girls, iron needs do not peak as sharply as ir boys because the maximal yearly weight gain is somewhat less than in boys and because the haemoglobin concentration in girls increases slightly durin this period. But the onset of menses usually follows the peak of adolescen growth and contributes to increased iron requirements (INACG, 1979).

Pathological iron losses

The previous discussion on iron requirements dealt with physiological iror losses, but in developing countries it is necessary to take into accoun additional iron losses related to pathological blood losses. The mos common cause of chronic blood loss in tropical context is parasitic infection.

Hookworm. Hookworm infestation is probably the most important cause o bleeding from the gut. It affects millions of people in the world. *Necato americanus* is most widespread in tropical and subtropical areas. *Anky lostoma duodenale* is more common in countries around the Mediterranear sea. The frequency of hookworm is promoted by a hot, humid climate whicl enables the development of larvae. Transmission exists throughout the year, but is maximal after the rainy season. It occurs by contact between the skin and soil polluted by larvae. For this reason, people who live and work barefoot are at a particularly high risk of infestation.

The parasites *N. americanus* and *A. duodenale* attach themselves to the mucosa of the initial intestinal tract and suck blood from the submucosal vessels (Fleming, 1981). With a worm-load producing 1000 eggs per gram of faeces, the intestinal blood loss averages 2.4 ml blood per day or 1 mg of iron daily in infestation by *N. americanus*, and 4.5 ml blood per day or 2 mg of iron daily in infestation by *A. duodenale* (Roche and Layrisse, 1966). Although 30–40% of this iron is reabsorbed within the intestinal tract, hookworm is an important cause of iron imbalance.

Trichuris trichiura. T. trichiura is widespread, especially in children. Transmission occurs by consumption of food or water polluted with eggs of *T. trichiura*. Larvae are liberated from the eggs in the intestinal tract. Worms may be responsible for a daily blood loss of 5 μl per worm (Layrisse et al, 1967), corresponding to about 0.25 ml daily or 0.1 mg/day of iron for a worm-load of 1000 eggs per gram of faeces. In severe infection, daily iron losses may reach more than 1 mg.

Schistosomiasis. Schistosoma haematobium is present in all of Africa, but mainly in west Africa, southern Africa, north Africa and Madagascar. *Schistosoma mansoni* is mainly present in the Nile Valley, east Africa and southern Africa. Female worms of *S. mansoni* discharge eggs into the veins draining the large bowel. Female worms of *S. haematobium* discharge eggs into the veins draining the bladder. *S. mansoni* causes a chronic inflammatory reaction responsible for colon and rectal polyps, which result in blood loss (Prata, 1978). Iron losses may be considerable, corresponding to around 1–6 mg/day. *S. haematobium* is responsible for haematuria. Urinary blood loss in infected patients in Egypt has been estimated to range from 0.5 to 125 ml per day (Mahmoud, 1966; Farid et al, 1968). In Kenyan primary schools, mean iron losses in children varied from 149 to 652 μg/day, according to *S. haematobium* egg counts (Stephenson et al, 1985). This supplemental iron spoliation may contribute to an imbalance in the iron status.

Other causes. Other sources of gastrointestinal bleeding may contribute to increasing the iron requirements in individuals, but in developing countries they do not play a major role from a public health standpoint. These include hiatal hernia, gastric and duodenal ulcers, ulcerative colitis, polyps and tumours of the gastric cavity and intestinal tract, haemorrhoids, and the use of some drugs (aspirin, corticosteroids, anticoagulants).

Dietary iron intakes

Three factors determine the iron absorbed from the diet: the amount of iron ingested, its bioavailability and the iron status of the individual.

Dietary iron ingested

Iron is present in many foodstuffs (Table 3). Data on dietary iron intakes in developing countries are scant and present wide variations from one survey to another. Some caution must be exercised when comparing published estimates, since much of the iron content of certain foods is probably of extrinsic origin, either in the form of dirt or from the surfaces of containers or cooking utensils. Finally, in dietary surveys conducted in developing countries, extremes ranged from 8 to 400 mg/day, but current limits are considered to be from 12 to 19 mg/day. These data are consistent with an analysis of food balance sheets (FAO, 1980), which show that total iron per capita in the diet usually varies from 13 to 21 mg/day. Finally, most of the dietary iron in developing countries is provided by products of vegetal origin.

Typical western diets usually contain about 5.5–6.0 mg iron per 1000 kcal (Galan et al, 1990a); 85–87% of dietary iron corresponds to non-haem iron.

Table 3. Iron content of different foods.

Food	Iron content (mg/100 g of food)	Food	Iron content (mg/100 g of food)	Food	Iron content (mg/100 g of food)
Maize		Taro	1.2	Antelope	2.1
White	3.6	Plantain	1.3	Lamb	2.0
Yellow	4.9	Bean	1.4	Chicken	1.1
Sorghum		Soybean	6.1	Beef	2.9
Red	15.6	Lentil	7.0	Pork	2.0
White	5.8	Chickpea	11.1	Caterpillars	0.5
Yellow	5.0	Cowpea	7.6	Termites	52.0
Millet	39.0	Peanut	3.8	Grasshoppers	11.0
Teff		Pumpkin	1.4	Cake of lake	
Red	75.5	Amaranth	8.9	flies	65.6
White	20.9	Baobab leaves	24.0	Iguana	3.7
Rice		Shea butterseed	3.0	Snail	41.0
Brown	2.0	Tomato	0.6	Hen eggs	2.6
White	1.7	Pineapple	0.4	Milk	0.2
Acha	8.5	Monkey bread	7.4	Eel	2.4
Wheat	6.5	Soursop	2.0	Prawn	1.6
Cassava	1.9	Datte	6.0	Tilapia	3.2
Yam	0.8	Guava	1.3	Snapper	2.2
Gari	1.6	Mango	1.2	Sardine	1.3
Potato	1.1	Orange	0.1	Carp	1.1
Sweet potato	2.0	Papaya	0.6	Mackerel	1.2

Bioavailability of iron

While the amount of dietary iron intake is obviously important, an even greater factor is the varied bioavailability of food iron (Bothwell et al, 1979). It is necessary to distinguish between the two forms of iron present in food. Haem iron, derived exclusively from haemoglobin and myoglobin (present only in meat and fish), is easily absorbed whatever the composition of the diet, while non-haem iron is usually of low bioavailability. About 25–30% of haem iron is absorbed, compared with 1–7% for non-haem iron. Haem iron is thus of great nutritional significance.

Moreover, the absorption of non-haem iron may be markedly affected by other ingredients in the meal (Hallberg, 1981). The presence of ascorbic acid, citric acid, tartaric acid, lactic acid or fish and meat (striated muscle and liver) enhances the absorption of non-haem iron in a meal (Cook and Monsen, 1976; Layrisse et al, 1968). Ascorbic acid appears to be a very important promoter of non-haem iron absorption, and may play a particular role in diets in which the amounts of meat are negligible. The overall absorption of iron may be significantly increased if fruit or vegetables containing ascorbic acid are present in the meal. In this context, oranges, lemons, grapefruits, guavas, papayas, and green leafy vegetables, cauliflower, cabbage, beetroot, pumpkin and turnips, are important sources of ascorbic acid.

On the other hand, tannates and polyphenolic compounds (contained in tea, coffee and cereals), bran, calcium, phosphates, oxalates, egg yolk and isolated soy proteins decrease non-haem iron absorption (Disler et al, 1975; Cook et al, 1981; Simpson et al, 1981). Tea, widely consumed in many countries of the world, is a powerful inhibitor of non-haem iron absorption because of its tannate content.

The total bioavailability of iron in a meal therefore results from the combination of effects of all dietary factors promoting or inhibiting the absorption of the common non-haem iron pool. The bioavailability of contamination iron is low, and sometimes negligible (Hallberg et al, 1983; Guiro and Hercberg, 1988).

Finally, to estimate the bioavailability of the diet of most inhabitants of developing countries it is necessary to consider that the typical diet is based on cereals or roots/tubers with no or very small quantities of meat, fish or foods rich in ascorbic acid. This type of diet often contains high levels of inhibitors of iron absorption (for example a high content of tannates and polyphenolic compounds in maize and sorghum). The average iron absorption of this type of diet, typical for the majority of lower socioeconomic classes, can be estimated at between 1 and 5% (Galan et al, 1990b). Occasional intake of small amounts of meat and/or fish cannot significantly modify global bioavailability. For higher socioeconomic classes with some intake of fish, meat and foods containing high levels of ascorbic acid, iron bioavailability can be estimated at between 5 and 10%. Only a small number of people probably have a very high intake of meat, fish and ascorbic acid (such as in industrialized countries): the iron absorption of this type of diet (uncommon in developing countries) may vary from 10 to 15% (Galan et al, 1990a). This range is considered as the iron bioavailability in typical western diet.

The quantity of iron absorbed from the diet is also influenced by body iron status. In case of decreased body iron stores, a higher proportion of iron is absorbed, and vice versa, but this compensatory effect is limited.

Measurement of iron status of populations

Until recently, iron deficiency was considered as virtually synonymous with anaemia, and its identification was based on a decrease in the concentration of circulating haemoglobin. Recently, however, technical advances in haematology, biochemistry and nutrition have demonstrated that iron deficiency cannot be limited simply to anaemia. Apart from its lack of specificity (other causes such as folate deficiency, genetic disorders, or acute or chronic infections may be responsible for a low haemoglobin level), anaemia, even when related to iron deficiency, reflects a delayed stage of the deficiency. In this case, anaemia constitutes the visible part of the iceberg. But iron deficiency is a much wider concept, both in terms of the number of concerned subjects and in the range of deleterious effects upon health.

Fortunately, new and accurate indicators of iron status, which are more specific and more sensitive than haemoglobin, have appeared in the last few decades, and in particular during the last 20 years, enabling detection of early stages of iron deficiency even before its effect upon haematopoiesis (Cook et al, 1976; Cook, 1982; Hercberg and Galan, 1985). From an epidemiological point of view, the use of these iron indicators depends on their qualities, including feasibility, sensitivity, specificity and variability.

Feasibility of the tests

The feasibility of a test is linked to the compliance of the population, the cost and complexity of the tests, the qualifications and experience of available staff and the practical organization of the survey. Certain techniques, such as bone marrow or liver biopsy, phlebotomy and isotopic dilution, cannot be used in a population because of their traumatic or invasive character. Therapeutic iron trials are possible but, in practice, are difficult to perform on populations, especially over a long period of time. In a theoretically healthy population, only blood sampling is acceptable. For this reason, serum ferritin, serum transferrin, serum iron, erythrocyte protoporphyrin (EP), mean corpuscular volume (MCV) and haemoglobin (Hb), haematocrit (Ht) measurements can be easily carried out with less than 1 ml of blood eventually drawn out by fingerprick or heelprick (in children under 1 year).

Sensitivity of the indicators

The sensitivity of an indicator of iron deficiency may be defined by the probability that an iron-deficient subject can be identified as such by the use of that indicator. Decreases in haemoglobin or haematocrit (or the expression of clinical symptoms of anaemia) correspond to a delayed stage of the deficiency. They indicate severe iron deficiency and, from a diagnostic point of view, can be considered as having low sensitivity. They are less sensitive than those which indicate the iron supply to the marrow (such as serum iron, total iron binding capacity (TIBC) or EP. The latter are, however, less sensitive than indicators measuring the size of the iron stores (such as serum ferritin). Depletion of the iron stores (reduction of serum ferritin) reveals the inadequacy existing between iron supply and iron requirements. Therefore, the serum ferritin measurement appears to be the most sensitive indicator for assessing iron status in a population.

No single iron parameter can monitor the entire spectrum of iron deficiency. Under the most favourable conditions, the use of a single iron parameter reflects only one stage of iron deficiency. Moreover, under certain circumstances, biochemical sensitivity is reduced, thereby decreasing the value of a particular indicator. Such circumstances include various pathological conditions and therapeutic regimens. For instance, in a tropical context the usual inflammatory processes are responsible for an increase in serum ferritin measurement, leading to a false diagnosis of adequate iron status in possibly iron-depleted subjects. This tends to cause lower estimates of iron deficiency in epidemiological surveys.

Specificity of the indicators

The specificity of an indicator of iron deficiency is defined by the probability that a non-iron deficient subject will not be identified as a deficient subject. All iron indicators have poor specificity. For instance, anaemia may have causes other than iron deficiency (possibly nutritional aetiologies). For each biochemical parameter, certain confounding factors can modify their significance and be responsible for false-positive results. In these conditions, there is a risk of false positives thereby overestimating the true prevalence of iron deficiency.

This problem is particularly important in a tropical context, where infections and inflammatory processes are widespread and may affect the significance of iron parameters independently of real iron status (Fleming, 1982; Hercberg et al, 1987a). Inflammatory syndromes, even to a mild degree, may be responsible for a decrease in Hb, serum iron and transferrin saturation levels and for an increase in the EP concentration, leading to an eventual false diagnosis of iron deficiency. Moreover, we have just seen that these inflammatory syndromes may conversely affect the significance of serum ferritin measurement.

Variability

Instrumental variability varies according to indicators and the techniques used (Dallman, 1984). Hb, Ht and MCV have low instrumental variability (1–3%) and are decreased due to the use of electronic counters. Serum iron presents considerable instrumental variability linked to environmental contamination. The instrumental error is 9% using manual techniques, but can be considerably lowered by using automatic equipment. Instrumental variability for the TIBC is roughly equivalent to that of serum iron (5–6%). For the EP assay, the instrumental error is between 1.5 and 2.5% using haematofluorometer methods, and 5% using extraction techniques. Instrumental variability is about 3.5% for serum ferritin 1-day assays and twice that for sequential-day assays, whatever the method used (ELISA, IRMA, RIA).

Intraindividual variability for Hb and Ht over a short time in 'healthy' subjects is similar to that of analytical variability (1–3%). For serum iron measurements there is a pronounced diurnal variation, from 13 to 20%. Even when blood is collected within the same hour in the same subject, day-to-day variability is 30–50%. For TIBC, intraindividual variability is lower than for serum iron and remains similar to that of analytical error. EP measurement by the haematofluorometer reveals day-to-day variations which are lower than with extraction methods.

Intraindividual variability for serum ferritin is of the order of 6–10% for within-day variation and is lower than 15% for between-days variation.

Preinstrumental, instrumental and intraindividual variability can be minimized in epidemiological surveys by standardizing the sampling technique, for example through the use of the same conditions, the same arm, the same position, and the same hour for blood sampling, and the use of automatic equipment.

Interindividual variability represents a major problem in our understanding of the significance of parameters used for assessing the iron status of individuals and populations. There is an 'overlap' in the distribution values observed in 'normal' and in 'iron-deficient' subjects, especially when deficiency is mild. This is particularly true for Hb. The use of cut-off of 'normality' for Hb may be responsible for a large number of false negatives and false positives. The problem was clearly demonstrated by Garby and Irnell (1969), who defined anaemia in the population by the response (or lack of response) to oral iron therapy. Using a single cut-off point, they found that 17% of truly anaemic women were classified as normal, while 35% of normal women were classified as anaemic. Similar results were obtained by frequency distribution of Hb in pregnant women. One-fourth of both anaemic and normal women were misclassified when a single cut-off of 110 g/l of Hb was used.

Results of population studies indicate that the distribution of Hb values is Gaussian, with a standard deviation of about 7% when subjects with iron-deficiency are rigorously excluded (Bothwell and Charlton, 1982). The distribution curve is skewed to the left in an apparently normal population by the presence of anaemic individuals within such a population. It is difficult to find a clear-cut dividing line between normal and anaemic subjects. By administering iron and then repeating haematological measurements, it is possible to obtain a more precise definition of the lower limits of 'normality'. Garby and Irnell (1969) were able to show that only 2% of women with an initial Ht of 36% or higher responded to supplementation. In other words, a woman with a Ht of 36% or higher has a 98% chance of not being anaemic.

This is also true for other iron parameters, such as serum ferritin, and particularly for serum iron, transferrin saturation and EP. For all these reasons, the simplest way to define the prevalence of iron deficiency, using a single cut-off level for a given measurement, does not permit reliable characterization of the iron status of a population, particularly in tropical contexts where confounding factors are widespread.

Many of the limitations to defining the prevalence of iron deficiency using isolated measurements can be circumvented by using combinations of multiple criteria. Several authors have proposed the use of a combination of ndependent iron indicators to define iron status (Cook et al, 1976; Derman et al, 1978; Hercberg et al, 1986a, 1986b, 1987a). Most of these authors define iron deficiency by the coexistence of at least two abnormal values among the three (or four) independent parameters used: serum ferritin, transferrin saturation, EP (and MCV). This approach avoids considering as iron-deficient a subject with one single abnormal iron indicator, a situation which may be due to the presence of unknown confounding factors or to a misclassification of the subject linked to the arbitrary chosen cut-off point. It therefore takes into consideration a possible error for each test due to interindividual variability, and especially the overlap in distribution of values between normal and iron-deficient populations. This method decreases the risk of false positives and false negatives, and seems particularly advantageous in a tropical context and may be considered as validated by two facts.

First, the prevalence of iron deficiency, if defined by a single iron parameter, varies considerably according to the chosen indicator. For instance, in a survey performed on a representative sample of 2968 subjects in south Benin (Hercberg et al, 1988a), the prevalence of iron deficiency in children 6 months to 2 years old varied from 82% when iron deficiency was defined by an abnormal value for EP, to 36% if the definition was based on an abnormal serum iron value, to 61% if the definition was based on abnormal transferrin saturation. On the other hand, when iron deficiency was defined by a low serum ferritin value, the observed prevalence was only 19%. It is evident that the difference in sensitivity between iron indicators does not explain the differences observed in assessing the prevalence of iron deficiency. The most sensitive test, such as serum ferritin measurement (which assesses the iron stores), identifies fewer subjects than transferrin saturation (which assesses transport of iron in plasma). But theoretically, depletion of iron stores starts before any abnormalities occur in blood transport of iron. These differences according to the iron parameter chosen are not specific to young children but have been found for each age and sex group. These results might be explained by the presence of unrecognized confounding factors such as infections and inflammatory syndromes without clinical evidence.

Secondly, the validity of a combination of abnormal iron indicators was tested for predicting anaemia (Hercberg et al, 1986a). When only one iron indicator was abnormal, the percentage of anaemia was 40.5%, very close to that observed in the whole sample. However, when at least two iron parameters were abnormal, the prevalence of anaemia rose to 74%.

In a subsample of children, the frequency of inflammatory processes (not clinically evident) was assessed by the use of sensitive inflammatory markers such as orosomucoid and C reactive protein (Hercberg et al, 1987b). In anaemic children, 62% had evidence of biological inflammation. Iron deficiency and/or inflammation are associated with anaemia in 81% of cases. Serum ferritin assay was most affected by the presence of inflammation. Among children with high values for serum ferritin (more than $80\,\mu g/l$), 30.5% presented abnormal values for markers of inflammation. Correlations are found between serum ferritin and markers of inflammation, but also between most iron parameters and inflammatory markers.

Thus the use of serum ferritin as the only criterion may lead, in a tropical context, to a false diagnosis of iron sufficiency in truly iron-depleted subjects, While a low serum ferritin concentration corresponds exclusively to depleted iron stores, conversely, normal serum ferritin may not be sufficient to eliminate the diagnosis of iron deficiency.

Moreover, in inflammation, the rise in the serum ferritin level is usually very high, particularly compared with modifications in transferrin saturation or the EP level. Therefore, a moderate rise in the serum ferritin concentration, combined with a low percentage of transferrin saturation and/or a high EP, suggests iron deficiency in an inflammatory context. This approach was used in various epidemiological surveys performed in a tropical context (Assami et al, 1987; Hercberg et al, 1987a; Prual et al, 1988). The use of a combination of several independent laboratory measurements of iron status permits improvement in the accuracy of the assessment of iron status of individuals and populations, especially in an inflammatory context.

However, the definition of anaemia is always subject to controversy particularly concerning the cut-off point which distinguishes anaemic from non-anaemic subjects. Thus, apart from the cut-off point method, another statistical approach has recently been proposed to estimate more precisely the prevalence of anaemia and iron-deficiency anaemia by analysis of the Hb distribution (Meyers et al, 1983). This technique is based on the hypothesis that distributions of Hb values for anaemic and non-anaemic populations are different, and that the Hb values for non-anaemic subjects have a Gaussian distribution. When a cumulative Gaussian frequency distribution of Hb value is plotted on probability paper, it is linear. If anaemia exists in the population, the distribution curve is skewed to the left and the non-linear portion might be considered as a composite of the Hb distribution of anaemic and non-anaemic subjects with low Hb levels. The estimated proportion of anaemics might be calculated by determining the difference between the curved and linear populations at increasing Hb levels. The contribution of iron deficiency, folate deficiency and inflammatory processes to anaemia can be deduced by modifications in the distribution of Hb values, when subjects with laboratory tests suggestive of each type of anomaly are excluded. In a survey performed in Algeria on menstruating women (Hercberg et al, 1988b), we observed that the conventional cut-off point tended to overestimate the true frequency of anaemia: 7% of women with an Hb concentration level lower than WHO recommendations of 120 g/l were not found to be anaemic using the cumulative frequency method. According to this method, iron deficiency represented the most frequent cause of anaemia in the context of this sample: it contributed to 77% of anaemia.

Consequences of iron deficiency and iron-deficiency anaemia upon health

The deleterious effects of iron deficiency are classically defined in terms of anaemia which accompanies a marked reduction in body iron. But recent studies in animals and man have demonstrated that iron deficiency without anaemia may cause changes in different enzyme systems, and have pointed out the possible consequences of iron deficiency alone upon various functions (Dallman, 1982; Galan et al, 1984). It is often difficult to draw a distinction between the deleterious effects of anaemia itself and the adverse consequences of iron deficiency or other causes of the anaemia.

Effect upon work capacity

Anaemia is known to reduce the maximal oxygen transport and may limit work performance (Andersen and Barkve, 1970). Even mild anaemia may reduce near-maximal work capacity. Studies have shown a direct relationship between Hb concentration and the score on the Harvard test in sugar cutters in Guatemala (Viteri and Torun, 1974), and between Hb concentration and the work output of latex tappers and weeders in Indonesia (Basta et al, 1979) and tea pickers in Sri Lanka (Ohira et al, 1979). In both studies, after iron supplementation, the output of the anaemic groups increased to that of their non-anaemic colleagues. The precise contribution of iron deficiency *per se*, as distinct from that of anaemia, is not clear, but it was demonstrated that the physical activity of non-anaemic iron-deficient patients who received iron supplementation was significantly increased, without any significant changes in haemoglobin levels (Ericsson, 1970; Ohira et al, 1979). This phenomenon has been confirmed in animals (Finch et al, 1976). Iron deficiency results in a decrease in skeletal muscle iron-containing protein, e.g. myoglobin, cytochromes and α-glycerophosphate oxidase. The changes in the levels of α-glycerophosphate oxidase (rapidly reversed by iron therapy) may lead to a disturbance in glycolysis which results in excess lactate formation; at a high level, this can lead to cessation of physical activity,

From the public health standpoint it is important to consider that even moderate degrees of iron-deficiency anaemia may impair the well-being of individuals and may have far-reaching socioeconomic consequences by affecting the productivity of workers.

Effect on mental performance

Symptoms of decreasing intellectual performance and abnormalities in mental behaviour have been described in iron-deficient animals and children (Pollitt and Leibel, 1982). These include irritability, apathy, lack of attention, low school performance scores and reduced learning capacity. The contribution of iron deficiency to these types of abnormalities is difficult to demonstrate because of their multifactorial determinism.

In a study conducted in the USA on 24 iron-deficient anaemic children aged 9–26 months, 12 were given intramuscular iron and 12 a placebo (Oski et al, 1983). Significant improvements in tests of mental development and behaviour were found in the children who had received iron therapy; in particular, they became more responsive to their environment. In another study in Guatemala (Lozoff et al, 1982), children with iron-deficiency anaemia scored less well than other children on tests of mental development, but no improvement in test scores was observed after 1 week of iron supplementation. Studies in Egypt and Indonesia have also demonstrated deficits in mental performances in schoolchildren with iron deficiency; these were reversed after iron therapy (Pollitt et al, 1985). Oski and Honig (1978) observed an improvement in mental development scores 1 week after iron injection in iron-deficient but non-anaemic babies aged 9–12 months. In Chile (Walter et al, 1983), similar results were obtained in 15-month-old children after 11 days of oral iron supplementation.

Some symptoms of decreasing intellectual performance may indeed be related to a rise in the hydroxyindole compounds in the brains of iron deficient subjects. A marked decrease in the activity of aldehyde oxidase accompanied by an increase in the concentration of serotonin and 5 hydroxyindole compounds in the brain, has been reported in iron-deficient animals (Mackler et al, 1978).

Moreover, it seems possible that at least part of the cerebral disturbance attributed to iron deficiency in children is due to an alteration in monoamine oxidase function (Symes et al, 1971). This could result in an excess of catecholamines in the central nervous system.

Due to its consequences in terms of brain function, iron deficiency may also contribute to specific behavioural disturbances such as geophagia (or pica), a compulsion to eat soil common in young children and pregnant women in some rural areas, especially in north Africa. This trouble is usually reversed with iron supplementation (associated in some cases with zinc therapy).

Effect on pregnancy

It is well known that a significant increase in maternal and fetal mortality and a risk of premature delivery are related to severe anaemia in pregnant women. In Malaya, the maternal death rate among women with severe anaemia was 15.5 per thousand, compared with 3.5 per thousand among non-anaemic women (Llewelyn-Jones, 1965). In India, it was found that conditions such as abortion, premature births, post-partum haemorrhage and low birth weight were especially associated with low Hb levels in pregnancy: 20–40% of maternal deaths were related to anaemia (Devi 1966).

Adverse effects of mild degrees of anaemia are less well documented. However, premature delivery is considered as more common in mildly anaemic mothers than in non-anaemic mothers (Ratten and Beischer 1972). Maternal anaemia is also associated with placental hypertrophy (Beischer et al, 1968b) and with reduced oestriol excretion (Beischer et al 1968a). It is also suggested that iron deficiency *per se* may be a risk factor in prematurity.

Effect upon resistance to infections

The consequences of iron deficiency and iron-deficiency anaemia on the liability to develop infections are subject to controversy. Anaemic individuals are usually considered at higher risk for developing infections than non-anaemic ones. There is a decreased resistance to infection in iron deficiency, but few epidemiological surveys exist which relate the incidence of infection to iron deficiency. Several epidemiological and clinical studies have shown a high incidence of infections in iron-deficient subjects and a decrease in this incidence after iron therapy (Fortuone, 1966; Arbeter et al, 1971; Fletcher et al, 1975; MacDougall et al, 1975; Chandra et al, 1977). Some surveys performed in adults and children have shown that higher morbidity rates due to infections have been found in anaemic subjects compared with non-anaemic subjects (INACG, 1977; Keusch et al, 1983). Iron supplementation has been shown to have a beneficial effect upon the incidence of infections (Mackay, 1928; Salmi et al, 1963; Andelman and Sered, 1966; Higgs and Wells, 1972; Fletcher et al, 1975; INACG, 1977). Recently, iron supplementation in infants, preschool and school-aged children was demonstrated to have a beneficial effect upon the incidence of infections (Heresi et al, 1985; Hussein et al, 1985). But other authors did not find this positive effect of iron supplementation (Cartwright and Lee, 1971; Burman, 1972; Damsdaran et al, 1979; Harvey et al, 1987). In Tanzania, Masawe et al (1974), on the basis of an analysis of hospitalized subjects, found that bacterial infections were more common in those with megaloblastic anaemia than in those with iron-deficiency anaemia. But it has been demonstrated (Baker, 1975) that there is an increase in folate needs in bacterial infection. Thus, a higher prevalence of megaloblastic anaemia than iron deficiency in patients with infection did not signify that iron deficiency protects against infection (Baker and DeMaeyer, 1979). Furthermore, the same authors relied on the absence of stainable iron in bone marrow as an index of iron deficiency, whereas it is now well known that in cases of infection there is impairment of iron release from the reticuloendothelial cells (Bothwell and Finch, 1962). Subjects with infections are thus more likely to have stainable marrow iron than those without infection. Masawe et al (1974) also reported that malaria was more frequent in patients with megaloblastic anaemia. However, trophozoites have a special need for folate for growth, so it is not surprising that patients with megaloblastic anaemia most likely due to folate deficiency had more evidence of malaria than those with iron deficiency. Moreover, the apparently increased incidence of malaria after supplementation of iron-deficient subjects which these authors reported may be explained by an increase in the number of young red cells which are more heavily parasitized (Baker and DeMaeyer, 1979). The same explanation may be applied to the results of Murray et al (1975), who observed quiescent infections and increased susceptibility to malaria after iron supplementation in subjects recently arrived at a refugee camp. Malarial and bacterial infections which developed in refugee camps could result from exposure to antigens not previously experienced, so that clinical infections would be apparent after several days, during which, coincidentally, the subjects had received iron supplementation (Fleming, 1982). Finally, these studies cannot be considered as suggesting either that iron deficiency protects against infection or that iron supplementation *per se* increases the incidence of malaria.

Most authors are in agreement concerning the effects of iron deficiency on cellular immunity in humans and in murine species. Humoral immune responses seem far less affected than cellular responses in iron-deficient humans, but they are impaired in iron-deficient animals. There is virtually no effect upon phagocytosis, but bactericidal activity is decreased in most studies on iron-deficient subjects (Chandra, 1973). Natural killer activity is decreased in iron-deficient mice. Iron deficiency also affects lymphokine production in mice, rats and humans.

The bacteriostatic and bactericidal roles of transferrin and lactoferrin have recently been emphasized. These iron-binding proteins prevent the utilization of iron by microorganisms. In one group of iron-deficient subjects, Vet and Ten Hoopen (1978) observed a decrease in lactoferrin concentration in neutrophilic polymorphonuclear leukocytes. After iron supplementation, these patients showed a significant increase in their leukocyte lactoferrin levels.

Other effects of iron deficiency

Iron deficiency probably has many consequences in terms of bodily functions, as suggested by the various enzymes in which iron is involved. It has been clearly demonstrated that iron-deficient animals exposed to cold temperature are unable to maintain their body temperature, as compared with a control group of non-iron-deficient animals (Dillman et al, 1980). It is possible that iron deficiency modifies the conversion of T_4 into T_3, which could be responsible for hypothermia.

FOLATE DEFICIENCY

Folate balance

Folate is present in most body tissues and fluids, and is particularly heavily concentrated in liver. Folate is required for one-carbon unit transfer, including that in the synthesis of nucleic acid. Hence, folate is of particular importance for cell division and growth. Intracellular folates are required as cofactors for enzymes responsible for synthesis of certain vital products and the removal of others. Folate-dependent enzymes mediate synthesis of thymidylate, purine and methionine, and prevent accumulation of homocysteine, forminoglutamic acid (FIGlu), urocanic acid and glycine. It was demonstrated that when the intake of dietary folate was reduced to a low level, the serum folate concentration fell within 3 weeks; increased FIGlu excretion was noted after 14 weeks; the red cell folate concentration fell after 17 weeks; and early megaloblastic anaemia was evident after 19 weeks (Herbert, 1962). It thus appears that well-nourished adults may have folate stores which can meet normal body requirements for up to 4–5 months.

Folate losses

Folate is excreted in the bile in a considerably higher concentration than is found in the plasma (Baker et al, 1965), but most of this folate is probably reabsorbed. Large amounts of folate are normally present in stools, but this is probably derived from bacterial synthesis in the colon and does not represent true excretion from the body folate pool. Folate is also excreted in the urine, but this does not amount to more than a few micrograms per day (Swensdeid et al, 1947). Unlike iron, folate is used in intermediary metabolism and this appears to represent the major need of normal subjects. Various studies suggest that the average basal requirement for adult males is about 60 μg/day, and the normal storage requirement would appear to be about 160 μg/day. There is considerable evidence that folate requirements increase during pregnancy and lactation.

Dietary folate

Folate is supplied by liver, meat, yeast, fermented cheese and especially green vegetables, which contain large amounts (Paul and Southgate, 1978). It exists both in a free form and a polyglutamate form. Folic acid is present only in very low quantities in human milk and is totally absent from goat's milk. Dietary intake of folate is influenced by the method of cooking and storage of foods: prolonged cooking results in considerable losses (Cheldelin et al, 1943).

Absorption of pteroylmonoglutamic acid can occur in the entire human small intestine, but is maximal in the upper jejunum (Hepner et al, 1968). About 85% of the ingested pteroylmonoglutamic acid is absorbed (Butterworth et al, 1969). Reduced folate monoglutamates are better absorbed than pteroylmonoglutamic acid (Chanarin and Perry, 1977). When both monoglutamate and polyglutamate forms of folate are available for absorption, on an average approximately 70% of total dietary folate is absorbed (Babu and Srikantia, 1976).

Assessment of folate status of populations

The introduction of assays for measurement of folate in plasma and erythrocytes permitted identification of subjects in whom megaloblastic anaemia was caused by folate deficiency (Cooper, 1990). Intracellular folate is derived from plasma folate, and the folate concentration in erythrocytes reflects the plasma folate available to cells during their maturation. Serum (or plasma) folate decreases rapidly when folate absorption is decreased, and in many patients with general illness, serum folate levels are in the range associated with deficiency (< 3 μg/l). The erythrocyte level decreases during folate deficiency as folate-deficient erythrocytes replace those produced before deficiency. In subjects with 'deficient' concentrations of plasma folate for 2–3 months, the concentration of folate in erythrocytes decreases in the range observed in deficient subjects (< 150 μg/l). Since megaloblastic anaemia develops only after 3–4 months of folate deficiency in previously repleted subjects, 'deficient' erythrocyte folate levels are expected in patients with megaloblastic anaemia due to folate deficiency. In patients with severe folate deficiency of short duration (e.g. pregnancy, alcohol intake, intensive care), megaloblastic anaemia may precede the descent of erythrocyte folate into the 'deficient' range. In addition, many subjects with 'deficient' concentrations of folate in red blood cells cannot be shown to have metabolic abnormalities caused by folate deficiency. These observations indicate that the association of low erythrocyte folate level with clinical deficiency is a chance occurrence rather than the cause of the deficiency.

Folate deficiency may be recognized by demonstrating megaloblastic anaemia, multilobe neutrophils, homocystinaemia, urinary FIGlu, or changes in these or in the erythrocyte volume after supplementation with folate (Lindenbaum et al, 1988; Stabler et al, 1988). When serum and red blood cell folate levels are assessed in populations of apparently normal subjects, 'deficient' values are observed in some. But among the subjects with these 'deficient' values of serum and erythrocyte folate, only a minority can be shown to have folate deficiency by the former criteria.

Consequences of folate deficiency and folate-deficiency anaemia on health

Folate deficiency may produce no symptoms before the development of anaemia. However, glossitis and hyperpigmentation of skin and mucosa may occur before there is any evidence of anaemia (Baker, 1966). In acutely developing folate deficiency, symptoms such as sleeplessness, irritability and forgetfulness have been described (Herbert, 1962).

Pregnancy

During pregnancy, folate deficiency may be associated with an increased prevalence of a variety of obstetric conditions such as abruptio placentae, abortion, fetal malformation, stillbirth, neonatal deaths, low birth weight, prematurity, toxaemia, and post-partum haemorrhage (Baker and DeMaeyer, 1979). However, the evidence is conflicting and at present the associations must be considered as unproven.

Immunological status

Several observations have shown that folate deficiency in humans is associated with decreased resistance to infections. Clinical studies have reported increased susceptibility to malaria (Seeler and Ott, 1945; Hamilton et al, 1972). Other clinical reports have associated megaloblastic anaemia related to folate deficiency with gastroenteritis, diarrhoeas and respiratory infections (Rodriguez, 1978). Bacterial and viral infections may also affect folate status (Matoh et al, 1964; Cook et al, 1974). The folate concentration in erythrocytes and serum was depressed in children with diarrhoeas or acute bacterial infections (Matoh et al, 1964) and in adults with tuberculosis (Roberts et al, 1966), malaria (Stickland and Kostinas, 1970) and hyperplastic candidiasis (Jenkins et al, 1977). Several factors associated with infection can increase folate requirements: an alteration in absorption is a major additional factor in gastrointestinal infections; other factors include cellular multiplication (lymphocyte and neutrophil precursors), increased immunoglobulin synthesis and synthesis of other specific proteins, and the need for repair of lesions produced in the respiratory tract or in the skin.

Most studies using animal models concluded that folate deficiency affected the immune system and increased the susceptibility to infection. Alterations in cell-mediated immunity, a decrease in lymphokine and monokine production and an alteration in phagocytosis have been described in folate deficiency.

Neurological and psychiatric illnesses

Folate-related neurological disorders have been a controversial issue for many years. Even at present, the role of folate deficiency in inducing neurological and mental symptoms is not fully understood. Some neuropsychiatric problems have been demonstrated to be folate-responsive (Botez and Botez, 1990): these include subacute combined degeneration of the spinal cord, folate-induced polyneuropathies, some organic brain syndromes and certain exogenous forms of depression with minor neurological signs and atrophy of the jejunal mucosa. Some neuropsychiatric disorders have been found to be associated with folate deficiency, including mental symptoms in epileptics, some cognitive disorders in alcoholics, and certain depressive states and emotional psychoses.

CONCLUSION

For more than 30 years, numerous studies have contributed to our knowledge of the assessment of nutritional anaemias, particularly iron and folate status, the role of determining factors and the consequences of deficiencies in haematopoietic factors upon public health. The significance of these deficiencies, especially when present in mild forms, is not yet accurately defined but there is mounting evidence that they have a considerable influence upon individual health and community life. Control of iron and folate deficiencies is theoretically possible by providing the deficient nutrients, either in the form of therapeutic supplements or by fortifying commonly used foodstuffs. However, the solving of specific short-term problems, along with prevention programmes aimed at specific deficiencies, should go hand-in-hand with the development of long-range realistic programmes for improving the conditions which cause these deficiencies.

SUMMARY

Nutritional anaemia is recognized as a major public health problem throughout the world, especially in developing countries. Infants, young children, menstruating women and, in particular, pregnant women are most frequently affected. Sufficient evidence suggests that iron deficiency is the most common cause of nutritional anaemia in the world. Folate deficiency is considered as the second most common cause. In this chapter we discuss the factors determining nutritional inadequacy in iron and folate requirements versus iron and folate intake, particularly in different age/sex categories; the amounts of iron and folate involved in daily exchange and the role of the diet and physiological and pathological variations in losses and requirements are reviewed. The consequences in terms of health of iron and folate deficiencies and methods for assessing iron and folate status of populations are also presented.

REFERENCES

Andelman MB & Sered BR (1966) Utilization of dietary iron by term infants. *American Journal of Diseases of Children* **3**: 45–55.

Andersen HT & Barkve H (1970) Iron deficiency and muscular work performance. An evaluation of the cardio-respiratory function of iron deficient subjects with and without anaemia. *Scandinavian Journal of Clinical and Laboratory Investigation* **114** (supplement 25): 9–62.

Apte SV & Venkatachalam PS (1963) Iron losses in Indian women. *Indian Journal of Medical Research* **51**: 958–962.

Arbeter A, Echeverri L, Fransco D, Munson D, Velez H & Vitale JJ (1971) Nutrition and infection. *Federation Proceedings* **30**: 1421–1428.

Assami M, Hercberg S, Assami S, Galan P, Assami A & Potier de Courcy G (1987) Evaluation de l'état nutritionnel de femmes algériennes en age de procréer vivant en zone urbaine, rurale et semi-rurale. *Annals of Nutrition and Metabolism* **31**: 237–244.

Aug-Than-Batu, Hla-Pe & Thein-Than (1971) Iron balance in young Burmese women. *Union of Burma Journal of Life Sciences* **4**: 327–333.

Babu S & Srikantia SC (1976) Availability of folates from some foods. *American Journal of Clinical Nutrition* **29**: 376–379.

Baker SJ (1966) The recognition of vitamin B_{12} and folate deficiency. *New Zealand Medical Journal* **65**: 884.

Baker SJ (1975) Nutrition and diseases of the blood. The megaloblastic anaemias. *Progress in Food and Nutrition Science* **1**: 241–459.

Baker SJ & Demaeyer EM (1979) Nutritional anemia. Its understanding and control with special reference to the work of the World Health Organization. *American Journal of Clinical Nutrition* **32**: 368–417.

Baker SJ, Kumar S & Swaminathan SP (1965) Excretion of folic acid in bile. *Lancet* **i**: 685.

Basta SK, Soekirman MS, Karyadi K & Scrimshaw NS (1979) Iron deficiency anemia and the productivity of adult males in Indonesia. *American Journal of Clinical Nutrition* **32**: 916–925.

Beaton GHM, Thein M, Milne H & Veen MJ (1970) Iron requirements of menstruating women. *American Journal of Clinical Nutrition* **23**: 275–283.

Beischer NA, Bhargava VL, Brown JB & Smith MA (1968a) The incidence and significance of low oestriol excretion in an obstetric population. *Journal of Obstetrics and Gynaecology of the British Commonwealth* **75**: 1024–1030.

Beischer NA, Holsman M & Kitchen WH (1968b) Relation of various forms of anaemia to placental weight. *American Journal of Obstetrics and Gynecology* **101**: 801–809.

Botez MI & Botez T (1990) Neurologic and psychiatric illness and folate deficiency. A review. In Hercberg S, Galan P & Dupin H (eds) *Aspects Actuels des Carences en Fer et en Folates dans le Monde*, Vol. 197, pp 429–440. Colloque INSERM.

Bothwell TH & Charlton RW (1982) Nutritional aspects of iron deficiency. In Saltman P & Hagenauer J (eds) *The Biochemistry and Physiology of Iron*, pp 749–766. Amsterdam: Elsevier/North-Holland.

Bothwell TH & Finch CA (1962) *Iron Metabolism*. Boston: Little Brown.

Bothwell TH, Charlton RW, Cook JD & Finch CA (1979) *Iron Metabolism in Man*. Oxford: Blackwell.

Brune M, Magnusson B, Persson H & Hallberg L (1986) Iron losses in sweat. *American Journal of Clinical Nutrition* **43**: 438–443.

Burman D (1972) Haemoglobin levels in normal infants aged 3–24 months and the effect of iron. *Archives of Disease in Childhood* **47**: 261–271.

Butterworth CE Jr, Baugh CM & Krumdieck C (1969) A study of folate absorption and metabolism in man utilizing carbon-14-labelled polyglutamates synthesized by the solid phase method. *Journal of Clinical Investigation* **48:** 1131–1142.

Cartwright GE & Lee GR (1971) The anaemia of chronic disorders. *British Journal of Haematology* **21:** 147–152.

Chanarin I & Perry J (1977) Mechanisms in production of megaloblastic anaemia. Folic acid. In National Academy of Sciences (ed) *Biochemistry and Physiology in Relation to the Human Requirement*, pp 156–168. Washington DC.

Chandra RK (1973) Reduced bactericidal capacity of polymorphs in iron deficiency. *Archives of Disease in Childhood* **48:** 864–866.

Chandra RK, Woodford B, Au B & Hyam P (1977) Iron status immune response and susceptibility to infection. *Ciba Foundation Symposium* **51:** 249–268.

Cheldelin VH, Woods AM & Williams RJ (1943) Losses of B vitamins due to cooking of food. *Journal of Nutrition* **26:** 477.

Cole SK, Billewicz WZ & Thomson AM (1971) Sources of variation in menstrual blood loss. *Journal of Obstetrics and Gynaecology of the British Commonwealth* **78:** 933–939.

Cook GC, Morgan JO & Hoffbrand AV (1974) Impairment of folate absorption by systemic bacterial infections. *Lancet* **ii:** 1416–1417.

Cook JD (1982) Clinical evaluation of iron deficiency. *Seminars in Hematology* **19:** 8–18.

Cook JD & Monsen ER (1976) Food iron absorption. III. Comparison of the effect of animal proteins on nonheme iron absorption. *American Journal of Clinical Nutrition* **29:** 859–867.

Cook JD, Finch CA & Smith NJ (1976) Evaluation of the iron status of a population. *Blood* **48:** 449–455.

Cook JD, Morck TA & Lynch SR (1981) The inhibitory effect of soy products on nonheme iron absorption in man. *American Journal of Clinical Nutrition* **34:** 2622–2629.

Cooper BA (1990) Recognition of folate deficiency in human nutrition. In Hercberg S, Galan P & Dupin H (eds) *Aspects Actuels des Carences en Fer et en Folates dans le Monde*, Vol. 197, pp 17–25. Colloque INSERM.

Dallman PR (1982) Manifestations of iron deficiency. *Seminars in Hematology* **19:** 19–30.

Dallman PR (1984) Diagnosis of anemia and iron deficiency: analytic and biological variations of laboratory tests. *American Journal of Clinical Nutrition* **39:** 937–941.

Dallman PR, Siimes MA & Steckel A (1980) Iron deficiency in infancy and childhood. *American Journal of Clinical Nutrition* **33:** 86–118.

Damsdaran M, Naidu AN & Sarma KVR (1979) Anemia and morbidity in rural preschool children. *Indian Journal of Medical Research* **69:** 448–456.

DeMaeyer EM & Adiels-Tegman M (1985) The prevalence of anemia in the world. *World Health Statistics Quarterly* **38:** 302–316.

Derman DP, Lynch SR, Bothwell H, Charlton RW, Torrance JD & Brink BA (1978) Serum ferritin as an index of iron nutrition in rural and urban South African children. *British Journal of Nutrition* **39:** 383–389.

Devi PK (1966) Observations of anaemia in pregnancy in India. *Israel Journal of Medical Sciences* **2:** 494–498.

Dillman E, Gale C, Green W, Johnson DG, Mackler B & Finch C (1980) Hypothermia in iron deficiency due to altered triiodothyronine metabolism. *American Journal of Physiology* **269:** 377–381.

Disler PB, Lynch SR, Charlton RW, Torrance JD & Bothwell TH (1975) The effect of tea on iron absorption. *Gut* **16:** 193–200.

Ericsson P (1970) The effect of iron supplementation on the physical work capacity in the elderly. *Acta Medica Scandinavica* **188:** 361–374.

Estrella R, Hercberg S, Maggy G, Larreatergui J & Yepez R (1987) Evaluation of iron-deficiency anemia by an iron supplementation trial in children living at a 2800 m altitude. *Clinica Chimica Acta* **164:** 1–6.

FAO (1980) *Food Balance Sheets and Per Capita Food Supplies (1967 to 1977)*. Rome: FAO.

FAO/WHO (1988) *Requirements of vitamin A, iron, folate and vitamin B_{12}*. Report of a Joint FAO/WHO Expert Consultation. FAO Food and Nutrition Series No. 23. Rome: FAO.

Farid Z, Bassily S, Schulbert AR, Zeind AS, McConnel E & Abdel Wahab MF (1968) Urinary blood loss in *Schistosoma haematobium* infection in Egyptian farmers. *Transactions of the Royal Society of Tropical Medicine and Hygiene* **62:** 496–500.

Finch CA (1959) Body iron exchange in man. *Journal of Clinical Investigation* **38:** 392–396.

Finch CA, Miller LR, Inamdar AR, Person R, Seiler K & Mackler B (1976) Iron deficiency in the rat. Physiological and biochemical studies of muscle disfunction. *Journal of Clinical Investigation* **58:** 447–453.

Fleming AF (1981) Haematological manifestations of malaria and other parasitic diseases. *Clinical Haematology* **10:** 983–1011.

Fleming AF (1982) Iron deficiency in the tropics. *Clinical Haematology* **11:** 365–388.

Fletcher J, Mather J, Lewis MJ & Withing G (1975) Mouth lesions in iron-deficient anemia: relationship to *Candida albicans* in saliva and to impairment of lymphocyte transformation. *Journal of Infectious Diseases* **131:** 44–50.

Fortuone R (1966) Acute purulent meningitidis in Alaskan natives: epidemiology, diagnosis and prognosis. *Canadian Medical Association Journal* **94:** 1922.

Galan P, Hercberg S & Touitou Y (1984) The activity of tissue enzymes in iron-deficient rat and man. An overview. *Comparative Biochemistry and Physiology* **77B:** 647–653.

Galan P, Cherouvrier F, Fernadez-Ballart J, Marti-Henneberg C & Hercberg S (1990a) Bioavailable iron density in French and Spanish meals. *European Journal of Clinical Nutrition* **44:** 157–163.

Galan P, Cherouvrier F, Zohoun I, Zohoun T, Chauliac M & Hercberg S (1990b) Iron absorption from typical West African meals containing contaminating Fe. *British Journal of Nutrition* **64:** 541–546.

Garby L & Irnell I (1969) Iron deficiency in women of fertile age in Swedish community. III. Estimation of prevalence based on response to iron supplementation. *Acta Medica Scandinavica* **185:** 107–117.

Green R, Charlton R & Seftel H (1968) Body iron excretion in man. A collaborative study. *American Journal of Medicine* **45:** 336–353.

Guiro A & Hercberg S (1988) Iron exchangeability from pearl millet and Senegalese pearl millet meals. *Nutrition Reports International* **38:** 231–238.

Hallberg L (1981) Bioavailability of dietary iron in man. *Annual Review of Nutrition* **1:** 123–147.

Hallberg L, Hogdahl AM, Nilsson L & Rybo G (1966) Menstrual blood loss. A population study, *Acta Obstetrica et Gynecologica Scandinavica* **45:** 25–56.

Hallberg L, Bjorn-Rasmussen E, Rossander L, Suwanik R, Pleemachinda R & Tuntawiroon M (1983) Iron absorption from some Asian meal containing contamination iron. *American Journal of Clinical Nutrition* **37:** 272–277.

Hamilton PJS, Gebbie DAM, Wilks NE & Lothe F (1972) The role of malaria, folic acid efficiency and haemoglobin AS in pregnancy at Mulago hospital. *Transactions of the Royal Society of Tropical Medicine and Hygiene* **66:** 594–602.

Harvey P, Heywood MC, Peisheim JB, Habicht JP & Alpers M (1987) Iron repletion and malaria. *Federation Proceedings* **46 (abstract):** 1161.

Hefnawi F, El-Zayat AF & Yacout MM (1980) Physiologic studies of menstrual blood loss. I. Range and consistency of menstrual blood loss in and iron requirements of menstruating Egyptian women. *International Journal of Gynaecology and Obstetrics* **17:** 343–352.

Hepner GW, Booth CC, Cowan J, Hoffbrand AV & Mollin DL (1968) Absorption of crystalline folic acid in man. *Lancet* **ii:** 302.

Herbert V (1962) Experimental nutritional folate deficiency in man. *Transactions of the Association of American Physicians* **75:** 307–320.

Hercberg S & Galan P (1985) Assessment of iron deficiency in populations. *Revue d'Epidémiologie et Santé Publique* **33:** 228–239.

Hercberg S & Galan P (1989) Biochemical effects of iron deprivation. *Acta Paediatrica Scandinavica* **361:** 63–70.

Hercberg S, Chauliac M, Devanlay M et al (1986a) Evaluation of the iron status of a rural population in South Benin. *Nutrition Research* **6:** 627–634.

Hercberg S, Chauliac M, Galan P et al (1986b) Relationship between anaemia, iron and folacin deficiency, haemoglobinopathies and parasitic infestation. *Human Nutrition, Clinical Nutrition* **40:** 371–379.

Hercberg S, Galan P, Chauliac M et al (1987a) Nutritional anaemia in Beninese pregnant women. Consequence on haematological profile of newborn. *British Journal of Nutrition* **57:** 185–193.

Hercberg S, Galan P, Chauliac M, Zohoun I & Masse-Raimbault AM (1987b) Iron status and inflammatory process in anemic children. *Journal of Tropical Pediatrics* **33:** 168–172.

Hercberg S, Chauliac M, Galan P et al (1988a) Prevalence of iron deficiency and iron deficiency anemia in Benin. *Public Health* **102**: 72–83.

Hercberg S, Galan P, Assami M & Assami S (1988b) Evaluation of the frequency of anemia and iron-deficiency anemia in a group of Algerian menstruating women by a mixed distribution analysis. Contribution of folate deficiency and inflammatory processes in the determination of anemia. *International Journal of Epidemiology* **17**: 136–141.

Heresi G, Olivaress M, Pizzaro F et al (1985) Effect of iron fortification on infant morbidity. In *Abstracts of the XIIIth International Congress of Nutrition*, Brighton, England, p 129.

Higgs JM & Wells RS (1972) Chronic mucocutaneous candidiasis; associated abnormalities of iron metabolism. *British Journal of Dermatology* **86**: 88–102.

Hurtado A, Merino C & Deldago E (1945) Influence of anoxemia on the hematopoietic activity. *Archives of Internal Medicine* **75**: 284–323.

Hussein MA, Hassan MA, Salem S, Scrimshaw N, Keresche G & Pollit E (1985) Field work on the effects of iron supplementation. In *Abstracts of the XIIIth International Congress of Nutrition*. Brighton, England, p 129.

International Nutritional Anemia Consultative Group (1977) *Guidelines for the eradication of iron deficient amemia*. A report of the INACG. Washington: Nutrition Foundation.

International Nutritional Anemia Consultative Group (1979) *Iron deficiency in infancy and childhood*. A report of the INACG, 49 pp. Washington: Nutrition Foundation.

International Nutritional Anemia Consultative Group (1981) *Iron deficiency in women*. A report of the INACG, 68 pp. Washington: Nutrition Foundation.

Jenkins WMM, MacFarlane TW, Fergusson MM & Mason DK (1977) Nutritional deficiency in oral candidiasis. *International Journal of Oral Surgery* **6**: 204–210.

Keusch GT, Wilson CS & Waksal SD (1983) Nutrition, host defenses and the lymphoid system. In Gallin JI & Fauci AS (eds) *Advances in Host Defense Mechanisms*, vol. 2, pp 275–359. New York: Raven Press.

Layrisse M, Aparcado L, Martines-Torres C & Roche M (1967) Blood loss due to infection with *Trichuris trichiura*. *American Journal of Tropical Medicine and Hygiene* **16**: 613–619.

Layrisse M, Martines-Torres C & Roche M (1968) The effect of interaction of various foods on iron absorption. *American Journal of Clinical Nutrition* **21**: 1175–1183.

Lindenbaum J, Healton EB, Savage DG et al (1988) Neuropsychiatric disorders caused by cobalamin deficiency in the absence of anemia or macrocytosis. *New England Journal of Medicine* **318**: 1720–1728.

Llewelyn-Jones D (1965) Severe anaemia in pregnancy. *Australian and New Zealand Journal of Obstetrics and Gynaecology* **5**: 191–197.

Lozoff B, Britenham GM, Viteri FE, Wolf AW & Urratia JJ (1982) The effects of short term oral iron therapy on developmental deficits in iron-deficient anemic infants. *Journal of Pediatrics* **100**: 351–357.

MacDougall LG, Anderson R, MacNab GM & Katz J (1975) The immune response in iron-deficient children: impaired cellular defense mechanisms with altered humoral components. *Journal of Pediatrics* **86**: 833–843.

Mackay HMM (1928) Anaemia in infancy: its prevalence and prevention. *Archives of Disease in Childhood* **3**: 117–147.

Mackler B, Person R, Miller LR, Inandar AR & Finch CA (1978) Iron deficiency in the rat. Biochemical studies of brain metabolism. *Pediatric Research* **12**: 217.

Macy IG, Kelly HJ & Sloan RE (1953) *The composition of milks*. Publication No. 254, p 27. Washington DC: National Academy of Sciences National Research Council.

Mahmoud A (1966) Blood loss caused by helminthic infections. *Transactions of the Royal Society of Tropical Medicine and Hygiene* **60**: 766–769.

Masawe AEJ, Muindi JM & Swal GBR (1974) Infections in iron deficiency and other types of anaemia in the tropics. *Lancet* **ii**: 314–317.

Matoh Y, Zamir R, Bar-Shani S & Grossowitcz N (1964) Studies on folic acid in infancy: folic and folinic acid blood levels in infants with diarrhea, malnutrition and infection. *Pediatrics* **33**: 694–699.

Meyers LD, Habitcht JP, Johnson CL & Brownie C (1983) Prevalence of anaemia in black and white women in the United States estimated by two methods. *American Journal of Public Health* **73**: 1042–1049.

Murray MJ, Murray AB, Murray NJ & Murray MB (1975) Refeeding-malaria and hyperferraemia. *Lancet* **i**: 653–654.

Ohira Y, Edgerton VR, Gardner GW, Senewiratne RJ, Barnard RJ & Simpson DR (1979) Work capacity heart rate and blood lactate responses to iron treatment. *British Journal of Haematology* **41:** 365–372.

Oski FA & Honig AS (1978) The effect of therapy on the developmental scores of iron deficient infants. *Journal of Pediatrics* **92:** 21–25.

Oski FA, Honig AS, Helu BM & Hoanitz P (1983) Effect of iron therapy on behavior and performance of non-anemic iron deficient infants. *Pediatrics* **71:** 877–880.

Paul AA & Southgate DAT (1978) *McCance and Widdowson's The Composition of Foods*, 4th edn of MRC Special Report No. 297. Amsterdam: Elsevier/North-Holland.

Pollitt E & Leibel RL (1982) *Iron Deficiency. Brain Biochemistry and Behavior*. New York: Raven Press.

Pollitt E, Soematri AG, Yunis F & Scrimshaw NS (1985) Cognitive effects of iron deficiency anaemia. *Lancet* **i:** 158–159.

Prata A (1978) Schistosomiasis mansoni. *Clinical Gastroenterology* **7:** 49–75.

Prual A, Galan P, de Bernis L & Hercberg S (1988) Evaluation of iron status in Chadian pregnant women: consequence of maternal iron deficiency on the haematopoietic status of newborns. *Tropical and Geographical Medicine* **40:** 1–7.

Ratten GJ & Beischer NA (1972) The significance of anaemia in an obstetric population in Australia. *Journal of Obstetrics and Gynaecology of the British Commonwealth* **79:** 228–237.

Roberts PD, Hoffbrand AV & Mollin DL (1966) Iron and folate metabolism in tuberculosis. *British Medical Journal* **2:** 198–205.

Roche M & Layrise M (1966) The nature and causes of hookworm anemia. *American Journal of Tropical Medicine and Hygiene* **15:** 1029–1102.

Rodriguez MS (1978) A conspectus of research on folacin requirements of man. *Journal of Nutrition* **108:** 1983–2075.

Salmi T, Hanninen P & Peltonen T (1963) Applicability of chelated iron in the case of prematures. *Acta Pediatrica Scandinavica, Supplement* **140:** 114.

Seeler AO & Ott WH (1945) Studies on nutrition and avian Malaria. III. Deficiency of folic acid and other unidentified factors. *Journal of Infectious Diseases* **77:** 82–84.

Simpson KM, Morris ER & Cook JD (1981) The inhibitory effect of bran on iron absorption in man. *American Journal of Clinical Nutrition* **34:** 1469–1478.

Stabler SP, Marcell PD, Podell ER & Allen RH (1988) Elevation of total homocysteine in the serum of patients with cobalamin and folate deficiency detected by capillary gas chromatography–mass spectrometry. *Journal of Clinical Investigation* **810:** 4660–4740.

Stephenson LS, Latham MC, Kurz KM, Miller D, Kinoti SN & Oduori ML (1985) Urinary loss and physical fitness of Kenyan children with urinary schistosomiasis. *American Journal of Tropical Medicine and Hygiene* **34:** 322–330.

Stickland GT & Kostinas JE (1970) Folic acid deficiency complicating malaria. *American Journal of Tropical Medicine and Hygiene* **19:** 910–915.

Swendseid ME, Bird OD, Brown RA & Bethell FH (1947) Metabolic function of pteroylglutamic acid and its hexaglutamyl conjugate. II. Urinary excretion studies on normal persons. Effect of a conjugase inhibition. *Journal of Laboratory and Clinical Medicine* **32:** 23.

Symes AL, Missala K & Sourkes TL (1971) Iron and riboflavin-dependent metabolism of a manoamine in the rat in vivo. *Sciences* **174:** 153–155.

Tufts DA, Haas JD, Beard LJ & Spielvogel H (1985) Distribution of hemoglobin and functional consequences of anemia in adult males at high altitude. *American Journal of Clinical Nutrition* **42:** 1–11.

Vet BJ de & Ten Hoopen CH (1978) Lactoferrin in human neutrophilic polymorphonuclear leukocytes in relation to iron metabolism. *Acta Medica Scandinavica* **203:** 197–203.

Viteri FE & Torun B (1974) Anaemia and physical work capacity. *Clinical Haematology* **3:** 609–626.

Walter T, Kovalskys J & Steel A (1983) Effect of mild iron deficiency on infant mental develpment scores. *Journal of Pediatrics* **102:** 509–522.

WHO (1968) *Nutritional anaemias*. Technical Report Series No. 405, Geneva: WHO.

8

Hereditary and nutritional iron overload

VICTOR R. GORDEUK

Systemic iron overload in the absence of iron-loading anaemia or blood transfusions has been described in two population groups, Caucasians and sub-Saharan Africans. In Caucasians iron overload results from an inborn error of metabolism which leads to abnormally increased absorption of iron, and the condition is termed 'hereditary haemochromatosis'. Iron overload among Africans is thought to be caused solely by increased dietary iron derived from traditional home-brewed beer. Usually referred to as 'siderosis' or 'dietary iron overload', the clinical picture of the African condition differs in some respects from that of hereditary haemochromatosis. While they are important medical problems in the populations at risk, these conditions are often overlooked in the clinical setting. Here we look at the geographic distribution, prevalence and presentation of these two common types of iron overload, and consider evidence that African siderosis may also be a genetic

Table 1. A global view of systemic iron overload.

Condition	Population at risk	Usual age group	Mechanism of iron loading	Relative occurrence
Hereditary haemochromatosis	Europe	Adults	Increased iron absorption	Common
Dietary iron overload	Africa	Adults	Increased dietary iron and absorption	Common
Thalassaemias	Asia, Middle East, Mediterranean	Children	Ineffective erythropoiesis, transfusions	Common
Kaschin–Beck (Urov) disease	Central and north Asia	Adults	Unknown	?Common
Non-thalassaemic hyperplastic refractory anaemias*	Worldwide	Children and adults	Ineffective erythropoiesis, transfusions	Uncommon
Hypoplastic refractory anaemias†	Worldwide	Children and adults	Transfusions	Uncommon
Atransferrinaemia	Sporadic	Children	Absence of transferrin	Rare
Neonatal iron overload	Sporadic	Newborns	Unknown	Rare

* Examples include sideroblastic anaemias, congenital dyserythropoietic anaemias, pyruvate kinase deficiency.
† Examples include aplastic anaemia, pure red cell aplasia, Blackfan–Diamond syndrome.

Baillière's Clinical Haematology—
Vol. 5, No. 1, January 1992
ISBN 0–7020–1626–8

169

condition, the clinical expression of which is enhanced by elevated dietary iron content.

Our discussion of hereditary haemochromatosis and dietary iron overload can be placed into perspective by briefly reviewing the global picture of systemic iron overload (Table 1). The thalassaemias are relatively common hyperplastic refractory anaemias in Asia, the Middle East and the Mediterranean (see Chapter 10); they are characterized by increased iron absorption which is somehow stimulated by high degrees of ineffective erythropoiesis (Pootrakul et al, 1988). Kaschin–Beck or Urov disease, prevalent in certain parts of northern and central Asia, is marked by widespread siderosis and skeletal deformities of uncertain aetiology (Hiyeda, 1939; Block, 1958; Rosin et al, 1982). The following conditions in general do not have a predilection for particular populations: non-thalassaemic refractory anaemias with hyperplasia of the bone marrow such as the sideroblastic anaemias (Bothwell et al, 1979), hypoplastic refractory anaemias such as aplastic anaemia (Schafer et al, 1981), congenital absence of transferrin (Goya et al, 1972) and neonatal forms of iron overload (Blisard and Bartow, 1986). In hypoplastic refractory anaemias the iron present in repeated blood transfusions builds up in the body, causing iron overload, while in refractory anaemias with marrow hyperplasia excess iron usually derives from a combination of increased absorption and transfusions.

HEREDITARY HAEMOCHROMATOSIS

Hereditary haemochromatosis is caused by an inborn error of metabolism which is characterized by (1) excessive iron absorption (Walters et al, 1975), (2) elevated plasma iron concentration (Milder et al, 1980), and (3) altered distribution of storage iron with high amounts of iron in parenchymal cells and relatively low quantities in cells of the mononuclear-phagocyte system (Valberg et al, 1975; Brink et al, 1976). The genetic transmission of hereditary haemochromatosis was clarified 15 years ago in France through the work of Marcel Simon and colleagues, who demonstrated that the haemochromatosis locus is linked to the HLA locus on the short arm of chromosome 6, and that the mode of inheritance is autosomal recessive (Simon et al, 1976, 1977). Thus the abnormal iron metabolism of hereditary haemochromatosis is caused by homozygosity for a defective gene resulting in deficient activity of a protein which directly or indirectly affects iron metabolism. However, the exact location and product of the gene for hereditary haemochromatosis have not been identified.

Geographic distribution and prevalence

Hereditary haemochromatosis has been described only in populations derived from Europe; its incidence in population groups from other parts of the world is not known. Based on the pattern of association of the haemochromatosis locus with certain HLA haplotypes, it has been hypothesized that the haemochromatosis mutation was a rare or unique mutation in ancestral Caucasians, that it has been transmitted to subsequent generations and that it has been scattered geographically by population migrations (Simon et al, 1987). The persistence of the haemochromatosis gene in the population is thought to be explained by the premise that increased iron absorption could protect women of child-bearing years from the adverse effects of iron deficiency. Since, in general, the devastating effects of hereditary haemochromatosis do not appear until later in life, the gene would provide a selective survival advantage during the reproductive years (Motulsky, 1979; Cox, 1980).

Hereditary haemochromatosis appears to be one of the most common genetic abnormalities affecting Caucasian populations. For example, in a prospective screening programme conducted among over 5000 adult male blood donors in the predominantly northern Europe-derived population of Utah in the United States, the prevalence of homozygosity for hereditary haemochromatosis was estimated to be 4.5 per 1000, corresponding to a gene frequency of 0.067 and a carrier rate in the population of 12.5% (Edwards et al, 1988). Table 2 summarizes the estimated prevalence of hereditary haemochromatosis in six countries, based on surveys of predominantly Caucasian populations. Most of these studies used elevated transferrin saturation, often in combination with elevated serum ferritin concentration, as evidence for the presence of hereditary haemochromatosis; in some studies the diagnosis was confirmed by liver biopsy documenting the presence of iron overload. There is considerable variation in estimated prevalence between and within countries, ranging from 0.5/1000 in Finland to 11.7/1000 among World War II veterans in Australia. The explanation for these differences is probably twofold, reflecting (1) variations in the true prevalence of hereditary haemochromatosis among different population groups, and (2) different definitions of hereditary haemochromatosis. If the condition is defined as homozygosity for the mutant gene, whether or not substantial iron loading has occurred (Edwards et al, 1988), a higher prevalence will be estimated than if hereditary haemochromatosis is defined as the presence of established iron overload (Hallberg et al, 1989). The latter definition excludes individuals who are homozygous for hereditary haemochromatosis, but who have not accumulated a heavy iron burden due to younger age, iron loss in the form of menstruation and child-bearing, or other unknown factors. It has been estimated that only one-fifth of homozygotes for the condition will progress to overt tissue damage and symptomatic disease (Finch and Huebers, 1982).

Pathogenesis

The search for the exact location of the haemochromatosis gene

As noted above, the haemochromatosis gene is linked to the HLA locus on the short arm of chromosome 6 but the precise location is not known. Strong associations between hereditary haemochromatosis and the A3, B7 and B14 HLA antigens have been described (Ritter et al, 1984). Simon and colleagues (1987) proposed that the gene for hereditary haemochromatosis is located more closely to the HLA-A locus than the HLA-B locus because

Table 2. The estimated prevalence of hereditary haemochromatosis in predominantly Caucasian populations of six countries.

Country	Region	Group studied	n	Sex*	Age	Estimated prevalence (no./1000)	Reference
Australia	Brisbane	Company employees	1968	M, F	Adult	3.6	Leggett et al (1990)
	Brisbane	World War II veterans	343	M	>57 years	11.7	Elliot et al (1986)
England	Southampton	Blood donors	1800	NS	Adult	2.8	Tanner et al (1985)
Finland	Nationwide	Population survey	22070	M, F	>15 years	0.5	Karlsson et al (1988)
South Africa	Cape Province	Population survey	1783	M	>40 years	9.5	Baynes (1989)
Sweden	Stockholm, Göteborg and Malmö (urban)	Population survey, hospital patients and necropsy series	23355	M	Adult	0.7	Hallberg et al (1989)
	Jamtland (rural)	Employees, blood donors and outpatients	5323	M, F	Adult	2.6	Hallberg et al (1989)
United States	Utah	Blood donors	5840	M	Adult	4.5	Edwards et al (1988)
			5225	F	Adult	2.7	
	Nationwide	Population survey	3540	M, F	Adult	1.4	Expert Scientific Working Group (1985)

* M, male; F, female; NS, not stated.

of findings in the French population that HLA-A3 is an independent marker for hereditary haemochromatosis, whereas HLA-B7 and B14 are not. On the basis of pedigrees in which recombination events are thought to have occurred, investigators have assigned a position for the haemochromatosis gene on the short arm of chromosome 6 proximal (centromeric) to the HLA-A locus but distal (telomeric) to the HLA-B locus (Edwards et al, 1980, 1982, 1986, 1990), or alternatively a location which is distal to the HLA-A locus (David et al, 1986; Powell et al, 1988). Direct evidence for either of these proposed locations is lacking.

The search for the metabolic defect

In the search for the identity of the metabolic defect in hereditary haemochromatosis, the following abnormalities affecting the mononuclear-phagocyte system have emerged: (1) relatively decreased amounts of mononuclear-phagocyte iron, as has already been mentioned (Yam et al, 1968; Valberg et al, 1975; Brink et al, 1976), and (2) increased release of iron from the mononuclear-phagocyte system (Fillet et al, 1989). Over the past decade, the explosion of knowledge of cytokines and growth factors has provided insights that some of these molecules have a role in the modulation of iron metabolism. Lee (1983) summarized the information then available, indicating that interleukin 1 is a mediator of the changes in iron metabolism which occur with chronic inflammation. Since then, evidence has accumulated that tumour necrosis factor-α (TNF-α), another cytokine largely derived from cells of the mononuclear-phagocyte system, is a modulator of iron homeostasis (Table 3). Recently it was reported that the release of

Table 3. Tumour necrosis factor-α as a modulator of iron homeostasis.

1. TNF-α induces expression of ferritin H mRNA and synthesis of ferritin H protein in adipocytes and muscle cells by a mechanism different from that of iron (Torti et al, 1988).
2. TNF-α leads to increased transferrin receptor mRNA expression and protein synthesis in fibroblasts by a growth-independent mechanism (Tsuji et al, 1991).
3. TNF-α inhibits release of iron from macrophages (Alvarez-Hernandez et al, 1989).
4. TNF-α reduces incorporation of plasma iron into newly synthesized erythrocytes (Moldawer et al, 1989).
5. Administration of TNF-α leads to reduction of plasma iron concentration (Tanaka et al, 1987; Girardin et al, 1988; Michie et al, 1988a, 1988b; Bertini et al, 1989; Demetri et al, 1989; Johnson et al, 1989; Moldawer et al, 1989; Morimoto et al, 1989; Bird et al, 1990).

TNF-α by monocytes is selectively impaired in hereditary haemochromatosis (Gordeuk et al, 1991), raising the possibility that deficient activity of this cytokine may contribute to the disordered iron metabolism of hereditary haemochromatosis. Consistent with this possibility are the observations that the depressed plasma iron concentration and decreased release of mononuclear-phagocyte iron, seen with increased TNF-α activity (Table 3), can be contrasted with the elevation in plasma iron (Milder et al, 1980) and the increased release of mononuclear-phagocyte iron (Fillet et al,

1989) which mark hereditary haemochromatosis. It is interesting to note that the gene for TNF-α is located approximately 200 kilobases proximal (centromeric) to the HLA-B gene on the short arm of chromosome 6 (Spies et al, 1986), a position which is near but somewhat proximal to sites which have been proposed for the haemochromatosis locus (Edwards et al, 1980, 1982, 1986, 1990; David et al, 1986; Powell et al, 1988).

Clinical picture

Abnormally increased iron absorption in homozygotes for hereditary haemochromatosis leads to progressive accumulation of iron which eventually overwhelms the cellular mechanisms for safe storage (Walters et al, 1975). The result is multisystem iron toxicity, which is usually manifested in the liver first (Edwards et al, 1977) but eventually may affect the heart, joints, pancreas and other endocrine organs. Clinical expression of haemochromatosis is more common in males than females and typically appears during middle to late adult years, but may occur in adolescents. Untreated, early mortality caused by hepatocellular carcinoma, cirrhosis, cardiomyopathy or diabetes mellitus is common. If the condition is diagnosed before cirrhosis has developed, and is treated with phlebotomy to remove excess body iron and to prevent reaccumulation, life expectancy is normal (Niederau et al, 1985).

The earliest laboratory abnormalities in homozygotes for hereditary haemochromatosis are elevated plasma iron concentration and transferrin saturation. The serum ferritin rises later as a reflection of the degree of iron loading (Milder et al, 1980). The transferrin saturation is regarded as the best single test to screen for hereditary haemochromatosis. Individuals with transferrin saturations greater than 50 to 62% should have repeat fasting determinations performed for confirmation (Dadone et al, 1982; Borwein et al, 1983) and assay of serum ferritin and liver enzymes. In patients with persistently elevated transferrin saturation in combination with elevated serum ferritin (Leggett et al, 1990), liver biopsy is the definitive test for documenting iron overload. Sampling of liver tissue permits histochemical visualization of the cellular distribution of iron, quantitative determination of the hepatic iron concentration, and pathological examination of the extent of injury (Bassett et al, 1986).

Some heterozygotes for hereditary haemochromatosis may develop mild iron overload, and this has not been regarded as pathologically important in the past (Cartwright et al, 1979). However, a recent report raises the possibility that the heterozygous state may increase the risk for certain forms of cancer. Participants in the United States National Health and Nutrition Survey who later developed carcinoma of the bladder, oesophagus, colon or lung had moderate elevations in mean transferrin saturations (Stevens et al, 1988) similar to values found in people who are heterozygous for hereditary haemochromatosis (Borwein et al, 1983). Since over 10% of the Caucasian population may be carriers of the haemochromatosis gene, the heterozygous state might be epidemiologically important in carcinogenesis.

Phlebotomy is the standard therapy for homozygotes for hereditary haemochromatosis: weekly removal of 450 ml of blood (200–250 mg of iron)

is continued until storage iron has been depleted and then lifelong maintenance therapy is needed, usually involving phlebotomy every 3 to 4 months
(Niederau et al, 1985).

DIETARY IRON OVERLOAD

Dietary iron overload is a condition of excess body iron which is common in
sub-Saharan African populations who have the custom of drinking a
fermented beverage with high iron content. Africa is virtually the only part
of the world where iron overload due to increased dietary iron has been
recognized. One possible exception is Kaschin–Beck or Urov disease in Asia
(see Table 1) (Block, 1958). Iron overload has been reported in at least 15
countries of sub-Saharan Africa (Table 4). The traditional beer which

Table 4. Countries in Africa in which iron overload has been reported.

Country	Reference
Southern Africa	
Angola	Gerritsen and Walker (1953)
Botswana	MacPhail et al (1979a)
Lesotho	MacPhail et al (1979a)
Malawi	Gerritsen and Walker (1953)
Mozambique	Gerritsen and Walker (1953)
South Africa	Bothwell and Bradlow (1960)
Swaziland	Friedman et al (1990)
Zambia	V. R. Gordeuk, personal observation (1991)
Zimbabwe	Buchanan (1967)
East Africa	
Ethiopia	Hofvander et al (1972)
Kenya	Senba et al (1985)
Tanzania	Haddock (1965)
Uganda	Owor (1974)
West Africa	
Ghana	Edington (1954)
Nigeria	Isah and Fleming (1985)

provides the excess dietary iron in Africa is home-brewed in steel drums
from locally-grown crops, and the iron is in an ionized, highly bioavailable
form. In two studies, the mean concentration of iron in traditional beer was
approximately 80 mg per litre (Bothwell et al, 1964; Buchanan, 1967). Many
individuals commonly drink several litres per day on weekends, leading to
the ingestion of 320 mg or more of iron per week in the form of traditional
beer alone. For comparison, the typical western diet contains a total of
about 14 mg of iron per day (Stevens et al, 1988) and the iron is in a less
bioavailable form (Bothwell et al, 1979).

Two observations are important in characterizing dietary iron overload in
Africa. (1) Although the excess iron is derived from a beverage containing
alcohol, the condition is distinct from alcoholic liver disease. Hepatic iron
concentrations do not exceed 90–180 μmol/g dry weight in alcoholic liver

disease (Chapman et al, 1982; Bassett et al, 1986). In dietary iron overload, liver iron concentrations often exceed these levels (Bothwell and Bradlow, 1960; Bothwell and Isaacson, 1962; MacPhail et al, 1979b; Friedman et al, 1990) and histological changes of alcohol effect are almost always absent (Gordeuk et al, 1986; Friedman et al, 1990). (2) The pattern of iron accumulation in dietary iron overload differs from that of hereditary haemochromatosis, in that iron deposition is prominent both in cells of the mononuclear-phagocyte system and in hepatic parenchymal cells (Isaacson et al, 1961; Brink et al, 1976). By contrast, hereditary haemochromatosis is marked by relatively reduced amounts of iron in cells of the mononuclear-phagocyte system (Valberg et al, 1975; Brink et al, 1976).

Prevalence

Southern Africa

Dietary iron overload has been studied most thoroughly in southern Africa, and it is there that the association with traditional beer containing high concentrations of iron was clearly established (Bothwell et al, 1964; Buchanan, 1967). The condition was first described in black South Africans in 1929, and by the 1950s it was recognized to have a high prevalence in the population (Bothwell and Charlton, 1988). A necropsy study of adult black South Africans dying in Baragwanath Hospital, near Johannesburg, from 1959 to 1960 showed that 21% of males and 7% of females had hepatic iron concentrations greater than 360 μmol/g dry weight, similar to levels found in symptomatic hereditary haemochromatosis (Bothwell and Isaacson, 1962) (Table 5). (The normal hepatic iron concentration is less than 17 μmol/g dry weight.) A follow-up study conducted at the same institution in 1976 suggested that the prevalence and severity of dietary iron overload had

Table 5. Prevalence of iron overload in urban southern Africa.

Sex	Age (years)	n	Liver non-haem iron concentration (μmol/g dry weight)		
			>90[a] (%)	>180[b] (%)	>360[c] (%)
Bothwell and Isaacson (1962)					
Male	20–39	128	32.0	17.2	12.5
	40+	190	64.7	50.0	26.3
Female	20–39	115	12.2	8.7	6.1
	40+	154	18.8	13.6	7.8
MacPhail et al (1979b)					
Male	20–39	61	24.6	3.3	3.3
	40+	190	47.9	32.1	13.2
Female	20–39	57	3.5	3.5	0
	40+	119	21.0	11.8	7.6

[a] Distinctly elevated (normal < 17 μmol/g dry weight).
[b] Levels higher than found with alcoholic liver disease.
[c] Severe iron loading; high risk of cirrhosis.

decreased substantially (MacPhail et al, 1979b) (Table 5). For example, in males 40–49 years of age, mean hepatic iron concentration decreased by more than one-half over the 17 years between the two studies. The lowered prevalence of iron overload was attributed to decreased consumption of iron-laden traditional beer and its substitution with commercially-prepared beer with low iron content. Although there was a decreased prevalence, severe hepatic iron-loading was found in 11% of males and 5% of females in the 1976 study. Nevertheless, the report contributed to a waning interest in dietary iron overload within the medical community, due to a perception that the condition had become a rare finding (Friedman et al, 1990).

Two community surveys conducted in rural Zimbabwe and South Africa since 1985 indicate that a high prevalence of dietary iron overload persists in non-urban areas of southern Africa (Gordeuk et al, 1986; Friedman et al, 1990) (Table 6). In these studies, elevated values for serum transferrin saturation and ferritin concentration were used as markers of iron overload, and apparently healthy individuals in the community as well as patients in hospital were tested. Predominantly men were surveyed. In addition to indicating a high prevalence of iron overload, these studies support the association of iron overload in Africa with traditional beer in the diet: mean values for transferrin saturation and serum ferritin were markedly elevated among traditional beer drinkers, and were highly significantly greater than the values for non-drinkers. Among drinkers over 45 years of age in the Zimbabwe study (Gordeuk et al, 1986), 23 of 111 men (21%) had high serum ferritin and a transferrin saturation of over 70%, a combination which indicates that liver toxicity from excess iron may be present (Bothwell et al, 1979; Finch, 1982). The role of iron overload in the genesis of the elevated transferrin saturations and serum ferritin concentrations in these reports was confirmed by studying 31 patients in hospital undergoing diagnostic liver biopsies, 23 of whom gave a history of traditional beer consumption. Twenty-two subjects had histological evidence of moderate to severe hepatic siderosis, and in 19 hepatic fibrosis or cirrhosis was present. Alcoholic hepatitis was found in only two patients (Gordeuk et al, 1986; Friedman et al, 1990).

In summary, iron overload is a condition which achieves a strikingly high prevalence in the population of southern Africa. Although a necropsy study in an urban population in 1976 suggested that the incidence of iron overload was decreasing because of reduced consumption of traditional beer, severe iron overload was still present. Recent community surveys indicate that iron overload persists as a common problem among rural populations who continue to drink traditional beer. Up to one-fifth of male traditional beer drinkers have serological evidence of iron overload of sufficient severity to pose a risk for liver disease and other pathological effects of excess iron.

East and west Africa

Iron overload has been reported in both east and west Africa (Table 7), but the prevalence appears to be lower than in southern Africa and the association with the consumption of a fermented beverage with high iron

Table 6. Community surveys of iron overload in rural southern Africa since 1985.

	Transferrin saturation (%)[a]			Serum ferritin (µg/l)[b]		
	Traditional beer drinkers	Non-drinkers	P	Traditional beer drinkers	Non-drinkers	P
Zimbabwe[c]						
Males, community	49±24	34±12	<0.001	476 (163–1385)	75 (35–185)	<0.001
n	173	99		173	99	
Males, hospital	49±26	28±13	<0.01	698 (213–2289)	102 (42–240)	<0.01
n	72	17		72	17	
South Africa[d]						
Males, community	48±21	36±14	0.001	584 (154–2213)	145 (30–693)	0.0001
n	102	25		102	25	
Males, hospital	55±26	39±25	0.0004	2062 (600–7088)	765 (205–2829)	0.0001
n	130	50		130	50	
Normal[e]		35±10			100 (40–160)	

[a] Mean ± standard deviation.
[b] Geometric mean and standard deviation range.
[c] Gordeuk et al (1986).
[d] Friedman et al (1990).
[e] Jandl (1991).

Table 7. Prevalence of iron overload in east and west Africa.

Country	Source of study	n	Sex[a]	Age	Excess hepatic iron[b] (%)	Heavy siderosis[c] (%)	Siderosis and cirrhosis[d] (%)	Reference
East Africa								
Ethiopia	Necropsies, accident victims	147	M	Mostly adult	—	2.7	0.7	Hofvander et al (1972)
Kenya	Necropsies, hospital patients	68	M*	NS	48.5	—	14.7	Senba et al (1985)
Tanzania	Diagnostic liver biopsies	495	M*	Mostly adult	10.3	—	5.3	Haddock (1965)
Tanzania	Necropsies, routine	71	NS	NS	15.5	—	—	Haddock (1965)
Uganda	Necropsies, unselected	579	M, F	>15 years	29.9	3.5	2.2	Owor (1974)
West Africa								
Ghana	Necropsies, all causes	111	M	>15 years	38.7	19.8	11.7	Edington (1954)
		59	F	>15 years	22.0	6.8	3.4	
Ghana	Necropsies, unselected	314	M	>15 years	36.3	13.7	7.0	Edington (1959)
		132	F	>15 years	19.7	3.8	1.5	
Nigeria	Community survey	26	M	Adult beer drinkers	—	7.7[e]	—	Isah and Fleming (1985)

[a] M, male; F, female; NS, not stated; M*, predominantly male.
[b] Iron visualized in hepatocytes by histochemical staining.
[c] Iron present in large amounts in hepatocytes, Kupffer cells and portal tracts.
[d] The finding of cirrhosis and increased liver iron.
[e] Transferrin saturation >90% and serum ferritin >600 µg/l.

content has not been thoroughly explored (Isah and Fleming, 1985). Heavy siderosis, as determined histochemically, has been described in 3–20% of adults, and the combination of siderosis and cirrhosis in 0.7–15%.

It is of note that the reported prevalence of severe hepatic iron loading is substantially higher among Africans than among Caucasians: this observa tion holds for east and west Africans as well as southern Africans, and i appears to be valid for urban dwellers, among whom dietary iron overload was reported to have decreased, as well as the rural population. Although i has received less attention from the medical community than hereditary haemochromatosis in recent years, severe iron overload of a degree potentially to cause damage to the liver and other organs appears to be ove ten times more common in many parts of Africa than is homozygosity fo hereditary haemochromatosis among Caucasians.

Clinical picture

The spectrum of iron loading in African dietary iron overload ranges from mild to severe. In individuals with mild to moderate degrees of exces hepatic iron (36–180 μmol/g dry weight), adverse consequences are no known to occur. With more marked hepatic siderosis (180–360 μmol Fe/g dry weight), there is an increased prevalence of portal fibrosis but cirrhosis i not common. In persons with severe iron loading (greater than 360 μmol Fe/g dry weight), a definite risk for hepatic damage is present and the prevalence of portal cirrhosis is high. Iron accumulates in parenchymal cell of the pancreas, thyroid, adrenal and heart after cirrhosis develops, and the histological and clinical picture may be similar to symptomatic hereditary haemochromatosis among Caucasians (Isaacson et al, 1961; Bothwell and Isaacson, 1962). Dietary iron overload is more common in men than women, and the prevalence and severity of the condition increases with advancing age (Bothwell and Isaacson, 1962).

To the clinician, the typical presentation of dietary iron overload i hepatic portal fibrosis and cirrhosis (Bothwell and Bradlow, 1960; Isaacson et al, 1961). Cirrhosis in dietary iron overload has been described as 'active and severe' and is thought to have a high mortality (Isaacson et al, 1961) Other clinical manifestations include scurvy and osteoporosis, apparently caused by large deposits of iron which accelerate oxidative metabolism o ascorbic acid, leading to chronic vitamin C deficiency along with impaired formation of collagen and new bone (Seftel et al, 1966). Dietary iron overload is also implicated in the development of diabetes mellitus (Seftel et al, 1961), idiopathic heart failure (MacPhail et al, 1979b), oesophagea carcinoma (MacPhail et al, 1979b) and infections (Buchanan, 1970; Robins Browne et al, 1979; Bothwell et al, 1984). Although an association between dietary iron overload and hepatocellular carcinoma has not been empha sized, it seems likely that iron loading may have a role in the high prevalence of this malignancy in Africa, possibly by serving as a cocarcinogen with chronic hepatitis B infection.

The diagnosis of dietary iron overload can be suspected on the clinica grounds of a history of traditional beer consumption, hepatomegaly with o without ascites, and hyperpigmentation. On laboratory testing, the serum iron, transferrin saturation and serum ferritin are usually elevated and the total iron binding capacity may be depressed. As in hereditary haemo-chromatosis, the presence of excess hepatic iron is confirmed by liver biopsy, which permits histological and chemical determination of iron content as well as histological assessment of hepatic damage.

Phlebotomy to remove excess body iron would be the logical approach to the therapy of dietary iron overload, and the single report of its use described benefit among the 12 individuals who underwent repeated venesections (Speight and Cliff, 1974).

Possible interaction between a gene and dietary iron content

In the Zimbabwe community survey, serological evidence for toxic iron overload was found in only a minority of community members, and these individuals did not appear to be different in age, sex and pattern of traditional beer consumption from the other community members (Gordeuk et al, 1986). This finding led to the hypothesis that, in addition to increased amounts of dietary iron, an inborn error of metabolism may be involved in the excessive iron absorption in African dietary iron overload. Recently a study was conducted to test for such an interaction between genotype and environment (Gordeuk et al, 1990). Transferrin saturations, serum ferritin concentrations and HLA haplotypes were determined, and traditional beer consumption estimated in 234 members of 36 African families chosen because of index cases with iron overload. As is typical of dietary iron overload, increased liver iron in index cases was present in both hepatocytes and cells of the mononuclear-phagocyte system. Among family members with increased dietary iron due to traditional beer consumption, transferrin saturations were distributed bimodally, with 55 values normal (less than 60%) and 44 elevated. Since mean serum ferritin concentrations were five times higher in subjects with elevated compared with normal transferrin saturations, the transferrin saturation appeared to be a marker of iron-loading in these families.

Likelihood analysis was used to test for an interaction between a gene (hypothesized iron-loading locus) and an environmental factor (increased dietary iron), which would determine transferrin saturation in the pedigrees. The analysis provided evidence with high statistical significance for both a genetic effect and an effect of increased dietary iron on transferrin saturation. In the most likely model, increased dietary iron raised the mean transferrin saturation from 29 to 34% in individuals without the hypothesized iron-loading allele, from 29 to 87% in persons heterozygous at the locus, and from 67 to 87% in subjects homozygous at the iron-loading locus. Linkage to the HLA region, tested using lod scores, was rejected for recombination frequencies of 0.1 or less; this finding suggested that the proposed iron-loading locus in Africans is distinct from the hereditary haemochromatosis locus in Caucasians.

To summarize, a recent pedigree study (Gordeuk et al, 1990) suggests that in African dietary iron overload an inborn error of metabolism, distinct from the HLA-linked haemochromatosis gene, may lead to iron loading in homozygotes, and make possible a genotype-by-environment interaction in which heterozygotes who ingest excess dietary iron in the form of traditional beer also develop iron overload. Based on an earlier Zimbabwe community survey (Gordeuk et al, 1986), one-fifth of the African population may be at risk for this interaction.

CONCLUSIONS

A contemporary perspective on systemic iron overload not secondary to other pathological processes can now be offered, subject to further investigations which are needed in both the epidemiology and pathogenesis of dietary iron overload. As summarized in Table 8, hereditary haemochromatosis and dietary iron overload represent two different clinical entities. A distinct inborn error of metabolism that results in iron loading may underlie each condition. The defective gene in hereditary haemochromatosis is linked to the HLA locus on the short arm of chromosome 6, but the specific location and product are not known. The possible defective gene in dietary iron overload likewise is not known, but it does not appear to be linked to the HLA locus. While the metabolic defect has not been identified for either condition, fruitful lines of research may be to investigate the molecular biology of cytokines that modulate iron metabolism.

Table 8. A perspective on hereditary haemochromatosis and dietary iron overload.

	Hereditary haemochromatosis	Dietary iron overload
Geography	Europe-derived populations	Sub-Saharan Africa
Genetics	Iron-loading gene linked to HLA locus, chromosome 6	Possible iron-loading locus not linked to HLA region
Environmental interaction	Possibly exacerbated by food fortification iron	Clinical expression strongly enhanced by iron in traditional beer
Inheritance	Autosomal recessive	Appears to be autosomal dominant in presence of increased dietary iron
Metabolic defect	Unknown	Unknown
Prevalence	Approximately 5/1000 in the general population	Approximately 20/100 among male traditional beer drinkers
Pattern of iron loading	Predominantly parenchymal cells	Both parenchymal cells and cells of the mononuclear-phagocyte system
Typical patient	Male of middle to late adult years with cirrhosis, cardiomyopathy, arthritis, or endocrinopathy	Male of middle to late adult years with hepatic portal fibrosis or cirrhosis
Treatment	Phlebotomy	Phlebotomy probably helpful
Prevention	Early diagnosis of homozygous status and phlebotomy before development of cirrhosis	Decrease consumption of traditional beer or develop appropriate technology to prepare traditional beer with low iron content

Hereditary haemochromatosis is a common genetic defect in populations derived from Europe, while the possible genetic defect of dietary iron overload is prevalent in sub-Saharan Africans. The clinical expression of the African condition is markedly affected by increased bioavailable dietary iron. Hereditary haemochromatosis and dietary iron overload have distinct patterns of iron accumulation, with hereditary haemochromatosis marked by relatively decreased storage iron in cells of the mononuclear-phagocyte system. There are broad similarities to the clinical presentation and management of each condition, and there is considerable overlap in the potential complications that affected patients may encounter.

In the populations at risk, dietary iron overload appears to be considerably more common than hereditary haemochromatosis, but the condition has received scant attention by the medical community in recent years. Renewed efforts at diagnosis, prevention and therapy of dietary iron overload are needed. Furthermore, research to understand the metabolic abnormality and to identify the possible genetic defect in dietary iron overload may hold one of the keys to unlocking the mystery of the fundamental regulation of iron metabolism.

REFERENCES

Alvarez-Hernandez X, Liceaga J, McKay IC & Brock JH (1989) Induction of hypoferremia and modulation of macrophage iron metabolism by tumor necrosis factor. *Laboratory Investigation* **61:** 319–322.

Bassett ML, Halliday JW & Powell LW (1986) Value of hepatic iron measurements in early hemochromatosis and determination of the critical iron level associated with fibrosis. *Hepatology* **6:** 24–29.

Baynes RD (1989) Aspects of iron overload in Southern Africa. *Transactions of the College of Medicine of South Africa.* **January–June:** 27–30.

Bertini R, Bianchi M, Erroi A, Villa P & Ghezzi P (1989) Dexamethasone modulation of in vivo effects of endotoxin, tumor necrosis factor, and interleukin-1 on liver cytochrome P-450, plasma fibrinogen, and serum iron. *Journal of Leukocyte Biology* **46:** 254–262.

Bird GLA, Sheron N, Goka AKJ, Alexander GJ & Williams RS (1990) Increased plasma tumor necrosis factor in severe alcoholic hepatitis. *Annals of Internal Medicine* **112:** 917–920.

Blisard KS & Bartow SA (1986) Neonatal hemochromatosis. *Human Pathology* **17:** 376–383.

Block M (1958) Hemosiderosis and hemochromatosis, II. In Wallerstein RO & Mettier SR (eds) *Iron in Clinical Medicine*, pp 115–130. Berkeley: University of California Press.

Borwein ST, Ghent CN, Flanagan PR, Chamberlain MJ & Valberg LS (1983) Genetic and phenotypic expression of hemochromatosis in Canadians. *Clinical and Investigative Medicine* **6:** 171–179.

Bothwell TH & Bradlow BA (1960) Siderosis in the Bantu. A combined histopathological and chemical study. *Archives of Pathology* **70:** 279–292.

Bothwell TH & Charlton RW (1988) Historical overview of hemochromatosis. *Annals of the New York Academy of Sciences* **526:** 1–10.

Bothwell TH & Isaacson C (1962) Siderosis in the Bantu. A comparison of incidence in males and females. *British Medical Journal* **1:** 522–524.

Bothwell TH, Seftel H, Jacobs P, Torrance JD & Baumslag N (1964) Iron overload in Bantu subjects. Studies on the availability of iron in Bantu beer. *American Journal of Clinical Nutrition* **14:** 47–51.

Bothwell TH, Charlton RW, Cook JD & Finch CA (1979) *Iron Metabolism in Man.* Oxford: Blackwell Scientific.

Bothwell TH, Adams EB, Simon M et al (1984) The iron status of black subjects with amoebiasis. *South African Medical Journal* **65**: 601–604.

Brink B, Disler P, Lynch S et al (1976) Patterns of iron storage in dietary iron overload and idiopathic hemochromatosis. *Journal of Laboratory and Clinical Medicine* **88**: 725–731.

Buchanan WM (1967) Bantu siderosis with special reference to Rhodesian Africans. *University College of Rhodesia Faculty of Medicine Research Series* **1**: 5–30.

Buchanan WM (1970) Peritonitis and Bantu siderosis. *South African Medical Journal* **44**: 43–44.

Cartwright GE, Edwards CQ, Kravitz K et al (1979) Hereditary hemochromatosis: phenotypic expression of the disease. *New England Journal of Medicine* **301**: 175–179.

Chapman RW, Morgan MY, Laulicht M et al (1982) Hepatic iron stores and markers of iron overload in alcoholics and patients with idiopathic hemochromatosis. *Digestive Diseases and Sciences* **27**: 909–916.

Cox TM (1980) Prevalence of the hemochromatosis gene. *New England Journal of Medicine* **302**: 695–696.

Dadone MM, Kushner JP, Edwards CQ, Bishop DT & Skolnick MM (1982) Hereditary hemochromatosis: analysis of laboratory expression of the disease by genotype in 18 pedigrees. *Journal of Clinical Pathology* **78**: 196–207.

David V, Paul P, Simon M et al (1986) DNA polymorphism related to the idiopathic hemochromatosis gene: evidence in a recombinant family. *Human Genetics* **74**: 113–120.

Demetri GD, Spriggs DR, Sherman ML et al (1989) A phase I trial of recombinant human tumor necrosis factor and interferon-gamma: effects of combination cytokine administration in vivo. *Journal of Clinical Oncology* **7**: 1545–1553.

Edington GM (1954) Haemosiderosis and anaemia in the Gold Coast African. *West African Medical Journal* **3**: 66–70.

Edington GM (1959) Nutritional siderosis in Ghana. *Central African Journal of Medicine* **5**: 186–189.

Edwards CQ, Carroll M, Bray P & Cartwright GE (1977) Hereditary hemochromatosis. Diagnosis in siblings and children. *New England Journal of Medicine* **297**: 7–13.

Edwards CQ, Cartwright GE, Skolnick MH & Amos DB (1980) Genetic mapping of the hemochromatosis locus on chromosome six. *Human Immunology* **1**: 19–20.

Edwards CQ, Skolnick MH, Dadone MM & Kushner JP (1982) Iron overload in hereditary spherocytosis: association with HLA-linked hemochromatosis. *American Journal of Hematology* **13**: 101–109.

Edwards CQ, Griffen LM, Dadone MM, Skolnick MH & Kushner JP (1986) Mapping the locus for hereditary hemochromatosis: localization between HLA-B and HLA-A. *American Journal of Human Genetics* **38**: 805–811.

Edwards CQ, Griffen LM, Goldgar D et al (1988) Prevalence of hemochromatosis among 11 065 presumably healthy blood donors. *New England Journal of Medicine* **318**: 1355–1362.

Edwards CQ, Griffen LM & Kushner JP (1990) Southern Blood Club symposium: an update on selected aspects of hemochromatosis. *American Journal of the Medical Sciences* **300**: 245–250.

Elliott R, Lin BPC, Dent OF, Tait A & Smith CI (1986) Prevalence of haemochromatosis in a random sample of asymptomatic men. *Australian and New Zealand Journal of Medicine* **16**: 491–495.

Expert Scientific Working Group (1985) Summary of a report on assessment of the iron nutritional status of the United States population. *American Journal of Clinical Nutrition* **42**: 1380.

Fillet G, Beguin Y & Baldelli L (1989) Model of reticuloendothelial iron metabolism in humans: abnormal behavior in idiopathic hemochromatosis and in inflammation. *Blood* **74**: 844–851.

Finch CA (1982) The detection of iron overload. *New England Journal of Medicine* **307**: 1702–1703.

Finch CA & Huebers H (1982) Perspectives on iron metabolism. *New England Journal of Medicine* **306**: 1520–1528.

Friedman BM, Baynes RD, Bothwell TH et al (1990) Dietary iron overload in southern African rural blacks. *South African Medical Journal* **78**: 301–305.

Gerritsen T & Walker ARP (1953) Serum iron and iron-binding capacity in the Bantu. *South African Medical Journal* **27**: 577–581.

Girardin E, Grau GE, Dayer J-M et al (1988) Tumor necrosis factor and interleukin-1 in the serum of children with severe infectious purpura. *New England Journal of Medicine* **319:** 397–400.

Gordeuk VR, Boyd RD & Brittenham GM (1986) Dietary iron overload persists in rural sub-Saharan Africa. *Lancet* **i:** 1310–1313.

Gordeuk VR, Mukiibi J, Hasstedt SJ et al (1990) Iron overload in Africa: evidence for an interaction between a gene and dietary iron content. *Blood* **76:** 32a.

Gordeuk VR, Ballou S, Lozanski G & Brittenham GM (1991) Decreased release of tumor necrosis factor by monocytes from homozygotes for hereditary hemochromatosis. *Clinical Research* **39:** 238a.

Goya N, Mizyazaki S, Kodate S & Ushio B (1972) A family of congenital atransferrinemia. *Blood* **40:** 239–245.

Haddock DRW (1965) Bantu siderosis in Tanzania. *East African Medical Journal* **42:** 67–73.

Hallberg L, Bjorn-Rasumssen E & Jungmer I (1989) Prevalence of hereditary haemo-chromatosis in two Swedish urban areas. *Journal of Internal Medicine* **225:** 249–255.

Hiyeda K (1939) The cause of Kashin–Beck's disease. *Japanese Journal of Medical Sciences (V. Pathology)* **4:** 91–106.

Hofvander Y, Olding L & Westermark P (1972) Liver changes in medico-legal autopsies in Addis Ababa, Ethiopia. *Acta Medica Scandinavica* **191:** 167–170.

Isaacson C, Seftel HC, Keeley KJ & Bothwell TH (1961) Siderosis in the Bantu: the relation-ship between iron overload and cirrhosis. *Journal of Laboratory and Clinical Medicine* **58:** 845–853.

Isah HS & Fleming AF (1985) Anaemia and iron status of symptom-free adult males in northern Nigeria. *Annals of Tropical Medicine and Parasitology* **79:** 479–484.

Jandl JH (1991) *Blood: Pathophysiology*. Boston: Blackwell Scientific.

Johnson RA, Waddelow TA, Caro J, Oliff A & Roodman GD (1989) Chronic exposure to tumor necrosis factor in vivo preferentially inhibits erythropoiesis in nude mice. *Blood* **874:** 130–138.

Karlsson M, Ikkala E, Renunanen A et al (1988) Prevalence of haemochromatosis in Finland. *Acta Medica Scandinavica* **218:** 299–304.

Lee GR (1983) The anemia of chronic disease. *Seminars in Hematology* **20:** 61–80.

Leggett BA, Halliday JW, Brown NN, Bryant S & Powell LW (1990) Prevalence of haemo-chromatosis amongst asymptomatic Australians. *British Journal of Haematology* **74:** 525–530.

MacPhail AP, Derman DP, Bothwell TH et al (1979a) Serum ferritin concentrations in black miners. *South African Medical Journal* **55:** 758–760.

MacPhail AP, Simon MO, Torrance JD et al (1979b) Changing patterns of dietary iron overload in black South Africans. *American Journal of Clinical Nutrition* **32:** 1272–1278.

Michie HR, Manogue KR, Spriggs DR et al (1988a) Detection of circulating tumor necrosis factor after endotoxin administration. *New England Journal of Medicine* **318:** 1481–1486.

Michie HR, Spriggs DR, Manogue KR et al (1988b) Tumor necrosis factor and endotoxin induce similar metabolic responses in human beings. *Surgery* **104:** 280–286.

Milder MS, Cook JD, Sunday S & Finch CA (1980) Idiopathic hemochromatosis, an interim report. *Medicine* **59:** 34–49.

Moldawer LL, Marano MA, Wei H et al (1989) Cachectin/tumor necrosis factor-alpha alters red blood cell kinetics and induces anemia in vivo. *FASEB Journal* **3:** 1637–1643.

Morimoto A, Sakata Y, Watanabe T & Murakami N (1989) Characteristics of fever and acute-phase response induced in rabbits by IL-1 and TNF. *American Journal of Physiology* **256:** PR35–41.

Motulsky AG (1979) Genetics of hemochromatosis. *New England Journal of Medicine* **301:** 1291.

Niederau C, Fischer R, Sonnenberg A et al (1985) Survival and causes of death in cirrhotic and noncirrhotic patients with primary hemochromatosis. *New England Journal of Medicine* **313:** 1256–1262.

Owor R (1974) Haemosiderosis in Uganda: autopsy study. *East African Medical Journal* **51:** 388–391.

Pootrakul P, Kitcharoen K, Yansukon P et al (1988) The effect of erythroid hyperplasia on iron balance. *Blood* **71:** 1124–1129.

Powell LW, Basset ML, Axelsen E, Ferluga J & Halliday JW (1988) Is all genetic (hereditary) hemochromatosis HLA-associated? *Annals of the New York Academy of Sciences* **526:** 23–33.

Ritter B, Safwenberg J & Olsson KS (1984) HLA as a marker of the hemochromatosis gene in Sweden. *Human Genetics* **68:** 62–66.

Robins-Browne RM, Rabson AR & Koornhof HG (1979) Generalized infection with *Yersinia enterocolitica* and the role of iron. *Contributions in Microbiology and Immunology* **5:** 277–282.

Rosin IV, Butko VS & Kalabuhov EP (1982) Several biochemical and biophysical aspects of the pathogenesis of Kaschin–Beck disease. *Terapevticheskii Arkhiv* **54:** 80–82.

Schafer AI, Cheron RG, Dluhy R et al (1981) Clinical consequences of acquired transfusional iron overload in adults. *New England Journal of Medicine* **304:** 319–324.

Seftel HC, Keeley KJ, Isaacson C & Bothwell TH (1961) Siderosis in the Bantu: the clinical incidence of hemochromatosis in diabetic subjects. *Journal of Laboratory and Clinical Medicine* **58:** 837–844.

Seftel HC, Malkin C, Schmaman A et al (1966) Osteoporosis, scurvy, and siderosis in Johannesburg Bantu. *British Medical Journal* **1:** 642–646.

Senba M, Nakamura T & Itakura H (1985) Statistical analysis of relationship between iron accumulation and hepatitis B surface antigen. *American Journal of Clinical Pathology* **84:** 340–342.

Simon M, Bourel M, Fauchet R & Genetet B (1976) Association of HLA-A$_3$ and HLA-B$_{14}$ antigens with idiopathic haemochromatosis. *Gut* **17:** 332–334.

Simon M, Bourel M, Genetet B & Fauchet R (1977) Idiopathic hemochromatosis. Demonstration of recessive transmission and early detection by familial HLA typing. *New England Journal of Medicine* **297:** 1017–1021.

Simon M, Le Mignon L, Fauchet R et al (1987) A study of 609 HLA haplotypes marking for the hemochromatosis gene: (1) mapping of the gene near the HLA-A locus and characters required to define a heterozygous population and (2) hypothesis concerning the underlying cause of hemochromatosis-HLA association. *American Journal of Human Genetics* **41:** 89–105.

Speight ANC & Cliff J (1974) Iron storage disease of the liver in Dar Es Salaam: a preliminary report on venesection therapy. *East African Medical Journal* **51:** 895–902.

Spies T, Morton CC, Nedospasov SA et al (1986) Genes for tumor necrosis factors alpha and beta are linked to the major human histocompatibility complex. *Proceedings of the National Academy of Sciences of the USA* **83:** 8699–8702.

Stevens RG, Torres DY, Micozzi MS & Taylor CR (1988) Body iron stores and the risk of cancer. *New England Journal of Medicine* **319:** 1047–1052.

Tanaka T, Araki E, Nitta K & Tateno M (1987) Recombinant human tumor necrosis factor depresses serum iron in mice. *Journal of Biological Response Modifiers* **6:** 484–488.

Tanner AI, Desai S, Lu W & Wright R (1985) Screening for haemochromatosis in the UK: preliminary results. *Gut* **26:** 1139–1140 (abstract).

Torti SV, Kwak EL, Miller SC et al (1988) The molecular cloning and characterization of murine ferritin heavy chain, a tumor necrosis factor-inducible gene. *Journal of Biological Chemistry* **263:** 12638–12644.

Tsuji Y, Miller LL, Miller SC, Torti SV & Torti FM (1991) Tumor necrosis factor-alpha and interleukin 1-alpha regulate transferrin receptor in human diploid fibroblasts. *Journal of Biological Chemistry* **266:** 7257–7261.

Valberg LS, Simon JB, Manley PN, Corbett WG & Ludwig J (1975) Distribution of storage iron as body iron stores expand in patients with hemochromatosis. *Journal of Laboratory and Clinical Medicine* **86:** 479–489.

Walters GO, Jacobs A, Worwood M, Trevett D & Thompson W (1975) Iron absorption in normal subjects and patients with idiopathic haemochromatosis: relationship with serum ferritin concentration. *Gut* **16:** 188.

Yam LT, Finkel HE, Weintraub LR & Crosby WH (1968) Circulating iron-containing macrophages in hemochromatosis. *New England Journal of Medicine* **279:** 512–514.

9

The elliptocytoses, ovalocytosis and related disorders

G. T. NURSE
T. L. COETZER
J. PALEK

The healthy mammalian red cell is a readily deformable biconcave disc with rheological properties which permit it during circulation to undergo compression, elongation, shear and angular transformation in response to varying physical forces, but regularly to return to its normal shape at rest. The sole exception is found in the *Camelidae*; in them the normal shape of the red cell is a biconcave ovoid; the properties of such cells and the cytoskeletal basis for their shape are unknown, but the cell shape does not appear to be attended with rheological alterations or to have any obvious effect on red cell function. By contrast, the appearance of a similar red cell shape is unusual (though not everywhere uncommon) in man, and is associated with an inconstant, and not always greatly deleterious, set of functional changes. Where consistently present in the same individual, the shape is invariably genetically determined.

Heritable ovoid or elliptical deformation of the human erythrocyte is virtually world-wide in its distribution. Its frequency and clinical manifestations follow no uniform pattern; it is a category rather than a condition, and embraces haematological expressions ranging from severe haemolysis to innocuity (Dacie, 1985). Most types of this deformation are dominantly inherited; in consequence each mutation may be expected to, but does not invariably, show irregularities in both penetrance and expression. Some which are heterozygously innocuous may produce adverse symptoms when homozygous (Nielsen and Strunk, 1968). Most occur sporadically and, where they appear to be without advantage to their possessors, may be expected to disappear over a variable number of generations.

Some populations appear either to be unusually susceptible to such mutations, or to conserve them for longer than others, and it has been suggested that these may sometimes constitute polymorphisms. Polymorphism, the presence in a population of a mutant gene at a frequency of 0.01 or higher, is an arbitrary concept (Sheppard, 1958), and polymorphisms may be kept in existence either by selective processes or by the completely random survival of usually neutral variants. Variants which are neutral in one environment may nevertheless be subject to strong selective forces in another. By accepted standards, the only strictly polymorphic variants of regular ovoid or elliptical red cell elongation are those which are found in south-east Asia and the western Pacific; but in populations of Black African descent in Africa and elsewhere there appear to be one or more polymorphisms in the making.

Normal red cell membrane structure

The shape and many of the rheological properties of red cells derive from the submembranous protein network known as the membrane skeleton. This structure is a highly ordered two-dimensional hexagonal lattice consisting predominantly of spectrin, protein 4.1 and actin (Liu et al, 1987). The major component, spectrin, is a heterodimer formed by lateral association of an α and a β chain. Each heterodimer self-associates in the head region of the molecule, forming tetramers and to a lesser extent oligomers (Ungewickell and Gratzer, 1978; Morrow and Marchesi, 1981). At the distal end, spectrin binds to a junctional complex composed of oligomeric actin, protein 4.1 and other minor proteins (Liu et al, 1987). The skeleton is attached to the membrane lipid bilayer through ankyrin, which has a high affinity for both β-spectrin and the transmembrane anion channel, band 3 (Bennett, 1982). Other minor modes of skeletal attachment involve protein 4.1 and the integral sialoglycoproteins (glycophorins C and A) (Mueller and Morrison, 1981; Anderson and Lovrien, 1984; Anstee et al, 1984), interaction between 4.1 and band 3 (Pasternack et al, 1985) and binding of phosphatidylserine, a lipid of the inner bilayer, to 4.1 and spectrin (Palek and Lambert, 1990).

The DNA sequences coding for all the major skeletal proteins have recently been cloned and the chromosomal loci of the genes identified (Table 1).

Table 1. Chromosomal localization of human red cell membrane protein genes.

Gene	Chromosome	Reference
α-Spectrin	1q 22–25	Huebner et al (1985)
β-Spectrin	14q	Prchal et al (1987)
Ankyrin	8p 11.2	Lux et al (1990)
Band 3	17q 21-ter	Showe et al (1987)
4.1	1p 32-ter	Conboy et al (1986)
β-Actin	7p ter-q22	Ng et al (1985)
Glycophorin A	4q 28–31	Cook et al (1980)
Glycophorin B	4q 28–31	Cook et al (1980)
Glycophorin C	2q 14–21	Mattei et al (1986)

CLASSIFICATION OF HERITABLE ERYTHROCYTE SHAPE VARIATION

We propose to deal here with those heritable variants of erythrocyte shape which are caused by primary molecular defects of either the integral proteins or the skeletal proteins of the red cell membrane, and to ignore those secondary alterations of the red cell membrane which accompany either other inherited red cell conditions, such as the thalassaemias and other haemoglobinopathies, or acquired red cell disorders. These membrane conditions may be divided into several broad overlapping classes, separable on morphological, clinical, epidemiological, and ultimately molecular criteria. It was on primarily morphological grounds that they were first classified: the small globular red cells of *spherocytosis* (Dacie, 1985), and the axial deformations or shape elongations. There has been a longstanding epidemiological tendency to use the terms *elliptocytosis* and *ovalocytosis* interchangeably (Fleming, 1988), probably because most people concerned in the study of elliptocytosis have had little experience of the geographically circumscribed principal foci of ovalocytosis. Conversely, some of those who have studied the ovalocytosis of the western Pacific appear unfamiliar with the appearance of the red cells in elliptocytosis and unaware that 'classical' elliptocytosis is not uncommon there. For instance, Cattani et al (1987) do not even mention the latter as a possible source of confusion in their study.

Spherocytosis

Hereditary spherocytosis is usually dominantly inherited, though patients with the recessive form of the disease have also been identified (reviewed in Palek and Lambert, 1990). It may be present in persons of European origin (Dacie, 1985), in Blacks, Japanese and others. The molecular basis of hereditary spherocytosis is heterogeneous. Mutant α-spectrin leading to severe spectrin deficiency, mutant β-spectrin which binds poorly to protein 4.1, deficiency of ankyrin due to a synthetic defect of this protein, and deficiency of band 3 protein (reviewed in Palek and Sahr, 1991) can be responsible. This form of red cell deformation may or may not be accompanied by splenomegaly; it is usually of mild effect or asymptomatic, though occasionally it may be associated with severe haemolysis.

Palek and Lux (1983) divide the elliptocytoses and ovalocytoses into three major clinical phenotypes, based on red cell morphology.

Elliptocytosis and ovalocytosis

Common elliptocytosis

In *common elliptocytosis*, also known as hereditary elliptocytosis, the majority of the red cells are abnormal. Their shape is predominantly elliptical, with the long axis more than twice the transverse axis, though ovalocytes may be present and some cells may be rod-shaped (Figure 1) (Dacie, 1985). The shape change occurs as the cells mature; their nucleated precursors are round, and a slight elongation only is present in some reticulocytes (Florman and Wintrobe, 1938). The condition is usually dominantly inherited. In a typical case, elliptocytes and occasional rod-shaped cells are present in the blood film, and the patient either has no obvious signs of haemolysis or shows minimal signs of haemolytic anaemia (Figure 2).

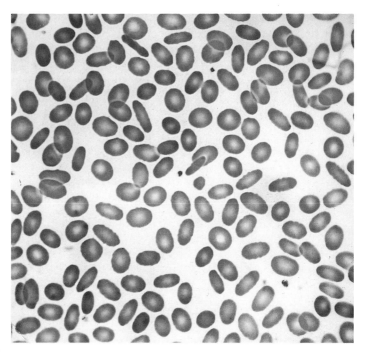

Figure 1. Benign non-haemolytic common elliptocytosis. From Dacie (1985) with permission.

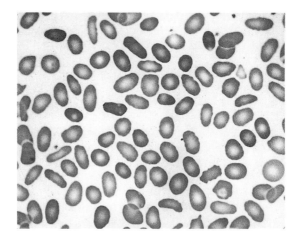

Figure 2. Common elliptocytosis showing signs of mild haemolysis. From Dacie (1985) with permission.

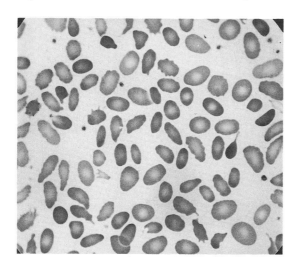

Figure 3. Common elliptocytosis showing signs of pronounced haemolysis. From Dacie (1985) with permission.

Additional shape abnormalities, including poikilocytes and cell fragments, may be seen in some patients with a clinical haemolytic anaemia; these may reflect either the interaction of two genetic defects, typically a spectrin mutation and another unrelated defect, or interaction of a genetic with an acquired abnormality such as microcirculatory stress (Figure 3). Common elliptocytosis is of wide distribution; it occurs mostly sporadically, most commonly in persons of African descent, but in a variety of other populations as well. The underlying molecular defect has been intensely studied and found to involve mutation of either α- or β-spectrin, which weakens the contact of spectrin heterodimers to tetramers, or protein 4.1 deficiency or dysfunction, or occasionally abnormalities of glycophorin C (Anstee et al, 1984; Lecomte et al, 1988; reviewed by Palek and Lambert, 1990). The suggestion by Mueller and Morrison (1981), that the cytoplasmic portion of erythrocyte sialoglycoprotein β provides a membrane attachment for the skeleton through protein 4.1, has been supported by the finding of several sporadic kinships in which absence of the Gerbich blood group antigens determined by glycophorin C are associated with elliptical red cells (Reid et al, 1987).

Palek and Lux (1983) include *hereditary pyropoikilocytosis*, in which the red cell membrane is unusually sensitive to thermal stress (Zarkowsky et al, 1975), as a variant of common elliptocytosis. It is inherited as an autosomal recessive, and often occurs without elliptocytes but with a bizarre cell morphology closely resembling that of thermally damaged red cells. Like spherocytosis, it nowhere attains frequencies approaching the polymorphic. It is found predominantly in persons of Black African, southern European or western Asian descent. Pyropoikilocytosis is sometimes reported in patients homozygous or doubly heterozygous for spectrin defects (Palek, 1987).

Spherocytic elliptocytosis

The so-called 'haemolytic ovalocytosis' (Cutting et al, 1965) or *spherocytic elliptocytosis* is a rare disorder, a phenotypic hybrid of elliptocytosis and spherocytosis. The peripheral blood smear shows variable numbers of rounded elliptocytes and some spherocytes. Mild to moderate haemolysis is present even where the red cells show no morphological changes (Palek and Lux, 1983). The molecular defect in this condition has not been fully elucidated, and it is too uncommon to disclose any particular distribution pattern.

South-east Asian ovalocytosis

South-east Asian ovalocytosis (Lie-Injo, 1965) has a more restricted distribution than common elliptocytosis. It appears to be confined to south-east Asia and to certain islands of the western Pacific, where it is often, though not invariably, found at polymorphic frequencies. It is characterized by oval red cells in which the long axis is less than twice the transverse axis, by the tendency of such cells to present as stomatocytes (where there is a transverse slit-shaped central pallor) and/or knizocytes (where the pallor is replaced by a well-haemoglobinized central area flanked by two patches of pallor) (Bessis, 1974), and by the almost invariable presence of darkly-staining oval macrocytes without any other stigmata of megaloblastic anaemia (Figure 4)

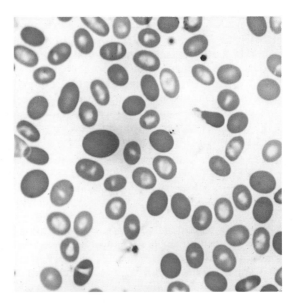

Figure 4. Typical south-east Asian ovalocytosis from Melanesia. Note the high proportion of cells with a transverse axis less than half the long axis; the oval macrocyte just to left of centre, and the knizocyte on the same level but closer to the right-hand edge; and the numerous stomatocytes, of which perhaps the most typical is shown overlapping the lower edge towards the left. From Dacie (1985) with permission.

(Amato and Booth, 1977). The cell membrane is more rigid than in normo-cytes: there are decreased osmotic fragility and an increased tendency to lysis on prolonged incubation. The condition is dominantly inherited (Baer et al, 1976; Nurse, 1980). There is some controversy about the proportion of oval cells which should be present before the condition may be diagnosed on morphological grounds, as well as about whether all cases invariably fail to form rouleaux. Related to the latter is the failure to sediment.

SOUTH-EAST ASIAN OVALOCYTOSIS

Molecular background

The molecular basis of this condition involves a structurally and functionally abnormal anion transporter with an altered cleavage pattern with trypsin and other agents and an increase in the binding of band 3 to ankyrin (Zhai et al, 1989; Liu et al, 1990).

Inheritance

Unanimity about the mode of inheritance is likely only with a relatively unusual phenotype; the fact that hereditary ovalocytosis, where it is mostly found, is seen at fairly high frequencies, at first produced some doubt as to how it was inherited. Baer et al (1976), though without giving details of family studies, described it as dominant, while Amato and Booth (1977), with their excellent opportunity to observe far greater numbers, were less inclined to commit themselves. It was not until Nurse (1980) described it in three generations of a single lineage in a New Guinea Highland population, in which it otherwise did not occur, that its dominant inheritance became obvious.

That lineage gave no history of any connection with those parts of Papua New Guinea where ovalocytosis is common, and so there remained, despite its morphological identity with the polymorphic type, the possibility that this ovalocytosis might represent a recent mutation and not display a typical inheritance pattern. Such doubts were to some extent resolved by the description by Castelino et al (1981) of the ovalocytic progeny of ovalocytic Melanesian mothers and normocytic (presumably Australian) Caucasoid fathers. The investigation of only parental couples and their immediate offspring hardly constitutes an acceptable genetic study, however, and without a more thorough investigation of the paternal families than appar-ently took place one cannot regard those conclusions as definitive either.

Possible clinical features

Hereditary ovalocytosis of the south-east Asian type is generally agreed not to be deleterious to those who manifest it (Isbister et al, 1975; Baer et al, 1976; Amato and Booth, 1977). Nevertheless, there have been occasional reports, none of them published as such, of haemolysis associated with ovalocytosis in the western Pacific (J. C. White, personal communication).

It is probable that all or most of these represent a combination of elliptocytosis and ovalocytosis; the illustrations facing p. 126 in Pryor and Pitney (1967) show ovalocytosis (complicated by the poikilocytosis and microcytosis of iron deficiency) with a few stomatocytes in the father and brother, and frank elliptocytosis in the mother of their case 2, whose own blood picture demonstrates the presence both of undoubted elliptocytes, ovalocytes, stomatocytes and a single oval macrocyte.

Baer (1988) has noted that although mothers with ovalocytosis tend in south-east Asia to live longer and to have larger families, presumably due to the protection against malaria afforded by the trait, there are among their children fewer who manifest the trait than should have been expected. She takes this to represent a loss of homozygotes, and suggests that ovalocytosis may be a balanced polymorphism. It has been suggested by one of us (J.P.) that homozygosity for the trait may be incompatible with viability, and that loss of the fetus occurs very early in intrauterine life, due to circulatory inefficiency, on account of exceptional rigidity of the red cell. To date, he and his team have tested more than 120 subjects with south-east Asian ovalocytosis and found all of them to be heterozygote carriers of the abnormal band 3 protein (Liu et al, 1990). Furthermore, preliminary studies of three couples, heterozygous carriers of this mutation, disclosed a higher frequency of miscarriages than was found where only one, or neither, parent carried the mutation. In a total of 242 pregnancies for the entire group, the proportion of miscarriages was 16% (22 out of 136) where both parents were normal, 10% where one parent carried the mutation (9 out of 90) and 25% (4 out of 16), consistent with the predicted proportion of homozygotes, for the carrier couples.

Geographical distribution and prevalence

Hereditary ovalocytosis is not confined to the south-east Asian mainland and Melanesia: it has been found also in places in between, such as the Philippines (Honig et al, 1971) and Kelimantan. Amato and Booth (1977) quote reports at the 1975 meeting in Jakarta of the Asian and Pacific Division of the International Society of Haematology, of its presence in the Dyaks of Sarawak (J. Ganesan, L. E. Lie-Injo, B. P. Ong) and in Medan in North Sumatra (P. Sembiring, A. Siregar, E. N. Kosasih). Probably the earliest record of the condition is that of its incidental finding in Celebes (Sulawesi) by Bonne and Sandground (1939). Its distribution in Papua New Guinea has received a great deal of attention; it was supposed at first that it occurred only where selection kept it in existence as a defence against malaria, but Holt et al (1981) showed that it was present even in mountain areas other than the one in which Nurse (1980) had found it. They related its presence to linguistic evidence of the directions of spread of certain of the Papuan languages from the north to the south coast of the island. One of us (G.T.N.) has observed its presence in Solomon Islanders, and it may extend out further into the Pacific, possibly into Micronesia. It has not been detected in Australian aborigines.

This distribution does, in fact, pose a more than usually difficult problem in epidemiological genetics. There is no close recent common ancestry among the people who now manifest the trait, and interbreeding among them, though it occurs, is not pronounced. For the responsible allele to have reached its modern frequencies in, for instance, coastal New Guinea would require a coefficient of selection incompatible with the fairly modest degree of protection against *Plasmodium falciparum* actually afforded by the trait. The answer could lie in the suggestion by Serjeantson et al (1977) that the protection is greater against *P. vivax* than against *P. falciparum*, which would not be incompatible with the hypothesis (Nurse, 1985) that the extension of *P. falciparum*, especially into the Pacific, has been relatively recent, and that the spread of *P. vivax* happened much earlier. The trait might consequently be a rather ancient one, possibly dating from a population influx into the Pacific from south-east Asia which took place some 4000 years ago (Bellwood, 1989) and left the inhabitants of Australia and most of those of the New Guinea Highlands relatively unaffected. It is possible that *P. vivax* could have arrived with the same migration.

Even where it is most common, the distribution of hereditary ovalocytosis is by no means uniform, suggesting either that it is still spreading into certain areas where it is advantageous, or that its frequencies are kept labile by fluctuating selective pressures. Assuming that it has been present longer in the Malay peninsula than anywhere else, and that certain malarious areas of New Guinea, such as the upper Sepik and middle Fly valleys, have only recently become colonized by man as spread of the gene from coastal peoples has afforded some measure of protection, makes it easier to understand the contrast between the 25–40% frequencies found among the Temuan by Baer et al (1976) and those of around 50% reported by Bonne and Sandground (1939) from Sulawesi, the 5–27% reported among New Guinea coastal peoples and recent migrants inland from the coast (Booth and Hornabrook, 1972; Amato and Booth, 1977; Booth et al, 1977; Serjeantson et al, 1977), and the 1–16% Holt et al (1981) observed along the inland waterways. The distribution in south-east Asia, as summarized by Livingstone (1985), appears to radiate with similar patchiness outwards from the foci on the mainland and on the islands stretching towards Melanesia; there are moderate frequencies among the Dyaks of Kelimantan (9–12%), but only around 1% in the populations of northern Sumatra.

The suggestion by the anonymous writer in the *Lancet* (Editorial, 1988), that the gene might, if it proved entirely benign, progress ultimately to fixation, and that this would provide 'the first identified example in man of eugenics in the wild', is neither historically nor genetically tenable. It presupposes closed populations in a state of constant expansion, similar to that population expansion in Africa which nearly, but not quite, produced monomorphism for absence of the Duffy blood group antigens. Li (1979) has pointed out that the survival of even a neutral mutation will depend on the extent to which fluctuations in the environment affect its neutrality, on the number of offspring produced by the person in whose germ plasm the mutation first occurs, the sex of that person and the proportion of the sexes among his or her offspring, and on the size and other demographic features of the mating population affected. Completely closed small communities, growing constantly in size and free of all environmental fluctuation, are unlikely to be found anywhere outside advanced mathematical genetics and similar imaginative fiction.

The extent to which unrelated haematological stress may accentuate or elicit the expression of a gene for axial deformation, especially ovalocytosis, requires further investigation. In Papua New Guinea it is widely accepted that persons who appear normocytic when well may manifest a considerable degree of ovalocytosis following a bout of malaria or in the presence of a nutritional anaemia; consequently apparent ovalocytics successfully treated for nutritional anaemia may subsequently appear normocytic. Such people are not the flamboyant ovalocytics with well-marked cell populations of almost 100% ovalocytes, but can manifest different proportions of oval cells at different times, and may be responsible for differences of opinion about the diagnosis of the condition and for the confusion which may attend surveys for ovalocytosis such as that of Cattani et al (1987).

Despite the relative continuity of the region of endemicity of hereditary ovalocytosis, a possibility which needs to be considered is that of repeated mutations producing not necessarily identical genes of similar phenotypic effect. There are differences even between lineages in the manifestations of the condition. Family differences between healthy ovalocytics tend to remain constant to an extent which makes it hard to blame them on variations in the expression of a single dominant gene. There is not nearly as much within-family variation in morphology as occurs in common elliptocytosis. The possibility of a controller or modifier gene or genes, in close linkage with a structural gene, has been suggested by Holt et al (1981) and Nurse (1981). This may not be as extravagant a suggestion as it may seem. After all, changes in the membrane skeleton are known to be brought about by mutations either producing changes in the constituent proteins or their modes of association or in the sialoglycoproteins which affect their linkages. Even on a level where single gene changes govern single defects one has also to consider the possibility of within-gene modifiers or interactions of alleles at different loci.

Hereditary ovalocytosis and malaria

Any polymorphism featuring an allele found mainly or only in the malarious tropics deserves to be scrutinized for evidence of any association with malaria. Even where the population in which the allele occurs is no longer exposed to malaria but is known or presumed on good evidence to have been so in the past, it is worth while considering the role it may have played in the conservation of the polymorphism. Several genetic systems have been identified as including alleles protective against malaria. One of them is south-east Asian ovalocytosis.

The suggestion was first made by Baer et al in 1976, and independently in the same year by Babona and Amato (1976). Serjeantson et al (1977) demonstrated a notable difference in parasitaemia rates between normocytic and ovalocytic individuals on the north coast of Papua New Guinea, and Booth et al (1977), investigating a widespread depression of blood group antigens in persons from Papua, found this always to be associated with ovalocytosis. Not all antigens were depressed: a number still reacted normally to the appropriate antibodies. The mechanism of this reduced agglutinability is unclear. Antibody-induced agglutination appears to require a relatively unrestricted lateral mobility of surface antigens followed by their clustering (Kuettner et al, 1976). It is interesting to note that the fractional mobility of ovalocyte band 3 protein is markedly reduced, while the mobility of glycophorin molecules remains unrestricted (Liu et al, 1990). Booth et al (1977) suggested that the mechanism of the protection might lie in just this antigenic depression, on the analogy of the absence of Duffy determinants denying receptors to *P. vivax*. The Duffy antigens, however, are not among those depressed in hereditary ovalocytosis, though the U antigen is, and absence of this has been found to protect against invasion by *P. falciparum* (Pasvol, 1984). It is also possible that Wr(b) and En(a), which are depressed, could play a protective part.

Kidson et al (1981) demonstrated the in vitro resistance of Melanesian ovalocytes from Papua New Guinea to invasion by malarial parasites in culture. They did this by comparing the invasibility of Melanesian ovalocytes to that of normocytes from other Melanesians and from non-Melanesian blood donors in Brisbane, Australia. Their study does not distinguish between the results for the two sets of normocytes; this is unfortunate, since the normocytic cells drawn from members of the Papua New Guinea Defence Force would inevitably have contained some chloroquine, the prophylactic taking of which is obligatory for all such men, and which is unlikely to have been present in the cells from Queensland blood donors. The majority of the ovalocytic cells also came from Papua New Guinean soldiers. Consequently, the irrespective lumping together of all normocytic cells could have resulted in a dilution effect, which might easily produce a still apparently significant difference, but, because of failure to consider this extra variable, could be unreal. Such considerations might also be responsible for the lack of uniformity in resistance of cells from different individuals. Kidson et al (1981) postulate that either an altered cytoskeleton leading to increased membrane rigidity could inhibit merozoite invasion of the ovalocyte, or that membrane deformation might result in the failure of merozoites to recognize receptor sites. This study needs properly controlled validation.

An investigation of Malayan ovalocytes was carried out by Mohandas et al (1984). The cells came from Malayan aborigines who were unlikely to have been taking chloroquine. Cells from different individuals differed in deformability; in general, a reduction in deformability paralleled a reduction in parasitic invasion. The role of cell rigidity was tested by artificially reducing the deformability of normocytes, determining that this resulted in a more rigid membrane, and testing the extent to which this affected the ability of merozoites to penetrate the cell wall; once more a direct relationship was found. The authors suggest that the increased rigidity could produce such results mechanically, either by preventing proper apposition of cell and parasite surfaces or by blocking parasite entry into the cytoplasm.

A study by Saul et al (1984) investigated the deformability of ovalocytes, and concluded that it was resistance to undergoing localized deformation which was probably most significant in reducing susceptibility to invasion. On the other hand, Rangachari et al (1989) showed that chemically-induced reductions in deformability of the normocyte under shear still permitted considerable invasion by merozoites, and suggested that the gross mechanical properties of the membrane *per se* were unlikely to be the primary determinants of malarial invasion, which could be linked instead to the freedom of membrane proteins to undergo topological changes during entry of the parasite.

COMMON ELLIPTOCYTOSIS

The molecular basis

In common elliptocytosis spectrin dimer self-association defects are the most common, usually involving an α-chain, or more rarely β-chain, mutant which changes the conformation of the αI or head region of the protein, resulting in a decreased functional capacity to form tetramers. The degree of impairment depends on the structural change: on this level the defect is manifested by an abnormal limited tryptic digest map, in which there is a decrease in the normal 80 kDa αI domain of spectrin and a concomitant increase in one or more lower molecular weight peptides.

So far, seven distinct structural abnormalities have been identified and defined according to the size of the abnormal peptide (reviewed in Palek and Lambert, 1990). Of the three most common, Sp αI/74 leads to the most severe clinical and biochemical consequences, while Sp αI/65, also known as Sp αI/T68, is relatively mild, producing only slight increases in the spectrin dimer content of the membrane. Sp αI/46, or Sp αI/T50, is of intermediate severity (Coetzer et al, 1990). It is the 65 and 46 kDa defects which appear in west Africa and the Maghrib to be increasing towards polymorphic frequencies. For several of the mutants the precise mutation has been identified either by amino acid sequencing (Marchesi et al, 1987) or more recently by cDNA analysis. Considerable heterogeneity has been found in the amino acid substitution, especially of Sp αI/74, where the primary defect resides either in the α- (Garbarz et al, 1990; Morlé et al, 1990; Coetzer et al, 1991) or, more rarely, the β-spectrin (Tse et al, 1990). In contrast, the 65 kDa mutation appears to be homogeneous and to involve a duplication of a leucine codon at position 154 (Roux et al, 1989; Sahr et al, 1989). Truncated forms of β-spectrin can also influence spectrin dimer self-association (reviewed in Palek and Lambert, 1990).

A partial spectrin deficiency, together with a spectrin self-association defect, have been observed in all the hereditary pyropoikilocytosis patients investigated (Coetzer and Palek, 1986). It appears that the condition results from the combination of a dysfunctional mutant spectrin, inherited from one parent with mild or symptomless common elliptocytosis, and an α-spectrin defect without phenotypic effect inherited from the other (Palek, 1985). Defective spectrin–ankyrin interaction has also been detected in common elliptocytosis, but the precise molecular basis of this is unknown (Zail and Coetzer, 1984).

Several protein 4.1 defects have been implicated in common elliptocytosis; a homozygous total absence, which is rare, leads to severe haemolytic anaemia, but the heterozygous state is much milder. The molecular basis of the deficiency is heterogeneous, resulting from aberrant mRNA splicing (Conboy et al, 1986), gene rearrangement (Lambert et al, 1988), in vivo degradation (Garbarz et al, 1984), or an as yet unidentified defect. Structural and functional defects of protein 4.1 have also been described: the mutant protein is either shortened or elongated due to a deletion or a duplication of the spectrin binding domain respectively (reviewed in Palek and Lambert, 1990).

Inheritance

Common elliptocytosis, diverse as it is in type and as distinct from pyropoikilocytosis, is almost universally acknowledged to be dominantly inherited. From this we can draw the conclusion that though some types may vary in expression (Gomperts et al, 1973), there is high degree of, and often complete, penetrance. It is rarely that family studies of a case do not disclose close relatives who show the condition, though often without clinical signs.

Clinical features

Hereditary (common) elliptocytosis is usually symptomless, and rarely detected except by chance. Only about 12% of cases display clinical features; these may vary from mild haemolysis with periodic slight jaundice to signs and symptoms similar to those present in severe hereditary spherocytosis. There may be pronounced variation in the expression of a gene for the condition within a single family (Jensson et al, 1967; Gomperts et al, 1973); in some cases the first clinically apparent haemolysis may be provoked by intercurrent infection. Some degree of splenomegaly is usually present where there is haemolysis, which, if it is frequent or severe enough, may also lead to the formation of gallstones. Some neonatal cases show abundant poikilocytosis following severe haemolysis, with cell fragmentation probably due to increased concentrations of unbound 2,3-diphosphoglycerate (Mentzer et al, 1987). Not uncommonly, when the condition presents with severe haemolysis in infancy, it may improve as the child gets older (Dacie, 1985).

There are great fluctuations in the degree of elliptocytosis between cases and even within the same individual at different times. In general there are relatively few cells of normal shape; the milder the clinical picture the more uniform the elliptocytosis (Wyandt et al, 1941). Haemolysis and the consequent stress on the erythropoietic system tend to accentuate the proportion of abnormal cells, though this may be masked to some extent in the immediate aftermath of a haemolytic episode by an increase in the proportion of discoid younger cells.

A distinction has often been drawn not only between haemolytic and non-haemolytic elliptocytoses but also between the type commonly inherited in linkage with the Rhesus blood group system (Fujii et al, 1955; Lovric et al, 1965) and the types which show no such linkage. It has been hypothesized that Rhesus-linked elliptocytosis represents a relatively mild subset of the haemolytic types (Nielsen and Strunk, 1968). Genetic studies have placed this gene (*El1*) close to the Rhesus locus on the short arm of chromosome 1 (1p32–36), which is the location of the protein 4.1 gene (Conboy et al, 1986; McGuire et al, 1988). Another elliptocytosis gene (*El2*) is located on the long arm of chromosome 1, close to the Duffy blood group locus (1q24), at the region of the α-spectrin gene (1q22–25) (Keats, 1979; Huebner et al, 1985). The sporadic and widespread nature of the condition indicates a multiplicity of unconnected mutations, and not all cases of the Rhesus-linked or Duffy-linked types can be shown to descend from recognized common ancestors, or to be associated with extended non-penetrance of single dominant genes.

The relatively frequent occurrence of common hereditary elliptocytosis means that, in both haemolytic and non-haemolytic forms, it is likely to be found in association with any of several other common heritable blood disorders. It has been reported with hereditary spherocytosis, where the effect is additive, and with the sickle-cell trait (but not sickle-cell anaemia), where it is not; when found with haemoglobin C there is no increase of haemolysis (Dacie, 1985). Aksoy and Erdem (1968) found that, in a family in which both β-thalassaemia and elliptocytosis were segregating, the combined heterozygotes were more anaemic than were their siblings with only one or the other gene. Co-existence with deficiency of glucose-6-phosphate dehydrogenase does not produce enhancement of haemolysis (Pryor and Pitney, 1967). Other conditions with which elliptocytosis has been associated include hereditary haemorrhagic telangiectasia, autoimmune haemolytic anaemia, acquired sideroblastic anaemia and primary renal acidosis (Dacie, 1985). Such associations are rare.

The palliative treatment of haemolytic hereditary elliptocytosis, in the absence of identifiable alloantibodies, is by blood transfusion. Complete cessation of haemolysis often follows splenectomy, which almost invariably produces marked improvement. Nevertheless, splenectomy is often not advisable in malarious areas. The abnormal cell shape may afford some protection against entry of the merozoites through reduced accessibility of the parasite receptors in the cell membrane, but following splenectomy this is likely to be offset by persistence in the circulation of such cells as may become infected. The cumulative effect of this could culminate in massive malarial rather than elliptocytic haemolysis. Splenectomy should only be carried out where effective malarial prophylaxis is available and the patient is likely to persist in taking it.

Epidemiological and population genetic patterns

The distribution within west Africa of the elliptocytoses is suggestive not so much of a single polymorphism evolving through darwinian selection, as of a pair of private polymorphisms, both of restricted distribution and neither with a sufficiently high frequency of the mutant allele to suggest that it has been in existence for very long. The strict criteria of Lecomte et al (1988) meant that they did not diagnose elliptocytosis unless at least 70% of the red cells were elliptical and there was evidence of familial transmission. They found that the 65 kDa α-spectrin variant was the most common; it occurred in Benin, Togo, the Ivory Coast and Burkina Faso, and its presence in the Sahel might well indicate it as responsible for the 'ovalocytosis' in the Tuaregs (Barnicot et al, 1954), and so relate to its being found also in the peoples of the Maghrib, north of the Sahara, where it is the most common cause of hereditary elliptocytosis (Alloisio et al, 1986), though there is no evidence that it has yet attained truly polymorphic frequencies (Roux et al, 1989). It is most probably the cause of the elliptocytosis described in the Ivory Coast at relatively high frequency by Sangare et al (1988). The 46 kDa α-spectrin pattern was restricted to certain divisions of the Ewe-speakers along the border between Togo and Benin. The molecular basis of the near-polymorphic elliptocytosis of Nigeria (Osamo et al, 1979) is not known; nor is that of the elliptocytoses described in Senegal by Derrien et al (1978), two of whose cases, however, showed signs of haemolysis not attributable to other causes.

The frequency of common elliptocytosis is conspicuously higher among west African peoples than in the rest of Africa or anywhere else in the world. Sporadic cases nevertheless abound, and not only in the familiar populations of Caucasoid descent in which they were first detected (Dacie, 1985); Haggitt and Rising (1971) have described hereditary elliptocytosis in a

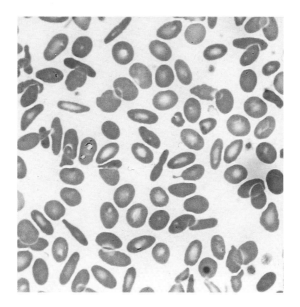

Figure 5. Common elliptocytosis in a Melanesian from Papua New Guinea. Note the occasional ovalocytes but the absence of knizocytes, stomatocytes or oval macrocytes. From Dacie (1985) with permission.

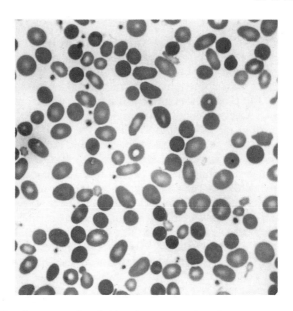

Figure 6. Melanesian reported as having 'homozygous hereditary elliptocytosis'. Note the predominance of elliptocytes and the abundant microspherocytes and fragmented cells. From Dacie (1985) with permission.

Chinese family; Fujii et al (1955) refer to its presence in Japan; Garrido-Lecca et al (1957) report its occurrence in Amerindians; and Aksoy and Erdem (1968) have discussed it in a Turkish family. In Papua New Guinea, where hereditary ovalocytosis reaches polymorphic frequencies, more than one type of hereditary elliptocytosis has also been observed (Figures 5 and 6) (Nurse, 1981), and P. Jarolim and J. Palek (unpublished data) detected the Sp αI/74 variant in two cases of common elliptocytosis from that country. Baker et al (1961) found elliptocytosis among southern Indians, and it has been observed in central as well as west Africa (van Ross et al, 1976). A large Icelandic kinship was studied by Jensson et al (1967); Breckenridge and Riggs (1968) describe the condition in a family of Greek descent; there are innumerable other accounts in a diversity of languages from many other parts of the world.

Common elliptocytosis and malaria

There is rather less agreement about the extent to which hereditary elliptocytosis, or at least certain types of it, may protect against malaria, than there is in the case of south-east Asian ovalocytosis. Rangachari et al (1989) record considerable invasion of cells from patients with two types of elliptocytosis. The elliptocytosis described by Osamo et al (1979) appears to be identical with the 'elliptocytosis or ovalocytosis' recorded by Fleming (1988) in 2–3% of the population in both southern and northern Nigeria. It seems unlikely that the occurrence at frequencies verging on the polymorphic can have arisen over a wide area otherwise than through natural selection, and the first candidate as a selective agent, as in all such instances, must be malaria. Evidence for this is furnished by Schulman et al (1990), who investigated the growth of *P. falciparum* in a variety of human erythrocytes containing abnormal proteins, and concluded that a functionally and structurally normal host membrane is indispensable for parasite growth and development. Nevertheless, they did observe normal parasite growth in one spherocytic subject with normal membrane spectrin content, and Fleming (1988) records the finding of a Nigerian 'ovalocytic' infant with intense parasitaemia.

The spectrin variants Sp αI/65 and Sp αI/46 described in west African populations by Dhermy et al (1989) may, as Facer (1989) suggests, be relevant to partial protection against malaria, since her work with her colleagues Palek and Prchal on the variant Sp αI/74 revealed that the pyropoikilocytic cells associated with defective spectrin tetramerization of that variant were significantly resistant to invasion by *P. falciparum* merozoites. The number of patients involved in this study was, however, very small, and it is in need of independent verification. The precise mechanism and molecular basis of reduced malaria invasion remain obscure. That the Sp αI/65 variant appears to be homogeneous at both the protein and the DNA level would imply that selection for this single variant, from whatever cause, is strong enough to offset any haematological disadvantages. Alloisio et al (1986) found that in the cases they studied from Algeria and Morocco there was a correlation between the proportion of the 65 kDa peptide, the defect in spectrin self-association and the extent of changes in the shape of the red cell. They suggest that clinical expression might depend on 'silent' defects of the spectrin β chain conducing to differences in the proportions of the α defect in different patients. This is unlikely, however, to influence protection against malaria in any way.

CONCLUSIONS AND SUMMARY

A sharper distinction than in the past can now be made between the contrasting types of hereditary axial deformation. There should no longer be any need to use the terms elliptocytosis and ovalocytosis interchangeably, and with increasing understanding of the underlying molecular defects and the prospect of defining these diverse conditions more accurately, it is probable that even these two terms will either be more generally accepted as referring to categories rather than to single entities, or else be discarded in favour of a wider classification based on biochemical alterations in the membrane skeleton.

Changes in red cell shape which depend on alterations in the red cell membrane integral or skeletal proteins are heritable, usually dominantly. The elliptocytoses and spherocytosis result from a variety of skeletal biochemical defects, and generally occur sporadically, but as far as is known the widespread ovalocytosis of south-east Asia and the western Pacific is homogeneously due to a single membrane skeleton defect, though this may be subject to local phenotypic modifications. This is the only one of these conditions which is strictly polymorphic, but the 65 and 46 kDa α-spectrin variants found in elliptocytosis in west and north Africa may represent polymorphisms in the making. There is good evidence that the south-east Asian ovalocytosis gene is selected for on account of the protection it affords against malaria; the evidence that this may be the case with certain types of elliptocytosis is at least suggestive.

Acknowledgements

We are grateful to Sir John Dacie for supplying originals of the illustrations, and to him and Dr Dominic Amato, and to Churchill Livingstone, the publishers of Sir John Dacie's *The Haemolytic Anaemias*, volume I part 1, for permission to reproduce them. We are also indebted to Dr David L. Wesche of the Walter Reed Hospital, Washington, DC, for pointing out the relevance of the metabolism of chloroquine to the conclusions drawn in one of the papers cited by us.

REFERENCES

Aksoy M & Erdem S (1968) Combination of hereditary elliptocytosis and heterozygous β-thalassaemia: a family study. *Journal of Medical Genetics* **5:** 298–301.
Alloisio N, Guetarni D, Morlé L et al (1986) Sp α1/65 hereditary elliptocytosis in North Africa. *American Journal of Hematology* **23:** 113–122.
Amato D & Booth PB (1977) Hereditary ovalocytosis in Melanesians. *Papua New Guinea Medical Journal* **20:** 26–32.
Anderson RA & Lovrien RE (1984) Glycophorin is linked by band 4.1 protein to the human erythrocyte membrane skeleton. *Nature* **307:** 655–658.
Anstee DJ, Ridgwell K, Tanner MJA, Daniels GL & Parsons SF (1984) Individuals lacking the Gerbich blood group antigen have alterations in the human erythrocyte membrane sialoglycoproteins beta and gamma. *Biochemical Journal* **221:** 97–104.
Babona D & Amato D (1976) Hereditary ovalocytosis and malaria in children. *Proceedings of the 12th Annual Symposium of the Medical Society of Papua New Guinea.* Lae.
Baer A (1988) Elliptocytosis, malaria and fertility in Malaysia. *Human Biology* **60:** 909–915.
Baer A, Lie-Injo LE, Welch QB & Lewis AN (1976) Genetic factors and malaria in the Temuan. *American Journal of Human Genetics* **28:** 179–188.
Baker SJ, Jacob E, Rajan KT & Gault E (1961) Hereditary haemolytic anaemia associated with elliptocytosis: a study of three families. *British Journal of Haematology* **7:** 210–222.
Barnicot NA, Ikin EW & Mourant AE (1954) Les groupes sanguins ABO, MNS et Rh des Touareg de l'Air. *L'Anthropologie* **58:** 231–240.
Bellwood PS (1989) The colonization of the Pacific: some current theories. In Hill AVS & Serjeantson SW (eds) *The Colonization of the Pacific: A Genetic Trail*, pp 1–59. Oxford: Oxford University Press.
Bennett V (1982) The molecular basis for membrane–cytoskeleton association in human erythrocytes. *Journal of Cell Biochemistry* **18:** 49–65.
Bessis M (1974) *Corpuscles—Atlas of Red Blood Cell Shapes.* Berlin: Springer-Verlag.
Bonne C & Sandground JH (1939) Echinostomiasis in Celebes veroorzaakt door het eten van zoetwatermosselen. *Geneeskundige Tijdschrift voor Nederlands-Indien* **79:** 3016–3034.
Booth PB & Hornabrook RW (1972) Weak I(T) red cell antigen in Melanesians: family and population studies. *Human Biology in Oceania* **1:** 307–309.
Booth PB, Serjeantson S, Woodfield DG & Amato D (1977) Selective depression of blood group antigens associated with hereditary ovalocytosis among Melanesians. *Vox Sanguinis* **32:** 99–110.
Breckenridge RL & Riggs JA (1968) Hereditary elliptocytosis with hemolytic anemia complicating pregnancy. *American Journal of Obstetrics and Gynecology* **101:** 861–862.

Castelino D, Saul A, Myler P et al (1981) Ovalocytosis in Papua New Guinea—dominantly inherited resistance to malaria. *Southeast Asian Journal of Tropical Medicine and Public Health* **12**: 549–555.

Cattani JA, Gibson FD, Alpers MP & Crane GG (1987) Hereditary ovalocytosis and reduced susceptibility to malaria in Papua New Guinea. *Transactions of the Royal Society of Tropical Medicine and Hygiene* **81**: 705–709.

Coetzer TL & Palek J (1986) Partial spectrin deficiency in hereditary pyropoikilocytosis. *Blood* **67**: 919–924.

Coetzer T, Palek J, Lawler J et al (1990) Structural and functional heterogeneity of α spectrin mutations involving the spectrin heterodimer self-association site: relationships to hematologic expression of homozygous hereditary elliptocytosis and hereditary pyropoikilocytosis. *Blood* **75**: 2235–2243.

Coetzer TL, Sahr K, Prchal J et al (1991) Four different mutations in codon 28 of α spectrin are associated with structurally and functionally abnormal spectrin αI/74 in hereditary elliptocytosis. *Journal of Clinical Investigation* (in press).

Conboy J, Mohandas N, Tchernia G et al (1986) Molecular basis of hereditary elliptocytosis due to protein 4.1 deficiency. *New England Journal of Medicine* **315**: 680–685.

Cook PJL, Noades JE, Lomas CG et al (1980) Exclusion mapping illustrated by the MNSs blood group system. *Annals of Human Genetics* **44**: 61–73.

Cutting HO, McHugh WJ, Conrad FG & Marlow AA (1965) Autosomal dominant hemolytic anemia characterized by ovalocytosis. A family of seven involved members. *American Journal of Medicine* **39**: 21–34.

Dacie J (1985) *The Haemolytic Anaemias* vol. I, part 1, 3rd edn, pp x, 440. Edinburgh: Churchill Livingstone.

Derrien J-P, Gaultier Y, Lartisien D et al (1978) L'helliptocytose constitutionelle au Senegal. *Bulletin de la Société Médicale de l'Afrique Noire de la Langue Française* **23**: 276–281.

Dhermy D, Carnevale P, Blot I & Zohoun I (1989) Hereditary elliptocytosis in Africa. *Lancet* **i**: 225.

Editorial (1988) Ovalocytosis and malaria. *Lancet* **ii**: 608–610.

Facer CA (1989) Malaria, hereditary elliptocytosis, and pyropoikilocytosis. *Lancet* **i**: 897.

Fleming AF (1988) Ovalocytosis and malaria. *Lancet* **ii**: 857.

Florman AL & Wintrobe MM (1938) Human elliptical red corpuscles. *Bulletin of the Johns Hopkins Hospital* **63**: 209–220.

Fujii T, Moloney WC & Morton NE (1955) Data on linkage of ovalocytosis and blood groups. *American Journal of Human Genetics* **7**: 72–75.

Garbarz M, Dhermy D, Lecomte M-C et al (1984) A variant of erythrocyte membrane skeletal protein band 4.1 associated with hereditary elliptocytosis. *Blood* **64**: 1006–1015.

Garbarz M, Lecomte M-C, Feo C et al (1990) Hereditary pyropoikilocytosis and elliptocytosis in a White French family with the spectrin αI/74 variant related to a CGT to CAT codon change (Arg to His) position 22 of the spectrin αI domain. *Blood* **75**: 1691–1698.

Garrido-Lecca G, Merino C & Luna G Jr (1957) Hereditary elliptocytosis in a Peruvian family. *New England Journal of Medicine* **256**: 311–314.

Gomperts ED, Cayanis F, Metz J & Zail SS (1973) A red cell membrane protein abnormality in hereditary elliptocytosis. *British Journal of Haematology* **25**: 415–420.

Haggitt RC & Rising JA (1971) Hereditary ovalocytosis in a Chinese family. *Archives of Pathology* **21**: 225–227.

Holt M, Hogan PF & Nurse GT (1981) The ovalocytosis polymorphism on the western border of Papua New Guinea. *Human Biology* **53**: 23–34.

Honig GR, Lacson PS & Maurer HS (1971) A new familial disorder with abnormal erythrocyte morphology and increased permeability of the erythrocytes to sodium and potassium. *Pediatric Research* **5**: 159–166.

Huebner K, Palumbo AP, Isobe M et al (1985) The alpha-spectrin gene is on chromosome 1 in mouse and man. *Proceedings of the National Academy of Sciences of the USA* **82**: 3790–3793.

Isbister JP, Amato D & Woodfield DG (1975) The blood film in the investigation of anaemia. *Papua New Guinea Medical Journal* **18**: 47.

Jensson O, Jonasson T & Olafsson O (1967) Hereditary elliptocytosis in Iceland. *British Journal of Haematology* **13**: 844–854.

Keats BTB (1979) Another elliptocytosis locus on chromosome 1? *Human Genetics* **50**: 227.

Kidson C, Lamont G, Saul A & Nurse GT (1981) Ovalocytic erythrocytes from Melanesians are resistant to invasion by malaria parasites in culture. *Proceedings of the National Academy of Sciences of the USA* **78:** 5829–5832.

Kuettner CA, Staehelin LA & Gordon JA (1976) Receptor distribution and the mechanism of enhanced erythrocyte agglutination by soybean agglutinin. *Biochimica et Biophysica Acta* **448:** 114–120.

Lambert S, Conboy J & Zail S (1988) A molecular study of heterozygous protein 4.1 deficiency in hereditary elliptocytosis. *Blood* **72:** 1926–1929.

Lecomte M-C, Dhermy D, Gautero H et al (1988) L'elliptocytose héréditaire en Afrique de l'Ouest: fréquence et repartition des variants de la spectrine. *Cahiers des Recherches de l'Académie des Sciences, Paris* **306, série III:** 43–46.

Li W-H (1979) Maintenance of genetic variability under the pressure of neutral and deleterious mutations in a finite population. *Genetics* **92:** 647–667.

Lie-Injo LE (1965) Hereditary ovalocytosis and haemoglobin E-ovalocytosis in Malayan aborigines. *Nature* **208:** 1329.

Liu S-C, Derick LH & Palek J (1987) Visualization of the hexagonal lattice in the erythrocyte membrane skeleton. *Journal of Cell Biology* **104:** 527–536.

Liu S-C, Zhai S, Palek J et al (1990) Molecular defect of the band 3 protein in Southeast Asian ovalocytosis. *New England Journal of Medicine* **323:** 1530–1538.

Livingstone FB (1985) *Frequencies of Hemoglobin Variants: Thalassemia, The Glucose-6-Phosphate Dehydrogenase Deficiency, G6PD Variants, and Ovalocytosis in Human Populations.* New York: Oxford University Press.

Lovric VA, Walsh RJ & Bradley MA (1965) Hereditary elliptocytosis: genetic linkage with the Rh chromosome. *Australian Annals of Medicine* **14:** 162–166.

Lux S, Tse W, Menninger J et al (1990) Hereditary spherocytosis associated with deletion of human erythrocyte ankyrin gene on chromosome 8. *Nature* **345:** 736–739.

McGuire M, Smith BL & Agre P (1988) Distinct variants of erythrocyte protein 4.1 inherited in linkage with elliptocytosis and Rh type in three white families. *Blood* **72:** 287–293.

Marchesi SL, Letsinger JT, Speicher DW et al (1987) Mutant forms of spectrin α-subunits in hereditary elliptocytosis. *Journal of Clinical Investigation* **80:** 191–198.

Mattei MJ, Colin Y, Le van Kim C et al (1986) Localization of the gene for human erythrocyte glycophorin C to chromosome 2, q14–21. *Human Genetics* **74:** 420–422.

Mentzer WC Jr, Iarocci TA & Mohandas N (1987) Modulation of erythrocyte membrane mechanical fragility by 2,3-diphosphoglycerate in the neonatal poikilocytosis/elliptocytosis syndrome. *Journal of Clinical Investigation* **79:** 943–949.

Mohandas N, Lie-Injo LE, Friedman M & Mak JW (1984) Rigid membranes of Malayan ovalocytes: a likely genetic barrier against malaria. *Blood* **63:** 1385–1392.

Morlé L, Rowe AF, Alloisio N et al (1990) Two elliptocytogenic αI/74 variants of the spectrin alphaI domain. Spectrin Culez (GGT → GTT, αI40 Gly → Val) and Spectrin Lyon (CTT → TTT, αI43 Leu → Phe). *Journal of Clinical Investigation* **86:** 548–554.

Morrow JS & Marchesi VT (1981) Self-assembly of spectrin oligomers in vitro: a basis for a dynamic cytoskeleton. *Journal of Cell Biology* **88:** 463–468.

Mueller TJ & Morrison M (1981) Glycoconnectin (PAS 2) a membrane attachment site for the human erythrocyte cytoskeleton. *Progress in Clinical and Biological Research* **56:** 95–116.

Ng SY, Gunning P, Eddy R et al (1985) Evolution of the functional human β-actin gene and its multi-pseudogene family: conservation of non-coding regions and chromosomal dispersion of pseudogenes. *Molecular Cell Biology* **5:** 2720–2732.

Nielsen JA & Strunk KW (1968) Homozygous hereditary elliptocytosis as the cause of haemolytic anaemia in infancy. *Scandinavian Journal of Haematology* **5:** 486–496.

Nurse GT (1980) Hereditary ovalocytosis in a Highland family. *Papua New Guinea Medical Journal* **23:** 66–69.

Nurse GT (1981) Haematological genetics in the tropics: Oceania. *Clinics in Haematology* **10:** 1051–1067.

Nurse GT (1985) The pace of human selective adaptation to malaria. *Journal of Human Evolution* **14:** 319–326.

Osamo NO, Photiades DP & Haddock DRW (1979) Hereditary elliptocytosis in Nigerians. *Nigerian Journal of Medical Science* **2:** 141–146.

Palek J (1985) Hereditary elliptocytosis and related disorders. *Clinics in Haematology* **14:** 45–87.

Palek J (1987) Hereditary elliptocytosis, spherocytosis and related disorders: consequences of a deficiency or a mutation of membrane skeletal proteins. *Blood Reviews* **1:** 147–168.

Palek J & Lambert S (1990) Genetics of the red cell membrane skeleton. *Seminars in Haematology* **27:** 290–332.

Palek J & Lux S (1983) Red cell membrane skeletal defects in hereditary and acquired hemolytic anaemias. *Seminars in Haematology* **20:** 189–224.

Palek J & Sahr KE (1991) Disorders of the red cell membrane skeleton. *Blood* (in press).

Pasternack GR, Anderson RA, Leto TL et al (1985) Interactions between protein 4.1 and band 3. An alternative binding site for an element of the membrane skeleton. *Journal of Biological Chemistry* **260:** 3676–3683.

Pasvol G (1984) Receptors on red cells for *Plasmodium falciparum* and their interaction with merozoites. *Philosophical Transactions of the Royal Society of London, Series B* **307:** 189–200.

Prchal JT, Morley BJ, Yoon S-H et al (1987) Isolation and characterization of cDNA clones for human erythrocyte β-spectrin. *Proceedings of the National Academy of Sciences of the USA* **84:** 7468–7472.

Pryor DS & Pitney WR (1967) Hereditary elliptocytosis: a report of two families from New Guinea. *British Journal of Haematology* **13:** 126–134.

Rangachari K, Beaven GH, Nash GB et al (1989) A study of red cell membrane properties in relation to malarial invasion. *Molecular Biochemistry and Parasitology* **34:** 63–74.

Reid ME, Anstee DJ, Tanner MJA, Ridgewell K & Nurse GT (1987) Structural relationships between human erythrocyte sialoglycoproteins beta and gamma and abnormal sialoglycoproteins found in certain rare human erythrocyte variants lacking the Gerbich blood-group antigens. *Biochemical Journal* **244:** 123–128.

Roux AF, Morlé F, Guetarni D et al (1989) Molecular basis of Sp α1/65 hereditary elliptocytosis in North Africa: insertion of a TTG triplet between codons 147 and 149 in the α-spectrin gene from five unrelated families. *Blood* **73:** 2196–2201.

Sahr KE, Tobe T, Scarpa A et al (1989) Sequence and exon–intron organization of the DNA encoding the αI domain of human spectrin. Application to the study of mutations causing hereditary elliptocytosis. *Journal of Clinical Investigation* **84:** 1243–1252.

Sangare A, Cowpli-Boni M, Sanogo I et al (1988) Contributions à l'étude de l'elliptocytose héréditaire en Côte d'Ivoire. *Médecine Tropicale* **48:** 253–257.

Saul A, Lamont G, Sawyer WH & Kidson C (1984) Decreased membrane deformability in Melanesian ovalocytes from Papua New Guinea. *Journal of Cell Biology* **98:** 1348–1354.

Schulman S, Roth EF Jr, Cheng B et al (1990) Growth of *Plasmodium falciparum* in human erythrocytes containing abnormal membrane proteins. *Proceedings of the National Academy of Sciences of the USA* **87:** 7339–7343.

Serjeantson S, Bryson K, Amato D & Babona D (1977) Malaria and hereditary ovalocytosis. *Human Genetics* **37:** 161–167.

Sheppard PM (1958) *Natural Selection and Heredity*. London: Hutchinson.

Showe LC, Ballantine M & Huebner K (1987) Localization of the gene for the erythroid anion exchange protein, band 3 (EPMB3), to human chromosome 17. *Genomics* **1:** 71–76.

Tse WT, Lecomte M-C, Costa FF et al (1990) Point mutation in the β spectrin gene associated with αI/74 hereditary elliptocytosis. *Journal of Clinical Investigation* **86:** 909–916.

Ungewickell E & Gratzer W (1978) Self-association of human spectrin. A thermodynamic and kinetic study. *European Journal of Biochemistry* **88:** 379–385.

van Ross G, Seynhaeve V & Fiase L (1976) Beta-plus thalassaemia, haemoglobin S and hereditary elliptocytosis in a Zairean family. *Acta Haematologica* **56:** 241–252.

Wyandt H, Bancroft PM & Winship TP (1941) Elliptic erythrocytes in man. *Archives of Internal Medicine* **68:** 1043–1065.

Zail SS & Coetzer TL (1984) Defective binding of spectrin to ankyrin in a kindred with recessively inherited elliptocytosis. *Journal of Clinical Investigation* **74:** 753–762.

Zarkowsky HS, Mohandas N, Speaker CB et al (1975) A congenital haemolytic anaemia with thermal sensitivity of the erythrocyte membrane. *British Journal of Haematology* **29:** 537–543.

Zhai S, Liu SC, Amato D et al (1989) Molecular defect of the anion transporter in Southeast Asian ovalocytosis: alterations of the cytoplasmic domain involved in ankyrin binding. *Blood* **74** (supplement 1): 220a (abstract).

10

Molecular epidemiology of the thalassaemias (including haemoglobin E)

ADRIAN V. S. HILL

Since the thalassaemias were last reviewed in this series 10 years ago (Luzzatto, 1981) an enormous amount of new information has become available on the distribution and the molecular basis of these conditions, which are now recognized as the most common genetic disorders in humans. Several reviews of this extensive field are available, covering in some detail the molecular nature of globin gene variants, their distribution, genotype–phenotype correlations and implications for clinical practice (Higgs et al, 1989; Weatherall et al, 1989; Kazazian, 1990). In this chapter, I shall take a more molecular epidemiological perspective of the thalassaemias, attempting to survey briefly the global picture now emerging of the molecular diversity of these disorders and trying to draw some inferences about the origin, spread and selective advantage of these globin gene mutations. No short review can now do justice to the wealth of population data accumulating and the examples given are a selection, reflecting in part my own interests. After outlining the molecular nature of the mutations responsible for the α and β thalassaemias I shall focus on their distribution in four geographical regions: Asia, Oceania, the Mediterranean and Africa, with reference to findings in derivative populations. Then I shall look at how well these distributions fit with the malaria hypothesis as applied to the thalassaemias, including haemoglobin (Hb)E, and end with some remarks on the progress in and prospects for attempts to control these disorders through prenatal diagnosis programmes.

MOLECULAR BASIS

α Thalassaemia

The α thalassaemias result from reduced (α^+ thalassaemia) or absent (α^0 thalassaemia) globin chain production by the duplicated α-globin genes (Figure 1), situated on the tip of the short arm of chromosome 16 (16p13.3) (Buckle et al, 1988). The lack of α-globin chains leads to an excess of γ- or

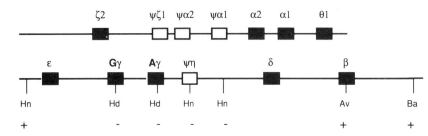

Figure 1. Gene map of the α-globin (above) and β-globin (below) gene clusters. Expressed sequences are shown as filled rectangles, pseudogenes as open rectangles. In the β-globin gene cluster the positions of some frequently studied restriction enzyme site polymorphisms are marked. These enzymes are Hn: *Hinc* II, Hd: *Hind* III, Av: *Ava* II, Ba: *Bam* HI. An example of a common restriction enzyme haplotype, $+ - - - - + +$, is shown below the enzyme sites.

β-chains which produce Hb Bart's (γ_4) and HbH (β_4) in fetal or adult life, respectively. The severity of the α thalassaemia phenotype reflects the number of α-globin genes affected. Homozygotes for the large DNA deletions, which remove both the α2- and α1-globin genes, are born with signs of chronic intrauterine hypoxia and usually die at or soon after birth, a condition known as the Hb Bart's hydrops fetalis syndrome. Loss of three of the normal complement of four α-globin genes leads to HbH disease, a chronic haemolytic anaemia, whereas loss of just one or two genes leads to a healthy carrier state with varying degrees of mild to very mild anaemia with hypochromia and microcytosis (reviewed in Weatherall and Clegg, 1981).

α Thalassaemia most commonly results from deletion of various segments of the α-globin gene cluster. Deletions removing one of the duplicated α-globin genes (denoted $-\alpha$) are common throughout almost all tropical and subtropical regions (Figure 2). It seems likely that the structure of the α-globin gene complex facilitates the occurrence of mutations which lead to such deletions. The α-globin genes are embedded in two highly homologous 4 kilobase (kb) duplication units which may be divided into homologous subsegments (X, Y and Z boxes). A relatively high rate of recombination between these homologous segments (Michelson and Orkin, 1983) leads to conservation of sequence identity and, intermittently, to unequal crossover events, generating (single) gene deletions of about 3.7 or 4.2 kb in size (Figure 3), depending on whether the crossover occurred in the X or Z homology boxes (Embury et al, 1980). $-\alpha^{3.7}$ Thalassaemia deletions may be further subdivided into subtypes I, II and III according to precisely where in the Z homology box the crossover occurred (Higgs et al, 1984). At the same time reciprocal triple α gene (ααα) chromosomes are generated, which may also be of two types. The relatively high frequency of such recombination events between homology blocks in the globin gene clusters is emphasized by the finding of chromosomes with from one to four α-globin genes (Gu et al, 1987), one to four ζ-globin genes (Winichagoon et al, 1982; Titus et al 1988), and one to five γ-globin genes (Sukumaran et al, 1983; Fei et al 1989): the ζ and γ gene variants having no adverse clinical effects. More

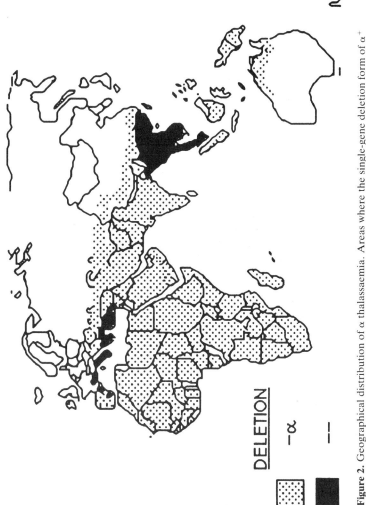

Figure 2. Geographical distribution of α thalassaemia. Areas where the single-gene deletion form of α^+ thalassaemia ($-\alpha$) is prevalent are shown as stippled. Areas where the more severe α^0 thalassaemias (double gene deletions, $--$) are found as well as α^+ thalassaemias are shown in black.

DELETION

$-\alpha$

$--$

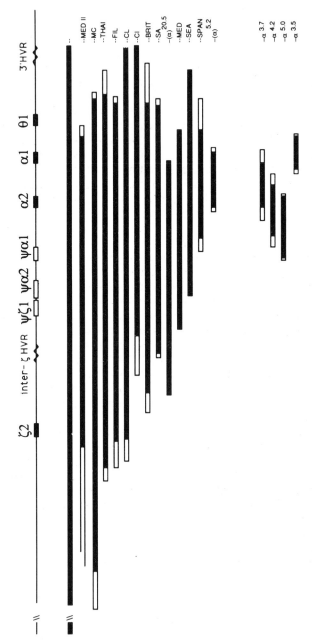

Figure 3. Summary of the positions and extents of the large deletions causing α⁰ thalassaemia by removing both α-globin genes (above), and the four smaller deletions which have been found to produce α⁺ thalassaemia (below). Three other deletions causing α thalassaemia by removing DNA upstream (to the left in the diagram) of the α-globin gene cluster are described in the text. The positions of important regions of length variation in this gene cluster, between the embryonic ζ-globin genes and at the 3′ end of the cluster, are also shown (adapted from Higgs et al, 1989).

recently two further small deletions producing α^+ thalassaemia have been described (Figure 3). Measurement of mRNA levels and Hb Bart's data indicate that, although normally the $\alpha2$ gene produces about three times as much globin as the $\alpha1$ gene, the output of $-\alpha$ chromosomes is intermediate, with the $-\alpha^{3.7}$ chromosome probably producing slightly more α-globin than the $-\alpha^{4.2}$ variant (Liebhaber et al, 1985, 1986; Bowden et al, 1987).

Deletions of both α genes (denoted $--$) produce α^0 thalassaemia, and at least 15 different deletions of this type are known (Figure 3, reviewed in Higgs et al, 1989). Epidemiologically, these differ from the $-\alpha$ deletions in being confined to particular geographical areas and, in general, are much less common. The exceptions to the latter are the $--^{SEA}$ and $--^{MED}$ defects, which are usually associated with HbH disease in south-east Asia and the Mediterranean, respectively. Hence, homozygotes for these $--$ defects, with the Hb Bart's hydrops fetalis syndrome, are most frequent in these regions. Detailed molecular analysis of the breakpoints of most of these deletions (Nicholls et al, 1987) have shown that they result from non-homologous or illegitimate recombination events which are probably very rare occurrences. This fits very well with the finding of particular deletions in restricted geographical areas.

Several of these large deletions remove both the ζ-globin genes as well as the α-genes; although carriers of these variants survive and develop normally, no homozygotes have been observed, and it is unlikely, in the absence of any α-like globin chain, that such fetuses would survive early gestation. Some of the most interesting of these mutations are three recently identified deletions, giving rise to α^0 thalassaemia, in which both α-globin genes are intact but varying amounts of upstream DNA is deleted (Hatton et al, 1990; Wilkie et al, 1990; Liebhaber et al, 1990). It appears likely that these deletions interfere with the regulation of globin gene expression by removing a controlling region of DNA located upstream of the α-globin gene complex (Higgs et al, 1990), similar to that described upstream of the β-like globin genes (Grosveld et al, 1987).

Less commonly α thalassaemia results from non-deletion defects, mainly point mutations (denoted $\alpha^T\alpha$ or $\alpha\alpha^T$, depending on whether the $\alpha2$- or $\alpha1$-gene is affected). Fifteen of these have now been characterized (reviewed in Higgs et al, 1989). Like the mutations affecting the β-globin gene these may affect RNA processing, RNA translation or the stability of the translated chain. However, no α-globin gene promoter mutations have yet been identified, perhaps because the phenotype of these would be very mild. Of the non-deletion mutations identified on $\alpha\alpha$ chromosomes, ten affect the dominant $\alpha2$-gene and only one involves the $\alpha1$-globin gene. However, unlike $-\alpha$ deletion forms of α thalassaemia, there is no up-regulation of the expression of the unaffected α gene in these cases so that, in general, non-deletion α^+ thalassaemia gives rise to a more severe reduction in α-chain synthesis than $-\alpha$ chromosomes. This is most clearly seen in the presence of an α^0 thalassaemia deletion on the other chromosome, so that HbH disease of the $\alpha^T\alpha/--$ genotype is more severe than deletional HbH disease $-\alpha/--$ (Kattamis et al, 1988). The predominance of $\alpha2$-gene mutations amongst non-deletional defects may in part reflect ascertainment bias, because individuals with more severe disease are more likely to come to medical attention. However, there may also be stronger selection pressure by malaria for α2-gene mutations which produce a larger reduction in α-globin synthesis than α1-gene mutations.

The most important non-deletion form of α thalassaemia is that associated with the haemoglobin variant, Hb Constant Spring, which is commonly found in parts of south-east Asia. This, like three other less common variants, results from a termination codon mutation in the α2-globin gene, which leads to an elongated α-chain (reviewed in Weatherall and Clegg, 1981). The abnormal mRNA is unstable, leading to the phenotype of a fairly severe α thalassaemia. The low level of Hb Constant Spring in carriers leads to difficulty in identifying these phenotypically, but polymerase chain reaction (PCR) amplification of the α2-globin gene with oligonucleotide hybridization now allows reliable diagnosis prenatally and postnatally (Kropp et al, 1989).

β Thalassaemia

β Thalassaemia results from mutations which lead to diminished β-globin chain production by the single β-globin gene on chromosome 11 (see Figure 1). Unlike the α thalassaemias most of these are point mutations, of which over 100 have now been described and it is estimated that these probably account for over 95% of the β thalassaemia genes worldwide (Huisman, 1990). These are classified into β^+ and β^0 thalassaemias according to whether the β-chain production is reduced or absent. With rare exceptions (see below) the β thalassaemias are recessive so that carriers, despite having hypochromic and microcytic red blood cells, are healthy with normal life spans (Gallerani et al, 1990). Most homozygotes are severely affected with thalassaemia major, a severe transfusion-dependent anaemia presenting in early childhood (Weatherall and Clegg, 1981). However, other homozygotes are less severely affected and not transfusion-dependent (thalassaemia intermedia), and considerable information is available on the genetic basis of this phenotypic variation. The severity of the homozygous state is determined by several factors, principally the nature of the mutation, β^0 thalassaemia being more severe than β^+ thalassaemia, and particular β^+ thalassaemias being more or less severe. Other important modulators are the level of HbF produced (which is controlled by both linked and unlinked genetic factors), higher levels being beneficial, and the presence of α thalassaemia, which can ameliorate particularly the homozygous state for β^+ thalassaemia (reviewed in Weatherall et al, 1989). The presence of additional α-globin genes can, on the other hand, be deleterious, so that heterozygotes for β thalassaemia with five or six α-globin genes (either ααα/αα, ααα/ααα or αααα/αα) have been found with thalassaemia intermedia (Galanello et al, 1983; Thein et al, 1984a; Camaschella et al, 1987; Kulozik et al, 1987; Thompson et al, 1989).

Over 100 mutations in the β-globin gene leading to β thalassaemia have provided a unique picture (Figure 4) of the variety of natural lesions which can partially or completely inactivate a mammalian gene. These have been

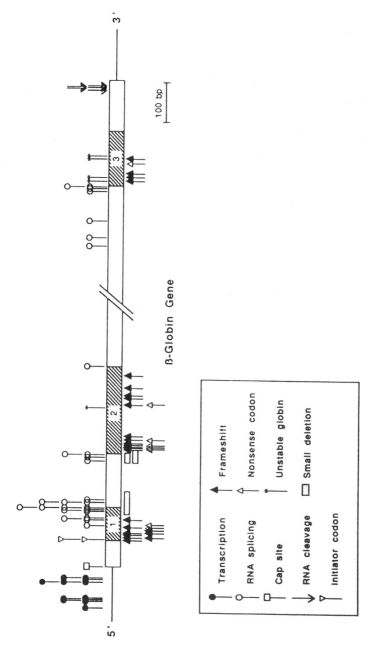

Figure 4. Positions of point mutations in the β-globin gene causing β thalassaemia. From Kazazian (1990) with permission.

reviewed recently by Kazazian (1990), who lists the 91 identified up to that time, with the original references. Slightly more than half produce β^0 thalassaemia. Most of these are frameshift mutations which alter the translational reading frame by inserting or deleting 1, 2, 4 or 7 nucleotides (nt). Eight others are nonsense mutations which terminate translation. Recently, two different mutations altering the codon for translation initiation have been found to produce β^0 thalassaemia.

Perhaps of more functional interest are the numerous mutations which affect RNA processing. Mutations in the canonical GT and AG sequences which mark the beginning and end of introns (twelve examples) lead to the complete loss of properly spliced message and a β^0 thalassaemia. However, mutations in nucleotides which flank these splice junctions (ten examples) and form part of consensus sequences for RNA splicing, leads to inefficient splicing and usually a β^+ thalassaemia. Other mutations within the intron sequences lead to the creation of new splice sites which can partially or completely prevent normal RNA splicing. Within the first exon of the gene, at codons 24–27, lies a so-called cryptic splice site, one which may become activated by a point mutation which makes it more closely resemble a true splice site. An important example of this is the mutation in codon 26 (gly→lys) which leads to the production of HbE, the only haemoglobin variant found in over half of any large population (Livingstone, 1985). As well as producing an amino acid change, this mutation activates the cryptic splice site in exon 1 (Orkin et al, 1982b) so that about 25% of mRNA splices into the mutant site. This, together with an associated overall reduction in splicing leading to reduced globin production, is the molecular basis for regarding HbE as one of the thalassaemias.

Finally, point mutations affecting the flanking promoter and polyadenine addition signal sequences in the β-globin gene have been identified (reviewed in Kazazian, 1990). The nucleotides AATAAA, at the end of most mammalian genes, form a signal sequence for addition of a poly A tail to the transcript. Mutations affecting this sequence were first described for the α2-globin gene in Middle Eastern individuals with α thalassaemia (Higgs et al, 1983), and five different mutations in this sequence have now been shown to produce β^+ thalassaemia. It appears that the elongated transcripts produced from these genes are unstable, leading to reduced globin production. Twelve promoter region mutations have been identified, all of which reduce transcription. These are concentrated in three areas: the TATA box situated about 30 nt upstream of the gene, and in the proximal and distal CACACCC sequences about 85 and 100 bp from the mRNA cap site. All of these produce β^+ thalassaemias and they are in general mild phenotypically. A striking example is a black individual homozygous for the –29 promoter mutation with a normal haemoglobin level (Safaya et al, 1989). However, a Chinese homozygote for the same mutation has been observed with thalassaemia major, emphasizing the importance of other interacting genes (Huang et al, 1986). One of these modulators appears to be a single base change at position –158 in the promoter of the Gγ-globin gene, associated with increased Gγ-globin production. The –101 mutation has been associated with the rare silent carrier state for β thalassaemia in which carriers have normal HbA_2 levels (Gonzalez-Redondo et al, 1989). The existence of a β thalassaemia with an entirely normal β-globin gene sequence (Semenza et al, 1984) may be explained by a polymorphism in a region 530 bp upstream (Murru et al, 1990). Recently, Huisman (1990) has classified these point mutations into four groups of increasing clinical severity, but it remains to be seen how useful this will be in view of the importance of other interacting genes.

At the severe end of the spectrum of β thalassaemia alleles are those which are dominant and produce thalassaemia intermedia in heterozygotes, often with inclusion bodies seen in normoblasts. The molecular nature of several of these rare alleles has been elucidated recently (Kazazian et al, 1989; S. Fucharoen et al, 1990; Ristaldi et al, 1990; Thein et al, 1990a; Murru et al, 1991). Almost all are associated with mutations in exon 3 which produce abnormal β-chains, and it has been proposed that the difference in phenotype from recessive β thalassaemia relates to the length and stability of these abnormal chains, in particular whether they are capable of binding haem and producing aggregations that are relatively resistant to proteolytic degradation (Thein et al, 1990a).

Deletions which affect the β-globin gene mostly also involve other genes in the β-globin cluster giving rise to δβ thalassaemia and the syndrome of hereditary persistence of fetal haemoglobin (HPFH) and these are reviewed elsewhere (Weatherall et al, 1989). A few deletions affecting the β-globin gene alone have been found, of which only one is common: that producing a 619 bp deletion in Asian Indians (Thein et al, 1988a).

DISTRIBUTION

One striking result from molecular analysis of the thalassaemias is remarkable molecular heterogeneity. The other is that of geographical clustering. Each population has its own group of common β thalassaemia mutations and a smaller number of α^0 thalassaemia deletions, with few examples of the same variant at high frequency in different global regions. The inference must be that the selective force amplifying the frequencies of all these alleles was introduced after the human racial divergence. I shall consider particular examples by discussing four areas in more detail. Before doing so, it is useful to review the nature of restriction enzyme haplotypes which have been helpful in tracing the origin and spread of variants in the α- and β-globin gene clusters.

Since the description of the first restriction enzyme site polymorphism by Kan and Dozy (1978), numerous polymorphic restriction sites have been identified in non-coding DNA of both the α- and β-globin gene clusters (Antonarakis et al, 1982; Higgs et al, 1986). In the β-globin cluster the seven most frequently studied restriction fragment length polymorphisms (RFLPs) may be grouped into two sets on each side of a region of relatively frequent recombination, or 'hot spot' near to the δ-globin gene (see Figure 1). The 5′ or upstream part of the haplotype consists of five RFLPs (denoted e.g. +−−−−) and the 3′ region of two (e.g. ++). This 3′

haplotype, in which the β-globin gene itself is situated, is strongly associated with other non-coding polymorphisms within the gene which together delineate 'frameworks', frameworks 1, 2 and 3 being identified by the $++$, $+-$ and $-+$ 3' RFLP patterns, respectively. Because frameworks span the β-globin gene they are more strongly associated with particular β thalassaemia point mutations than the RFLP haplotype as a whole, and the 5'-haplotype, on the other side of the recombination hot spot, in particular. As well as restriction enzyme site polymorphisms the α-globin restriction enzyme haplotype (Higgs et al, 1986) includes several regions of length variation, due to the presence of variable copy numbers of short tandem repeat sequences. Because some of these have high recombination rates, leading to new length variants, they provide a powerful marker for tracing the origin and, potentially, the age of α-globin gene variants.

Asia

It is appropriate to consider the thalassaemias in Asia first because this continent bears by far the greatest burden of severe thalassaemia alleles. The α^0 thalassaemias reach their highest frequency in south-east Asia. The common two-gene-deletion form $--^{SEA}$, like other deletions due to illegitimate recombination events, appears to have had a single origin, judging by its geographical distribution and the pattern of flanking polymorphic restriction enzyme sites. Its association with seven length alleles of the region of length variation at the 3' end of the α-globin gene complex (the 3' HVR) (Winichagoon et al, 1984) probably indicates subsequent recombination and an 'early' origin). The other two south-east Asian α^0 thalassaemia deletions, $--^{THAI}$ and $--^{FIL}$, are less common, with the latter accounting for perhaps a third of such defects in the Philippines; a deletion of the complete gene cluster is encountered rarely. No haplotype data are available on the Hb Constant Spring alleles but, again, geography suggests a single origin in south-east Asia leading to frequencies of 0.05 to 0.15 in parts of Thailand today (Hundrieser et al, 1990). Both $-\alpha^{3.7}$ and $-\alpha^{4.2}$ single gene deletions are found, with the former (mainly subtype I with rare IIs) accounting for more than 85% of these. Recent DNA studies in Thailand found frequencies of the $-\alpha$ defect of 0.10–0.15, much higher than the $--$ deletions, 0.025 (Hundrieser et al, 1988b, 1990).

Although α^0 thalassaemia appears to be very rare in India, the highest reported frequencies of α^+ thalassaemia (0.71–0.95) have been found in some of the tribal populations (Brittenham et al, 1980; Kulozik et al, 1988; Labie et al, 1989), with $-\alpha^{4.2}$ deletions being almost as frequent as $-\alpha^{3.7}$ defects. Very high $-\alpha$ frequencies, 0.78, have also been found in the Tharu people of Nepal (Modiano et al, 1991). In eastern Saudi Arabia $-\alpha$ frequencies reach 0.37, mainly $-\alpha^{3.7}$, with lower frequencies in the north (El-Hazmi, 1987). HbH disease is seen occasionally in this area and has a distinct molecular basis. Such individuals are homozygous for a polyadenylation signal mutation in the α2-globin gene (Thein et al, 1988b), a variant also sporadically found in people of Mediterranean origin. The $--\alpha^0$ thalassaemia determinant has never been found in Arabia, explaining the absence of the Hb Bart's hydrops fetalis syndrome (Pressley et al, 1980). Recent studies have provided extensive information on the molecular basis of β thalassaemia in several Oriental (Chan et al, 1987; Antonarakis et al, 1988; Fucharoen et al, 1989; Laig et al, 1989; Lie-Injo et al, 1989; Yang et al, 1989; Thein et al, 1990b; Lin et al, 1991) and Indian populations (Thein et al, 1988a; Parikh et al, 1990), in which carrier rates of up to 9% are found (Wasi et al, 1980; Livingstone, 1985). Some of these data, which provide a basis for prenatal diagnosis programmes, are presented in Table 1. There are several different point mutations and one small (619 bp) deletion common in India. The question of the origin of these mutations has been addressed, as in Mediterranean populations (Kazazian et al, 1984b), by determining the association beween particular mutations and the linked β-globin restriction enzyme haplotype. A clear-cut example is the Indian 619 bp deletion which is invariably associated with a single haplotype: $+----+$ (Thein et al, 1984b). More difficult to interpret are alleles associated with several haplotypes. Where only the 5'-haplotype varies this is usually assumed to indicate a single origin with subsequent recombination between the 5'- and 3'-haplotypes. An association with different 3'-haplotypes or frameworks makes multiple origins more likely. An example of the latter is the IVS-1 nt5 G→C mutation which is found at high frequency in India, Malaysia, Indonesia and Melanesia, at low frequency in Thailand and China and sporadically in the eastern Mediterranean. It is associated with framework 3 in Indians (Thein et al, 1988a), framework 1 in Melanesians (Hill et al, 1988) and with both in Indonesia and Malaysia (Lie-Injo et al, 1989; Yang et al, 1989). An alternative explanation of the finding of the same mutation on different β-globin gene frameworks is that of a single origin with a small recombination (gene conversion) event transferring the mutation from one chromosome to another. This seems particularly likely to have occurred when a mutation confined to a particular geographical area is there associated with more than one framework. An example of this is the common Chinese codon 41–42 frameshift mutation which is associated with both frameworks 1 and 2 (Kazazian et al, 1986). Indeed, several Oriental mutations are associated with multiple haplotypes, whereas mutation–haplotype associations in the Mediterranean appear to be stronger. This may indicate that the mutations in Asia are older, but different population structure, relative selection coefficients, and migration patterns in the two regions could also have produced this difference.

Several of these molecular markers are now helpful in measuring population affinities and tracing gene flow in particular regions. Most attention has been focused on the origin of HbE, which reaches remarkably high frequencies in the 'haemoglobin E triangle' of Laos, Kampuchea and Thailand (Flatz, 1967; Livingstone, 1985). Antonarakis et al (1982) found HbE to be associated with three different haplotypes in south-east Asians, representing both frameworks 2 and 3. They argued for at least two origins on the basis that a double crossover to move the HbE mutation from one framework to another was very improbable. A possible gene conversion was not considered. More extensive studies of Thais, Kampucheans (Hundrieser et al, 1988c; Yongvanit et al, 1989) and some Vietnamese (Nakatsuji et al,

Table 1. Percentage frequencies of the various molecular types of β thalassaemia alleles in some Asian and Melanesian populations.

Mutation	Indian (n=102)	Indian (n=110)	Malaysian (n=41)	Thai (n=116)	Thai (n=123)	Thai (n=71)	Chinese (n=93)	Taiwanese (n=74)	Melanesian (n=24)
Frameshift 41/42	12	9	12	51	40	44	48	29	0
-28 A→G	0	0	0	10	3	3	8	11	0
IVS-2 nt654	0	0	7	11	2	13	22	46	0
$\beta^0 17$	0	0	2	10	41	20	10	11	0
IVS-1 nt5	23	35	49	5	2	11	0	0	88
IVS-1 nt1	14	5	7	2	0	1	0	0	0
619 bp deletion	21	23	0	0	0	0	0	0	0
Frameshift 8/9	20	16	0	0	0	0	0	0	0
$\beta^0 15$	5	3	0	0	0	0	0	0	0
Frameshift 71/72	0	0	0	1	0	3	0	0	0
Codon 19 A→G	0	0	15	2	0	4	0	0	0
Codon 35 C→A	0	0	0	3	0	1	0	0	0
Frameshift 35	1	0	5	0	0	0	0	0	0
Frameshift 16	1	5	0	0	0	0	0	0	0
-88 C→T	2	1	0	0	0	0	0	0	0
-86 C→G	0	0	0	1	0	0	0	0	0
CAP +1	2	2	0	0	0	0	0	0	0
Other/unknown	2	1	2	3	13	0	0	4	12

The number of abnormal β-globin genes studied (n) is shown. From: India (Thein et al, 1988a; Parikh et al, 1990), Malaysia (Yang et al, 1989), Thailand (Fucharoen et al, 1989; Laig et al, 1989; Thein et al, 1990b), China (Chan et al, 1987), Taiwan (Lin et al, 1991) and Melanesia (Hill et al, 1988). In some series not all the alleles listed were tested for, so some of the mutations listed as 0% may be included as others.

1986) have indicated that HbE on framework 3 is almost confined to Kampuchea, where the framework 3 haplotype is in fact predominant. This suggests that the mutation in Kampuchea is relatively new compared with the framework 2 associated mutation, which is found with multiple 5'-haplotypes in several populations of the Austroasiatic language group. Although an independent origin for the mutation in Kampuchea has been advocated on the grounds that a small gene conversion event transferring the mutation from one haplotype to another is 'much less likely' (Nagel and Ranney, 1990), there is currently no useful estimate of this probability. Looked at another way, it would appear improbable, given the widespread distribution of malaria, that if an advantageous mutation has occurred and been selected to high frequency only twice, this should have happened in neighbouring populations. An independent source for the high frequency of the HbE mutation in certain Tibeto-Burman speaking populations of Assam, India, was also advocated on the basis of their lack of known Mongoloid ancestry (Deka et al, 1988). Here, however, molecular analysis has been more helpful, with the same framework 2 haplotypes as in northern Thailand strongly supporting an Oriental origin (Hundrieser et al, 1988a). The uneven distribution of HbE in Assam may reflect differential selection by malaria following the introduction of this allele from the East (Saha, 1990). In contrast, a case of HbE in a European may well represent a separate mutation (Kazazian et al, 1984c) because this is associated with a framework 1 β-globin gene, which has not been found in Asians, with one unconfirmed exception (G. Fucharoen et al, 1990).

Oceania

The globin genes of Pacific Islanders have been studied in some detail, both because of the ethnic distinctiveness of these groups and the opportunity to look at the epidemiology of the thalassaemias and malaria in an area with a reasonably well-defined population history. The striking impression is of how different their haemoglobinopathies are from south-east Asians (reviewed in Hill et al, 1989). HbE and Hb Constant Spring are absent, as are the α^0 thalassaemia determinants found in most of south-east Asia, and even the very common mild α^+ thalassaemia deletions are of separate origin. The $-\alpha$ frequency reaches about 0.70 on the north coast of Papua New Guinea and, uniquely, this is predominantly the $-\alpha^{4.2}$ deletion (Flint et al, 1986a). In most of island Melanesia and all of Polynesia the $-\alpha^{3.7}$ deletion is the more frequent. However, throughout Melanesia, Polynesia and Micronesia this $-\alpha^{3.7}$ deletion is mainly or exclusively of the $-\alpha^{3.7}$III subtype, which has been found in no other population (Hill et al, 1985; O'Shaughnessy et al, 1990). Restriction enzyme haplotype analysis has supported the proposal that this mutation has had a single origin, probably some 4–5000 years ago, in the Austronesian-speaking population that colonized coastal and island Melanesia before spreading westwards to colonize Polynesia. The high frequency of α thalassaemia in many Melanesian populations makes it a major cause of anaemia (Bowden et al, 1985), as is increasingly being recognized in other tropical and subtropical areas

(Chidoori et al, 1989; Stevens et al, 1989). HbH disease is very rare in Papua New Guinea and the only family studied proved to have a non-deletional form (Hill et al, 1987).

β Thalassaemia is found in most of coastal Papua New Guinea at carrier rates of on average 5%, and also in about 20% of the population of one island in Vanuatu, Maewo. The molecular defect in all of the Maewo cases and in most of the small number of New Guineans studied was the IVS1 nt5 G→C mutation (Hill et al, 1988), which is the commonest β thalassaemia defect in Malaysia and Indonesia (Lie-Injo et al, 1989; Yang et al, 1989). This mutation was on a haplotype and framework quite different to that in Asian Indians (Kazazian et al, 1984a), but identical to the less frequent haplotype in Indonesia. Although it is tempting to assume that the Melanesian variant simply reflects gene flow from Indonesia, this particular mutation appears to have had separate origins in India, the Mediterranean (Chehab et al, 1987), and south-east Asia, so an additional one in Melanesia is at least a possibility. However, in their ζ-globin gene variants and α-globin restriction enzyme haplotypes, Austronesian-speaking populations of the Pacific reveal clearer evidence of their Asian origins (Hill et al, 1989).

The Mediterranean

The molecular basis of thalassaemia was first investigated systematically in Mediterranean populations, and we now have a detailed picture of the mutations prevalent in this region. Single α-gene deletion forms of α thalassaemia, almost always $-\alpha^{3.7}I$, are found at relatively low frequencies and a handful of rare non-deletional forms of α^+ thalassaemia have been characterized (reviewed in Higgs et al, 1989). Although five α^0 thalassaemia deletions have been found in this region (see Figure 3), the $--^{MED}$, followed by $-(\alpha)^{20.5}$, are the most frequent. Rare cases of HbH disease seen in the absence of a $--$ deletion have been described (Henni et al, 1987; Thein et al, 1988b).

The nature and distribution of β thalassaemia mutations in Mediterranean populations have been reviewed by Cao et al (1989) and Huisman (1990). The highest carrier rates are in the islands of Cyprus (18%) and Sardinia (13%), with 7.5% in Greece. Of the 20 or so known mutations, only one is a β-globin gene deletion (Diaz-Chico et al, 1987). In general the correlation between particular mutations and restriction enzyme haplotypes is strong (Orkin et al, 1982a; Kazazian et al, 1984b). However, there are several exceptions, the most striking of which is the $\beta^0 39$ mutation, which accounts for 95% of β thalassaemia alleles in Sardinia, where it has been found associated with nine different chromosomal haplotypes (Pirastu et al, 1987). Inspection of the less frequent haplotypes suggests strongly that they have been derived from the most common type by recombination, indicating, despite the observation elsewhere of a spontaneous mutation in this position (Chehab et al, 1986), that there is no need to invoke multiple origins on the one island. Although the more common mutations appear to be associated with more haplotypes (Kazazian et al, 1984b), suggesting that they may be older, this may at least in part reflect the fact that fewer examples of the rarer mutations have had associated restriction enzyme haplotypes determined.

The same set of common mutations are, in general, found throughout most of the Mediterranean, except in Algeria where the three most common mutations (IVS-1 nt110, $\beta^0$39, and IVS-1 nt6) accounted for only 37% of mutations. The IVS-1 nt110 mutation is the most common in all of the eastern Mediterranean (Greece, Turkey, Cyprus, Yugoslavia, Bulgaria and the Lebanon: original references in Huisman, 1990) with the 'Sardinian' mutation, $\beta^0$39, being most common in the west. Cao et al (1989) have suggested that the IVS-1 nt110 mutation arose in ancient Greece and then spread with the expansion of Greek civilization, and that the $\beta^0$39 mutation may have been spread to the western Mediterranean by Phoenician sailors. The third most common allele, IVS-1 nt6, which causes a relatively mild β^+ thalassaemia, is fairly evenly distributed and, like other mild (e.g. promoter region) mutations, is found more frequently amongst cases of thalassaemia intermedia (Murru et al, 1991).

Africa

Our knowledge of thalassaemias in Africa has lagged behind that of other continents. It has become clear only fairly recently that α^+ thalassaemia, not HbS, is the most common haemoglobinopathy in Africa. DNA studies in several sub-Saharan African populations (tabulated in Muklwala et al, 1989) have found $-\alpha$ frequencies ranging from 0.10 to 0.27, compared with frequencies of 0.05–0.08 in north Africans. As for HbS, there appears to be a general geographical correlation of $-\alpha$ frequency and malarial endemicity, with lower frequencies in southern Africa, particularly among the !Kung San (0.06) (Ramsey and Jenkins, 1987). In almost all cases these deletions have been of the $-\alpha^{3.7}$ type, but about 10% of the $-\alpha$ deletions in The Gambia, west Africa are of the $-\alpha^{4.2}$ type (A. V. S. H. and B. M. Greenwood, unpublished data). Hence, the occasional detection of this variant in American Blacks is probably not due to admixture, as previously suggested (Muklwala et al, 1989). Some of these studies addressed the question of the frequency of $-\alpha$ deletions amongst HbS homozygotes. Although an increased frequency of α thalassaemia was found in Benin and the Central African Republic, this was not found in patients from Senegal (Pagnier et al, 1984) and Nigeria (Falusi et al, 1987). Most of these studies were small and the possible confounding effect of population stratification was not addressed: for example, ethnic groups with higher sickle frequencies might also have higher $-\alpha$ frequencies. Hence, it is still unclear to what extent, if any, α thalassaemia prolongs the life span of subjects with homozygous sickle-cell anaemia in Africa.

No cases of HbH disease or Hb Bart's hydrops fetalis have been found in sub-Saharan Africa (and no $--$ deletions identified by gene mapping), raising the question as to why α^0 thalassaemia alleles have not been selected in this region of hyperendemic malaria. A large deletion removing both α- and ζ-globin genes has been identified in an American Black (Felice et al, 1984), but in view of the large combined DNA/Hb Bart's surveys done in

Blacks this deletion must be very rare. The single report of the caucasian $--^{BRIT}$ deletion in an American Black presumably results from admixture (Steinberg et al, 1986).

Although β thalassaemia is uncommon in most of sub-Saharan Africa, there are significant frequencies in parts of west Africa, particularly in Liberia where carrier rates of 9% have been recorded (Willcox, 1975). It has long been recognized that homozygous cases in this region were particularly mild (Willcox et al, 1975) and molecular surveys of American Blacks have revealed the probable molecular basis for this mild African phenotype (Gonzalez-Redondo et al, 1988). The most frequent mutations are of the promoter, at positions −29 (Antonarakis et al, 1984) and −88 (Orkin et al,1984), a codon 24 mutation activating a false splice site (Goldsmith et al, 1983) and a polyadenylation signal mutation (Orkin et al, 1985). These are all mild $β^+$ thalassaemia alleles with limited reduction in β-globin production. It would be of particular interest to know which of these alleles is found in the northern Liberian population, from which we have the only estimate of the degree of protection β thalassaemia provides against malaria (Willcox et al, 1983).

NATURAL SELECTION BY MALARIA

Population studies

It was the distribution of thalassaemia in malarious areas of the Mediterranean that led Haldane (1949) to propose that carriers were less susceptible to malaria and that this might lead to a balanced polymorphism. Although there has been relatively little evidence to support his proposal from case-control studies or in vitro experiments on red cells from carriers of thalassaemia, the accumulated data on the distribution and molecular basis of the thalassaemias now form a convincing case for a relationship with malaria. Essentially there are three types of supporting data; microepidemiological studies in Sardinia and Melanesia, a global correlation of the endemicity of malaria with the distribution of thalassaemia and, thirdly, the observation of extensive molecular diversity.

The classical microepidemiological study is that of Siniscalco and colleagues (1961), who found a decreasing frequency of β thalassaemia with increasing altitude (and decreasing endemicity of malaria) amongst villages in Sardinia. This was true also for glucose-6-phosphate dehydrogenase deficiency but not for several other polymorphisms. This study has been criticized on the grounds that migrational history suggests that thalassaemia might have been introduced from outside and have not reached the more isolated highland populations (Brown, 1983). We know now that the predominant $β^039$ mutation *is* found elsewhere in the Mediterranean, and a greater diversity of mutations common in coastal populations would have been more convincing, but selection remains a likely explanation for the observation. Less well known are studies from Papua New Guinea, where the accumulated data on over 3000 subjects from a variety of highland and coastal populations show a striking difference in frequencies between malaria-free highland and malarious coastal populations (collated in Hill et al, 1988). These New Guinean populations also formed part of the most convincing study on α thalassaemia and the malaria hypothesis (Flint et al, 1986a). Gene frequencies for −α alleles were found to range from 0.24 to 0.69 amongst malarious Papua New Guinea coastal populations, but were always less than 0.05 in the malaria-free highlands, a result confirmed by Yenchitsomanus et al (1986). Moreover, a steady decline in −α frequencies was demonstrated from the north to south of island Melanesia, correlating with a marked decrease in the endemicity of malaria (Figure 5; Hill, 1986). Detailed restriction enzyme haplotype analysis and documentation of other DNA polymorphisms indicated that the malaria–thalassaemia association was unlikely to be due to migration or genetic drift. For HbE, Flatz et al (1964) demonstrated a positive geographical correlation between frequencies of this variant and high endemicity of malaria in Thailand.

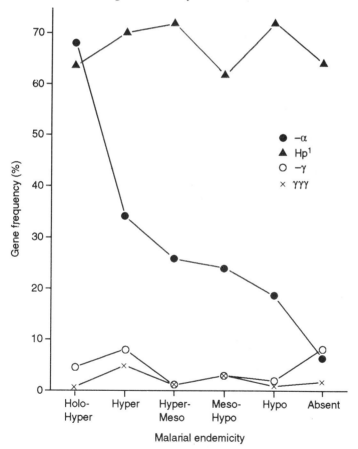

Figure 5. Percentage gene frequency of α⁺ thalassaemia, shown in filled circles, plotted against malarial endemicity in various islands and regions of Melanesia (Hill, 1986). Also shown are the gene frequencies of presumably non-selected genetic markers in the same populations: Hp^1 a haptoglobin allele, and the frequencies of the single- and triple-γ-globin gene variants.

It has been clear for some decades that Hbs S, C and E and thalassaemia major are confined to regions of the world where malaria was or is prevalent (Weatherall and Clegg, 1981; Livingstone, 1985). Only more recently has it been possible to study α^+ thalassaemia reliably. Surveys in Japanese (Nakashima et al, 1990), Koreans (Shimizu et al, 1989), Icelandics and Britons (Flint et al, 1986b) have confirmed that $-\alpha$ deletions are very rare in these populations. An apparent exception to this rule is the finding that most populations in malaria-free Polynesia and Micronesia have frequencies of α thalassaemia of 0.01–0.15 (O'Shaughnessy et al, 1990). However, analysis of these α thalassaemias has shown them to be almost exclusively the $-\alpha^{3.7}$III deletion prevalent in malarious Melanesia, indicating that the Polynesians' ancestors probably acquired this variant through admixture before they colonized Polynesia (Hill et al, 1985). Amerindians are the only tropical populations apparently free of thalassaemias (Livingstone, 1985), consistent with the belief that *falciparum* malaria did not reach the Americas before Columbus (Dunn, 1965).

The extensive data on the molecular diversity of the thalassaemias now form part of the supporting evidence for the 'malaria hypothesis', or at least for natural selection acting on these variants. A single mutation causing thalassaemia might spread widely through a founder effect and genetic drift, but it is quite implausible to suggest that a great variety of mutations could have reached high frequencies in diverse populations without the involvement of some selective agent. This argument for selection is stronger for the β^0 thalassaemias, which are lethal in the homozygous state, than for the mild α thalassaemias. A very mild selective pressure, along with the tendency of the α-globin genes to misalign and recombine, could lead to a gradual elevation in α^+ thalassaemia frequencies because there is no apparent counterbalancing force (α^+ thalassaemia heterozygotes and possibly even homozygotes appearing fully fit). Only a substantial increase in fitness of carriers could maintain high frequencies of β^0 thalassaemia and HbS (Cavalli-Sforza and Bodmer, 1971).

In vitro studies

Although evidence for the correctness of the 'malaria hypothesis' can only come from epidemiological or clinical (see below) studies, the mechanism of protection can be investigated by in vitro experiments. With the development of the in vitro culture system for *Plasmodium falciparum* it has been possible to look at invasion and growth of the parasite in a variety of abnormal red cells (reviewed by Nagel and Roth, 1989). Although decreased growth has been demonstrable in the highly abnormal cells of patients with HbH disease (Ifediba et al, 1985) or β thalassaemia/HbE double heterozygotes (Brockelman et al, 1987), most workers have failed to find diminished growth in red cells from thalassaemia heterozygotes. The exceptions are the early report of Friedman (1979), who used conditions of marked oxidant stress, and the report of Brockelman et al (1987), who used a different culture medium. This disparity highlights the main difficulty with this work, which is to know whether a difference observed under particular conditions in culture is of importance in vivo. Another example is the relevance of the impaired growth of *P. faciparum* in cells with increased concentrations of HbF (Pasvol et al, 1977) to the protection of β thalassaemia carriers. The epidemiological data suggest that the selective advantage of heterozygous α^+ thalassaemia is very small and this may be below the sensitivity of current assays.

Despite these reservations, the recent data of Luzzi et al (1991a,b) are of particular interest. They failed to find any altered growth of parasites in red cells from individuals with α^+ thalassaemia, even under conditions of oxidant stress. However, red cells from cases of both α^+ and β thalassaemia were found to display increased amounts of malaria 'neoantigens' on the red cell surface. Antibodies to these parasite antigens, which are inserted into the red cell membrane, have been associated with resistance to malaria (Marsh et al, 1989). This raises the possibility of more rapid immune clearance of parasitized red cells as the protective mechanism in thalassaemia, consistent with the observations of Yuthavong et al (1990) on increased phagocytosis of infected red cells from individuals with thalassaemia. With red cells from HbE heterozygotes Nagel et al (1981) found no reduction in parasite growth, but Bunvaratvej et al (1986) have reported increased phagocytosis of such cells by peripheral blood monocytes.

Measuring fitness

Although the most convincing evidence for the protective effect of HbS against malaria came from observations that carriers were almost absent amongst children dying of malaria (reviewed by Allison, 1964), only one case-control study of any size has been reported for clinical malaria and the thalassaemias. This was performed in Liberia by Willcox et al (1983) who found that, amongst 558 cases of malaria, children who were carriers of β thalassaemia had half the risk of developing an attack of clinical malaria compared with children without thalassaemia, and that carriers appeared to have still greater protection from severe malaria. The HbAS genotype was even more protective. The single case-control study of children with fairly severe malaria from south-east Asia included only 122 children and results were inconclusive (Kruatrachne et al, 1970). I am unaware of any published case-control studies on malaria and α thalassaemia (defined by DNA analysis). Our own preliminary data, on over 1000 malaria cases from the Gambia and Malawi, showed no significant protection for α thalassaemia carriers against uncomplicated or cerebral malaria. However, there may be some protection against severe malarial anaemia, the other commonly fatal form of severe malaria in sub-Saharan Africa (A.V.S.H. et al, unpublished data). In any case, the amount of protection afforded is very small compared to HbS or β thalassaemia carriers. The recent observation from Nepal (Modiano et al, 1991) that α thalassaemia is very frequent amongst the Tharu population, who enjoy relative protection from malaria compared to their neighbours, provides no means of assessing how much, if any, of this relative protection is caused by α thalassaemia. An increasing number of other loci are implicated in malaria resistance (e.g. Hill et al, 1991).

This modest degree of protection against malaria is in keeping with the very mild phenotype of α^+ thalassaemia, and also suggests that, unlike HbS and β thalassaemia alleles which are balanced polymorphisms, the $-\alpha$ allele may be a transient polymorphism, i.e. still increasing in frequency. The rate at which an advantageous gene should increase in frequency can be calculated if the mortality from malaria and the degree of protection afforded to carriers is known (Cavalli-Sforza and Bodmer, 1971). A frequent difficulty in such calculations is to estimate the starting frequency, before selection occurred. However, the cross-over mechanism generating $-\alpha$ deletions suggests that the frequency of the $\alpha\alpha\alpha$ chromosome (which is found at a remarkably constant 0.002–0.006 in different regions) may be a reasonable estimate. For the $-\alpha$ frequency to be as low as 0.1–0.2 in Africa after at least 2000 years of malarial selection, its associated fitness increment (in heterozygotes) must be very small, <0.02, compared with about 0.15 for HbAS. An intriguing observation is that of the populations observed to have $-\alpha$ frequencies >0.25, many are very high, >0.60. This may reflect the fact that the fitness of the $-\alpha/-\alpha$ homozygote is substantially greater than the heterozygote, leading to rapid selection once homozygotes become common.

Modelling selection

A complete understanding of the nature of selection of the thalassaemias and other haemoglobinopathies by malaria would lead to a model describing the temporal evolution of these variants, incorporating the effects of mutation, selection, migration and genetic drift. Several such simulations have been described and, although incomplete, they have highlighted the measurements that need to be made to produce more realistic models. Livingstone's (1976) model of the evolution of Hbs S and C and β thalassaemia attempted to reproduce the geographical clines seen in west Africa, assuming various fitness values for the nine different β-globin genotypes found in this region. He showed that it was possible to generate such clines after about 200 generations, a plausible length of time for malarial selection, using selected fitness values. However the direction of the frequency change, i.e. whether HbS was replacing HbC or vice versa, depended on the fitness values chosen. As well as indicating the importance of having reasonable models of population structure in addition to estimates of the age of the various alleles, the central need for plausible estimates of fitness or, at least, relative fitness of the various genotypes was made clear. Similarly, Yokoyama's (1983) attempt to model the evolution of the various types of α thalassaemia in south-east Asia was severely limited by the rather implausible fitness values chosen for the various genotypes (Livingstone, 1985).

More recently, Livingstone (1989) presented simulations of the generation of the distribution of β-globin variants (including HbE) in the Old World, assuming multiple origins for β thalassaemia alleles but only one for HbS (in the Middle East) and one for HbC. The distributions were again unstable and, with the chosen fitness parameters, best approximated the real distributions after 100–150 generations of diffusion and selection. The result was seen to justify Livingstone's view that there may have been just a single origin for HbS, in contrast to the evidence from restriction enzyme haplotype data for at least four origins (reviewed by Nagel and Ranney, 1990). However, a multiple mutation model for HbS would appear equally capable of generating realistic distributions.

There are several parameters in these models for which the current estimates are uncertain. These include genotype fitness, the number of origins particular variants have had, the lengths of time these have been present in different populations, and, for older alleles, the frequencies of these at the onset of malarial selection. Hence, it is not clear how valuable current models can be in placing constraints on how the present distributions may have evolved.

Overview

Overall, Haldane's proposal that high frequencies of thalassaemia are the result of natural selection by malaria has stood up very well to the onslaught of molecular epidemiology. However, simply implicating malaria as the primary selective agent is a long way from understanding the details of how and why this has occurred. Although natural selection by malaria is of great biological interest in itself, it also serves as a paradigm for the study of the evolution of the enormous number of other disease resistance and susceptibility genes.

There appear to be three areas where further data may be usefully obtained in the near future. Foremost amongst these is the need to achieve some measurements of the fitness of the various globin genotypes (other than HbS) before malaria control or eradication makes this impossible. This is most efficiently done through case-control studies of children with severe malaria (rather than comparisons of parasitaemia levels). The more severely ill the cohort of malaria cases, the smaller the sample size needed. For example, such a study in Ghana should allow a realistic estimate of the current resistance to malaria of HbC heterozygotes and homozygotes to be made. Likewise, a large case-control study in a suitable south-east Asian population should not only provide information on HbE, Hb Constant Spring and the severe α and β thalassaemias but might give some idea of the nature of the interaction of these variants in terms of protection from malaria. Does, for example, a β thalassaemia heterozygote enjoy more or less protection from malaria if he or she is also a carrier of α^+ thalassaemia?

Secondly, it may soon be possible to produce some estimates of the age, or at least the relative ages, of particular globin gene variants. The numerous molecular markers in the β-globin and, particularly, the α-globin gene clusters, together with increasing knowledge of rates of recombination between various parts of the gene clusters, may be used with population studies of the frequencies of haplotypes associated with each variant to derive estimates of the age of mutations. Currently, our estimates of absolute recombination rates are too imprecise for this to be very useful, but further data, perhaps from analysis of germline DNA by PCR as well as family studies, may overcome this limitation. Already, the observation that

most common β thalassaemia mutations are associated with one predominant restriction enzyme haplotypes plus a few less common ones,
suggests a generally similar age for these variants, compatible perhaps with
the sudden (in evolutionary terms) arrival of *falciparum* malaria in human
populations.

Thirdly, exploitation of the exquisite sensitivity of the PCR may allow
direct estimates of the mutation rate, at least in males, by analysis of sperm
DNA. Even relative rates of mutation for unequal crossovers and various
point mutations would be invaluable. Differences in mutation rates to
particular variants may, for example, account for the relatively low frequency of HPFH alleles in Africans. This phenotypically mild disorder
might give substantial malaria resistance, but its molecular basis suggests
that the illegitimate recombination events giving rise to the known deletions
may be rare occurrences, so that a recent origin has prevented it reaching
high frequency. Ramsay and Jenkins (1984) proposed that the $-\alpha$ deletion
was present earlier in Africa than the HbS allele, based on the distribution of
these variants in southern African populations, and this is quite consistent
with the impression that unequal crossovers between homologous globin
genes occur more frequently than particular point mutations.

Finally, little attention has been given to the possibility of natural
selection by the other human malarias, despite the striking association
between absence of the Duffy blood group and complete resistance to *P.
vivax* malaria (Miller et al, 1976). Nurse (1985) speculated on the possibility
of α thalassaemia providing resistance to *vivax* malaria, apparently based on
the evidence that both were 'old', compared with, say, *falciparum* malaria
and HbS. More intriguing is the observation that very high frequencies of
α^+ thalassaemia are found mainly in areas where *P. vivax* is the predominant parasite, such as Papua New Guinea and parts of the Indian
subcontinent.

PRENATAL DIAGNOSIS

Despite the increasing interest in gene therapy and bone marrow transplantation, prenatal diagnosis programmes remain the only realistic option for
large scale control of thalassaemia major. The potential for control of the
thalassaemias has been demonstrated by the highly successful prenatal
diagnosis programmes in some Mediterranean populations. In Sardinia,
publicity campaigns and education programmes, combined with, initially,
fetal blood analysis and, later, first trimester diagnosis by chorionic villus
biopsy and DNA analysis, led to a 90% decline in thalassaemia major births
(Cao et al, 1989). Similar programmes in Cyprus and Greece have also been
highly effective (WHO, 1985).

Many of the difficulties facing prenatal diagnosis have been solved or
ameliorated by technical advances over the last decade. The introduction of
chorionic villus sampling with first trimester diagnosis has increased the
acceptance rate of the procedure, allows much earlier terminations and can
have a fetal loss rate (2%) similar to that of amniocentesis (2.6%) and lower

than that of fetal blood sampling (6%) (Cao et al, 1989). Molecular methods of diagnosis of the thalassaemias have rapidly tracked advances in molecular biology over the last decade, moving from linkage analysis using RFLPs to direct detection of the mutations by oligonucleotides following gene amplification by the PCR. The multiplicity of mutations in the populations served by certain laboratories has been a particular challenge. In the UK, for example, thalassaemias are seen in populations originating in Cyprus, other parts of the Mediterranean, the Middle East, the Indian subcontinent, south-east Asia and some other parts of the world, covering between them an enormous range of common mutations (Old et al, 1989). The amplification refractory mutation detection system has been found useful in this setting (Old et al, 1990), and the direct detection of new mutations by sequencing amplified genes as part of a prenatal diagnosis has been found to be feasible (Kazazian, 1990). An alternative rapid technique, when mutations are defined, may be to use denaturing gradient gel electrophoresis to detect characteristic homo- and heteroduplexes of PCR amplification products (Cai and Kan, 1990).

A more complex problem is the difficulty of precisely predicting the phenotype prenatally from the molecular defects in the case of many thalassaemias, particularly when there are several interacting globin gene variants. Although considerable progress has been made in this area there are clearly other linked and unlinked genetic modifiers still to be defined.

Most encouraging have been the numerous data sets appearing on the molecular basis of β thalassaemia in the Oriental populations. The techniques and molecular details are now available to begin to take on the huge challenge of reducing the burden of the more severe thalassaemia syndromes in this region. Clearly there are enormous financial, educational, organizational and, sometimes, cultural hurdles to be overcome in implementing prenatal diagnosis programmes in developing countries. However, the experience in the Mediterranean encourages the belief that, with sufficient motivation, it should be possible to make a considerable impact on the frequency of these diseases.

SUMMARY

The thalassaemias are the most common genetic disorders of man, and over the last decade the molecular epidemiology of these defects has been studied in detail. After briefly reviewing the great diversity of mutations giving rise to these conditions, four global regions are discussed in more detail. The thalassaemias, of which haemoglobin E is one, are most frequent in Asia, where recent work has defined the molecular basis of the β thalassaemias and the frequencies of the various types of α^+ and α^0 thalassaemia. Oceanic populations have a range of globin gene variants remarkably different to those of south-east Asia. Most is known about the nature and frequencies of thalassaemia mutations in Mediterranean countries, where prenatal diagnosis programmes have been very successful in reducing the frequency of new cases of thalassaemia major. α^+ Thalassaemia is the most common haemoglobinopathy in sub-Saharan Africa, and molecular studies of American Blacks with β thalassaemia have elucidated the probable molecular basis of the mild form of this disorder in Africans.

Although each geographical region has its own group of common β thalassaemia mutations, with little overlap, most of these appear to have had a single origin. The question of single or multiple origins for HbE in south-east Asia is unresolved. Recombination events producing α^+ thalassaemia deletions are frequent, whereas α^0 thalassaemia is produced by a variety of large deletions, each of which has had a single origin.

The evidence favouring natural selection by *P. falciparum* malaria as the primary cause of high frequencies of the thalassaemias throughout the tropics and subtropics is reviewed. While the mechanism of protection remains unclear, epidemiological evidence supporting the hypothesis is strong, but more information is required from case-control studies on the amount of protection provided by the various thalassaemia genotypes.

Acknowledgements

I am grateful to several members of the Institute of Molecular Medicine for discussions and comments on the manuscript: Douglas Higgs, who provided Figures 2 and 3, Swee Lay Thein, John Old, John Clegg and Sir David Weatherall. Unpublished work referred to has been supported by the Wellcome Trust.

REFERENCES

Allison AC (1964) Polymorphism and natural selection in human populations. *Cold Spring Harbor Symposium on Quantitative Biology* **29:** 137–149.

Antonarakis SE, Boehm CD, Giardina PJV & Kazazian HH (1982) Non-random association of polymorphic restriction sites in the β-globin gene cluster. *Proceedings of the National Academy of Sciences of the USA* **79:** 137–141.

Antonarakis SE, Orkin SH, Chen T-C et al (1984) β-thalassemia in American Blacks: novel mutations in the 'TATA' box and an acceptor splice site. *Proceedings of the National Academy of Sciences of the USA* **81:** 1154–1158.

Antonarakis SE, Kang J, Lam VMS, Tam JWO & Li AMC (1988) Molecular characterization of β-globin gene mutations in patients with β-thalassaemia intermedia in South China. *British Journal of Haematology* **70:** 357–361.

Bowden DK, Hill AVS, Higgs DR, Weatherall DJ & Clegg JB (1985) The relative role of genetic factors, dietary deficiency and infection in anaemia in Vanuatu, Southwest Pacific. *Lancet* **ii:** 1025–1028.

Bowden DK, Hill AVS, Higgs DR et al (1987) Different haematologic phenotypes are associated with leftward ($-\alpha^{4.2}$) and rightward ($-\alpha^{3.7}$) α^+-thalassaemia deletions. *Journal of Clinical Investigation* **79:** 39–43.

Brittenham G, Lozof B, Harris JW et al (1980) Alpha globin gene number: population and restriction endonuclease studies. *Blood* **55:** 706–708.

Brockelman CR, Wongsattayanont B, Tan-Ariya P & Fucharoen S (1987) Thalassemic erythrocytes inhibit in vitro growth of *Plasmodium falciparum*. *Journal of Clinical Microbiology* **25:** 56–60.

Brown PJ (1983) New considerations on the distribution of malaria, thalassemia, and glucose-6-phosphate dehydrogenase deficiency in Sardinia. *Human Biology* **53:** 367–382.

Buckle V, Higgs DR, Wilkie AOM, Super M & Weatherall DJ (1988) Localization of human α-globin to 16p13.3-pter. *Journal of Medical Genetics* **25:** 847–849.

Bunvaratvej A, Butthep P, Yuthavong Y et al (1986) Increased phagocytosis of *Plasmodium falciparum*-infected erythrocytes with haemoglobin E by peripheral blood monocytes. *Acta Haematologica* **76:** 155–158.

Cai SP & Kan YW (1990) Identification of multiple β-thalassemia mutations by denaturing gradient gel electrophoresis. *Journal of Clinical Investigation* **85:** 550–553.

Camaschella C, Bertero MT, Serra A et al (1987) A benign form of thalassaemia intermedia may be determined by the interaction of triplicated alpha locus and heterozygous beta thalassaemia. *British Journal of Haematology* **66:** 103–107.

Cao A, Rosatelli C, Galanello R et al (1989) The prevention of thalassemia in Sardinia. *Clinical Genetics* **36:** 277–285.

Cavalli-Sforza LL & Bodmer WF (1971) *The Genetics of Human Populations*, 965 pp. San Francisco: WH Freeman.

Chan V, Chan TK, Cheha FF & Todd D (1987) Distribution of β-thalassemia mutations in South China and their association with haplotypes. *American Journal of Human Genetics* **41:** 678–685.

Chehab FF, Honig GR & Kan YW (1986) Spontaneous mutation in β-thalassaemia producing the same nucleotide substitution as that in a hereditary form. *Lancet* **i:** 3–5.

Chehab FF, Der-Kaloustian V, Khouri FP, Deeb SS & Kan YW (1987) The molecular basis of β-thalassaemia in Lebanon: application to prenatal diagnosis. *Blood* **69:** 1141–1145.

Chidoori C, Paul B & Gordeuk VR (1989) Homozygous α⁺ thalassaemia in Zimbabwe: an unrecognised cause of hypochromia and microcytosis. *Central African Journal of Medicine* **35:** 472–476.

Deka R, Reddy AP, Mukherjee BN et al (1988) Hemoglobin E distribution in ten endogamous population groups of Assam, India. *Human Heredity* **38:** 261–266.

Diaz-Chico JC, Yang KG, Kutlar A et al (1987) A 300 bp deletion involving part of the 5′ β-globin gene region is observed in members of a Turkish family with β-thalassemia. *Blood* **70:** 583–586.

Dunn FL (1965) On the antiquity of malaria in the western hemisphere. *Human Biology* **37:** 385–393.

El-Hazmi MAF (1987) α-Thalassaemia in Saudi Arabia: deletion pattern. *Human Genetics* **76:** 196–198.

Embury SH, Miller JA, Dozy AM et al (1980) Two different molecular organizations account for the single α-globin gene of the α-thalassaemia-2 genotype. *Journal of Clinical Investigation* **66:** 1319–1325.

Falusi AG, Esan GJF, Ayyub H & Higgs DR (1987) Alpha-thalassaemia in Nigeria: its interaction with sickle cell disease. *European Journal of Haematology* **38:** 370–375.

Fei YJ, Kutlar F, Harris HF et al (1989) A search for anomalies in the zeta, alpha, beta, and gamma globin gene arrangements in normal black, Italian, Turkish and Spanish newborns. *Hemoglobin* **13:** 45–65.

Felice AE, Cleek MP, McKie K, McKie V & Huisman THJ (1984) The rare α-thalassemia-1 of blacks is a ζα-thalassaemia-1 associated with deletion of all α- and ζ-globin genes. *Blood* **63:** 1253–1257.

Flatz G (1967) Haemoglobin E: distribution and population dynamics. *Humangenetik* **3:** 189–234.

Flatz G, Pik C & Sundharagiati B (1964) Malaria and haemoglobin E in Thailand. *Lancet* **ii:** 385–387.

Flint J, Hill AVS, Bowden DK et al (1986a) High frequencies of α thalassaemia are the result of natural selection by malaria. *Nature* **321:** 744–749.

Flint J, Hill AVS, Weatherall DJ, Clegg JB & Higgs DR (1986b) Alpha-globin genotypes in two North European populations. *British Journal of Haematology* **63:** 796–796.

Friedman MJ (1979) Oxidant damage mediates variant red cell resistance to malaria. *Nature* **280:** 245–247.

Fucharoen G, Fucharoen S, Jetsrisuparb A et al (1990) Molecular basis of Hb E-β-thalassemia and the origin of Hb E in northeast Thailand: identification of one novel mutation using amplified DNA from buffy coat specimens. *Biochemical and Biophysical Research Communications* **170:** 698–704.

Fucharoen S, Fucharoen G, Sriroongrueng W et al (1989) Molecular basis of β-thalassemia in Thailand: analysis of β-thalassemia mutations using the polymerase chain reaction. *Human Genetics* **84:** 41–46.

Fucharoen S, Kobayashi Y, Fucharoen G et al (1990). A single nucleotide deletion in codon 123 of the β-globin gene causes an inclusion body β-thalassaemia trait: a novel elongated globin chain βMakebe. *British Journal of Haematology* **75:** 393–399.

Galanello R, Ruggeri R, Paglietti E et al (1983) A family with segregating triplicated alpha globin loci and beta thalassaemia. *Blood* **62:** 1035–1040.

Gallerani M, Cicognani I, Ballardini P et al (1990) Average life expectancy of heterozygous beta thalassemic subjects. *Haematologica* **75:** 224–227.

Goldsmith ME, Humphries RK, Ley T et al (1983) Silent substitution in β⁺-thalassemia activating a cryptic splice site in β-globin RNA coding sequence. *Proceedings of the National Academy of Sciences of the USA* **80:** 2318–2322.

Gonzalez-Redondo JM, Stoming TA, Lanclos TD et al (1988) Clinical and genetic heterogeneity in Black patients with homozygous β-thalassaemia from the Southeastern United States. *Blood* **72:** 1007–1014.

Gonzalez-Redondo JM, Stroming TA, Kutlar A et al (1989) A C→T substitution at nt−101 in a conserved DNA sequence of the promotor region of the β-globin gene is associated with 'silent' β-thalassaemia. *Blood* **73:** 1705–1711.

Grosveld F, Blom Van Assendelft G, Greaves Dr, Kollias G (1987) Position-independent high level expression of the human β-globin gene in transgenic mice. *Cell* **51:** 975–985.

Gu YC, Landman H & Huisman THJ (1987) Two different quadruplicated α-globin gene arrangements in man. *British Journal of Haematology* **66:** 245–250.

Haldane JBS (1949) Disease and Evolution. *La Ricerca Scientifica* **19 (supplement):** 68–75.

Hatton C, Wilkie AOM, Drysdale HC et al (1990) Alpha thalassemia caused by a large deletion upstream of the α globin gene cluster. *Blood* **76:** 1–7.

Henni T, Morle F, Lopez B, Colonna P & Godet J (1987) α-Thalassemia haplotypes in the Algerian population. *Human Genetics* **75:** 272–276.

Higgs DR, Goodbourn SEY, Lamb J et al (1983) α Thalassaemia caused by a polyadenylation signal mutation. *Nature* **306:** 398–400.

Higgs DR, Hill AVS, Bowden DK, Weatherall DJ & Clegg JB (1984) Independent recombination events between the duplicated human α-globin genes: implications for their concerted evolution. *Nucleic Acids Research* **12:** 6965–6977.

Higgs DR, Wainscoat JS, Flint J et al (1986) Analysis of the human α-globin gene cluster reveals a highly informative genetic locus. *Proceedings of the National Academy of Sciences of the USA* **83:** 5165–5169.

Higgs DR, Vickers MA, Wilkie AOM et al (1989) A review of the molecular genetics of the human α-globin gene cluster. *Blood* **73:** 1081–1104.

Higgs DR, Wood WG, Jarman AP et al (1990) A major positive regulatory region located far upstream of the human α-globin gene locus. *Genes and Development* **4:** 1588–1601.

Hill AVS (1986) The population genetics of alpha thalassaemia and the malaria hypothesis. *Cold Spring Harbor Symposium on Quantitative Biology* **51:** 489–498.

Hill AVS, Bowden DK, Trent RJ et al (1985) Melanesians and Polynesians share a unique α thalassaemia mutation. *American Journal of Human Genetics* **37:** 571–580.

Hill AVS, Thein SL, Mavo B, Weatherall DJ & Clegg JB (1987) Non-deletion haemoglobin H disease in Papua New Guinea. *Journal of Medical Genetics* **24:** 767–771.

Hill AVS, Bowden DK, O'Shaughnessy DF, Weatherall DJ & Clegg JB (1988) β Thalassaemia in Melanesia: association with malaria and characterization of a common variant. *Blood* **72:** 9–14.

Hill AVS, O'Shaughnessy DF & Clegg JB (1989) Haemoglobin and globin gene variants in the Pacific. In Hill AVS & Serjeantson SW (eds) *The Colonization of the Pacific: A Genetic Trail*, pp 246–285. Oxford: Oxford University Press.

Hill AVS, Allsopp CEM, Kwiatkowski D et al (1991) Common West African HLA antigens are associated with protection from severe malaria. *Nature* **352:** 595–600.

Huang S-Z, Wong C, Antonarakis SE et al (1986) The same TATA box thalassemia mutation in Chinese and US blacks: another example of independent origins of mutation. *Human Genetics* **74:** 152–164.

Huisman THJ (1990) Frequencies of common β-thalassaemia alleles among different populations: variability in clinical severity. *British Journal of Haematology* **75:** 454–457.

Hundrieser J, Deka R, Gorgoi BC, Papp T & Flatz G (1988a) DNA haplotypes and frameworks associated with the beta-globin gene in the Kachiri population of Assam (India). *Human Heredity* **38:** 240–245.

Hundrieser J, Sanguansermsri T, Papp T & Flatz G (1988b) Alpha-thalassaemia in northern Thailand. *Human Heredity* **38:** 211–215.

Hundrieser J, Sanguansermsri T, Papp T, Laig M & Flatz G (1988c) β-globin gene linked DNA haplotypes and frameworks in three South-East Asian populations. *Human Genetics* **80**: 90–94.

Hundrieser J, Laig M, Yongvanit P et al (1990) Study of alpha-thalassaemia in northeastern Thailand at the DNA level. *Human Heredity* **40**: 85–88.

Ifediba TC, Stern A, Ibrahim A & Rieder RF (1985) *Plasmodium faciparum* in vitro: diminished growth in hemoglobin H disease erythrocytes. *Blood* **65**: 454–455.

Kan YW & Dozy AM (1978) Polymorphism of DNA sequence adjacent to the human β-globin structural gene: relationship to sickle mutation. *Proceedings of the National Academy of Sciences of the USA* **75**: 5631–5635.

Kattamis C, Kanavakis E, Tzotzos S, Synodinos J & Metaxotou-Mavrommati A (1988) Correlation of phenotype to genotype in haemoglobin H disease. *Lancet* **i**: 442–444.

Kazazian HH (1990) The thalassemia syndromes: molecular basis and prenatal diagnosis in 1990. *Seminars in Haematology* **27**: 209–228.

Kazazian HH, Orkin SH, Antonarakis SE et al (1984a) Molecular characterization of seven β-thalassaemia mutations in Asian Indians. *EMBO Journal* **3**: 593–596.

Kazazian HH, Orkin SH, Markham AF et al (1984b) Quantification of the close association between DNA haplotypes and specific β-thalassaemia mutations in Mediterraneans. *Nature* **310**: 152–154.

Kazazian HH, Waber PG, Boehm CD et al (1984c) Hemoglobin E in Europeans: further evidence for multiple origins of the β^E-globin gene. *American Journal of Human Genetics* **36**: 212–217.

Kazazian HH, Dowling CE, Waber PG, Huang S & Lo WHY (1986) The spectrum of β-thalassaemia mutations in China and Southeast Asia. *Blood* **68**: 964–966.

Kazazian HH, Dowling CE, Hurwitz RL, Coleman M & Adams JG (1989) Thalassemia mutations in exon 3 of the β-globin gene often cause a dominant form of thalassemia and show no predilection for the malarial-endemic regions of the world. *American Journal of Human Genetics* **45**: 242 (abstract).

Kropp GL, Fucharoen S & Embury SH (1989) Selective amplification of the α2-globin DNA for detection of the hemoglobin Constant Spring mutation. *Blood* **73**: 1987–1992.

Kruatrachne M, Sriripanich B & Sadudee N (1970) Haemoglobinopathies and malaria in Thailand: a comparison of morbidity and mortality rates. *Bulletin of the World Health Organization* **43**: 348–349.

Kulozik AE, Thein SL, Wainscoat JS et al (1987) Thalassaemia intermedia: interaction of the triple alpha-globin gene arrangement and heterozygous beta-thalassaemia. *British Journal of Haematology* **66**: 109–112.

Kulozik A, Kar BC, Serjeant BE, Serjeant, GR & Weatherall DJ (1988) The molecular basis of α-thalassaemia in India: its interaction with sickle cell disease. *Blood* **71**: 467–472.

Labie D, Srinivas R, Dunda O et al (1989) Haplotypes in tribal Indians bearing the sickle gene: evidence for the unicentric origin of the β^s mutation and the unicentric origin of the tribal populations of India. *Human Biology* **61**: 479–491.

Laig M, Sanguansermsri T, Wiangnon S et al (1989) The spectrum of β-thalassaemia mutations in northern and northeastern Thailand. *Human Genetics* **84**: 47–50.

Lie-Injo LE, Cai S-P, Wahidijat I et al (1989) β-thalassaemia mutations in Indonesia and their linkage to β haplotypes. *American Journal of Human Genetics* **45**: 971–975.

Liebhaber SA, Cash FE & Main DM (1985) Compensatory increase in α1 globin gene expression in individuals heterozygous for the α-thalassaemia-2 deletion. *Journal of Clinical Investigation* **76**: 1057–1064.

Liebhaber SA, Cash FE & Ballas SK (1986) Human α-globin gene expression. The dominant role of the α2-locus in mRNA and protein synthesis. *Journal of Biological Chemistry* **261**: 15327–15333.

Liehaber SA, Griese E-U, Weiss I et al (1990) Inactivation of human α-globin gene expression by a de novo deletion located upstream of the α-globin gene cluster. *Proceedings of the National Academy of Sciences of the USA* **87**: 9431–9435.

Lin L-I, Lin K-S, Lin K-H & Chang H-C (1991) The spectrum of β-thalassaemia mutations in Taiwan: identification of a novel frameshift mutation. *American Journal of Human Genetics* **48**: 809–812.

Livingstone FB (1976) Hemoglobin history in west Africa. *Human Biology* **48**: 487–500.

Livingstone FB (1985) *Frequencies of Hemoglobin Variants.* Oxford: Oxford University Press.

Livingstone FB (1989) Simulation of the diffusion of the β-globin variants in the Old World. *Human Biology* **61:** 297–309.

Luzzatto L (ed.) (1981) Haematology in tropical areas. *Clinics in Haematology* **10(3).**

Luzzi GA, Merry AH, Newbold CI et al (1991a) Surface antigen expression on *Plasmodium falciparum*-infected erythrocytes is modified in α- and β-thalassemia. *Journal of Experimental Medicine* **173:** 785–791.

Luzzi GA, Merry AH, Newbold CI et al (1991b) Protection by α thalassaemia against *Plasmodium falciparum* malaria: modified surface antigen expression rather than impaired growth or cytoadherence. *Immunology Letters* (in press).

Marsh K, Otoo L, Hayes RJ, Carson DC & Greenwood BM (1989) Antibodies to blood stage malaria antigens of *Plasmodium falciparum* in rural Gambians and their relation to protection against infection. *Transactions of the Royal Society of Tropical Medicine and Hygiene* **83:** 293–303.

Michelson AM & Orkin SH (1983) Boundaries of gene conversion within the duplicated human α-globin genes. Concerted evolution by segmental recombination. *Journal of Biological Chemistry* **258:** 15245–15254.

Miller LH, Mason SJ, Clyde DF & McGinniss MH (1976) The resistance factor to *P. vivax* in Blacks. The Duffy blood-group genotype. *New England Journal of Medicine* **295:** 302–304.

Modiano G, Morpurgo G, Terrenato L et al (1991) Protection against malaria morbidity: near-fixation of the α-thalassemia gene in a Nepalese population. *American Journal of Human Genetics* **48:** 390–397.

Muklwala EC, Banda J, Siziya S et al (1989) Alpha thalassaemia in Zambian newborn. *Clinical and Laboratory Haematology* **11:** 1–6.

Murru S, Loudianos G, Cao A et al (1990) A β-thalassemia carrier with normal sequence within the β-globin gene. *Blood* **76:** 2164–2165.

Murru S, Loudianos G, Deiana M et al (1991) Molecular characterization of β-thalassemia intermedia in patients of Italian descent and identification of three novel β-thalassemia mutations. *Blood* **77:** 1342–1347.

Nagel RL & Ranney HM (1990) Genetic epidemiology of structural mutations of the β-globin gene. *Seminars in Hematology* **27:** 342–349.

Nagel RL & Roth EF (1989) Malaria ànd red cell genetic defects. *Blood* **74:** 1213–1221.

Nagel RL, Raventos-Suare C, Fabry ME, Tanowitz H, Sicard D & Labie D (1981) Impairment of the growth of *Plasmodium falciparum* in Hb EE erythrocytes. *Journal of Clinical Investigation* **68:** 303–305.

Nakashima H, Fujiyama, A, Kagiyama S & Imamura T (1990) Genetic polymorphism of gene conversion within the duplicated human alpha-globin loci. *Human Genetics* **84:** 568–570.

Nakatsuji T, Kutlar A, Kutlar F & Huisman THJ (1986) Haplotypes among Vietnamese hemoglobin E homozygotes including one with a γ-globin gene triplication. *American Journal of Human Genetics* **38:** 981–983.

Nicholls RD, Fischel-Ghodsian N & Higgs DR (1987) Recombination at the human α-globin gene cluster: sequence features and topological constraints. *Cell* **49:** 369–378.

Nurse GT (1985) The pace of human selective adaptation to malaria. *Journal of Human Evolution* **14:** 319–326.

Old JM, Thein SL, Weatherall DJ et al (1989) Prenatal diagnosis of the major haemoglobin disorders. *Molecular Biology and Medicine* **6:** 55–63.

Old JM, Varawalla NY & Weatherall DJ (1990) Rapid detection and prenatal diagnosis of β thalassaemia: studies in Indian and Cypriot populations in the UK. *Lancet* **336:** 834–837.

Orkin SH, Kazazian HH, Antonarakis SE, Goff SC & Boehm CD (1982a) Linkage of β-thalassaemia mutations and β-globin gene polymorphisms in the human β-globin gene cluster. *Nature* **296:** 627–631.

Orkin SH, Kazazian HH, Antonarakis SE et al (1982b) Abnormal RNA processing due to the exon mutation of the β^E-globin gene. *Nature* **300:** 768–769.

Orkin SH, Antonarakis SE & Kazazian HH (1984) Base substitution at position -88 in a β-thalassemic globin gene. *Journal of Biological Chemistry* **259:** 8678–8681.

Orkin SH, Cheng T-C, Antonarakis SE et al (1985) Thalassemia due to a mutation in the cleavage-polyadenylation signal of the human β-globin gene. *EMBO Journal* **4:** 453–456.

O'Shaugnessy DF, Hill AVS, Bowden DK et al (1990) Globin genes in Micronesia: origins and affinities of Pacific island peoples. *American Journal of Human Genetics* **46:** 144–155.

Pagnier T, Dunda-Belkhodja O, Zohoun I et al (1984) α-Thalassemia among sickle cell anaemia patients in various African populations. *Human Genetics* **68**: 318–319.

Parikh P, Cotton M, Boehm C & Kazazian HH (1990) Ethnic distribution of β-thalassaemia in Indian subcontinent. *Lancet* **336**: 1006.

Pasvol G, Weatherall DJ & Wilson RJM (1977) Effects of foetal haemoglobin on susceptibility of red cells to *Plasmodium falciparum malaria*. *Nature* **270**: 171–173.

Pirastu M, Galanello R, Doherty MA et al (1987) The same β-globin gene mutation is present on nine different β-thalassemia chromosomes in a Sardinian population. *Proceedings of the National Academy of Sciences of the USA* **84**: 2882–2885.

Pressley L, Higgs DR, Clegg JB et al (1980) A new genetic basis for Hb H disease. *New England Journal of Medicine* **303**: 1383–1388.

Ramsay M & Jenkins T (1984) α-Thalassaemia in Africa: the oldest malaria protective trait? *Lancet* **ii**: 410.

Ramsay M & Jenkins T (1987) Globin gene associated restriction-fragment-length polymorphisms in southern African peoples. *American Journal of Human Genetics* **41**: 1132–1144.

Ristaldi MS, Murru S, Casula L et al (1990) A spontaneous mutation produced a novel elongated β-globin chain structural variant (Hb Agnana) with a thalassemia like phenotype. *Blood* **75**: 1378–1379.

Safaya S, Rieder RF, Dowling CE, Kazazian HH & Adams JG (1989) Homozygous β-thalassemia without anaemia. *Blood* **73**: 324–328.

Saha N (1990) Distribution of hemoglobin E in several mongoloid populations of northeast India. *Human Biology* **62**: 535–544.

Semenza GL, Delgrosso K, Poncz M et al (1984) The silent carrier allele: β-thalassaemia without a mutation in the β-globin gene or in its immediate flanking regions. *Cell* **39**: 123–128.

Shimizu K, Park KS & Omoto K (1989) The DNA polymorphisms of the β-globin gene cluster and the arrangements of the α- and γ-globin genes in Koreans. *Hemoglobin* **13**: 137–146.

Siniscalco M, Bernini L, Latte B & Motulski AG (1961) Favism and thalassaemia in Sardinia and their relationship to malaria. *Nature* **190**: 1179–1180.

Steinberg MH, Coleman MB, Adams JG et al (1986) A new gene deletion in the α-like globin gene cluster as the molecular basis for the rare α-thalassaemia-1 ($--/\alpha\alpha$) in Blacks: HbH disease in sickle cell trait. *Blood* **67**: 469–473.

Stevens DW, Wainscoat JS, Ketley N et al (1989) The pathogenesis of hypochromic anaemia in Saudi infants. *Journal of Tropical Pediatrics* **35**: 301–305.

Sukumaran PK, Nakatsuji T, Gardiner MB et al (1983) Gamma thalassaemia resulting from the deletion of a γ-globin gene. *Nucleic Acids Research* **11**: 4635–4643.

Thein SL, Al-Hakim I & Hoffbrand AV (1984a) Thalassaemia intermedia: a new molecular basis. *British Journal of Haematology* **56**: 333–337.

Thein SL, Old JM, Wainscoat JS et al (1984b) Population and genetic studies suggest a single origin for the Indian deletion β⁰ thalassaemia. *British Journal of Haematology* **57**: 271–278.

Thein SL, Hesketh C, Walace RB & Weatherall DJ (1988a) The molecular basis of thalassaemia major and thalassaemia intermedia in Asian Indians: application to prenatal diagnosis. *British Journal of Haematology* **70**: 225–231.

Thein SL, Wallace RB, Pressley L et al (1988b) The polyadenylation site mutation in the α-globin gene cluster. *Blood* **71**: 313–319.

Thein SL, Hesketh C, Taylor P et al (1990a) Molecular basis for dominantly inherited inclusion body β-thalassaemia. *Proceedings of the National Academy of Sciences of the USA* **87**: 3924–3928.

Thein SL, Winichagoon P, Hesketh C et al (1990b) The molecular basis of β-thalassaemia in Thailand: application to prenatal diagnosis. *American Journal of Human Genetics* **47**: 369–375.

Thompson CC, Ali MA, Vacovsky M & Boyadjian S (1989) The interaction of the anti-3.7 type quadruplicated α-globin genes and heterozygous β-thalassaemia. *Hemoglobin* **13**: 125–135.

Titus EA, Tsia YE & Hunt JA (1988) Alpha-thalassaemia screening reveals quadruple zeta-globin genes in a Laotian family. *Hemoglobin* **12**: 539–550.

Wasi P, Pootrakul S, Pootrakul P et al (1980) Thalassemia in Thailand. *Annals of the New York Academy of Sciences* **344**: 352–363.

Weatherall DJ & Clegg JB (1981) *The Thalassaemia Syndromes* 3rd edn. Oxford: Blackwell Scientific.

Weatherall DJ, Clegg JB, Higgs DR et al (1989) The haemoglobinopathies. In Scriver CR, Beaudet AL & Sly WS (eds) *The Metabolic Basis of Inherited Disease* 6th edn, pp 2281–2339. New York: McGraw-Hill.

WHO (1985) *Report of WHO working group on hereditary anaemias: update on the progress of haemoglobinopathies control.* WHO document HMG/WG/85.8. Geneva: World Health Organization.

Wilkie AOM, Lamb J, Harris PC, Finney RD & Higgs DR (1990) A truncated human chromosome 16 associated with α thalassaemia is stabilized by addition of telomeric repeat (TTAGGG)n. *Nature* **346**: 868–871.

Willcox MC (1975) Thalassaemia in northern Liberia: a survey in the Mount Nimba area. *Journal of Medical Genetics* **12**: 55–63.

Willcox MC, Weatherall DJ & Clegg JB (1975) Homozygous β thalassaemia in Liberia. *Journal of Medical Genetics* **12**: 165–173.

Willcox M, Bjorkman A, Brohult J et al (1983) A case-control study in northern Liberia of *Plasmodium falciparum* malaria in haemoglobin S and β-thalassaemia traits. *Annals of Tropical Medicine and Parasitology* **77**: 239–246.

Winichagoon P, Higgs DR, Goodbourn SEY et al (1982) Multiple arrangements of the human embryonic zeta globin genes. *Nucleic Acids Research* **10**: 5853–5868.

Winichagoon P, Higgs DR, Goodbourn SEY et al (1984) The molecular basis of α-thalassaemia in Thailand. *EMBO Journal* **3**: 1813–1818.

Yang KG, Kutlar F, George E et al (1989) Molecular characterization of β-globin gene mutations in Malay patients with Hb E-β-thalassaemia and thalassaemia major. *British Journal of Haematology* **72**: 73–80.

Yenchitsomanus PT, Summers KM, Board PG et al (1986) Alpha thalassaemia in Papua New Guinea. *Human Genetics* **74**: 432–437.

Yokoyama S (1983) Selection for the α-thalassaemia genes. *Genetics* **103**: 143–148.

Yongvanit P, Sriboonlue P, Mularlee N et al (1989) DNA haplotypes and frameworks linked to the β-globin locus in an Austro-Asiatic population with a high prevalence of hemoglobin E. *Human Genetics* **83**: 171–174.

Yuthavong Y, Bunyaratvej A & Kamchonwongpaisan S (1990) Increased susceptibility of malaria-infected variant erythrocytes to the mononuclear phagocyte system. *Blood Cells* **16**: 591–597.

Index

Note: Page numbers of article titles are in **bold** type.